The History of
Clinical Psychology
in Autobiography

◆

Volume II

Brooks/Cole Professional Books

◆

Consulting Editor: C. Eugene Walker

Family Therapy and Beyond: A Multisystemic Approach to Treating the Behavior Problems of Children and Adolescents
Scott W. Henggeler and Charles M. Borduin

Changing Expectations: A Key to Effective Psychotherapy
Irving Kirsch

Panic Disorders and Agoraphobia: A Comprehensive Guide for the Practitioner
John R. Walker, G. Ron Norton, and Colin A. Ross, Editors

The History of Clinical Psychology in Autobiography, Volumes I and II
C. Eugene Walker, Editor

*Helping Young Children Develop Social Skills:
The Social Growth Program*
Cheryl A. King and Daniel S. Kirschenbaum

*Programmed Writing: A Self-Administered Approach for Interventions
with Individuals, Couples, and Families*
Luciano L'Abate and Janet Cox

The History of
Clinical Psychology
in Autobiography

◆

Volume II

Edited by

C. Eugene Walker

University of Oklahoma Health Sciences Center

Brooks/Cole Publishing Company
Pacific Grove, California

Consulting Editor: *C. Eugene Walker*
Brooks/Cole Publishing Company
A Division of Wadsworth, Inc.

Printed in the United States of America
10 9 8 7 6 5 4 3 2 1

Library of Congress Cataloging-in-Publication Data
(Revised for volume 2)

The history of clinical psychology in autobiography.

(Brooks/Cole professional books)
Includes bibliographical references.
1. Clinical psychologists—Biography. 2. Clinical psychology—History. [DNLM: 1. Psychology, Clinical—biography. 2. Psychology, Clinical—history.
WZ 112.5.P6 H673] I. Walker, C. Eugene (Clarence Eugene), [date].
RC466.8.H57 1990   616.89′0092′2   90-2241
ISBN 0-534-14436-5 (v. 1)

ISBN 0-534-14437-3 (v.2)

Sponsoring Editor: *Claire Verduin*
Editorial Associate: *Gay C. Bond*
Production Coordinator: *Fiorella Ljunggren*
Production: *Sara Hunsaker, Ex Libris*
Manuscript Editor: *Lorraine Anderson*
Permissions Editor: *Marie DuBois*
Interior Design: *Katherine Minerva*
Cover Design: *Lisa Berman*
Typesetting: *BookPrep*
Cover and Jacket Printing: *Phoenix Color Corporation*
Printing and Binding: *Arcata Graphics/Fairfield*

To James D. Linden,
Professor, Mentor, Friend

Preface

◆

The modern era of clinical psychology spans a scant 45 or 50 years, having grown largely from the impetus of the need for mental health services for military personnel during World War II and for veterans after the conflict. Thus, the individuals who pioneered the field and shaped the current course of the discipline are still very much with us. Many are still professionally active, while others are enjoying active retirement. With this in mind, the present editor determined to begin a series of volumes of autobiographical essays by these founders of the field. Volume 1 appeared in 1991 and contained contributions by Albert Ellis, Hans J. Eysenck, Sol L. Garfield, Molly Harrower, Margaret Ives, Alan O. Ross, Edwin Shneidman, and Hans H. Strupp. New volumes will appear periodically, as new contributors are identified.

Numerous individual works and series of autobiographical essays have already been published in the field of psychology. These have proved to be worthwhile and significant contributions. The present series, concentrating on the field of clinical psychology, is presented with the hope that it will be similarly valuable and yet unique. Although this series will attempt to present a history of clinical psychology in autobiography, it is not merely a history of clinical psychologists. We intend to include in this series many individuals who are primarily researchers but whose work has greatly influenced the thinking and work of clinical psychologists. We will also include representatives from other fields such as psychiatry, sociology, and education who have had a major impact on the field of clinical psychology.

My sincere appreciation is expressed to Division 12 of the American Psychological Association and its advisory board: Charles D. Spielberger, Chair, and board members Theodora M. Able, Norman Abeles, Roderick W. Pugh, Jerome Resnick, Donald Routh, and Rogers Wright. I am greatly impressed with the willingness of the authors of the essays included in the present volume to share their experiences and their thoughts with us. These authors tell us of their successes and their failures, their friends and their enemies, their contributions and their mistakes. It is my hope that those who are pursuing a career in clinical psychology, or who are simply interested in the field, will find these essays exciting and valuable.

C. Eugene Walker

Contents

◆

Theodora M. Abel, Ph.D.

Clinical Professor, Department of Psychiatry
School of Medicine, University of New Mexico

Director of Psychology Emeritus
Postgraduate Center for Mental Health, New York City

◆

A Career in Clinical Psychology

Early Years

I was born in Newport, Rhode Island, on September 9, 1899. My mother had gone up there to be matron-of-honor at the wedding of her best friend. I arrived on the scene unexpectedly. I was not supposed to be born until November. There had been some miscalculation, for I seemed to be as developed as a 9-month baby. My mother never forgave me for interfering with her plans. She generally liked to run the show. For once she could not. No one was prepared for a baby. I was wrapped in a towel and placed in a laundry basket.

My Grandparents and Parents

My parents were visiting my maternal grandparents at the time. My grandfather, Clement Cleveland, was a physician who was a graduate of Harvard and the Columbia Medical School. My grandmother was the one who had suggested her husband practice in Newport in the summers, as it was there that his rich patients from New York spent their summers. Early on my grandparents did not have a great deal of money, so they lived in a boarding house near the unfashionable second beach. My grandfather had a horse and buggy so he could get over to his patients, and he kept a room in the fashionable quarters in case there was a night delivery of a baby. His father had received a medical degree but never practiced, as he could not stand to inflict pain on patients; anesthetics had not yet come in. Instead, he ran a school for girls in Baltimore, Maryland. His younger brother was a genius. He made a German-model violin at the age of 16, using a piece of a beam from the attic of their house. It is still a good violin. I play it at times, although it is a little heavy for me. This uncle became a full professor of engineering at Cornell University at the age of 26; he died of pneumonia two years later.

My grandfather was very authoritative. Robert Louis Stevenson came to see him in New York on his way to the South Pacific islands. Stevenson had tuberculosis. The doctor told him he would die if he went to the South Seas; that he should go instead to the sanatorium in Saranac. Stevenson went to the South Seas and died.

When I was 11 and visiting my grandparents, I was very sick with a high fever. I ached all over; I couldn't move my neck and my fingers were in pain. I announced to my mother and grandmother over and over that I was dying. In desperation they asked my grandfather to speak to me. (He was not my doctor, as it was not the custom for a physician to treat a family member.) My grandfather came in the room and gave me hell. He shouted at me to shut up and not speak another word. He pointed out that I was "damn lucky" not to be paralyzed as was a friend of mine. I had nonparalytic polio. He did a lot of cussing if he thought someone was stupid. One time a colleague of his got lost in the woods for hours. When he was finally rescued, my grandfather used all the slang words in the English language pointing out that any fool could tell where North was by feeling the bark on the trees. Of course, he never did this swearing in front of my very religious grandmother.

My grandmother, whom we called Nonna, was very fat and had a pockmarked face. She had spent two years in Germany and Italy learning German and Italian. When at the age of 19 she was in London with her maiden aunts, they went to a doctor. He told them about the new vaccine against smallpox that had just come out. Because they were sailing for the States the next day, they didn't bother to be vaccinated. The ship took three weeks to get to Boston. On the ship Nonna came down with smallpox. When they reached Boston my grandmother was put off the ship on an island that was a quarantine island. She remained in bed two months in a sort of a barn. Each day the cows would peer in at her. She wrote in her diary when she got home "So glad to be home." She was very ashamed of her red and pockmarked face and wouldn't appear in public very much. One time, when she was 20, she finally decided to go down to dinner in a boarding house in New Hampshire. My grandfather was up there for the hiking. He fell in love with her and they married the next winter. He said, "I didn't marry her face." She was a great help to him in his profession. She had been a Presbyterian but she realized that all of "society" in New York was Episcopalian. So she had them join the Episcopal church. She never would admit the reason for her change of religious affiliation. Many years later, long after she died, my mother and grandfather were in church together in Palm Beach, Florida. One moment when it was quiet, my grandfather whispered very loud to my mother, "The goddamned Trinity. If it hadn't been for your mother, I'd have been a Unitarian." My mother was terribly embarrassed as he could be heard easily. He told me a few years before he died that since he had no problems with his heart and liver, he would die of kidney failure. This he did at the age of 91.

My mother was her father's favorite. She had an older and a younger brother. She was the only one of the three who became successful. She spent one year when she was 15 and another at 19 in Paris living with a French family. This family and their descendants have remained friends with most of us over the years. One member of this family was in the Chambre des députés. I was my mother's only child. She had several miscarriages. She was an Rh-negative and in those days there was no treatment for this condition. When I was 13 a cousin, Robert Cleveland, came to live with us, as his mother had died of TB. His father, the older brother of my mother, lived in Seattle. Robert became a member of our family. Now he lives in Washington, D.C., with his family, having retired from the State Department.

My mother, Elsie, married my father, Robert G. Mead, when she was 21. He was a banker but studied law at night at New York Law School and became a lawyer. I never knew his father. His mother died when I was quite young and I was never close to her. She was of Dutch descent. My father's family (Mead) had first migrated from France to England at the time the Huguenots were chased out of France. They changed their name to Mead from the Spanish *del Prado* (meadow). They came to America about two hundred years ago.

My mother never had to work for her living, but she was an organizer of all kinds of institutions and a money raiser. She and my grandfather founded the American Cancer Society in 1913. I was 13 then and I remember their discussing their plans in our living room. My mother was on the board of hospitals where my grandfather worked. She was continually giving suggestions for the better functioning of hospitals (the Memorial and the Women's hospitals in New York.) She would go around the country raising money; she raised a million dollars for cancer.

Mme. Marie Curie

Mme. Curie had a friend, Mrs. Maloney, editor of the *Ladies Home Journal* and later editor of the magazine of the *New York Tribune,* who worked with my mother raising money. In 1920 Mrs. Maloney was in Paris where she met Mme. Curie. Mme. Curie said she had one gram of radium to be used for treatment but she needed another gram for research purposes. Mrs. Maloney said she would raise the money. At that time one gram cost $100,000 in the Belgian Congo (now Zaire). With the help of my mother, the money was raised. It was arranged that there would be a ceremony in Washington, D.C., and President Harding would present Mme. Curie with the money. After the ceremony there was a reception at the White House.

Three of us girls from Vassar (we were seniors) were invited. We drew lots to see which one of us was to explain who we were to the president. I drew to do the job. I told him we came from Vassar. He said his sister had gone to Vassar.

Two years later when I was studying at the Sorbonne, I saw a good deal of Mme. Curie. She showed me around her laboratory. I would go to her house almost every Friday to play sonatas with her younger daughter, Eve. I played the violin, Eve the piano. Then we would have supper. Mme. Curie usually talked to us about French literature. At the end of the year after I received my grades from the university, I was quite ashamed to get the comment "assez bien"; that meant "pretty good." Mme. Curie said that any comment beyond "passed" was very good and that students didn't usually get any comment at all.

At that time Mme. Curie and her sister, Dr. Dluska, had organized a radium institute in her name in Warsaw. They needed a gram of radium. I nobly said I would get the money for her when I got back to America. At that time a gram cost only $50,000. Since I could never raise a penny, I relied on my mother and Mrs. Maloney to do the job. Mrs. Maloney told me to give her two weeks and come back to discuss the gram. This was after I had returned to New York. When I went back to Mrs. Maloney's office she said she had the $50,000. She had asked five millionaires to give $10,000 each. One of them was John D. Rockefeller, Jr.

Over the years my mother and I received letters from Mme. Curie. I kept 23 and made copies. One copy was for myself and one for Susan Quinn of Brookline, Massachusetts, who is writing the life of Mme. Curie. The originals I gave to the Polish government in 1990. You would think I had given them a gold mine. There was a reception for me at the Polish consulate in New York and I received a plaque. The letters are in the Mme. Curie Museum in Warsaw.

Just one more note. Mme. Curie came up to Vassar while I was a senior there and gave a talk in the physics department (a speech completely unintelligible to me). She said she would like to go to West Point and found that the superintendent, Douglas MacArthur, was away but his mother was there. Mrs. MacArthur ordered a dress parade (entirely against the rules). So we went to West Point. I went later that year to a prom there and danced once with the superintendent, MacArthur. In the early 1930s when I spent the summer in Poland (my husband was Polish), I stayed at the radium institute with Dr. Dluska. She was the director at that time. I remember looking out the window once. It was raining a little and two women outside in the park were fighting with their umbrellas, hitting each other. As they did so their wigs slipped half off. I take it they were orthodox Jewish women. It was the custom and still is for married women to shave their heads and wear a wig.

Age 3 Onward

I had a nurse named Minnie till I was about 3 years old. We lived in a brownstone house on West 11th Street, Manhattan, just next to the First Presbyterian Church on Fifth Avenue. I do not remember Minnie. Then came my nurse Rosie, who remained with me till I was 12, when she got married and left. I have two memories of when I was 3. I used to go to an Episcopal Sunday school around the corner. Can you imagine, the poor children went to the parish house for Sunday school while the middle class had their classes in the minister's house! Each week we were given a picture to color. One time I brought home a picture of the Three Wise Men. I colored their beards purple and was scolded by my nurse. This was sacrilegious she said; the beards should have been brown or black. Apparently that year a friend of mine, Louisa Cogswell (my best friend till I went to college), and I had some kind of a nursery school in my bedroom. One day the nursery school teacher demonstrated sunbeams. She shut the wooden blinds on the windows, then opened one blind slightly. This sent a sunbeam on the opposite wall. She kept opening and shutting the blind. I was very impressed, I guess, by cause and effect. My friends tell me that this was the beginning of my interest in science.

When I was 4 I went to the Froebel League Kindergarten. It was located on West 42nd Street about where the graduate school of City College is located today. I used to go up in the Sixth Avenue elevated train to get there. All I remember is hanging my coat up on a nail in the kindergarten. I suppose my nurse took me and came for me. The Sixth Avenue el doesn't exist anymore. The next year the kindergarten moved to Park Avenue about 60th Street. Three of us went there in a horse and carriage. I suppose that is the way we got home also. My only memory of that kindergarten is coming home one day and telling my mother we were shown the room of the first grade. When I was 6 I had lessons with a girl, Virginia Hagen, in her house on Ninth Street. One day she and the teacher laughed at me because I had written the word *cat* going uphill. I guess I was humiliated.

For the next two years I went to Miss Clark's school down the street from where I lived. There was one large room, first grade in front, third grade in the back, and second grade in the middle. Just for math, a class would go to another room with a different teacher. Miss Clark always wore black; she was fat. She had a feather boa around her neck. When she got excited, she would twirl this boa in the air.

The Farm at Ossining

Every summer till I was 10 we lived on a farm in Ossining, New York. This farm was my great security. It gave me more comfort than did any human being. When it had to be sold, I cried for days. I had a black pig as a pet. I would put blue ribbons around his neck. Once, when my mother was having company, I walked through the house followed by the pig; my mother shouted at me. We had four farm horses and a couple of horses to pull our carriages. When I was 8 I was able to harness Bill to a buggy and drive my father to the station to get a train to the city each morning. Once coming home there was a steamroller on the road. Bill got scared and I got out and led him around the steamroller. Another time I was sitting on a small stool under Bill in the stable, brushing his stomach. My father and Mr. John D. Rockefeller, Jr., were standing in the doorway. Mr. Rockefeller was horrified at what I was doing. My father reassured him that the horse and I were great friends. I used to lie down in a box stall with Bill (when he was lying down) and tell him my secrets. For a couple of years I had a donkey, Cadichon, that I rode or he pulled a cart.

We had fields of daisies. I remember several of us picked a lot of daisies; then five daisies were tied together with a string and put in a bucket. These bunches of daisies went down to Bellevue Hospital in New York for the patients. I have many more memories of those years. They would fill a book. Just one more . . . An older boy cousin of mine had a Ford car, a Tin Lizzie. He needed a cushion for the seat, so I went with him to a church in town. I stood outside the church, on guard, and he stole a crimson cushion from a small side pew for the car. We were not caught. When I had to leave the farm for good, I took small samples from the barn, from every room in the house (wall paper), and from favorite trees, etc. to keep as treasures. My mother thought this was a strange thing to do. But my grandmother bought me little labels with a string attached so I could record each piece. No wonder she was my favorite even though she annoyed me with her fussiness over my hair and nails. When I had therapy, many years later, I would speak of my grandmother with tears rolling down my cheeks.

Trips to Europe

First Trip

When I was 5 we went to Europe for three months. We had an apartment in Paris near the Arc de Triomphe with my great aunt and uncle and their daughter, who had just come out in society in Boston. I will mention two memories of this time. Every day I went to the park to play. My nurse and I passed a corner pharmacy in front of which was a large cage with a parrot. Each day the parrot said to me, "Vas-t'en à l'école?" I would reply in French that I didn't go to school but went to play in the park. I asked my nurse, when we first got to Paris, why people spoke French in the streets. She said because we were in France. My mother gave me the same answer. I was frustrated because in the States English was spoken in the streets and French only at home. Oh yes, another memory. One day at lunch Pierre, a 10-year-old French boy, sat opposite me. The day before he had asked me if there were any Chinese in America. I had said yes because I used to go with my mother to a Chinese laundry. The Chinese man there wore a queue, a long pigtail. Then Pierre had asked me if there were Japanese in America and I had replied that there were none. In the middle of lunch I suddenly remembered I had seen a Japanese woman in a kimono with a baby on her back crossing a street when I was coming back from playing in Washington Square. So I announced in French that after all there were Japanese in America. Everyone at the table burst out laughing. I was mortified. Then this boy asked me if I would marry him. I replied that I had a fiancé in America, and this made everyone laugh again.

That year the Russo-Japanese War had just ended. I went to a birthday party at the apartment of one of our French friends. A war game was played: some of us were to be Japanese, others Russian. The two teams stood at each end of the hall. We had a pail of water and a lot of newspapers. We were to make wads of wet paper and throw them at the enemy. I just remember we were told that the Japanese won. That hall must have been a mess.

Before coming back to the States we spent a few days in London. King Edward VII and Kaiser Wilhelm II were to parade down an avenue in an open carriage. A waiter from the hotel held me up in the crowd on the street so I could see the royalties. I had heard that people were afraid a bomb might be thrown. I remembered that in Paris a bomb had been thrown at the heir to the Spanish throne. I got it into my head that a bomb was a lion. At the parade in London I kept looking around for a lion.

Second Trip

In the summer of 1908 my mother, my nurse, and I went to France. My father came over later. We spent some time just by the sea and then in the mountains at Saint-Gervais, near Mont Blanc. My nurse and I, with some French boys and their nurse, would walk around the foothills. Near Mont Blanc some Italian workmen were digging a tunnel under the mountain. My nurse, who came from Northern Italy, knew both French and Italian. She would talk to these men in Italian. I was mad that I could not understand. I insisted my nurse teach me Italian. This she did. Every day I had a lesson in reading and writing both Italian and French.

In the fall I went into the fourth grade at the Chapin School. As I knew French so well, I started German. This suited my grandmother, as she said a person wasn't educated until she knew four languages. I kept telling her my mother knew only three, but her reply was that my mother knew other things.

Third Trip

In 1911 I went on my third trip to Europe. My mother had had a serious operation. She decided to accompany friends (the Macy family) for a six-month stay abroad. One of the Macy boys accused me of being in second class on the boat. His family had a suite of rooms, and my mother and I had only a stateroom. I got so mad at him that I began physically fighting with him on the stairs. A waiter came up and said that girls do not fight.

We went to Geneva, Switzerland, where we stayed in a hotel on a hill on the outskirts of town. As my mother and her friends went motoring around Europe, the Macy children were placed in various families, and my nurse looked after me. I went to a school in town that had one large room upstairs for girls; the boys were below. We were of different ages, from 9 to 13. Our teacher was a Russian. There were three German girls in the class, an Armenian, myself (the only American) and the rest were Swiss. I knew French well and had had German in school so I had no trouble in class. Except, at first I could not translate German into French directly without using English as the intermediary. Also, I had never learned the metric system. The first day I was puzzled by a problem of a man selling so many hectares of land. That night I got someone at the hotel to teach me the metric system. In school we studied irregular verbs, math, dictation, and sewing (putting in a patch). We went to school on Saturdays, as is done in Europe still today, and were off on Thursdays. I skipped school some afternoons when my mother and her friends were around and they took us all on little trips, such as up the mountain at Geneva or way off to see Mont Blanc. One afternoon the older Macy boy (the one I had fought with on the boat) and I played hooky and went to the amusement park. An attendant let us stay on the roller coaster for many spins, even though we had paid just for one ride. No one ever knew about this. I just went home at the regular expected time. After school each day I had Italian and French lessons with my nurse.

In May, for three weeks or so, I went with my mother and nurse all over Italy. I kept a diary of all the museums, etc., we went to and got postcards of various scenes and of my favorite paintings, statues, and buildings: the Sistine Chapel, the Roman Forum, the Duomo in Florence. My father had the book bound. The Chapin School was worried the next fall that I had not done sufficient schoolwork while away, but when the diary was seen, I was given full credit for the work I had missed. One teacher was concerned that I hadn't learned English history thoroughly, but the prinicipal ruled this complaint out.

Fourth Trip

In the summer after graduating from college, I went on a trip to Italy with 120 students from various universities around the United States. We had an Italian leader who had been my senior-year professor of Italian. We toured various universities around Italy, as well as visiting Milan, Venice, Florence, Naples, Capri, Pompey, and other places. Our goal had been to place a plaque at the tomb of Dante in Ravenna commemorating the 600th year of his death. At several universities I had to make a speech in Italian to the students who greeted us. Apparently I was the one fluent in Italian. Actually, when I got to France later that summer, I was told I spoke French with an Italian accent.

After leaving the student group in Paris, I went with my mother to Poland and Czechoslovakia. She had been invited by the head of the YMCA in Warsaw and Prague to discuss having women work in canteens for men as had been done during World War I. In Poland we went on a YMCA train to Baranowicze near the Russian border (now a part of the Ukraine), where the YMCA, among other organizations, was helping refugees who were coming back from Russia after wandering for seven years. On that trip we also visited Cracow and then Prague. We picked up a child in Warsaw who had been lost among refugees for several years and returned her to her mother in Prague. Also, I met my future husband, Theodore Abel, who had been in the Polish army fighting against the Russians and who was working for the YMCA in Cracow for the summer.

I have been to Europe and other parts of the world many times since, as I will describe later on.

The Chapin School

After my third trip to Europe in 1911, I entered the Chapin School, a private school in New York City. I went there on the recommendation of an old woman who used to wash our hair once a week. She dressed all in black, and I thought she was a witch. She told my mother that all nice girls went to that school. I was a month late getting to school. I started off badly in the fourth grade. When in math class I told the teacher that I already knew about long division, she stated that I was not to speak unless spoken to. I whispered to a friend that I knew the stuff. The teacher sent me down to my homeroom teacher with a note saying I had spoken out of turn. This school was very difficult. The art teacher was the only person that I felt acted like a human being and showed some empathy. In my psychoanalysis I suddenly remembered her warmth.

When I was in the sixth grade, we were studying English history and had to memorize the kings. A girl in the class brought the list up to date: "And after Queen Victoria's long reign was done, we see Edward VII and George V, his son." In the tenth grade I was taking German, French, Latin, and first-year Greek (the only student doing so). I had homework in these languages every night, as well as in history, math, and English. I finally got enough courage to speak to the principal about my work. She let me drop French, since I could read and write it as well as English. By the time I graduated, I had completed six years of Latin and three of Greek.

My best friend, Louisa Cogswell, and I were taken to school by a nurse on the Fifth Avenue bus. It wasn't until 14 years old that I could go to school alone. When I was 4 or 5 years old, the Fifth Avenue bus was drawn by two horses.

It's funny how I remember what history was taught beginning in the fifth grade: fifth grade, American; sixth grade, English; seventh grade, Greek; eighth, Roman; ninth and tenth, Western Europe. (In my freshman year at Vassar I took this same history, using the same book.) No history in the eleventh grade and ancient history in the twelfth grade.

During my senior year, the middle and upper school (fourth through twelfth grades) elected a president of the student body: Dorothy Caswell, one of my best friends. But she had to move to Boston and I was elected in her place. I was shy but I managed somehow to preside at student meetings and meetings with the principal. All this helped me gain a little confidence. My girl friends all had boyfriends, even steady ones, but not I. I was too shy. I did meet boys at dances, and in the senior year I did go around with one boy whom I didn't care for much. I remember once we were standing by the statue of some military man at Madison Square. Under the statue was written "Amor patriae." I told my date that I didn't believe in this, that I was a world citizen. He was shocked.

My Summers: 1912–1922

After our farm in Ossining was sold, I spent summers (when not in Europe) in various places: Tokeneke and Black Point, Connecticut; and Larchmont, New York. The summer before my senior year at Chapin, I went to summer music camp. Then the second month I went on a horseback trip through the Rockies and Yellowstone Park with a friend and her family. Before we finished the trip, I had run a sharp stick through my leg, which became badly infected. A nurse who was along with us was able to work on my leg and get a lot of pus out. But for two days I had to ride on the horse with my leg up on the saddle somehow. This was in the days long before penicillin. My leg got better, but I got several abscesses in different parts of my body. I was fortunate that the infection didn't travel all through my bloodstream. It took half a year to get over all the infection. When we got back to New York, there was a polio epidemic and schools did not open till November.

The summer of 1918, after my freshman year at Vassar, I went to secretarial school in New York, studying Pitman shorthand and typewriting. Both of these skills have served me in good stead ever since. This I did in the mornings. In the afternoons I worked at the YMCA, where my mother was volunteering. During World War I, women ran huts or canteens for the soldiers in France. In August that summer my mother went to Paris for a year. When the war was over, she was in charge of 3000 women working in the huts in France and along the Rhine.

The next summer my mother was still in France. My father was staying with a friend in the country, commuting to New York. My cousin and her husband, as well as two other cousins, lived in our house in Manhattan. I had a part-time job at the Manhattan Trade School for Girls. I assisted a secretary, who was a very disturbed person. She sent me out on work she was supposed to do, which was to find jobs for girls who finished the school. I remember going to Henri Bendels, a very fashionable store on 57th Street. The manager asked me to choose a dress for myself. I had the good sense to refuse. One day my boss asked me to bring her a chicken sandwich. When I did so, she threw it in my face. At the end of the summer I heard she had committed suicide.

In June 1922 Mr. Taylor of the YMCA in Poland reminded me that I had promised to come back to work the next summer. My parents objected to this; they saw Poland as a country full of disease, especially typhus. But I took all the money I had in a savings account ($157) and sailed for Europe tourist class. In Paris I stayed with French friends. In Warsaw Mme. Curie had arranged for me to live with her sister, Dr. Dluska, and her husband, Dr. Dluski. The YMCA gave me enough money for the train trip. I worked in the YMCA doing odds and ends: sorting out books, typing letters, and other kinds of secretarial work. I was asked to take visitors around and show them the city. I accompanied a Chinese person once and then an Argentinian student. The latter, I found out later, belonged to the richest family in Buenos Aires. We would go dancing at the Hotel Europa. He taught me the tango. Later in the summer I went to work in Cracow, where the workers from the YMCA were sent for further training. I boarded with the Fisher family in the Stary Rynek (the market square). I kept in touch with this family through the years. In 1957 I went to Toronto, where Mrs. Fisher had come to visit her son. When the Soviets had invaded Poland, her home had been taken away from her except for one room. In the summer of 1990 I went to an International Family Therapy meeting in Cracow and walked around the old market square. The town had remained the same, except that the houses had all been turned into business offices. I had tears in my eyes when I looked at the house I had lived in 68 summers ago.

Vassar College: 1917–1921

In my senior year at the Chapin School I applied to Vassar College. I had wanted to go to Bryn Mawr, where some friends were going, but my father did not like the president of the college. He had sat next to her at a dinner, and he said she was rude and masculine. So I went to Vassar. I majored in history and took two more years of Greek. In my sophomore year I had a course in psychology with Professor Margaret Washburn. I became very interested. I really had no idea what I wanted to do after college. When I was younger, I used to play pinochle every week with an older cousin. She was a secretary for the head of the Community Service Society. I knew this organization helped people. I decided I would become a social worker, and I thought psychology might be a requirement. But all of this was very vague.

Maybe a project I was involved in when I was 15 influenced me in my final choice of profession, even though I was not aware at all of this. A girl a year ahead of me at Chapin had been asked by her aunt to form a working girls' club. She invited me to join her as secretary and treasurer. We met in the basement of the church next to my home once a week, where we planned recreation for the weekends. We went to the Museum of Natural History and to the Metropolitan and walked around Staten Island and in other places. Then the girls decided they wanted to visit Sing Sing prison. They had heard that the new superintendent had made many prison reforms. So I wrote a letter to this superintendent saying a group of the working girls' club wished to visit the prison some Sunday. I guess he had no idea I was only 15 years old. All the girls were over 18, many in their 20s. We got permission to go up on a Sunday. I remember seeing the cell block when the doors were open. The prisoners were all out in the yard. I talked to one prisoner, who said he had heard that jobs were many in South America and that he would go there when his term was up and start a new life. I have no other memories of that visit.

The first year at Vassar I was very happy to be away from my mother. I liked her very much but she was very bossy and always wanted to know what I did and where I went. My second year at college my mother was in Paris for the whole year (when she was in charge of 3000 women who were running huts where American soldiers could relax and get food). At Vassar we were allowed only eight weekends a year away from school. I enjoyed these weekends, especially when my mother was away. My father was much more permissive, but he did ask questions about my whereabouts.

In college I continued taking more and more psychology. I liked abnormal and also applied, where we had a chance to give a Binet test of intelligence to children in an orphanage in Poughkeepsie.

The last semester at Vassar another student, Margaret Child, and I did a piece of research for credit in psychology. This study was on "The Effects of Immediate Repetition of the Pleasantness or Unpleasantness of Music." Several years later, Professor Washburn wrote up this study. It was published as Chapter 10 in a book entitled *The Effects of Music* (Washburn, Abel, & Child, 1927). Margaret and I did get credit for this work: Professor Washburn put our names after hers as authors of the paper. She never told us she had done this. It was about twenty years later that I came across the book and discovered that our study had been published.

The last semester at Vassar, I was coming back to college in the train, after a weekend in the city, when a fellow student came up to me and said that she and I had made Phi Beta Kappa. I thought she was kidding. I had received a C in math and three C's in economics. I had been told that no one who had had a C made Phi Beta. This changed my life. For the first time I thought I had a brain. I had heard about graduate school, and I went to Miss Washburn to ask her about it. She said I should go to Cornell, where she had received a degree. Professor E. B. Titchener was head of the psychology department there. But my father said I could not go away to graduate school; I would have to stay home. So I decided to go to Columbia instead. Miss Washburn told me to go down to Columbia in May and speak to the head of psychology about going there in the fall. When I spoke with Professor Woodworth he said, "Be my guest." That was my entrance exam for graduate school.

Columbia University—First Time Around: 1921–1922

In the fall I began full-time classes at Columbia. After two weeks I withdrew, much to my father's dismay, since he had already paid the tuition for the full term, because I had been invited by a professional quartet to practice with them. I played twice a week for three hours each as second violinist. I was terribly flattered at this opportunity, so I accepted. I took violin lessons and practiced as much as I could. Every Monday night I went to the Metropolitan Opera House with a young man. We paid $2 for standing room at the back of the orchestra seats. After the opera we went dancing on the roof of the then Pennsylvania Hotel. At the end of the year the young man told me I had cost him $5 a week! When the second semester came around I realized I was missing something in my life: it was psychology. So I took two courses at night (seven hours credit).

Le Sorbonne: 1922–1923

After the summer in Poland, my French friends had suggested I live with them in Paris the next fall instead of going back to Columbia. They explained how I could study at the Sorbonne. My father wrote that I was to go home first and sent me money to return. Instead, I spent this money on clothes and remained in Paris. I wanted to be able to see my fiancé, Theodore Abel, during vacations. He was studying sociology with Professor Florian Znaniecki at the University of Poznan.

When I went to the Institute of Psychology to register, I was told that without an M.A. I could not do so. But when the registrar saw I had had seven hours at Columbia, he said, "Seven hours at Columbia is worth a master's degree." Later, Columbia gave me 30 hours' credit for the work I did that year in Paris. I took a course on memory with Pierre Janet, who was very contemptuous of Freud. I had another course (Creativity) with Delacroix. A Jesuit priest was my partner in a laboratory course. He kept saying that, by working with him, I made his blood pressure go up. Simon of Binet-Simon fame gave a course on the psychology of mathematics. I was not interested in this topic, but once a week Simon took the class to visit different institutions, such as schools for the blind, the deaf, the delinquents, and the retarded.

Another professor, Dumas, lectured on the abnormal. Every Sunday morning he took the class to St. Anne's psychiatric hospital. There he would interview a patient in our presence. I shall never forget a red-haired paranoid woman being interviewed. She was 36 years old and had been picked up while sitting in a park. She claimed to be the daughter of the Duc de Guise, the supposed heir to the French throne. According to her, she was engaged to the son of the Kaiser of Germany. They would marry and unite the two countries. She stated that Clemenceau had recognized her standing in the crowd at some ceremony and invited her to stand next to him. Dr. Dumas asked the patient how she could be the daughter of the Duc de Guise as he was only 40 years old, four years older than she was. Her answer was, "Ça s'arrange" (That can be arranged). Earlier she had been a governess to the family of the czar in Russia. This had been verified as true.

At the Sorbonne we had both oral and written final exams. Thanks to Simon's trip to the institution for the blind, I was able to answer one oral question: What do the blind do with their left hand when they read Braille? I remembered a girl reading Braille with the first finger of her right hand and keeping track of the lines with her left hand. I passed all the questions. On the written we were told that if we made a single mistake in spelling or did not place the accents correctly, we would fail. The French language had to be written perfectly. I took a few lessons to practice writing essays, and I passed.

That same year I studied Polish at L'Ecole des Langues Vivantes Orientales. And I had violin lessons once a week, which meant practicing a couple of hours a day. I was not idle. My fiancé came to Paris for New Year, and I went to Poznan for Easter. On the way to Poland I had to go first through the German customs and then, after a further ten-minute ride in the train, through the Polish customs. I had my violin along. The German customs officer asked me in German where I had bought my violin. I guess he thought I had purchased it in Germany and wanted to sell it in Poland. When I told him I got it in the United States, he didn't believe me. He told me to play something. If I could play the violin, then he would assume it was mine. So in the middle of the night, pouring rain outside, in the customs hut, I played a slightly distorted version of the Marseillaise. The officer did not recognize the tune, but some others there laughed. I could keep my violin. As I said earlier, I returned to Columbia University in the fall.

Columbia University—Second Time Around: 1923–1925

Professor Washburn at Vassar had done a study on national differences and preferences in beliefs (Washburn, 1923). When I was in Paris, I thought it would be interesting to repeat this study among university students in different countries. I had contacts that enabled me to get answers to the questionnaire from 146 Polish, 115 French, 107 Czech, and 119 American Students.

When I started graduate school at Columbia in the fall of 1923, I showed my write-up of this experiment to Professor Woodworth. He said it would do for my master's thesis. The paper was published in the *Journal of Comparative Psychology* (Abel, 1926). To earn some money that year, I got a job working with classes of subnormal girls in the New York City school system twice a week. I was supposed to evaluate their intelligence level, as well as their emotional stability (using the Downey-Will Profile). My doctoral dissertation was about the work I did there.

A piece of advice Professor Washburn gave me at the time I received my doctorate was that I should continue doing research and produce three published articles a year. This I tried to do.

At one time during the winter, Mary Cover Jones invited graduate students over to her apartment to meet J. B. Watson. He came into the living room holding a large glass jar. In it was a snake. Watson picked up the snake by the neck and passed it around the group. Each one of us was to hold the snake and pass it along to his or her neighbor. Fortunately I was not afraid of snakes.

I got married in the fall of 1923. My husband got a fellowship to do graduate work in the sociology department of Columbia University. He also worked two days a week, and between us we made a living. He tutored me so I could pass the German exam. French was easy for me.

At this point, it might be of interest to tell about my relationship with Margaret Mead. Because my family name was Mead, Professor Woodworth put Margaret and myself next to each other in one of his classes. (He placed his students alphabetically.) Margaret, early on, told me I'd never be a success, because I did not minor in anthropology or some other subject besides psychology. I was narrow-minded, she said. When later in the fall I got married and took my husband's name, she said that would finish me. I was glad I did not keep the name of Mead. I would have been asked throughout the years if I was a relative of Margaret's. We did become good friends though. Her first husband, Luther Cressman, was getting a degree in sociology along with my husband. The four of us often went out to dinner together or to a show. In later years Margaret helped me get various research projects.

The next year, I wrote my dissertation (Abel, 1925) and worked part-time, still with the retarded girls, this time looking for jobs for them. My husband continued finishing up his class requirements. In February 1925 I took my final exam (oral) on my dissertation. I was also seven months' pregnant. I also taught history twice a week at the Chapin School to make a little more money. My son was born in April.

University of Illinois: 1925–1926

The next fall my husband got a job teaching sociology at the University of Illinois in Urbana. He had not finished his dissertation, which he completed two years later. I wanted to work part time at the university there, but at that time it was against the rules for a relative of a faculty member to work in the same university. The evening before classes were to begin, someone knocked at the door of our apartment. It was Professor Bentley, chairman of the psychology department. A part-time instructor had just eloped and an instructor was needed to take her place. The dean had said I could be asked to take the job. I was asked by Professor Bentley to teach quiz sections six hours a week and to begin the next morning at ten. I was to use his book *The Field of Psychology*. The next morning I bathed, nursed, and dressed my 4-month-old son and pushed him in his carriage to the university. I didn't know with whom I could leave him as we had only just arrived in Urbana. When I got to Professor Bentley's office he asked me what I wanted. He didn't recognize me all dressed up. I left my son asleep in his carriage and climbed up to the fourth floor to the class. My son was just under the window of the class. I asked a student to watch out to see if he was still asleep. Peter slept through the two hours. In the afternoon I returned for one quiz section and my husband looked after our son. I did this routine twice a week but soon found a neighbor to look after Peter while I was gone.

In the spring Professor Bentley had a picnic for the psychology department. Otto Rank was visiting the university and was invited to the picnic. At one point Bentley asked me to catch up with Rank, for he seemed to be walking off from the group. Bentley said Rank was very absentminded and would just walk off from a group. So I went to fetch him back.

The dean told me that I could not teach the next year. I applied for a National Research Council fellowship. My project was "Attitudes and the Galvanic Skin Reflex" (Abel, 1930). I received the fellowship, but then my husband was asked to teach at Cornell University for one year at an increased salary.

In the fall of 1926, I transferred my research to Cornell. Professor E. B. Titchener, the chairman of the psychology department, gave me permission to work in his laboratory but said I could expect no help from anyone in the department. I got a galvanometer from the physics department. Graduate students in psychology were willing to be my subjects. Professor Titchener never came up to the department but, instead, sent messages via a courier. I received a message from Titchener saying he expected me to attend his lectures on psychology. All his professors and graduate students had to attend each lecture. I was told I was to follow the teachers ahead of the graduate students into the classroom, where we sat in the front row. Titchener always wore his Oxford robes and cape for the lectures. At one point I received a note from him saying that he never lectured on emotions, only on sensations. He usually had Professor Neff from Clarke University lecture on emotions, but Neff could not come that year so I was to take his place. I worked very hard on this assignment, as I didn't want to give a bad impression. At the end of the semester, after the student exams for the course were corrected, I was teased a lot by the staff because one student had written "according to Aristotle and Abel . . ."

The second semester Titchener ran a seminar on humor one night a week. He wrote me a note saying he expected me to attend. I did so. Each student was to choose a book to review on humor or aesthetics. I wanted to review Bergson as I could read French easily. But Titchener said I was to take what was left over. And that was Lipps's *Aesthetik*. The German was very hard, but my husband's good German helped me greatly. I wanted to do a good job because several times during the seminar Titchener made fun of Columbia. Knowing that I had received a degree there, at various times he would ask the class if they knew the kinds of dissertations that were carried out at Columbia. Then he would proceed to give an example: a bunch of pins were thrown on the floor, and a student was timed picking the pins up. Then the subject drank a can of beer, the same number of pins were thrown on the floor, and he was timed on how fast he could pick them up. Everyone laughed. I said nothing. Titchener had said he would report on the introduction of the Lipps book. Two days before I was to report on the book, Titchener sent me a note saying he could not do the introduction and that I was to do so. I spent the next 48 hours working on the 40-page introduction. The fact is, I did not want to let down Columbia. I am not sure that Columbia has ever appreciated my efforts.

At the end of the year, Titchener must have forgotten about his opinion of Columbia for he nominated me for Sigma Xi, the honorary scientific society. I and one of his students, a Japanese who was very short (he came up to my shoulder, and I am not very tall), walked up together to receive our certificates (Abel, 1978a).

I realized during the year that Titchener was losing his memory. It showed up in some lectures. He died the next summer. A few years later when I was back at Cornell for the summer, I saw his brain in the physiology department. He had had a tumor on the medulla.

After Cornell, we returned to Illinois for two years (1927–1929). During that time I finished the research I had started at Cornell, and my older daughter was born.

Research 1: 1930–1946

The main thrusts of my research before I entered the clinical field were (1) a study of the role of visual, auditory, and kinaesthetic perception in short-term memory and (2) modes of thinking—a comparison of normal and subnormal adults as to moral judgments and social facilitation in motor tasks.

After teaching at Sarah Lawrence (where I taught from 1929 to 1935), I obtained two research projects. I took the one-year project (1935–1936) and postponed the four-year one for a year. The first project was a fellowship given by the Laura Spelman Rockefeller Fund to work with a group from the Progressive School Association under the leadership of Caroline Zachary. That year I also observed English, chemistry, and social science classes in the Bronxville High School in Bronxville, New York and math classes of the tenth grade in the Fielding School in Riverdale, New York. As Max Wertheimer was my supervisor, he suggested I do a research project on gestalt. I chose to study the recall of finished and unfinished tasks as carried on by Zeigarnik. Unfinished tasks were always remembered more easily than finished ones. My subjects came from the Fielding School (Abel, 1938, 1941).

The next four years my work was funded by the Keith Foundation. I was back at work again with the subnormals at the Manhattan Trade School. This time I was director of a group. A psychologist did intelligence and aptitude testing, a social worker visited the homes of the girls, a WPA doctor looked after their health, and a placement counselor found jobs for them when they finished their training on power machines in the garment trades. I talked to the girls who had various problems. I also did a piece of research. The fourth year the work was finished, and I spent the rest of the year writing a book entitled *The Subnormal Adolescent Girl* in collaboration with Elaine F. Kinder (Abel & Kinder, 1942), who was research psychologist at Letchworth Village, New York. In 1938 my second daughter, Zita, was born.

Letchworth Village: 1940–1946

The next year I was offered a position as research psychologist at Rockland State Hospital near my home. Dr. Kinder was interested in that same position, and I wanted to continue working with the retarded in an institution. So we traded places, and I spent some time doing research at Letchworth Village, an institution for the retarded. I learned the Rorschach test from both Klopfer and Piotrowski in New York. But I worked on problems such as why some adolescent girls in the school could learn fractions and why others could not although they were of the same chronological and mental ages. It turned out the latter had emotional difficulties that showed up on the Rorschach.

One of my assistants in Letchworth gave verbal and nonverbal intelligence tests to all the inmates of that institution. In fact, at Letchworth you couldn't die without taking an IQ test. I remember that once I was asked by the hospital there to send someone over quickly to give an intelligence test. A patient was very sick, in an oxygen tent, and had never been tested. I didn't send a psychologist to do the testing. Instead I found out that this patient had been tested at Bellevue Hospital in New York City, so I used the IQ she had received there before coming to Letchworth. No one questioned where the IQ had come from. The girl died.

I also did a study of why the black girls dominated the white girls in the institution—both in everyday life and in an experiment (Abel, 1943). What came out in my experiment and in observing the behavior of the black girls was that apparently institutionalization enhanced their aggressive tendencies. This was not because they were under restriction but because they found themselves, for the first time, on an equal footing socially with the white girls. The white girls were no longer the "master caste," and so the black girls put them in an inferior position.

Gregory Bateson invited me to talk about this study at an anthropological meeting at the New York Academy of Sciences. He invited me to come to dinner first at the home of Larry Frank. I started out that morning to get to Letchworth but a severe snowstorm impeded my way. I literally spent all day getting into New York City. I reached the home of Larry Frank at 6:00 P.M. Larry's wife, Mary, was not expecting me because Gregory had forgotten to tell her he had invited me. He did not appear. Mary Frank gave me supper and at 7:30, I went to the Museum of Natural History, where the meeting was to be held. There was Gregory. He was expecting me but had forgotten about the dinner. After my talk we went to a friend's house near the museum. Margaret Mead, at that time still Gregory's wife, was in Washington, D.C., where she worked during World War II. Several people had gathered at this home, and we talked till the early hours of the morning. I left the group alone. Gregory never offered to see me to a cab. It was very cold and it took me forever to find a cab to take me to my parents' home. I never would have made it to my home in Rockland County.

At Letchworth there were other psychologists, intern psychologists, and social workers handling all kinds of cases for placement in foster homes or to return them to their communities. I just want to mention one case, a blind baby, that made a lasting impression on me. One day the head matron at the hospital said there was a little blind boy, a year and a half old, in bed there. He had been abandoned by his family and was supposed to have very low intelligence. She remarked that he was shouting one word, "Eckie!" The doctor on the ward was a Dr. Malecki. I went over and found the boy was quite bright. He was then placed in a foster home where he remained till he was 6. When he was old enough, he went to the school for the blind. He was of at least normal intelligence.

I remained six years in Letchworth. However, one four-month period I took a leave and worked at the Manhattan Trade School again. During this time I gave Rorschachs to groups of about 15 girls at a time, using the Rorschach slides devised by Molly Harrower. From the protocols, I picked out those in which there were signs of anxiety, depression, and other disturbances (Abel, 1945) These girls were counseled by me and some teachers. Before leaving Letchworth I had heard about play therapy. One of my interns and I began doing play therapy with three little boys reported by their teacher as appearing upset. I was so intrigued by this new technique that I decided to get training. I also found a couple of psychiatrists who were willing to start me on analytically oriented psychotherapy. They supervised my therapeutic work with three adults. Later, I received supervision in play therapy.

Work During My Parents' Illnesses: 1946–1947

In 1946 both my parents became quite ill, so I left Letchworth. I tried to spend as much time as I could with them and still carry out my work. One year I received some money through the Benedict/Mead Fund to study attitudes toward menstruation in different cultures. I interviewed individuals from France, China, Ireland, and the United States (Abel & Joffe, 1950). I could set my own hours for this work.

The next year I spent one morning a week doing counseling at the Manhattan Trade School, with the normal girls. I just want to mention one girl who was sent to see me for counseling. Her teacher said she could not understand why this girl could not carry the American flag in a pageant. The day before, she had started crying, saying that it was impossible. I was quite puzzled until I asked her if it was the wrong day to carry the flag. She said yes. I realized she was of the orthodox Jewish faith and was menstruating. She felt she would contaminate the flag. I explained to her the flag was not part of religion.

After my mother died I moved my father and his nurses into my home in Palisades, New York. I spent that year at home straightening out the affairs of my parents. My father died in February of 1947.

The Postgraduate Center for Mental Health: 1947–1970

In April, after my father died, a psychiatrist friend of mine suggested I go to New York and see Dr. Larry Wolberg, who had opened a large outpatient mental health clinic, then called the Postgraduate Center for Psychotherapy. (Later the name was changed to the Postgraduate Center for Mental Health.) I said I did not want a job. I had a part-time job coming up the first of July doing research with Ruth Benedict and Margaret Mead. My friend persuaded me just to go and have a talk with Larry Wolberg, so I made an appointment. The first thing Larry did was to take up his appointment pad and ask me when I was going to start to work for him. I told Larry he didn't know me and I didn't want a job. Well, we kept on talking for almost an hour. Then Larry took up his pad again and repeated his question about my working there. This time I said I'd work ten hours a week, two evenings from 5 to 10 P.M.

I began the first of May. In August I went to see Larry and told him the psychologists doing diagnostic testing were over one hundred records behind. He asked me to be the director of psychology. I worked out some plan to get the records up to date. I did both therapy and diagnostic testing myself. I remained 23 years at the center. At first Dr. Wolberg supervised my work. A school was organized to train psychiatrists, psychologists, and social workers in psychoanalysis and psychoanalytically oriented psychotherapy. I took a couple of courses myself, including one in group therapy with Al Wolf. I opened a private office of my own near the center (the center moved three times during those 23 years). I took a course in supervision along the way and did supervising my last five years at that clinic. I taught courses in initial interviewing, dream interpretation, and, with an anthropologist, a course on taking the culture into account in doing therapy. The various departments at the center (group, child and adolescent, community, heads of the three disciplines) formed the executive committee. We met once a week with Dr. Wolberg as chairman. We were fed the same meal once a week for all the years I was there. Arguments were rife and the fur flew, but we did reach conflict resolutions.

I had my own psychoanalytically oriented psychotherapy twice a week for three and a half years in the early 1950s with Dr. Henry Grand. My therapy helped me see more clearly what my relationships had been with my father and mother. Also, I found out that the warmest parental relationship I had had was with my maternal grandmother. At the conscious level, I had found her fussy and a nuisance because she was always inspecting my nails, making me braid my hair, and dress for dinner each evening. I was sorry but did not cry at her death when I was 22. But in my therapy I began crying when I spoke of her. To this day I have tears in my eyes when I think of my grandmother. She gave me a lot of affection, kissing, and patting. I would sit on her fat lap and slide off even when I was 10 years old. By the way, this fatness killed her. She got diverticulitis. This was long before the days of antibiotics. She was too fat to have surgery, so she died of an intestinal infection.

In the 1950s Alexander Luria from Moscow visited the center along with a colleague, whose name I have forgotten. Luria gave a lecture. The evening after the lecture our executive committee invited Luria and his colleague for dinner at the Carlton House. Before dinner I talked with Luria. We clicked our glasses and began to laugh. I was drinking a vodka martini and Luria had a whiskey sour.

Psychologists in New York State had tried for some time to get state certification, but for several years they were blocked by psychiatrists. One time I went to Albany as representative of the Postgraduate Center to talk to a government committee about the certification of psychologists. Eric Fromm went to the same meeting as representative of the William Alyson White Institute. On the way back to New York on a train I sat next to Fromm. At one point he looked at his watch and excused himself. He said he had a supervisory hour. He went to the back of the car and sat down with a young man. After 45 minutes Fromm came back and sat next to me again, and we continued our conversation. Apparently the young man had gone all the way to Albany and back on the train so he could have supervision at his appointed hour.

For a few years in the 1960s a group of mental health professionals got together with some permanent members of the United Nations. We met about once a month. The question discussed was the extent to which U.N. members from different countries saw themselves as representing primarily their own nation or whether they felt they were world citizens.

Early in 1968 several of us from the Postgraduate Center heard Dr. Nathan Ackerman talk about family therapy at the New York Academy of Medicine. Four of us decided to take training in family therapy with Dr. Ackerman one night a week during the academic year 1968–1969. The class met part of the time at the Family Institute and the rest of the time at the Jewish Board of Guardians. The next year (1969–1970) Asya Kadis, a well-known group therapist, and I had the nerve to teach family therapy at the Postgraduate Center. Even though we had been supervised only a few times, we felt ready to teach and supervise. I also took a few families and couples in my private practice.

Research 2: 1947–1981

For two years, in my early days at the Postgraduate Center for Mental Health, I worked part-time on a research project of Mead and Benedict on the study of cultures at a distance. I gave Rorschach tests to Chinese males and females, some born in China and some born in the United States, and compared the two. Dr. Francis Hsu from Northwestern University kindly provided me with Rorschachs he had done to supplement my groups (Abel & Hsu, 1949). Then I interviewed a few Chinese, several French, and three or more Syrians who were either Jewish, Mohammedan, or Christian. The psychologists working with the Chinese and those in the French group met once a week to discuss their work. Many members of the team were studying the East European Jews who had migrated to the States. I wrote up my work, in some instances alone.

The next two years (1949–1951) I did research at Bellevue Hospital in the psychiatric aspects of facial disfigurement. This project was headed by a sociologist, Frances MacGregor, and a plastic surgeon. Besides myself, we had a psychiatrist, a social worker, and another psychologist on the team. My main job was to do diagnostic testing with patients before and after they had plastic surgery. Some patients were too disfigured to have surgery. These were tested also. I gave Rorschachs, figure drawing tests and Thematic Apperception Tests (TAT) to both the severely disfigured and the mildly disfigured. The study was financed by NIMH (Abel, 1952).

Over the New Year of 1954 I was invited by Rhoda Metraux to spend a month in a village on the island of Montserrat, British West Indies, and give projective tests to men, women, and children. Dr. Metraux had a fellowship for a year to make a complete cultural anthropological study of the village. I gave Rorschachs, TATs, figure drawing tests and some color preference tests (Abel & Metraux, 1957). In 1970, just before moving to Albuquerque, I was asked by Vera Reuben to spend a few days in Kingston, Jamaica, training a psychologist, Hillary Sherlock of the University of the West Indies, on how to give the Lowenfeld Mosaic. Reuben had a grant from the NIMH to make a study of a group of male smokers of cannabis and a group of male nonsmokers. I compared the results of this test to the results of the test on the adult male subjects from Montserrat (the study I had done earlier). The only difference I found between the two groups was that the cannabis smokers used many more colors than did the nonsmokers (Abel & Reuben, 1971).

Then when I was in Albuquerque I gave the Mosaic test to Indian children in St. Catherine's Indian School in Santa Fe. As I had children of the same chronological ages and with an equal sex distribution in both Montserrat and Santa Fe, I compared the two groups. I next compared a new group of Indian children at St. Catherine's on the Lowenfeld Mosaic and on her three-dimensional Kaleidobloc tests (Abel, 1981). The interesting finding of the comparison was that on the two-dimensional test the Indians made two-dimensional designs, as on rugs or pots. On the three-dimensional test they constructed modern buildings such as the Golden Gate Bridge, a shopping center, or a modern apartment building.

Last I gave the Mosaic test to students of both sexes in five cultures: Chicanos in Albuquerque; Navajo students (both groups were university students); students at universities in Mexico City (all born in Mexico City); Japanese students, who were tested at Hiroshima University in Japan; and nursing students and lab technicians from Shiraz, Iran (Abel, 1982–1983).

In the 1970s Joyce Wilson and I studied spinal-cord injured (both quadriplegics and paraplegics). We interviewed them along with members of their families in St. Joseph's Hospital after their accidents and again after they had returned home. The quadriplegics we monitored for some time (Abel & Wilson, 1979).

In 1980 Dr. George Vassiliou, director of the Anthropos Institute in Athens, Greece, asked me to find out if there were any Greeks living in Albuquerque and what they were doing. Joanna Major and I interviewed over one hundred Greeks of different ages both first and second generation (Abel & Major, 1980–1981). We asked about their work, their education, their interests, their participation in social and religious activities, their ideas about marriage (to Greeks or those from other cultures). All the adults stated that no young person should marry a non-Greek or even date a non-Greek.

Teaching

In 1928 my husband had received his Ph.D. in sociology from Columbia University and in 1929 was invited to teach at Columbia. So we moved back to New York. There I obtained a position teaching psychology at Sarah Lawrence College, where I remained until 1935. I enjoyed being what was called a "don," helping girls with personal problems. But I was not too happy teaching, because I taught what I thought was good, sound scientific psychology. The dean, instead, wanted me just to talk about adjustment problems. She was glad when I resigned. I bet I would have been fired if I had not resigned first.

While I was at Sarah Lawrence I took a course with Köhler at the New School for Social Research. Another year I attended lectures by Karen Horney.

For a few years in the early 1930s, Lawrence Frank organized a meeting run by Kurt Lewin during the Christmas holidays. One year the meeting was held at Bryn Mawr College, and I attended it. Erik Hamburgher, from Germany, who later changed his name to Erik Erikson, was present. One afternoon it was snowing hard.

At one point Hamburgher suggested we all go out and play in the snow. This we did.

When I was working in the Mead-Benedict project (1947–1949) I was asked to teach four hours a week at Fordham University (Fall 1947). Zygmunt Piotrowski had left that university to move to Philadelphia, and he suggested I take his place. I taught one Friday afternoon: two hours of class and then two hours of laboratory on the Rorschach test. Early the next week I was called up by the head of psychology. He told me I could not teach, because I had not been approved by the president of the university. We met at Columbia to talk this over. This chairman (I am sorry I have forgotten his name) told me I would have to retract two statements I had made in published material. In a book I have coauthored with Kinder, entitled *The Subnormal Adolescent Girl* (1942), I discussed sterilization saying it was not a good method of preventing retardation. Fordham objected to my using the term *sterilization*. I had also written that retarded women who had had at least three children should be prevented from getting pregnant again (they made poor mothers). This amounted to birth control and was forbidden. I announced I would not retract what I had written, so I had to resign. The head of psychology told me that I could say whatever I wanted in class but could not put it into print. I answered that I cared what I said both in class and in print. A priest who was a member of the psychology department at Fordham told me later at some meeting that he found firing me very foolish. A few years later my husband taught sociology at Fordham. At that time the university had become much more liberal and my teaching would have been tolerated then.

During several years in the 1950s and early 1960s I taught psychology at Long Island University one night a week. There I taught projective testing, mental retardation, and psychopathology, and I supervised master's theses. I stopped teaching when I realized I was working too many hours a week.

In 1978 I was invited by Dr. Hamadani, whom I had met earlier in Santa Barbara, to spend a month at his Neuropsychiatric Institute in Shiraz, Iran, to teach family therapy to his staff of mental health workers, including the psychiatric residents. This was two months before the Shah left. The revolution had started, and the medical school was on strike. For five days all doctors at the general hospital went on strike. I heard from a Tanzanian intern that during that time thirteen patients had died because of lack of care. This intern had to cope alone with the medical care. He could not cover the whole hospital. The psychiatric residents also went on strike. When I asked the latter what happened to the Hippocratic oath, they replied that it did not apply in Iran. I spoke also to Dr. Hamadani and he got the residents to return after a couple of days.

I gave talks to five or six individuals but they soon realized that what I had to say did not always apply in Iran. So it was arranged that I would see each of the day-hospital patients and their families in family therapy. A psychiatric nurse who knew English acted as cotherapist and did the translating. She was so good that I felt I was talking directly to the members of the family. I saw five families a few times, one family seven times. I have often wondered if the little boys I saw in these families lost their lives in the Iran–Iraq war (Abel, 1978b).

Diagnostic Testing

In the 1950s and 1960s I did diagnostic testing for two psychiatrists. One of them, Dr. Jack Millet (who had been and still was a supervisor of mine in therapy), lived in my town, Palisades, New York. He would ask me to do a diagnostic test for him on Saturdays, then I would spend a good part of Sunday writing up the report on the tests. I did this for a couple of years until I got up my courage to tell Dr. Millet that I could no longer do it. I felt it was about time I took a little vacation on weekends. I referred him to a friend of mine, Henry Werner. Jack Millet was very pleased with what Henry was able to do.

For about three years in the early 1950s I volunteered to do diagnostic testing one night a week in the Psychiatric Center of New York Hospital, where Dr. Thomas Rennie had organized the first outpatient clinic for veterans. It was to be a model for further veteran outpatient clinics.

In doing this testing I gave the Rorschach, the Thematic Apperception Test, figure drawings, and the Lowenfeld Mosaic.

Rockland Consultation Center

Dr. Millet, my guru, organized an outpatient clinic first in Nanuet and three years later moved it to Pearl River, New York. Two psychiatrists, three psychologists, and a social worker each bought a share in the house. We all practiced there part time. Dr. Millet was the director, and we also had an office manager. I began doing therapy there with adolescents, children, and some parents. Jack Millet supervised me when necessary. We had a staff meeting once a week where cases were discussed. Play therapy took place on a concrete floor. Water, fire, clay, sand, toys, you name it, were used. I worked there one afternoon, two evenings, and Saturdays till 3 P.M. The rest of the time I worked in New York at the Postgraduate Center and in private practice. After ten years I came to realize I was working much too much. I sold my shares at the Rockland Center and transferred all but four patients whom I continued to see in my home until I moved to Albuquerque.

Music

Languages were one of my two hobbies or leisure-time pursuits; the other was music. As I said earlier, I began violin lessons at the age of 8 in the summer, as my mother couldn't find a piano teacher in the country. This teacher taught me once a week also when we returned to the city. When I was 9 he suggested I play in the junior orchestra of the East Side Music School on the Lower East Side. He felt I should have contact with other musicians. I played in the first-violin section each week unitl I was 13, and then I was promoted to the senior orchestra. We occasionally gave concerts at different places—once at the Commodore Hotel (now gone; the Hyatt Regency stands in its place), where we played for the governor of the state of New York.

The vacation before senior year at Vassar, I spent at an inn in Blue Hill, Maine, where I took violin lessons from Franz Kneisl, the first violinist of a well-known quartet. Most of his pupils were more advanced than I was. I was scared but I managed to play in front of the teacher. I walked nearly a mile through the woods twice a week for lessons. I practiced four hours a day. I could do little else except rest. I went swimming only a couple of times all summer. A student who was already a professional discovered I could read music well so he got me to practice in a quartet. His mother accused me of being a rich girl who did nothing but ride horseback in college. I told her I never a saw horse at Vassar. She gradually accepted me as a person.

Over the years I played in orchestras wherever I was living—New York, Paris, Urbana, Cornell. When I was living in New York in the 1930s I played second violin in a quartet (the other players were professionals). Sometimes we were invited to play at a party at someone's house on the Upper West Side. I believe the professionals were paid. All those years I also played in a piano quartet with amateurs.

After we moved to Albuquerque in 1971 I played in the amateur orchestra, the Philharmonia, for many years. We gave concerts twice a year. Three years ago I stopped doing this. I got too tired playing so late at night and having the extra rehearsals for concerts. Up to that time I also played quartets once a week with friends from the orchestra. One year we had two violas so we played quintets all year. I have continued to play sonatas, as I had done all along, with a friend playing the piano, and at times her son playing duets for two violins with us. When I was in Paris my violin teacher said a pupil of his had to sell her violin. It was a genuine Stradivarius. I bought it for $2500. I had only $900 but my French host lent me the rest. My mother threw a fit and made me pay him back the whole amount within a year. Now I am planning to sell the violin, after it is repaired by the summer of 1992, for 120 times more than I paid for it!!

Foreign Languages

As I mentioned earlier, I had learned French, Italian, and German in my growing-up years. The graduate year I studied psychology at Le Sorbonne I also took Polish lessons twice a week at L'Ecole des Langues Vivantes Orientales (Polish was included as an oriental language!). Maybe under the shadow of my grandmother (she had long since died), I started to learn Arabic. I thought it would be interesting to learn a non-European language. So I went to a school where Persian and Arabic were taught. I worked for ten years with an orientalist. I translated one book on teaching in Egypt in the 12th century (Az-Zarnuji, 1947). Dr. von Grunebaum did the editing and coauthored the book. Then I translated a satire written by philosophers in Baghdad in the 10th century. When Dr. von Grunebaum got sick he had another editor help me, Dr. Lichtenstedter from Harvard. She wanted me to do the editing. Since I was not an orientalist I could not do it. So she found another editor, as she was too busy to edit it herself. I thought I was to be a coauthor. But I found out the book had been published under her name and the editor's, Goodman (Az-Zarnuji, 1947). They did acknowledge that I had worked on the book and had written an article on "Psychological Themes in the 10th Century Satire." My ego was hurt because I had spent ten years on this translation. But actually I don't think I mentioned to the Harvard professor that Dr. von Grunebaum expected me to be a cotranslator. I did write about the psychological theme in this satire.

While I was doing this Arabic translation, I began to study Spanish once a week at the Berlitz School. I had begun going to Mexico City to give talks and I wanted to be able to do some speaking. I found out that as I learned to talk Spanish I could no longer speak Italian. The languages are too similar. But I can now read and write both languages almost as well as French.

One day in New York, in a secondhand book shop, I found a book on Assyrian cuneiform writing. I had fun from time to time learning to translate some of the sentences. But it was also most confusing. An ideogram might stand for a whole word with three or more meanings or for a syllable only.

One summer in New York I took Japanese and learned the syllabic part of the writing. In Japan, when at a dinner, I could get off a short speech in Japanese thanking my hosts and saying I had come from America by airplane to Tokyo.

Albuquerque: 1971–Present

After reaching Albuquerque I planned to spend some time getting settled and fixing up the house. But within two weeks I was at work. Dr. Ross Snyder, who at that time was the psychiatrist at the Child Guidance Center, invited me to teach family therapy. I went there once a week, spending a couple of hours talking about the techniques of family therapy. Also, I began seeing a family once a week. An intern from the psychology department acted as cotherapist. The family gave permission for professionals to observe the sessions through a one-way screen. Dr. Snyder also invited me to participate in a program he was running on first-offender middle school boys, ages about 12–15. The students came with their families. The record of the offense was canceled by the police if the students and their parents attended our sessions.

In 1971 I went back to New York City to a meeting of the New York Society of Clinical Psychologists. I received a certificate from this organization as Psychologist of the Year (1969–1970).

I started teaching psychiatric residents family therapy. A social worker, Joyce Wilson, met me while I was doing this teaching. She and one of the residents, both of whom were then working with inpatients at the mental health center, suggested I do family therapy with them as cotherapists (Abel, Bruzzese, & Wilson, 1974).

I was first appointed assistant clinical professor in the Department of Psychiatry at the Medical School of the University of New Mexico, later associate clinical professor, and around 1980 I became clinical professor.

Private Practice: 1972–Present

I began private practice early on, for a while sharing offices with one group and then moving to another group, where I remained over ten years. I did individual therapy, couples, and family therapy. For two years I worked as a cotherapist in group therapy. I had never been trained in group therapy except for having taken a couple of courses back in New York earlier. But working with families served me in good stead. I saw a group gradually developing as a family. At one point I wrote up a comparison of group and family therapy (Abel, 1982). I ended up having at least 30 hours of private practice a week. I began reducing these hours in the early 1980s and met most of my patients in a room in my home, but maintaining an office one afternoon a week outside my home.

During the last four years I have reduced my patient load to three a week. I have also done therapy with another psychiatric resident. When the present fourth-year residents were in their first year, I saw seven of the eight once a week for a year. This was a support group where they told about their difficulties in their various assignments at work and they would complain about some of their supervisors. Now I keep in touch with this group a couple of times a year.

Many times in my professional life I have been to workshops (some of which I ran) and conferences. Frequently I presented a paper or was a member of a panel.

Meetings

Before entering the clinical field, I attended national and international meetings. I went to many meetings of the American Psychological Association, mostly in the United States but some in Canada; meetings of the Eastern Psychological Association (I was secretary of this organization for two years in the 1940s); the New York State Psychological Association (I was a member of the board at one time); the American Psychopathological Association (I was vice-president one year in the 1960s); the International Congress of Psychology in Copenhagen in 1932, and Stockholm in 1951.

In Stockholm I read a paper discussing an inconsistency in one of Piaget's concepts. Piaget was present at the meeting and refuted my ideas. Also at that meeting someone read a paper in French. I did the translating, as most of the audience didn't understand French. I remember being somewhat embarrassed by the presence of Piaget.

Just after Christmas in 1953 I attended a meeting of the InterAmerican Psychological Association in Santo Domingo. The dictator Rafael Trujillo had a limousine and chauffeur at the disposal of psychologists who were presenting papers. I rode around in a Cadillac. Trujillo had a reception for the group of psychologists. I shook Trujillo's hand saying, "Me gusta mucho conocerlo."

In 1976 I went to a psychiatric conference in Opatija, Yugoslavia. I chaired a meeting and also read a paper on family therapy. Dr. Hamadani from Shiraz, Iran, heard my paper. That is how he came to know me, and at a meeting in Santa Barbara of a regional world congress he came up to me and invited me to Shiraz.

I attended the World Congress of Social Psychiatry in Zagreb, Yugoslavia, in 1981, in Paris in 1982, and again in Brazil in 1986. This congress met just last October in Washington, D.C. At three I presented a paper (the last two with a coauthor, Dr. Sam Roll). In 1972 there was a conference in Cyprus (before the island was divided between Turkey and Greece) organized by the Drs. Vassiliou of Athens. Concepts of family interaction were discussed.

Ever since 1969 I have been to other parts of the world, giving lectures and demonstrating family therapy with patients and a cotherapist from the country I was visiting. I believe I have been to Mexico City invited by the Asociacion Mexicana de Psicoterapia Psicoanalitica at least twelve times. In 1984 I attended a meeting of the International Group Psychotherapy Association there. In earlier years I had gone to the Interamerican Association annual meetings in Mexico City. I went to Japan six times talking about therapy and family therapy in Tokyo, Osaka, and Hiroshima. Three times I showed up in Egypt. The first time I was invited by a psychologist at Al-Shams University to talk about cultural differences. Our book (coauthored with Rhoda Metraux and Samuel Roll), *Psychotherapy and Culture* (1987), had been seen by the professionals there. The next two times I spoke about family therapy.

I have been present at a number of annual meetings of the Society for the Study of Culture and Psychiatry. This society meets every other year or so in a foreign country. The society met in Mexico City a few years ago. In 1989 the meeting was held at Farnham Castle near London. In 1990 the group met at Timberline Lodge at Mt. Hood, Oregon.

Since living in New Mexico, I have frequently attended the South Western Group Psychotherapy Society annuals, usually in Texas. There I have given workshops and acted as consultant.

My Descendants

As for my family, two of my three children have careers unrelated to the mental health field. My son, Peter, is a lawyer for *TV Guide,* and my older daughter, Caroline Lalire, is managing editor at the Bookings Institution in Washington, D.C. My younger daughter, Zita Emerson, has an M.S. in psychology and does cognitive therapy at an outpatient mental health center in Albuquerque. I have ten grandchildren, two of whom followed me in the clinical field. My oldest granddaughter,

Vega Lalire, announced when she was 8 years old that she was going to do what I do. She had no idea what this was. She now has a doctorate in psychology and has been trained in neuropsychological testing for brain damage. She has a license to practice in New York State and works more than full time in her fields of testing and therapy. My oldest grandson, Bruce Abel, received an M.S.W. and a doctorate in social work. He is now the manager of a mental health center in Eugene, Oregon, and supervises mental health workers who do family therapy. His wife, Gail, is a family therapist. Another grandson, Walker Abel, received a masters in something called wilderness psychology. He takes groups of students from the University of California in Santa Cruz into the mountains to have an outward-bound experience. One grandson, Rex Lalire, is an architect; another, Ted Abel, a geologist; one granddaughter, Koren Emerson, is a landscape architect; another, Jessica Abel, is a science teacher in a middle school. My youngest grandson, Mark Emerson, is a scholar. He just received a master's in history, specializing in Roman and medieval history and is going on for a Ph.D. In his senior year at the university he received Phi Beta Kappa. He had never heard of it. He called me up to find out what kind of reception he was going to. Last year I tutored him in French, so he was able to pass the required language exam for his master's. He will be moving to California for his advanced degree, so I won't be able to tutor him in Latin!! Other grandsons: Tom Emerson is studying for a master's in biology, and Gregory Lalire is a writer. As of this writing I have three great grandchildren.

My husband died in 1988. A short time before he died, the Harvard University Press republished his book *Why Hitler Came to Power.* He was so pleased to see it.

Predictions for the Future of Clinical Psychology

I believe psychodiagnostic testing and individual, couples, and family therapy will go on for some time. Milieu therapy has begun in some places, especially in England. Dr. Josephine Lomax-Simpson in Wimbledon (a psychiatrist) includes in her therapeutic work a large group that meets once a month. This group consists of inpatients and outpatients at a psychiatric hospital as well as all the professional staff, psychiatrist, social workers, psychologist, nurses, and family members from the community who come with their children. There may be at least a hundred people in the group. I also understand there is a hospital in London where not only all the professionals meet with the patients but the household staff does so as well, including the cooks. Patients can complain about the food in these meetings.

I believe that there will be more and more group therapy and a great deal more milieu therapy, as well as groups for conflict resolution. I am hopeful that there will be political groups that get together to resolve conflicts locally, nationally, and internationally. These new milieu groups will not just get together to decide on boundaries or on limiting arms, nuclear weapons, etc. but meet to understand one another better. They will talk about feelings, their understanding of the others' positions and the various ways in which they can cooperate and help one another.

Russian and American astrophysicists work together today. In the future this is the way politicians and government members might work together for peace, improvement of the conditions of their peoples, and the environment.

References

Abel, T. M. (1925). Tested mentality as related to success in skilled trade training. In R. S. Woodworth (Ed.), *Archives of Psychology, 77.* New York: Columbia University Press.

Abel, T. M. (1926). National differences and preferences in beliefs. *Journal of Comparative Psychology, 6,* 21–41.

Abel, T. M. (1930). Attitudes and the galvanic skin reflex. *Journal of Experimental Psychology, 13,* 47–60.

Abel, T. M. (1938). Modes of thinking and classroom adjustment. *Journal of Social Psychology, 9,* 287–298.

Abel, T. M. (1941). Measurement of dynamic aspects of behavior among adolescents. *Journal of Genetic Psychology, 58,* 3–26.

Abel, T. M. (1943). Negro-white interpersonal relationships in a limited environment. *Transactions of the New York Academy of Sciences: Psychology Section, 9,* 90–113.

Abel, T. M. (1945). Group Rorschach testing in a vocational high school. *Rorschach Research Exchange, 9,* 178–188.

Abel, T. M. (1952). Personality characteristics of the facially disfigured. *Transactions of the New York Academy of Sciences: Psychology Section, 14,* 325–328.

Abel, T. M. (1971). Psychological themes in a 10th century Arabic satire on beasts and men. *Transnational Mental Health Research Newsletter, 8,* 2–11.

Abel, T. M. (1971). Report on the Lowenfeld Mosaic Test. In Vera Reuben: "Effects of Long Term Chronic Use of Cannabis in Jamaica" (pp. 375–382). (Report for the National Institute of Mental Health).

Abel, T. M. (1978a). An experience during the last year of E. B. Titchener. *American Psychologist, 13,* 47–60.

Abel, T. M. (1978b) Family therapy in Iran. *Transnational Mental Health Research Newsletter, 20,* 1–9.

Abel, T.M. (1981). A comparison of two-dimensional and three-dimensional designs of high school Pueblo-American Indians in New Mexico. *Transnational Mental Health Research Newsletter, 22,* 3–15.

Abel, T. M. (1982). Comparisons between group and family therapy. In L. Wolberg & M. Aronson (Eds.), *Group and Family Therapy.* New York: Brunner/Mazel.

Abel, T. M. (1982–1983). Psychodynamics as reflected in the Lowenfeld Mosaic Test among university students in five cultures. *Hiroshima Forum for Psychology, 9,* 3–16.

Abel, T. M., Bruzzese, D., & Wilson, J. E. (1974). Shorter term family therapy for short term hospitalized patients. A vehicle for training as well as treatment. In L. Wolberg & M. Aronson (Eds.), *Group Therapy* (Chap. 8). New York: Stratton Intercontinental Medical Corporation.

Abel, T. M., & Hsu, F. (1949). Some aspects of personality of Chinese as revealed by the Rorschach test. *Rorschach Research Exchange and Journal of Projective Techniques, 14*(3), 285–301.

Abel, T. M., & Joffe, N. (1950). Cultural background of female puberty. *American Journal of Psychotherapy, 9,* 90–113.

Abel, T. M., & Kinder, E. F. (1942). *The subnormal adolescent girl.* New York: Columbia University Press.

Abel, T. M., & Major, J. (1980–1981). Greeks in Albuquerque, New Mexico. *Transnational Mental Health Newsletter.*

Abel, T. M., & Metraux, R. (1957). Normal and deviant behavior in a peasant community: Montserrat, BWI. *American Journal of Orthopsychiatry, 27,* 167–184.

Abel, T. M., Metraux, R., & Roll, S. (1987). *Psychotherapy and Culture* (2nd ed.). Albuquerque: University of New Mexico Press.

Abel, T. M., & Wilson, J. E. (1979). Spinal-cord injured and family systems. A pilot study. In L. Wolburg & M. Aronson (Eds.), *Group Therapy* (Chap. 18). New York: Stratton Intercontinental Medical Corporation.

Az-Zarnuji. (1947, Orig. work 12th C.). Ta'lim al-Muta'Allim-Tariqi at-Ta-Allum [Instruction of the student: The method of learning.] G. E. von Grunebaum & T. M. Abel (Trans.). Published under the auspices of the Iranian Institute and School of Asian Studies. New York: King's Crown Press.

Gabaldon, J. L. (1980). Problems of an age: The psychological writing of Theodora M. Abel. Unpublished doctoral dissertation, The Fielding Institute, Santa Barbara, CA.

Stevens, G., & Gardner, E. (1982). *The Women of Psychology* (Vol. 2, Chap. 2). Cambridge, MA: Schenken.

Washburn, M. F. (1923). A questionary study of certain national differences in emotional trends among foreign born women in New York and Chicago. *Journal of Comparative Psychology, 3,* 413–430.

Washburn, M. F., Abel, T. M., & Child, M. (1927). The effects of immediate repetition on the pleasantness or unpleasantness of music. In M. Schoen (Ed.), *The Effects of Music* (Chap. 10). New York: Harcourt Brace.

Anne Anastasi, Ph.D.

Professor Emeritus
Fordham University, Bronx, New York

A Career in Psychological Measurement

When I was invited to contribute a biographical chapter to this book, my first reaction was to decline, with appreciation and regrets. My reason was simply that I am not a clinical psychologist: I have never studied, taught, or practiced clinical psychology and therefore have not earned such a title. The editor assured me, however, that there were a few other contributors to the volume "who are not, strictly speaking, clinical psychologists but who had a significant influence on the field." This was accompanied by the generous assurance that my contributions "in assessment and measurement were very influential in the field."[1] On that basis, I accepted the invitation and decided to concentrate on two aspects of my experiential history. First, I shall consider the conditions and persons that helped to shape my development, not only as a psychologist, but more particularly in the assessment and measurement areas.[2] Second, because I lived through the decades

---

[1] Personal communication from C. Eugene Walker, October 2, 1989.

[2] More detailed autobiographical accounts, written from diverse viewpoints, include Anastasi (1972b, 1980, 1982, 1983, August) and Sexton & Hogan (1990). Transcripts of oral history interviews, focusing on different aspects of my career (awards, academic life, publications, APA activities), are provided in Denton (1987), DeVito (1989, March), Robertson (1987, 1988), and Sexton (1987, March).

when clinical psychology began to emerge and then leaped into its spectacular growth period, I have some clear recollections of early clinical psychologists and of conditions in the field during its incipient stages. Although I was an outsider looking in, I did a good deal of interested looking and have some vivid memories to share.

Unconventional Beginnings

Familial Context

I was born on December 19, 1908, in New York City—more precisely in Manhattan. My earliest recollection of my family includes three characters: my grandmother, my mother, and my mother's brother. My grandmother was a grande dame, my uncle was a dilettante, and my mother was a realist. My father, who had been an attendance officer for the New York City Board of Education, died of an intestinal ailment when I was a year old. Although he was survived by his parents and a sister who was a high school teacher, the two families became estranged after my father's death and I never met any of his relatives.

Both my mother and my uncle had received an excellent education, predominantly in the humanities and the classics, but they had no readily marketable skills for earning a living. It was my mother who assumed the major responsibility as the family breadwinner. After a few attempts to utilize her educational background in the world of work, she decided that business was where the money is and that bookkeeping is essential to running a business. Accordingly, she taught herself bookkeeping with books borrowed from the public library. She was hired as a bookkeeper in a small piano factory, where she soon rose to business manager. When the owner retired and the company closed, she opened her own piano factory, of which she was president, my uncle was vice-president, and the best worker from the earlier factory was shop foreman. After a few years, when phonographs drove pianos out of the middle-class market, this company, too, had to shut down.

Following various intervening jobs, my mother eventually became office manager of one of New York's largest foreign-language newspapers, where she remained until her retirement. She had finally succeeded, but it had been a struggle. From this struggle came her indomitable resolve that I should receive a good professional education so that I would always be able to earn my living comfortably—a recurring goal in family discussions that is among my earliest childhood recollections.

I had no playmates of my own age. Our visitors were generally adults, for whom I was often expected to recite poetry, after dropping a proper curtsy. The repertoire ranged from a couple of humorous poems to excerpts from such classics as *Le Petit Savoyard* and the opening lines of Dante's *Divine Comedy*. We owned a huge volume of Dante with terrifying illustrations by Gustave Doré. My mother allayed my fears, however, by explaining that they were just make-believe, like figures of speech. Throughout my childhood, there was constant emphasis on the contrast between reality and myth.

From the standpoint of child psychology, there was much to criticize in my early upbringing. There was little opportunity for development in peer relations and in such common physical skills as skipping rope, roller skating, or bicycling. The one overriding positive feature, however, was the presence of adults who regarded child-rearing as a serious responsibility. For example, when my mother came home from work, although often very tired, she would muster the energy to play fascinating games with me, including word games that we made up and role-playing games that continued for months on end, like a private movie serial or soap opera.

Education

My grandmother took charge of my early education, which began as far back as I can recall. I do not know at what age I started to read, because reading and being read to seem to merge imperceptibly. Certainly by the age of 3 I recall daily lesson periods with my grandmother. The content ranged widely, from literature, history, and geography to arithmetic and natural science. Whether I was read to or read myself, there were always pauses for questions, explanations, exercises. My grandmother had a way of imbuing everything with glamor and drama, and I always looked forward to my lessons.

When I reached school age, in order to meet legal educational requirements, a public school teacher was engaged to tutor me in regular school subjects every afternoon. In the mornings and on weekends, I did homework. My grandmother was closely involved and became quite adept in drilling me with flash cards. She was reluctant to have me attend school because she believed I would learn bad manners from the other children. When I reached the age of 9, however, she was finally convinced that I could go to school, but under some unusual conditions. I was to enroll in the school where my private teacher taught, who was to escort me to and from school, and I was to have my lunch in the teachers' room. Although the teacher lived within a block of us, her school was a long subway ride away. Surprisingly enough, this arrangement was actually implemented and I was admitted to 3B (second half of third grade).

After two months, the classroom teacher decided that the work was too easy for me, and I was transferred to a 4A class. This move proved to be a disaster. The classroom was crowded, and I was assigned a seat in the last row. Although no one—including myself—suspected it, I was significantly myopic and could not read the blackboard from that distance. I complained that I felt lost and did not know what was going on in class. No one realized that I might need glasses; actually, I acquired my first pair of glasses during my freshman year at college. In all intervening schooling, I managed to sit in the front row. But as for that 4A class, I dropped out after a few days and resumed my private lessons. Parenthetically, one advantage I derived from my unusual and fragmented early education was that I learned how to be an independent, self-taught learner. During my subsequent formal education, through the college and graduate school levels, I often said that I went to class to find out what there was to learn, and then went home to learn it. I still think this is a good idea, and it has helped me to keep up with developments in my field throughout my professional life.

By the fall of 1918, my family finally decided that I should attend our neighborhood public school, where I was enrolled in a 4B class. After subsequently skipping 5A and 6A, I continued through the eighth grade in the same cohort, and was thus able to form a few continuing friendships with classmates. I graduated at the top of my class, being awarded the gold medal for general excellence. Together with many of my classmates, I then entered a large public high school in our neighborhood. Because the school had outgrown its own building, the entire entering class was assigned to temporary quarters in an abandoned elementary school building with deteriorated and inadequate physical facilities. In order to accommodate more students, classes where held on a double shift. My routine on three out of five school days was to leave home at 10:30 A.M., ride a trolley car to school, participate in a physical education period at 11:00, eat a box lunch in the school yard, and then attend classes from 1:00 to 5:00. There were no lockers, no showers, and meager washing facilities of any sort. Classes were overcrowded, teachers were overworked, and the whole environment was most unattractive. I stood all this for just two months.

During my dropout phase, there were many family conferences about what to do next. The solution was finally reached with the help of a close family friend, herself a brilliant and dedicated teacher. Upon hearing about my grim high school experience, she promptly exclaimed, "You don't want to go to high school. What you really want to do is go to college." There were alternative routes, she explained, such as the series of examinations offered by the College Entrance Examination Board. At that time, these examinations covered specific courses, such as intermediate algebra, solid geometry, or second-year French. There were, moreover, special schools offering courses in just the subjects required for college admissions, in which one-year courses were condensed into single semesters. By attending such a school, I was able to qualify for admission to Barnard College within two years. As a result, I entered Barnard at the age of 15, graduated at 19, and received the Ph.D. from Columbia University at 21. My graduate studies were in part funded by Barnard's Caroline Duror Graduate Memorial Fellowship, "awarded to that member of the graduating class showing greatest promise of distinction in her chosen line of work." To this day, I am not convinced that high school is necessary!

Why Psychology—and What Kind?

The College Period

When I entered Barnard in 1924, I was sure I would major in mathematics, which had been my first love since elementary school. I had taken all the math exams offered by the College Board and had also accumulated more overall credits than needed for college admission. Consequently, I was admitted with advanced standing in mathematics and was placed in a calculus course taught by the distinguished mathematician Edward Kasner. During my freshman year, I also took a required one-semester course in psychology—a subject about which I knew nothing at all, having hardly ever heard the word before. The textbook in this course was by Pillsbury (1921), and we were offered solid scientific fare. Although I thoroughly enjoyed the course, I certainly did not consider the possibility that I might choose psychology as my lifework.

Two significant events occurred in my sophomore year: I took a course in developmental psychology with Harry L. Hollingworth, then Chairperson of Barnard's Psychology Department; and I happened to read an article by the British psychologist Charles Spearman (1904). Hollingworth was a fascinating lecturer, with a lively scientific curiosity. He was also a vigorous critic of popular psychologizing and slipshod thinking. At that time, his redintegration theory was just taking shape and he sought applications of it in all behavior domains, from advertising to psychoneuroses (Hollingworth, 1913, 1920, 1926, 1927, 1928, 1930; Hollingworth & Poffenberger, 1917). He was one of the last of the generalists in psychology. Years later, one of my former classmates reminded me that after attending one of "Holly's" classes, I observed, "Once I get my Ph.D. in math, I'm going back to take some more psych courses." Then the Spearman article really clinched matters. In it I found out not only about correlation coefficients but also about some fascinating relationships among correlations that later led Spearman (1927) to develop his rationale for tetrad equations, itself an early step toward modern techniques of factor analysis. Here, then, I found a way of enjoying the best of two possible worlds: I could remain faithful to my first love, mathematics, while pursuing its applications in an exciting new field. I changed my major to psychology and embarked upon my chosen career.

Barnard offered specially qualified students an honors program that emphasized independent study in the junior and senior years. Departments differed in their attitudes toward this program; only some departments used it. I was offered honors by the departments of chemistry and history. Because I felt attracted to this type of program but did not wish to major in either of those subjects, I discussed these offers with Hollingworth. He explained that his department did not offer honors because of an unfortunate experience with an earlier graduate who, while academically successful, had become lonely and depressed under that system. I was unconvinced and argued that I was accustomed to independent study. He replied that if I wanted to undertake it at my own risk, he was ready to admit me to honors work in psychology. This program did not require attendance at any courses, but included a comprehensive examination in the senior year, sight reading knowledge of French and German, and the completion of an original research project.

I plunged into the honors program with zest. I took courses (without credit, but doing all the work) in psychology and anthropology at Barnard and then registered under the same conditions for graduate courses at Columbia, including Carl Warden's course in Comparative Psychology. I enrolled in a course in the Psychology of Advertising given by H. K. Nixon at the Columbia University School of Business Administration. I studied German in summer school with an excellent teacher who drilled us in Thuringian pronunciation while introducing us to German music and poetry. Then I passed the Barnard test in German even though I had already met the Barnard foreign language requirement in French in my freshman year. Both of these were more rigorous than the corresponding requirements for the Ph.D. in psychology. I purchased a copy of H. E. Garrett's (1926) statistics book and solved all the problems in it. And in my junior year I conducted an experimental study with Frederick H. Lund, then an instructor at Barnard. Suggested by the work of Bingham (1910) and Moore (1914) on the development of musical preferences, this study was concerned with the role of experiential factors in the esthetic judgment of visual forms. It was reported in a joint article in the *American Journal of Psychology* and represents my first publication (Lund & Anastasi, 1928).

My senior-year honors examination extended over five days and covered a variety of testing techniques: written, oral, and performance. One morning's task was for me to administer the Pintner-Paterson Scale of Performance Tests to a child. The volunteer I recruited for this purpose happened to be highly verbal and an irre-pressible talker. My unexpected instructions, however, were to give the test as though the examinee were a deaf-mute. My volunteer role-played admirably, never uttering a word during the whole period. Moreover, she was so bright that all I had to do was spread the test materials before her and wave my hands vaguely over them—and she would proceed to carry out each task. As for the written part of my comprehensive examination, administered in several sessions, I was later told by Hollingworth that he had used a copy of the Ph.D. qualifying examination for an earlier year—he didn't see why he should prepare a whole new examination for a single student. I recall commenting longingly that I wished it had been the current year's.

The Graduate School Period

After admission to the Columbia graduate school, my first objective was to integrate my undergraduate preparation with the Ph.D. requirements. In my first conference with A. T. Poffenberger, then chairperson of the Psychology Depart-ment, I raised two questions. First, could I skip the M.A. degree? Second, was it possible to obtain a Ph.D. in two years? My first request was quite out of line with the department's policy at that time. Nevertheless, by accepting my published research in lieu of a master's thesis and my honors examination in lieu of the M.A. comprehensives, the department granted the request. In answer to my second question, I was told that it was unlikely but not impossible, especially if I continued right through the summers.

I had already begun to take courses during the 1928 summer session, one of which was Poffenberger's own Applied Psychology. The course assistant was Mortimer J. Adler, who was completing his Ph.D. work in psychology. Because Poffenberger was absent in order to undergo some minor emergency surgery near the end of the course, Adler took over the last few lectures and the final examination.

During my first year of graduate work, I took R. S. Woodworth's Advanced Experimental Psychology, a full-year, intensive, doctoral-level course. Other regular academic-year courses included Woodworth's Contemporary Schools of Psychology, Gardner Murphy's History of Psychology, and a course on race differences with Otto Klineberg, who had just returned from Europe, where he had gathered the data for his comparative study of racial and national samples in test performance (Klineberg, 1931). Once a week, several students in our department rode the subway up to the Columbia Medical Center to take courses at the College of Physicians and Surgeons. One term the course I took was a survey of neuroanatomy given by Adolph Elwyn, with occasional lectures by Frederick Tilney. Another term it was a specialized course on the physiology of the nervous system, with laboratory demonstrations, conducted by F. H. Pike.

The summer of 1929 stands out as a peak period in my entire student history. Having just passed the Ph.D. comprehensives after my first year of graduate work, I became involved in a succession of three unrelated but equally memorable experiences. First, on Woodworth's recommendation, I was appointed as a research assistant to Charles B. Davenport at the Carnegie Institution of Washington's research center in Cold Spring Harbor, New York. Davenport, who had been Woodworth's biology teacher at Harvard, had for some years been interested in human heredity and comparative racial research (e.g., Davenport, 1928, 1929; Davenport & Craytor, 1923). During the 1920s and 1930s, psychologists, anthropologists, and geneticists were still looking hopefully toward the development of so-called culture-free tests; and it was on a project to devise this type of test that I was engaged as one of three summer research assistants. Actually, our work schedule had to be adjusted to accommodate two of us who were involved with university summer sessions. I was planning to take courses at Columbia, and another assistant was planning to teach a course elsewhere. Consequently, the research job for the two of us covered all of June and the last two weeks in August.

The "tests" we devised (or "test ideas," there being no standardization or validation) are included in a comprehensive report of the entire, much broader project. In the foreword to this report, there is a hint that the project may have helped to shake loose the faith in culture-free tests and innate abilities. The opening sentence read: "This volume is the outcome of a search for 'tests of innate ability.' It has developed into a revelation of the difficulties to be encountered when mental tests are used to measure mental endowment" (Schieffelin & Schwesinger, 1930, p. iv).

Our own, rather primitive, operating procedures may be of some intrinsic interest. From 9:00 to 5:00, the three of us sat at a long table in an office we shared with a German interpreter who was busy abstracting literature for another division of the institution. Here we worked assiduously at dreaming up new tests (or adaptations of existing tests) that would require no language, no numbers, and no paper and pencil. One of the tests I devised was an adaptation of the Woodworth-Wells Symbol-Digit Substitution Test (Schieffelin & Schwesinger, 1930, pp. 199–201). Instead of pairing the five simple figures with numbers, I decided to pair them with five colors. On a large sheet of bristol board, I pasted small squares of five colors, in random order; another set of five was used for the key at the top. What I needed next was a supply of circular wooden chips, on which the five forms could be drawn in India ink.

Just as we were wondering where to get 59 wooden chips, Davenport arrived for his daily visit. When he learned of our problem, he rushed out mumbling that he had an idea. Soon he was back, triumphantly flourishing an old broomstick and a saw. In two days we had the test materials ready for pilot testing.

Let me hasten to add that our project was a small and atypical segment of the research that was in progress at Cold Spring Harbor that summer. I met many of the summer researchers—students, postdoctorals, and senior scientists—as well as members of the permanent staff. Various fields, such as genetics, physiology, neurology, and chemistry were represented, and much excellent work was going on. It was at Cold Spring Harbor, for example, that I first heard about P.T.C. taste deficiency[3], which was then just beginning to intrigue geneticists.

In August, an international genetics group was apparently meeting in this country, and at Cold Spring Harbor there were elaborate preparations to receive visitors. Those of us who could speak any language besides English were pressed into service as interpreters and wore tags listing the appropriate languages. I recall an amusing incident in which a French geneticist was visiting the laboratory of a staff member who had been breeding rats for deafness. Since the local scientist seemed able to communicate in French, I stayed in the background. But pretty soon I perceived a mounting animation in the discussion, the French geneticist responding incredulously that the findings were completely out of line with other published research, including his own. At that point, I realized that, in his scientific zeal, the American geneticist had been saying *lourd* (fat) when he meant *sourd* (deaf). Of course, the rats had not been bred for obesity. When I timidly suggested, "Pas lourd, sourd," the difficulty was quickly cleared up by the replacement of one consonant.

In the 1929 summer session—during July and the first half of August—I took two courses with Clark Hull and one with R. M. Elliott. At that time, Columbia had one of the most active psychology departments in the country, with visiting professors and postdoctorals to enrich the local fare not only during the regular academic year but also—and especially—during the summer session. For several years, Elliott would come from Minnesota to teach two courses, one dealing with the nature of the introductory course in psychology and the other with theoretical issues in psychology. I took the latter and found it intensely stimulating. Hull's two courses dealt with aptitude testing and with psychological research on hypnosis. He was on his way from Wisconsin to Yale, where he was soon to begin his monumental research on learning. His book on aptitude testing (Hull, 1928) had recently been published and was the class text. The hypnosis book (Hull, 1933), which summarized the pioneer experimental research by him and his students, was in preparation. The course he gave in this area was unusually lively, controversial, and widely attended. It presented many opportunities to apply the scientific method in both discussions and demonstrations to test popular beliefs and misconceptions. My

---

[3] An accidental discovery in a chemistry laboratory revealed that the crystals of phenyl-thio-carbamide (P.T.C.) are tasteless to some persons, although decidedly bitter to most people. Studies of family pedigrees indicated a genetic basis for this taste deficiency, which also extends to several other, closely related chemicals (for ref., see Anastasi, 1958a; Snyder, 1951).

own contacts with both Hull and Elliott continued long after the completion of those summer courses, through correspondence, exchange of reprints, meetings, and personal conferences.

My remarkable summer of 1929 ended with attendance at the International Congress of Psychology at Yale. This congress was the first to be held in the United States, and it would be over three decades before another met in this country. The 1929 congress met jointly with the American Psychological Association. Karl S. Lashley was president of the APA and James McKeen Cattell was president of the congress. For us graduate students, it was a rare opportunity to hear and meet psychologists whose work we had been studying, including not only most of the leading American psychologists but also the live persons attached to such familiar names as Spearman, McDougal, Pieron, and Pavlov.

My Columbia Ph.D. was simply in "psychology," with no modifying adjectives. The Columbia Graduate School did not offer degrees in any psychological specialties. Actually, in view of the emphases in the department, the program could be best described as "experimental psychology." Although the variety of course offerings was fairly broad for that time, the basic program centered on carefully controlled laboratory work, expert use of apparatus (most of which came from Stoelting), and quantitative analysis of results. Both in major course content and in comprehensive degree examinations, the heavily represented topics were sensation, perception, and learning. In theoretical orientation, the Columbia department was officially eclectic. Woodworth was well known for his middle-of-the-road eclecticism and his receptivity to all new ideas and suggestions. We were certainly exposed to diverse approaches in our various courses. But many of us developed personal predilections and aversions among the many prevalent "schools" of psychology.

Among the postdoctoral experiences that influenced my own development, several stem from an event in my personal life. In 1933, I married John Porter Foley, Jr., of Bloomington, Indiana. After receiving his A.B. degree in psychology from Indiana University, John obtained the Ph.D. from Columbia, where we met. In various ways, John's experiential background complemented mine. For instance, in his graduate studies and for several years in his subsequent teaching and experimentation, John worked largely in animal psychology, in which my own training had been limited to a single graduate course. Similarly, his studies in anthropology and his research with Franz Boas at Columbia strengthened my own interest in a field that is highly relevant to differential psychology. A major influence in shaping my own psychological thinking was the work of J. R. Kantor of Indiana University, who played the same part in John's undergraduate education that Hollingworth played in mine. It was through John that I met Kantor and became interested in studying his published works (e.g., Kantor 1924, 1926, 1929, 1936, 1958). In several ways, Kantor resembled Hollingworth. He, too, was a generalist, with a remarkable breadth of knowledge extending over psychology and related fields. And he, too, formulated a comprehensive theoretical system, successively named organismic and interbehavioral psychology.

The 1920s witnessed the rise of behaviorism, with widespread interest in the work of its founder, John B. Watson. As a student, I was strongly attracted to this development and I avidly read all I could find by Watson and his students, ranging from studies of the homing behavior of the sooty tern and conditioned fears in young children to the comprehensive treatise *Psychology from the Standpoint of a Behaviorist* (e.g., Jones, 1924; Watson, 1913, 1919, 1924; Watson & Lashley, 1915; Watson & Raynor, 1920). My understanding of behaviorism was strengthened and modified through the work of other psychologists who influenced my thinking. Thus I regard Hollingworth's redintegration and Kantor's interbehavioral psychology, as well as certain more recent developments, as broadened, systematic, and comprehensive elaborations of the fundamental behaviorist approach.

In summary, I entered psychology via mathematics; I was trained as a generalist, with a strong experimental bent; and my basic theoretical identity is with behaviorism, although with a broad orientation and a continued openness to new developments that can be fitted into the system.

Focus on Measurement

How does a person who received a Ph.D. in psychology from Columbia University in 1930 become a specialist? How did I become a specialist in psychometrics? Insofar as I can judge in retrospect, I was able to assemble an unofficial specialization in this area by selecting all relevant courses from available offerings, by chosing a particular dissertation topic and mentor, by doing some postdoctoral study, and by continuing independent learning over my entire professional life. What did my specialization comprise? I define psychometrics methodologically as including statistics and psychological testing, and substantively as concerned with the nature and sources of individual and group differences in behavior.

Quantitative Methodology

Upon becoming a college psychology major, I soon discovered that a principal and expanding area for the use of mathematical methods in psychology was in test construction and the analysis of test results. In my independent honors studies, I became fairly widely acquainted with available tests, how they were administered and scored, and how they had been constructed and evaluated. As for statistics, it was still infrequently offered in separate courses in graduate psychology programs, and even more rarely at the undergraduate level. In fact, Henry Garrett's 1926 book, which I used in independent study, was largely instrumental in introducing statistics courses in psychology departments. In comparison with other textbooks available at the time, it was simpler and more clearly presented. Before entering psychology, Garrett had taught mathematics in high school. This experience undoubtedly helped him in communicating statistics to typical, mathematically uninterested psychology students.

My first meeting with Garrett occurred just before my registration for graduate school, when I requested that I be exempt from his required statistics course, because I had worked through his book while at Barnard. My request was granted after I had completed a final examination for the course with a perfect score. On this basis, I was also admitted to Garrett's advanced, one-year course on statistical problems in the construction and applications of tests. Conducted partly as a seminar, this course treated a wide diversity of statistical problems. It was in this course, for example, that I first heard of the path coefficient developed by Sewall Wright (1921, 1934) for use in genetics. At that time, this technique received little or no attention from psychologists. Recently, interest in it has been revived in connection with structural modeling—a statistical procedure now being widely explored in many fields of psychology to test hypotheses about causal interrelations among variables that cannot be experimentally manipulated (James, Mulaik, & Brett, 1982; Loehlin, 1987). During my first graduate school year, I also took Garrett's survey course on psychological tests, and I served as the lab assistant in the course in my second year. This course devoted considerable time to traditional early tests of "simple functions," including measures of physical and motor ability, attention, perception, association, learning, and memory; it also covered available instruments for assessing "complex functions," such as intelligence and personality.

During my second graduate school year, a major undertaking was the completion of my doctoral dissertation. Mine was one of a set of dissertations done under Garrett's direction with a special application of the tetrad equation to the identification of group factors. This technique had been described by T. L. Kelley (1928) in his *Crossroads in the Mind of Man*, in which he reported its use in identifying group factors in his studies with schoolchildren. My own study with college students concerned the identification of a group factor in tests of immediate memory for rote material (Anastasi, 1930). I recall arguing that the factor I had identified should be called *a* memory factor, rather than *the* memory factor, because I was convinced that there were several memory factors, a finding demonstrated in my own later study (Anastasi, 1932), as well as in factor analytic research by other investigators (e.g., Christal, 1958). One of the eight memory tests I prepared for use in my dissertation, the Picture-Number Paired Associates Test, was subsequently included in the ETS kit of factor-referenced tests (French, 1954; French, Ekstrom, & Price, 1963; Ekstrom, French, Harman, & Dermen, 1976, p. 94).

As for postdoctoral training, there was a single formal course that I attended, under rather unusual circumstances. This occurred in the summer of 1931, after I had been awarded the Ph.D. from Columbia in December 1930. The Department of Mathematics of the University of Minnesota circulated an announcement of "Special Lectures in Mathematics" for the 1931 summer quarter. This special program was organized to precede the annual joint meetings of the American Mathematical Society and the Mathematical Association of America, to be held at the University of Minnesota in September of that year. One of the offerings was a course by the British statistician R. A. Fisher. Labeled "Statistical Theory of Experimental Design," the course was described as "especially suited to research workers in biology, agronomy, and other experimental sciences." The announcement added that "the privilege of visiting these courses without credit and without cost will be extended as a courtesy to scholars who hold the Ph.D. degree from this or any other graduate school." The economic depression of the 1930s being well under way, anything that was offered without cost had a special appeal. Analysis of variance (ANOVA) was then largely unknown to psychologists. To be sure, the first edition of Fisher's book had been published as early as 1925. But most of the applications cited at that time (e.g., Snedecor, 1934) seemed to deal with fields of corn and litters of pigs; and some of the psychologists who had heard about this new statistical approach were skeptical about its value for psychological research. It was an easy decision for me. I booked a round-trip passage on the Great Lakes steamer (Buffalo to Duluth, with stopovers for sight-seeing) and set forth on a very full summer, combining my introduction to ANOVA with a delightful vacation.

Fisher's course was well attended, and the students included a relatively large representation of mathematics professors and agricultural researchers. Fisher lectured formally, speaking rapidly and softly and keeping close to the contents of his book (Fisher, 1925). There was little elaboration or explanation and no interaction with students, either as a group or individually. Some dissatisfaction about these conditions was expressed by the students among themselves but was never, to my knowledge, communicated to Fisher. For me, this proved to be one more opportunity for independent learning. I noted which portion of the text was covered during each class session and then adjourned to my dormitory room to learn the material.

Fisher's book (and his course) included much more than analysis of variance. The new material included such now familiar statistical concepts and procedures as the transformation of Pearson coefficients into the normally distributed Z function, degrees of freedom, t ratios, and the use of Student's tables for small samples. But it was analysis of variance and the related topic of experimental design that eventually opened up a vast new area of statistical analysis. That fall, I gave a talk at the Columbia departmental seminar on what I had learned about analysis of variance. The group noticeably relaxed when informed at the outset that the variance was really the square of the familiar standard deviation. Members of the audience appeared to follow without difficulty the basic elementary points about ANOVA, which is all I was qualified to provide at that time. But the typical reaction was still that this procedure held little promise for use in psychology!

Much of my subsequent development in psychometrics was achieved by keeping up with what was happening in factor analysis. In addition to the standard information sources provided by the published literature, I relied on contacts with major contributors through their occasional lectures, informal seminars, personal conferences, and extensive correspondence and exchange of reprints. I had considerable contact with Spearman by continuing correspondence, as well as in person when he was visiting at Columbia. In my own early research (Anastasi, 1930, 1932), I used Spearman's (1927) tetrad equation, not to test for g but, through Kelley's adaptation, to identify group factors (Kelley, 1928). I followed closely the development of early forms of factor analysis itself by Kelley (1935) in the United

States and by Burt (1941) and Vernon (1940, 1950) in England; and in the process, I reviewed some of Burt's and Vernon's books in this area (Anastasi, 1941a, 1941b, 1952).

It was the work of Thurstone (1935, 1947) that eventually gave factor analysis its strongest impetus. The application of this methodology in psychology was certainly encouraged by Thurstone's development of the simplified centroid procedure, which rendered the computations practicable in a precomputer era. Thurstone's introduction of rotation of axes also facilitated the psychological interpretation of factors and, with the inclusion of correlated factors, permitted a reconciliation of Spearman's g with the group factors identified by Thurstone and other researchers. Still later, comprehensive, hierarchical trait models (Humphreys, 1962; Vernon, 1961) provided for factors at different levels, from narrow to broad, which may be appropriate for different assessment purposes. Further advances include the development and application of more mathematically sophisticated methods of factor analysis, whose common use is now feasible through the widespread availability of high-speed computers. At the same time, different types of independently developed factor solutions were put on a more systematic, common mathematical foundation in terms of matrix algebra, and the results of the different solutions were shown to be convertible from one to another through the use of a computed transformation matrix (Harman, 1976, chap. 15).

Factor analysis has remained a focal interest in my research, teaching, and writing throughout my career. By the time I began to teach in graduate school, this methodology was so widely employed in psychology as to justify its treatment in a separate graduate course. I introduced such a course when in 1947 I joined the Graduate School of Arts and Sciences at Fordham University,[4] and I continued to teach it until my retirement in 1979. Although using texts that emphasized methodology (including successive editions of Harman, 1976), I always reserved some sessions at the end of the course for the psychological uses of factor analysis, with illustrative findings and theoretical interpretations of the nature of factors. This approach reflects my substantive interests, with which I identify as strongly as I do with methodology.

Differential Psychology

My interest in individual differences, as part of my personal orientation toward people, was discernible early in my life. I have stated elsewhere (Anastasi, 1980, p. 6) that "the conspicuous personality differences among the three significant

---

[4] My teaching, administrative, and association activities have been systematically reported elsewhere (Anastasi, 1972b, 1980, 1982; DeVito, 1989, March; Sexton, 1987, March; Sexton & Hogan, 1990). For the present purpose, the following chronological framework should suffice. I taught in the psychology department of Barnard College in 1930–1939; at Queens College of the City University of New York in 1939–1946 (as a one-member department the first year and as department chairperson until I left); and at Fordham University in 1947–1979, serving two terms in the rotating office of chair of the joint graduate and undergraduate departments. I was president of the Eastern Psychological Association in 1946–1947 and of the American Psychological Association in 1971–1972.

characters in my early family environment may well have contributed to my life-long interest in individual differences and their causes." However that may be, my personal concern with such differences certainly antedated my professional interest in their study, which began in graduate school. I have already referred to Garrett's course on statistical problems in the construction and applications of tests, which I took during my first year at Columbia. The last portion of that course dealt with critical analyses of the literature on individual and group differences in test performance. In that connection, I prepared a class report and paper on sex differences, which represents the first concrete expression of my burgeoning interest in differential psychology. This was also the occasion of my first encounter with Garrett's strongly hereditarian views, a subject of repeated friendly arguments over the years.

A later, related experience was my preparing a rough, preliminary draft for the last chapter of Garrett and Schneck's 1933 textbook on psychological tests. This chapter, titled "Some Applications of Psychological Tests," touched upon the major available findings on individual and group differences in ability. By that time, I had already been teaching a course on differential psychology, which I had introduced at Barnard when I was appointed as an instructor. Not surprisingly, the interpretations of findings were quite differently slanted in Garrett's final version of the chapter, and my contribution was acknowledged in general terms in the preface. It was while teaching differential psychology at Barnard that I decided to write my first book. I was dissatisfied with the one or two texts then available in the area designated as "individual differences," and I found it necessary from the outset to supplement the course text with outside reading assignments. I therefore embarked on the preparation of the first edition of my *Differential Psychology* (1937). I used this and its successive revised editions in all my subsequent teaching of differential psychology at both undergraduate and graduate levels.

A word may be in order about my use of the term *differential psychology*. At the time, this area was loosely described as "individual differences," or "human differences," which sounded more like a topic than like a field of psychology. But it was as a broad field of psychology that I envisaged it. For this reason I chose, for my courses as well as my textbook, a literal translation of the term introduced by William Stern (1900) in the first edition of his book and retained in subsequent German editions. I was interested to see that the German translation of my own book, published in two volumes in 1976, was titled *Differentielle Psychologie*. I had now come full circle!

What, essentially, does the field of differential psychology cover? In the closing chapter of my *Differential Psychology* (3rd ed., 1958a, p. 604), I wrote:

> The fundamental aim of differential psychology . . . is similar to that of all psychology, namely, the understanding of behavior. Differential psychology approaches this problem through a comparative analysis of behavior under varying environmental and biological conditions. By relating the observed differences in behavior to other known concomitant phenomena, it should be possible to tease out the relative contribution of different (variables) to

behavioral development. If we can determine why one person reacts differently from another, we shall know what makes people react as they do.

In my development of the field of differential psychology—in text, courses, and research—I can recognize the previously mentioned influence of Hollingworth, Kantor, and Watson. This influence is particularly evident in my concern with the contributions of learning, operating through the life-span reactional biography of individuals, to the development of their specific individuality. Other conspicuous influences on my thinking in this field stem from my contact with the work of Franz Boas at Columbia and the emerging group of cultural anthropologists and cross-cultural psychologists inspired by him. From another angle, I owe much to my various contacts with geneticists, notably Theodosius Dobzhansky (1950, 1951a, 1951b), whom I first met in a series of monthly, interdisciplinary seminars on human variation, held in the 1950s at Columbia University under the auspices of the Zoology Department.

My second textbook, *Psychological Testing* (1954), shows the influence of differential psychology in my treatment of testing. This is especially true of my emphasis on the proper interpretation of test scores, not only in terms of their statistical properties but also in terms of the behavior that the tests are designed to measure. For instance, a chapter entitled "Psychological Issues in Intelligence Testing" (Chap. 12, 1988b) touches upon several topics from differential psychology, such as age changes in test scores throughout life, population changes in intellectual performance, problems in cross-cultural testing, heritability and modifiability of intelligence, and interrelations between cognitive and affective variables (see also Anastasi, 1958b, 1985). My continuing efforts toward the prevention of test misuses and of the misinterpretation of test scores—in my writing, lecturing, and service on various committees and working groups—reflect essentially the implementation of the same concerns (Anastasi, 1990). In the same spirit, in my presidential address to the APA Division of Evaluation and Measurement (Div. 5), I argued that many popular criticisms and current misuses of tests arise from the progressive dissociation of psychological testing from the mainstream of psychology (Anastasi, 1967).

A research area that cuts across differential psychology and testing concerns the factor-analytic investigation of the nature and organization of human traits. Beginning with Spearman's pioneer quantitative investigations of the composition of human intelligence, which first drew me into psychology, this topic has remained a major focus of my own research interests. At the same time, my approach to this problem reflects my behaviorist tendencies. From the start, I resisted the early traditional view that aptitudes and other traits identified through factor analysis represent fixed, unchangeable, innately determined causal entities. Rather, I looked for the learning experiences that led to "factor formation" and that produced the kinds of factor patterns found in individuals and in culturally similar groups.

As early as 1932, in the conclusion to a study on memory factors conducted as an expanded follow-up on my Ph.D. dissertation, I referred to the "possibilities regarding environmental influences and training in relation to problems of mental organization" and added, "Especially fruitful in this connection would be the experimental study of the effect of special training on intertest correlations, as well as the comparison of correlation results in groups of widely diverse training and background" (Anastasi, 1932, p. 58).

In a subsequent study (Anastasi, 1936),[5] I undertook to demonstrate, in a condensed version, what may occur through everyday-life experience to produce the differences in factorial composition found by investigators who work with different populations. Essentially, my object was the experimental alteration of a factor pattern through a brief, relevant interpolated experience. Five short tests were administered to 200 sixth-grade children, who then received instruction in the use of special logical devices designed to facilitate performance on three of the tests. After 13 days, parallel forms of the five tests were administered. Intercorrelations and Hotelling's principal component analysis of the initial and final tests revealed differences in correlations (and possible factor structure) for the three "instructed" tests, negligible change for the two "noninstructed" tests, and slight changes in the relations between "instructed" and "noninstructed" tests. The study was offered as a simple demonstration that factor patterns may be experientially influenced and that they may be expected to vary in the same persons over time and among populations with different experiential histories. The publication of this study led to a minor skirmish with Thurstone (1938; see also Anastasi, 1938). This interchange was typical of the controversies of the time, especially with regard to factor analysis and the nature of human abilities. I subsequently had occasion to talk to Thurstone in person. He was most gracious and finally suggested that our real difference stemmed from his underlying conviction that "traits are really hereditary," although he had no direct evidence for that belief.

The mechanism of factor formation remained a life-long interest for me. It surfaced in student dissertations that I directed (e.g., Avakian, 1961; Filella, 1960) and in comparative surveys of research conducted at different age levels and in different cultural populations (Anastasi, 1970b, 1986a). In the effort to understand discrepancies in the findings of different investigators, my approach was to look for possible experiential differences that might account for the obtained differences in factor patterns. I have also speculated on the effects of major technological developments on the structure of human intelligence. Are we likely to find a verbal factor before the invention of phonetic writing systems or a quantitative factor before the invention of a number system? In what ways did the development of machinery influence the nature and scope of spatial aptitude factors? And what changes can be expected in the nature and composition of human intelligence with increasing exposure to computer technology? (Anastasi, 1988a). My own emerging concept of human intelligence reflects both the results of accumulated research over the decades and my enduring behaviorist orientation. In my view, intelligence is not an entity but a quality of behavior, and in the human species, "it comprises that combination of cognitive skills and knowledge demanded, fostered, and rewarded by

---

[5] For excerpt, see Anastasi (1982, pp. 109–116).

the particular culture within which the individual becomes socialized" (Anastasi, 1986b, p. 20).

Still a Generalist at Heart

I have tried to trace the steps whereby I became a specialist after my Columbia degree in general psychology. But the influence of my initial education in psychology and of my significant contacts with such eminent generalists as Hollingworth, Woodworth, and Kantor was not displaced in the process. Rather, the strands were intertwined. In several ways I have remained a generalist. For many years, I belonged to only one APA division, that of General Psychology (Div. 1). I eventually joined also the Division of Evaluation and Measurement (Div. 5), after I had been teaching graduate students for several years and some of my former students applied for fellowship status in Division 5, for which they asked me to submit a recommendation! Of course, during all those years I was not precluded from attending sessions or presenting papers in Division 5, or in any other APA division.

My generalist orientation is certainly evident in my teaching, at both undergraduate and graduate levels. The courses I taught included introductory general psychology, experimental psychology, psychological testing, general statistics, statistical methods in test construction, factor analysis, differential psychology, intellectual deviates, and applied psychology. The last-named course I taught at various times to undergraduates at Barnard College, Queens College, and Fordham College. My approach to this course differed somewhat from that current at the time. It was more consonant with the approach followed in early textbooks (e.g., Hollingworth & Poffenberger, 1917; Poffenberger, 1942; Burtt, 1946), which spanned all major areas of applied psychology. Later books appearing under this rubric diverged in two directions. Some of the more technically oriented became in effect books on industrial psychology. Another, rapidly growing type was popular books on how to get along with people and conduct one's life effectively. They ranged from general discussions of personal adjustment problems to superficial psychologizing and advice giving.

As the more solid, broadly oriented books became outdated and were no longer revised, it proved increasingly difficult to find a suitable text for my course. Hence, I decided to write my own. Understandably, I had some misgivings about undertaking such a huge task, with topics ranging from engineering psychology to clinical psychology. I decided to call my book *Fields of Applied Psychology* (Anastasi, 1964, 1979), and I defined its scope as what psychologists do when they are not engaged in either university teaching or basic research. I decided that I wanted to write a book, not *in* these various fields, but *about* them. It should provide the sort of information that would help a student to choose a career specialty in psychology. At the same time, I wanted to cite genuine research, with good methodology, to illustrate the proper foundation for each field of application. I recall a conversation with a colleague who, on learning that there would be three chapters on clinical psychology, commented, "How can you write three chapters on clinical psychology?"

Naively oblivious of the fact that the emphasis was meant to be on *you,* I responded, "It's very simple: one chapter on diagnosis, one on therapy, and one on research—it's a natural division." Apparently there was still a need for the kind of book I wrote on applied psychology—at least, some reviewers thought so. A review of my first edition in *Contemporary Psychology* (Dunnette, 1964) was titled "Achievements of Applied Psychology," and a review of my second edition in the same journal was titled "Selling Science to Undergraduates" (Biglan, 1980).

In my generalist role, one of the discernible themes in my activities—in teaching, research, and writing—was a "debunking" effort (Anastasi, 1982, Chap. 1). In addition to the critical evaluation of charlatanism and unsupported claims in my applied psychology text, some of my research was similarly motivated. One series of studies, conducted jointly with my husband and supported by a grant from the Columbia University Council for Research in the Social Sciences, concerned the relation between artistic productivity and psychopathology. The project was stimulated by the unbridled psychologizing in writings by artists and art critics, as well as by the unsubstantiated claims by some psychiatrists and clinical psychologists, regarding the "pathological signs" in art products. In the 1930s and 1940s, several New York art shows featured psychotic art, as well as the art products of children and "primitive" cultures. At least one gallery provided a copy of Prinzhorn's (1923) classic book on psychotic art as a handy reference for its visitors. In one part of our own project, using uniform data-gathering procedures and control groups, we found that many alleged indices of pathology tended to be associated, not with pathology, but with educational, occupational, and socioeconomic background (Anastasi & Foley, 1944).

Psychological writings of the period were also characterized by frequent overgeneralizations about human behavior from the data gathered within a single culture. Such overgeneralization is illustrated by descriptions of developmental stages, especially as applied to children's drawings. For instance, the Goodenough (1926) Draw-a-Man Test was originally designed as a nonverbal intelligence test appropriate for use with children from different cultures. On the basis of later cross-cultural data, that claim was eventually retracted (Goodenough & Harris, 1950; Harris, 1963). In the meantime, John and I had been doing some exploratory cross-cultural work on children's drawings, in a meager effort to refute the earlier overgeneralizations (Anastasi & Foley, 1936, 1938).

Another, long-term project with both "debunking" and behavioristic nuances approached artistic production from a different angle. Conducted in collaboration with some of my graduate students and funded by the Center for Urban Education (long-since disbanded), it dealt with the origin and development of creative talent in children (Anastasi, 1970a). In one part of this multifaceted project, we obtained biographical history data from high school students who had achieved distinction through artistic or literary production. We looked specifically for events or conditions in the individuals' past histories that differentiated them from comparable control cases (Anastasi & Schaefer, 1969).

Apart from the incidental questioning of popular beliefs regarding the esoteric origins of creative talents, the primary object of the creativity project was positive.

We were looking for variables associated with creative achievement and for ways to encourage the development of creative productivity. An enduring goal in my teaching and writing was likewise focused on the positive. Especially in the introductory course in psychology, I emphasized how the basic scientific approach can contribute to an understanding of behavior. This was also true of my differential psychology course, particularly in the analysis of behavioral differences among persons classified in terms of age, gender, and ethnic categories—where popular stereotypes abound.

To paraphrase the previously cited review of my applied psychology textbook, I was constantly trying to "sell science," not only to undergraduates but at all levels, from my fellow professionals to the general public. I have often argued that the most effective way we can "give psychology away" to the public—to borrow an apt phrase from George Miller's (1969) APA presidential address—is to promote the use of the basic scientific approach as a way of coping with problems and reaching decisions in daily life. In my own APA presidential address (Anastasi, 1972a), I cited some simple examples of the scientific way of thinking that could be taught to schoolchildren, from the kindergarten up. Among them were: the multiplicity of variables involved in cause-and-effect relations, which underlies the need for experimental designs; limitations and biases of human observation and memory, which necessitate objective record keeping; the multidimensionality of individual and group differences; and the overlapping of group distributions in any single variable.

In this account of my development as a psychologist, I have concentrated on those aspects of my work that were most meaningful to me. It is gratifying to find that my peers have generally chosen the same aspects as significant; this evaluation is reflected in the citations for the awards I have received over the years.[6] I played no part in providing or selecting data for these citations, nor did I know who wrote any of them. In fact, in no case did I know that I was being considered, in advance of my official notification of the award, as is the customary practice.

The first award I received during my professional career was the Award for Distinguished Service to Measurement, presented annually by Educational Testing Service to a recipient selected by the presidents of six organizations concerned with measurement.[7] This citation began with references to differential psychology and went on to mention psychological traits, heredity and environment, and my "sweeping away many of the presuppositions, myths, and fallacies generated by misconceptions. . . ." The same ideas recur in later award citations. There is

---

[6] In chronological order, these awards include: ETS Award for Distinguished Service to Measurement, 1977; APA Distinguished Scientific Award for the Applications of Psychology, 1981; AERA Award for Distinguished Contributions to Research in Education, 1983; APA Division 15 E. L. Thorndike Medal for Distinguished Psychological Contributions to Education, 1984; American Psychological Foundation Gold Medal, 1984; National Medal of Science, 1987.

[7] American Educational Research Association (Division D), Association for Measurement and Evaluation in Guidance, American Psychological Association (Divisions 5 and 15), National Council on Measurement in Education, Psychometric Society.

reference to the reconceptualization of psychological traits, the technology of psychological testing, and analyses of individual, cultural, and sex differences in performance. My three textbooks are cited, with the comment that "(t)hey frame the very questions scientists in these disciplines ask and the manner in which research is conducted" (American Psychological Foundation, 1985). For my most recent award, the National Medal of Science, the complete citation reads: "For her work in the development of the discipline of differential psychology as a behavioral science, which illuminates the way traits are influenced by heredity and environment and the methods by which traits and human characteristics are measured." That seems to sum up my life quite neatly.

About Clinical Psychology: Random Observations by an Onlooker

Primordial Era

During World War I, I was in elementary school and had never heard the word *psychology*. However, two psychologists who influenced my career, Hollingworth and Woodworth, had themselves been actively introducing clinical psychology into the military system during that war. Hollingworth worked with emotionally disturbed soldiers at the U. S. Army General Hospital in Plattsburg Barracks, New York. His work with some 1200 cases led to the publication of *The Psychology of Functional Neuroses* (Hollingworth, 1920). His findings and conclusions are also cited in detail in his *Abnormal Psychology* (1930, Chaps. 17, 18) and were duly incorporated in his comprehensive theory of redintegration, which considers the individual's learning history and motivation, as well as situational conditions.

Like other clinical psychologists of that period, Hollingworth gave primary attention to intelligence test performance in his data analyses, with mental ages and IQs conspicuously represented in the tables. The Stanford-Binet was used, along with the Army Alpha and several laboratory-type tests of simple cognitive processes. Neurotics averaged somewhat below the general army norms, and differences were also found among the types of neuroses. The rank order of these diagnostic categories in amount of education exactly equaled their rank order in average mental age; in interpreting this relation, Hollingworth favored mental age as causing the educational level attained, rather than vice-versa—a view also typical of psychologists in the 1930s. In other respects, however, Hollingworth sounds ahead of his time. For example, he wrote, "The success of therapy we explain in the main by the substitution of cortical for affective and postural responses. . . . This technique may also involve repetition, practice, and therefore a re-educational process" (Hollingworth, 1930, p. 488).

Hollingworth also reports results he obtained when he administered the Woodworth Personal Data Sheet to some of his neurotic cases, as part of the preliminary tryouts of this newly developed instrument. The most conspicuous finding was a marked drop in number of symptoms reported after the Armistice was announced. From other evidence, malingering did not appear to be a significant reason for this change; Hollingworth attributed the drop to a genuinely "thera-peutic" effect of the Armistice, which produced "a general buoyancy" shared by neurotics and normals, including the medical officers.

Woodworth developed the Personal Data Sheet (P.D. Sheet) as a rough screening device for identifying seriously disturbed recruits who were unsuited for military service. It was designed essentially in an attempt to standardize the usual psychiatric interview and to adapt it for mass testing. Accordingly, Woodworth gathered infor-mation regarding common neurotic and preneurotic symptoms from the psychiatric literature and through conferences with psychiatrists. The original inventory questions were formulated in reference to these symptoms. Final item selection, however, was based on empirical criteria. No item was retained if 25 percent of a "normal" sample answered it in the unfavorable direction. In addition, only symptoms reported at least twice as often in a previously diagnosed neurotic group as in a normal group were chosen. The 116 items thus assembled dealt with such behavioral deviations as abnormal fears, obsessions and compulsions, nightmares and other sleep disturbances, excessive fatigue and other psychosomatic symptoms, feelings of unreality, and motor disturbances such as twitchings.

Although the necessary research on the P.D. Sheet was not completed soon enough to use the instrument operationally for its intended military purpose, the P.D. Sheet was published in a civilian edition after the end of World War I (Woodworth, 1918; see also Franz, 1919; Symonds, 1931). Several later revisions and adaptations were also published, including an early questionnaire for use with children and teenagers (Woodworth & Mathews, 1923). In its specific content, form, and method of construction, the P.D. Sheet remained the prototype for self-report inventories for several decades.

My first personal involvement with anything labeled as clinical psychology occurred when, as a graduate student at Columbia, I enrolled in a course named Clinical Psychology. Today, that course would undoubtedly be called Individual Intelligence Testing. It covered chiefly the Stanford-Binet (1916 edition) and also included some practice with a few other instruments, such as the Pintner-Paterson Performance Scale and the Porteus Mazes. The course was given by Louise Poull at the Randall's Island Children's Hospital, where she was the only psychologist. This was a municipal institution for the mentally retarded of all ages and all degrees of intellectual disability. Dr. Poull explained that it had originally been named a "children's hospital" because the residents were all children in terms of mental age. Housed in dilapidated wooden buildings, the institution has long since disappeared. Randall's Island now houses a stadium and is accessible via the Triboro Bridge; at that time, it could be reached only by a diminutive ferry operated by the city.

In physical facilities, the institution at which I learned to administer the Stanford-Binet contrasted sharply with that located at Letchworth Village, New York, where I spent a week as one of two research assistants gathering data for Charles B. Davenport during the summer of 1929. Davenport's plan for test development included "tryouts" of our allegedly culture-free tests on samples of widely varying populations. These samples seem to have been selected partly for sheer diversity and partly for availability. They included, among others, children of research workers at Cold Spring Harbor, "criminally insane" adults in a New Jersey state prison, and institutionalized mentally retarded persons of all ages. Letchworth Village was a handsome place, with modern, attractive, well-kept buildings and extensive, beautifully landscaped grounds. The residents whom we encountered casually were neatly dressed, well groomed, active, and cheerful as they went about performing their daily indoor or outdoor tasks. There were also, of course, wards with more severely retarded persons and "sick wards" with permanently bedridden patients; but all seemed to be receiving good nursing care and presumably competent medical services.

All in all, this more recently established state institution was most unlike the much older, smaller, and inadequately funded city institution on Randall's Island. But as for clinical psychology, there was again a sole representative, a young woman who did not, I believe, have a Ph.D. and who constantly expressed general dissatisfaction with her job. She was, to be sure, a most gracious person and very cooperative toward us interlopers, who were on the premises only to gather data for Davenport's project and provided nothing in return.

After obtaining my Ph.D. and beginning to teach at Barnard, I had contact with several typical clinical psychologists of the 1930s. They were persons with a Ph.D. in psychology who had a solid foundation in general psychology and some training in testing, especially with individual intelligence scales. Most of them were women. An example was Clairette Armstrong, employed as a psychologist at the New York City Children's Court. There she administered tests, did some interviewing and pre-paration of case histories, and made recommendations regarding disposition of the cases. She worked in close cooperation with social workers and other professionals. The Children's Court handled a wide diversity of cases, from child custody to juvenile delinquency. The children were either passive or active objects of judicial concern; that is, the court was involved either to protect the children from neglect or mistreatment or to deal with criminal offenses by minors.

Another example was Rose Anderson, Director of the Clinical Division of The Psychological Corporation, then located in New York City. The work of that division consisted chiefly in testing and interviewing individual clients, followed by general educational or occupational counseling, or possibly referral for further diagnosis and therapy.

An outstanding example with significant practical impact is provided by the work of Emily Burr, for many years Director of the Vocational Adjustment Bureau (VAB)[8] in New York City. Founded in 1919, VAB derived its major support from a group of public-spirited New York women, presided over by Mrs. Henry Ittleson. With a multidisciplinary staff that included the full-time or part-time services of several psychologists, VAB provided assessment, counseling, training, and job placement for young women referred by social agencies or schools because of job failures. A sizeable number had been displaced from factories or offices by the

---

[8] Information about VAB was verified from a set of articles reprinted by VAB as a series of *Bulletins,* with references to original sources (e.g., Burr, 1924, 1932; Metcalfe & Burr, 1936).

introduction of machines that performed simple jobs such as packing and wrapping. Intellectually, the VAB clients were described as largely low normal or normal; many also had a variety of emotional and interpersonal problems. The cases actually accepted by VAB ranged widely in both chronological age (from mid-teens to the 40s) and IQ (from 40s to well over 100). Over the years, the number of cases handled came to several thousands.

For its period, VAB functioned with considerable psychometric sophistication. Testing included not only the usual measures of general intelligence but also tests of clerical and mechanical aptitudes and psychomotor skills. Some of the tests were developed or adapted through VAB research (often in collaboration with Columbia University graduate students); they were validated against highly specific job processes, identified through detailed job analyses. Case-history and personal information was also obtained through a series of intensive interviews covering a comprehensive array of physical, sensory, motor, cognitive, and personality items. The experienced interviewers were apparently able to establish good rapport with their type of client and accumulated a rich database on each individual.

Because these early clinical psychologists were essentially "mental testers," they could branch off into several emerging fields of applied psychology, such as educational, industrial, and forensic psychology. And several of them did, as these examples show.

My contacts with the primordial clinical psychologists of the 1930s include another, unofficial category whose members were less visible than the "mental testers" and were predominantly male. In graduate school, these were the students who came with the expectation of becoming practitioners, in the model of the medically trained psychiatrists of the time. To some extent, they reflected the then widespread popular confusion between psychologists and psychiatrists. Not surprisingly, these frustrated clinicians were generally dissatisfied with graduate school offerings, which hardly met their interests at all. In their efforts to supplement their formal courses with training in their own area of interest, they often relied on published works, contacts with individual practitioners, and informal small-group training programs. These special independent programs generally dealt with one of the several varieties of psychoanalysis; some were concerned with hypnosis, and still others with projective diagnostic techniques, especially the Rorschach. People kept referring to various Rorschach training programs that met "one evening a week in someone's living room." My recollections of what I heard about these various external programs evoke impressions of exaggerated claims, overgeneralization, and tendencies toward cultism.

Most of these students left graduate school after obtaining the M.A. degree; some took additional courses, but few obtained the Ph.D. at Columbia. Those who did usually took college teaching jobs in psychology and continued to pursue their clinical interests on the side. Another career pattern is exemplified by Frederick Thorne, who, after receiving a Columbia Ph.D. in psychology in 1934, went on to obtain an M.D. from Cornell. Eventually, he taught and practiced clinical psychology in several capacities during the postwar period, besides editing and publishing the *Journal of Clinical Psychology,* which he had founded in 1945.

Clinical Psychology as a Professional Specialty

One of the best established facts in the history of psychology is that, after World War II, clinical psychology emerged as a full-fledged professional specialty. The participation of well over a thousand psychologists in the armed forces during World War II demonstrated both the need for psychological services and the variety of services that psychologists could render. To be sure, some military psychologists worked in test development and the use of tests in personnel selection and classification; another group made significant contributions to equipment design, thereby launching the specialty of engineering psychology. A sizeable proportion of military psychologists, however, performed diversified counseling and clinical functions; it was partly this work that stimulated the expansion of postwar clinical psychology to include psychotherapy along with the original diagnostic activities.

The 1940s were a time of rapid development for the new professional specialty. A major influence was the initiation of government subsidized training and internship programs, particularly under the auspices of the Veterans Administration and the U.S. Public Health Service. The American Psychological Association formulated training requirements and began to accredit university programs in this specialty. The Boulder Conference (held in Boulder, Colorado, in 1949) defined the scientist-professional model for clinical psychologists, a model that was reaffirmed in subsequent conferences. I attended the Miami Conference in 1958 (together with other nonclinical psychologists), this being the first conference concerned with the training of all psychologists. Following the Boulder model, this conference emphasized that the clinical psychologist, like other psychological specialists, should be trained as a "psychologist first, a specialist second." The decade of the 1940s was also marked by the beginning of state licensing of psychologists and by the establishment of the American Board of Professional Psychology (ABPP),[9] with clinical psychology as one of its first professional specialties.

The Place of Mental Retardation

Many of the prewar clinical psychologists had worked with mentally retarded children or (less often) adults. In the postwar period, the primary focus shifted to emotional disorders. This change does not imply that mental retardation received less attention. On the contrary, work on mental retardation expanded and became a vigorous subspecialty of clinical psychology. As such, it was broadened to include intervention ("remedial") procedures and considerable research. Moreover, insofar as intervention programs had to be tailored to fit individual needs, diagnostic testing itself required the assessment of specific assets and liabilities to supplement traditional global measures of ability. The general shift in orientation resulted from the growing recognition that most mentally retarded persons *can* learn and thereby improve their performance level in schoolwork, in occupational tasks, and in other

---

[9] Originally called American Board of Examiners in Professional Psychology (ABEPP).

activities of daily life. This change itself reflected developments in differential psychology, as a belief in the modifiability of "the IQ" gradually replaced the earlier, rigidly hereditarian concept of intelligence.

I saw evidence of this changed orientation when I resumed my contacts with Letchworth Village, following my initial visit in 1929. In the 1950s, I began to give a graduate course called Intellectual Deviates, which covered the two extremes of the distribution of intelligence. I devoted the first two-thirds of the course to mental retardation and the last third to intellectually "gifted" children and adults. For the first part of the course, I arranged an annual field trip to Letchworth Village, on which I regularly accompanied the students. On these trips, I observed two conspicuous changes from my earlier visit. First, there was a stronger emphasis on training. Classroom schooling through the fourth grade was provided for the more mildly retarded children. These students were sectioned into two or more homogeneous groups within each grade, on the basis of individual qualifications. Those who successfully completed the fourth-grade work could be transferred to a regular public school to continue their education. There was also shop training, on a part-time schedule for those attending classes and full-time for those who could not profit from academic instruction. Every effort was made to prepare individuals for parole or discharge from the institution, an object that was achieved in a sizeable proportion of the cases.

The second change I observed at Letchworth Village was in the presence of a strong and active psychology department, headed by Thomas McCulloch, a Duke University Ph.D. in general psychology and an ABPP diplomate in clinical psychology. The psychological work included considerable ongoing research, much of it of the carefully designed, laboratory type on a diversity of basic questions in psychology.

Another outstanding example of the newly emerging subspecialty on mental retardation is to be found in the Kennedy Child Study Center in New York City. This center conducts a developmental and training program for retarded children between the ages of 4 and 7 on a day-care basis. When installed in its permanent quarters in 1959, it provided facilities for a daily attendance of some 70 children, as well as research laboratories and office space for a multidisciplinary staff. For many years, Olivia Hooker, a University of Rochester Ph.D. in Clinical Psychology, was Associate Administrator and Director of Psychological Services for the Kennedy Center.

A related development of the postwar decades was the establishment of the APA Division on Mental Retardation and Developmental Disabilities (Div. 33). By 1991, the membership of this division had grown to include 92 fellows, 762 members, and 114 associate members.

Observations over Three Decades of Growth

The effects of the many university training programs in clinical psychology that were started in the 1950s were clearly evident during the years from 1960 to 1990. Those were years of phenomenal growth in number of clinical psychologists, as well as improvement in the quality of their work as both scientists and professionals. From 1968 to 1974, I was Chairperson of the combined graduate and undergraduate psychology department at Fordham University. The year I assumed the Chair coincided with the appointment of Marvin Reznikoff as director of the department's clinical psychology training program. He came to us from the Institute of Living in Hartford, Connecticut, where he had been Director of Clinical Psychology since 1955. Our department had started a clinical training program shortly after the war, which was initially supported in part by VA funding. By 1968, the department had permanent APA approval for its program and was able to receive USPHS funding.

A noteworthy feature of the period was that the students enrolled in the clinical psychology programs were highly selected in all admission requirements, because of the excessively high ratio of applicants to admissions. In our department, we had 15 places reserved for incoming clinical students. The number of applicants during my six-year period as Chairperson rose from 173 in 1968 to 426 in 1974. This increase was partly due to our program becoming gradually better known, especially through the achievement of our graduates. Our program was closely integrated along the scientist-professional lines; each student had contact with professors in a diversity of areas. The qualifying examinations were truly comprehensive in coverage, and dissertation committees regularly included professors from statistical and experimental specialties, along with clinical representatives.

Our experience with high applicant-admission ratios was typical of that of universities in general. Everywhere, demand was extremely high and available facilities were limited. The ratios began to decline as some applicants were siphoned off through the introduction of additional Doctor of Psychology (Psy.D.) programs in a few universities, as well as the establishment of independent schools of psychology that offered one or both degree programs.

Another of my personal contacts with the growth of clinical psychology occurred through my election to the APA Board of Directors and Presidency. In one or another capacity, this gave me a continuous five-year period on the Board (1969–1973). This APA period coincided with the emergence of a subgroup of clinical psychologists, the full-time private practitioners, as distinguished from the clinical psychologists engaged primarily in university teaching or in institutional practice. Some of the private practitioners were just beginning to express concern that APA did not adequately meet the particular needs of their specialty in certain professional and business matters. A major concern was with the availability of insurance reimbursement for professional psychological services. In later years, these problems became more acute and led to some divisiveness within the APA.

My own closest involvement with the content of clinical psychology occurred during the preparation of the two editions of my textbook *Fields of Applied Psychology* (1964, 1979), in each of which I included three chapters about clinical psychology. As I compare the chapter titles and section headings in the two editions, I notice changes that reflect significant conceptual and methodological developments in both clinical practice and research over the intervening 15 years. That so much could happen in so short a time indicates the rapid rate of progress in the field. In the 1964 edition, the three chapters were titled simply "Diagnosis," "Therapy," and "Clinical Research." In the 1979 edition, they had become "Clinical Practice: Appraisal Procedures," "Clinical Practice: Intervention Procedures," and "Research in Clinical and Community Psychology." Obviously, the new titles for the first two chapters reflected the growing recognition of the inappropriateness of the medical, disease-oriented model for describing psychological dysfunction. At the time, the terms *appraisal* and *assessment* seemed about equally popular. I compromised by choosing *appraisal* for the more conspicuous chapter title and *assessment* for repeated use in several section headings. Subsequently, *assessment* appears to have won out in general usage.

As for section headings, the only one that remained completely unchanged in the first chapter was "Nature of Clinical Judgment," whose contribution to clinical assessment I emphasized all along. In this connection, I have periodically enjoyed stimulating discussions with Paul Meehl (1954), with whom I disagree that statistical procedures can now (or ever) completely replace clinical judgment in either data gathering or the final synthesis of information about the individual (see also Anastasi, 1988b, pp. 513–515).

In the chapter on intervention (therapy), the most significant second-edition changes are the inclusion of sections headed "Group Therapy and Other Group-Related Procedures," "Behavior Therapy," and "Community Psychology." In the first edition, the newly emerging area of behavior therapy received only a subsection, whose heading did not rate listing in the table of contents. Community psychology had surfaced in full vigor and many forms between the two editions. Hence, it appeared not only as a full-fledged new section but also in the title of the third chapter, dealing with research.

In both editions, the chapter on research includes sections on the validation of assessment (diagnostic) techniques and on outcome studies of interventions (therapy). Research findings on outcome, however, remained disappointing throughout and led to the abandonment of at least one major effort to evaluate the effectiveness of therapy, as the complexity of methodological problems became evident (Bergin & Strupp, 1972; see also Anastasi, 1979, pp. 380–386). Among the principal procedural obstacles are the choice of a criterion of improvement for measuring outcome and the dependence of outcome on higher-order interactions among variables of specific therapeutic techniques, of client problems and related personality characteristics, and of therapist orientation and training.

Another topic included in both editions as a separate section is the integration of clinical and experimental approaches. It may be of some significance that this formed the last section of the research chapter in the 1964 edition but the opening section of the chapter in the 1979 edition. In the earlier book, it represents a hopeful look into the future; in the later book, it set the tone for the whole chapter. Moreover, in the second edition, experimental research with patient data, as well as controlled studies with animals and normal persons, are cited throughout the chapter, including the last section. Among the most notable, long-term research projects that bridged the experimental and clinical fields are those directed by Neal Miller (Dollard & Miller, 1950; Miller, 1958), Harry Harlow (Suomi & Harlow, 1977), and Martin Seligman (1975).

Although not visible in chapter or section headings, another topic that received increased attention in the research chapter of the 1979 edition was the development of statistical techniques and experimental designs appropriate for clinical data (e.g., Barlow & Hersen, 1984; Campbell & Stanley, 1966; Gottman, 1973; Kazdin, 1982). Of particular interest are the techniques designed for the intensive study of individual cases, which I regard as the essence of the clinical method. There are techniques applicable, not only to N-of-one research, but also—in somewhat better controlled variants—to research with N-of-two or N-of-one-at-a-time.

Emerging Trends in 1990

For the past decade I have become increasingly interested in looking for convergences among psychological phenomena that have been investigated from different viewpoints and have often led to lively controversies (Anastasi, 1990, August). Within my own specialty, such convergences are illustrated by the development of comprehensive models of the composition of intelligence, which integrate general factors, group factors, and specific factors. This hierarchical model has been recognized for some time and has gradually been gaining acceptance (Humphreys, 1962; Vernon, 1961). Another example is the reconciliation of trait and situational approaches to individual differences in behavior (Anastasi, 1983; 1988b, pp. 555–558; Mischel, 1979; Mischel & Peake, 1982).

Recently, in looking for examples both in psychometrics and in other areas of psychology, I came upon the impressive convergence movement that is sweeping across psychotherapy with increasing vigor (Beitman, Goldfried, & Norcross, 1989; Goldfried, 1982; Norcross, 1986). As proposed by some of the leaders in this movement, the convergence and integration are most likely to occur at an intermediate level of abstraction, which focuses on psychotherapy strategies. It would be premature to expect unification in terms of an all-encompassing grand theory; and it would not be desirable to try to force all psychotherapy (or all psychology) into such a theory. At the other extreme, specific therapeutic techniques should still provide a sufficiently diverse repertoire to permit the most effective selection to fit the individual case.

The process of seeking common elements across widely varying types of traditional psychotherapy has directed attention to specific variables of client problems, of intervention procedures, and of outcome. The resulting identification of clearly defined variables in all three domains should also contribute to the design of appropriate research on the effectiveness of particular therapeutic procedures. There does, in fact, appear to be a resurgence of research in this area, which may itself be a side effect of the integration movement (e.g., Elkin et al., 1989; Luborsky, Crits-Christoph, Mintz, & Auerback, 1988).

From my observation post, if I were asked what changes I should most like to see in clinical psychology in the years ahead, I would emphatically reply: (1) well-designed research on the effectiveness of therapeutic interventions, with precise definition of both independent and dependent variables; and (2) integration among the bewildering array of "schools" of psychotherapy. When what one would like to see happen coincides with emerging trends that are rapidly gaining momentum, there is cause for optimism. And optimism is what I feel about the future of clinical psychology.

References

American Psychological Foundation awards for 1984 (1985). *American Psychologist, 40,* 340–341.

Anastasi, A. (1930). A group factor in immediate memory. *Archives of Psychology,* No. 120.

Anastasi, A. (1932). Further studies on the memory factor. *Archives of Psychology,* No. 142.

Anastasi, A. (1936). The influence of specific experience upon mental organization. *Genetic Psychology Monographs, 18*(4), 245–355.

Anastasi, A. (1938). Faculties *versus* factors: A reply to Professor Thurstone. *Psychological Bulletin, 35,* 391–395.

Anastasi, A. (1941a) [Review of C. Burt, *The factors of the mind*]. *American Journal of Psychology, 54,* 613–614.

Anastasi, A. (1941b). [Review of P. E. Vernon, *The measurement of abilities*]. *American Journal of Psychology, 54,* 154–155.

Anastasi, A. (1952). [Review of P. E. Vernon, *The structure of human abilities*]. *American Journal of Psychology, 65,* 143–145.

Anastasi, A. (1954). *Psychological testing.* New York: Macmillan. (Later eds. 1961, 1968, 1976, 1982, 1988)

Anastasi, A. (1958a). *Differential psychology* (3rd ed.). New York: Macmillan. (1st ed. 1937)

Anastasi, A. (1958b). Heredity, environment, and the question "How?" *Psychological Review, 65,* 197–208.

Anastasi, A. (1964). *Fields of applied psychology.* New York: McGraw-Hill. (Rev. ed. 1979)

Anastasi, A. (1967). Psychology, psychologists, and psychological testing. *American Psychologist, 22,* 297–306.

Anastasi, A. (1970a). *Correlates of creativity in children from two socio-economic levels.* (Final Project Report, CUE Subcontract No. 2, Under Contract No. OEC-1-7-062868-3060). New York: Center for Urban Education.

Anastasi, A. (1970b). On the formation of psychological traits. *American Psychologist, 25,* 899–910.

Anastasi, A. (1972a). The cultivation of diversity. *American Psychologist, 27,* 1091–1099.

Anastasi, A. (1972b). Reminiscences of a differential psychologist. In T. S. Krawiec (Ed.), *The psychologists* (pp. 3–37). New York: Oxford University Press.

Anastasi, A. (1980). (Autobiography). In G. Lindzey (Ed.), *A history of psychology in autobiography* (pp. 1–37). San Francisco: Freeman.

Anastasi, A. (Ed.). (1982). *Contributions to differential psychology: Selected papers.* New York: Praeger.

Anastasi, A. (1983). Traits, states, and situations. A comprehensive view. In H. Wainer & S. Messick (Eds.), *Principals of modern psychological measurement. A Festschrift for Frederic M. Lord* (pp. 345–356). Hillsdale, NJ: Erlbaum.

Anastasi, A. (1983, August). Chance encounters and locus of control. In A. N. O'Connell (Chair), *Eminent women in psychology: Personal and historical reflections.* Symposium conducted at the Annual Convention of the American Psychological Association, Anaheim, CA. [Also published in A. N. O'Connell & N. F. Russo (Eds.). (1988). *Models of achievement: Reflections of eminent women in psychology* (vol. 2, pp. 57–66). Hillsdale, NJ: Erlbaum.]

Anastasi, A. (1985). Reciprocal relations between cognitive and affective variables—with implications for sex differences. In T. B. Sonderegger & R. A. Dienstbier (Eds.), *Nebraska Symposium on Motivation, Vol. 32: Psychology and gender* (pp. 3–35). Lincoln: University of Nebraska Press.

Anastasi, A. (1986a). Experiential structuring of psychological traits. *Developmental Review, 6,* 181–202.

Anastasi, A. (1986b). Intelligence as a quality of behavior. In R. J. Sternberg & D. K. Detterman (Eds.), *What is intelligence?* (pp. 19–22). Norwood, NJ: Ablex.

Anastasi, A. (1988a). Explorations in human intelligence: Some uncharted routes. *Applied Measurement in Education, 1*(3), 207–213.

Anastasi, A. (1988b). *Psychological testing* (6th ed.). New York: Macmillan. (1st ed. 1954)

Anastasi, A. (1990). What is test misuse? Perspectives of a measurement expert. *Proceedings of the 1989 ETS Invitational Conference* (pp. 15–25). Princeton, NJ: Educational Testing Service.

Anastasi, A. (1990, August). *Are there unifying trends in the psychologies of 1990?* Invited address presented at the Annual Convention of the American Psychological Association, Boston.

Anastasi, A., & Foley, J. P., Jr. (1936). An analysis of spontaneous drawings by children in different cultures. *Journal of Applied Psychology, 20,* 689–726.

Anastasi, A., & Foley, J. P., Jr. (1938). A study of animal drawings by Indian children of the North Pacific Coast. *Journal of Social Psychology, 9,* 363–374.

Anastasi, A., & Foley, J. P., Jr. (1944). An experimental study of the drawing behavior of adult psychotics in comparison with that of a normal control group. *Journal of Experimental Psychology, 34,* 169–194.

Anastasi, A., & Schaefer, C. E. (1969). Biographical correlates of artistic and literary creativity in adolescent girls. *Journal of Applied Psychology, 53,* 267–273.

Avakian, S. A. (1961). An investigation of trait relationships among six-year-old children. *Genetic Psychology Monographs, 63,* 339–394.

Barlow, D. H., & Hersen, M. (1984). *Single case experimental designs: Strategies for studying behavior change* (2nd ed.). New York: Pergamon.

Beitman, B. D., Goldfried, N. R., & Norcross, J. C. (1989). The movement toward integrating the psychotherapies: An overview. *American Journal of Psychiatry, 146,* 138–147.

Bergin, A. E., & Strupp, H. H. (1972). *Changing frontiers in the science of psychotherapy.* Chicago: Aldine.

Biglan, A. (1980). Selling science to undergraduates [Review of A. Anastasi, *Fields of applied psychology*]. *Contemporary Psychology, 25,* 820–821.

Bingham, W. V. (1910). Studies in melody. *Psychological Monographs, 12*(3, Whole No. 50)

Burr, E. T. (1924). Minimum intellectual levels of accomplishment in industry. *Journal of Personnel Research, 3,* 207–212.

Burr, E. T. (1932). How a thousand girls were trained for self-support. *Personnel Journal, 10,* 344–346.

Burt, C. (1941). *The factors of the mind: An introduction to factor analysis.* New York: Macmillan.

Burtt, H. E. (1946). *Applied psychology.* New York: Prentice-Hall. (2nd ed. 1957)

Campbell, D. T., & Stanley, J. C. (1966). *Experimental and quasi-experimental designs for research.* Chicago: Rand McNally.

Christal, R. E. (1958). Factor analytic study of visual memory. *Psychological Monographs, 72*(13, Whole No. 466)

Davenport, C. B. (1928). Race crossing in Jamaica. *Scientific Monthly, 27,* 225–238.

Davenport, C. B. (1929). Do races differ in mental capacity? *Human Biology, 1,* 70–89.

Davenport, C. B., & Craytor, L. C. (1923). Comparative social traits of various races. Second study. *Journal of Applied Psychology, 7,* 127–132.

Denton, L. (1987). The rich life and busy times of Anne Anastasi. *APA Monitor,* 10–11.

DeVito, A. J. (1989, March). Interview with Anne Anastasi. Transcript No. 48, *Fordham University Sesquicentennial Oral History Project.*

Distinguished scientific award for the applications of psychology for 1981. (1982). *American Psychologist, 37,* 52–59.

Dobzhansky, T. (1950). The genetic nature of differences among men. In S. Persons (Ed.), *Evolutionary thought in America* (pp. 86–155). New Haven, CT: Yale University Press.

Dobzhansky, T. (1951a). *Genetics and the origin of species* (3rd ed.). New York: Columbia University Press.

Dobzhansky, T. (1951b). Mendelian populations and their evolution. In L. C. Dunn (Ed.), *Genetics in the twentieth century* (pp. 573–589). New York: Macmillan.

Dollard, J., & Miller, N. E. (1950). *Personality and psychotherapy: An analysis in terms of learning, thinking, and culture.* New York: McGraw-Hill.

Dunnette, M. D. (1964). Achievements of applied psychology [Review of A. Anastasi, *Fields of applied psychology*]. *Contemporary Psychology, 9,* 481–482.

Ekstrom, R. B., French, J. W., Harman, H. H., & Dermen, D. (1976). *Manual for kit of factor-referenced cognitive tests* (3rd ed.). Princeton, NJ: Educational Testing Service.

Elkin, I., et al. (1989). National Institute of Mental Health Treatment of Depression Collaborative Research Program: General effectiveness of treatments. *Archives of General Psychiatry, 46,* 971–983.

Filella, J. F. (1960). Educational and sex differences in the organization of abilities in technical and academic students in Colombia, South America. *Genetic Psychology Monographs, 61,* 115–163.

Fisher, R. A. (1925). *Statistical methods for research workers.* Edinburgh: Oliver and Boyd.

Franz, S. I. (1919). *Handbook of mental examination methods* (2nd ed.). New York: Macmillan.

French, J. W. (1954). *Kit of selected tests for reference aptitude and achievement factors.* Princeton, NJ: Educational Testing Service.

French, J. W., Ekstrom, R. B., & Price, L. A. (1963). *Kit of reference tests for cognitive factors* (rev. ed.). Princeton, NJ: Educational Testing Service.

Garrett, H. E. (1926). *Statistics in psychology and education.* New York: Longmans, Green. (Later editions 1937, 1947, 1953, 1958)

Garrett, H. E., & Schneck, M. R. (1933). *Psychological tests, methods, and results.* New York: Harper.

Goldfried, M. R. (Ed.). (1982). *Converging themes in psychotherapy: Trends in psychodynamic, humanistic, and behavioral practice.* New York: Springer.

Goodenough, F. L. (1926). *Measurement of intelligence by drawings.* Yonkers, NY: World Book Co.

Goodenough, F. L., & Harris, D. B. (1950). Studies in the psychology of children's drawings: II. 1928–1949. *Psychological Bulletin, 47,* 369–433.

Gottman, J. M. (1973). N-of-one and N-of-two research in psychotherapy. *Psychological Bulletin, 80,* 93–105.

Harman, H. H. (1976). *Modern factor analysis* (3rd ed.). Chicago: University of Chicago Press. (Earlier eds. 1960, 1967)

Harris, D. B. (1963). *Children's drawings as measures of intellectual maturity: A revision and extension of the Goodenough Draw-a-Man Test.* New York: Harcourt, Brace and World.

Hollingworth, H. L. (1913). *Advertising and selling: Principles of appeal and response.* New York: Appleton.

Hollingworth, H. L. (1920). *The psychology of functional neuroses.* New York: Appleton.

Hollingworth, H. L. (1926). *The psychology of thought.* New York: Appleton.

Hollingworth, H. L. (1927). *Mental growth and decline: A survey of developmental psychology.* New York: Appleton.

Hollingworth, H. L. (1928). *Psychology: Its facts and principles.* New York: Appleton.

Hollingworth, H. L. (1930). *Abnormal psychology: Its concepts and theories.* New York: Ronald.

Hollingworth, H. L., & Poffenberger, A. T. (1917). *Applied psychology.* New York: Appleton.

Hotelling, H. (1933). Analysis of a complex of statistical variables into principal components. *Journal of Educational Psychology, 24,* 417–441, 498–520.

Hull, C. L. (1928). *Aptitude testing.* Yonkers, NY: World Book Co.

Hull, C. L. (1933). *Hypnosis and suggestibility: An experimental approach.* New York: Appleton-Century.

Humphreys, L. G. (1962). The organization of human abilities. *American Psychologist, 17,* 475–483.

James, L. R., Mulaik, S. A., & Brett, J. M. (1982). *Causal analysis: Assumptions, models, and data.* Beverly Hills, CA: Sage Publications.

Jones, M. C. (1924). A laboratory study of fear: The case of Peter. *Pedagogical Seminary (later Journal of Genetic Psychology), 31,* 308–315.

Kantor, J. R. (1924). *Principles of psychology,* Vol. 1. New York: Knopf.

Kantor, J. R. (1926). *Principles of psychology,* Vol. 2. New York: Knopf.

Kantor, J. R. (1929). *An outline of social psychology.* Chicago: Follett.

Kantor, J. R. (1936). *An objective psychology of grammar.* Bloomington: Indiana University Publications (Science Series, No. 1).

Kantor, J. R. (1958). *Interbehavioral psychology: A sample of scientific system construction.* Chicago: Principia Press.

Kazdin, A. E. (1982). *Single-case research designs: Methods for clinical and applied settings.* New York: Oxford University Press.

Kelley, T. L. (1928). *Crossroads in the mind of man: A study of differentiable mental traits.* Stanford, CA: Stanford University Press.

Kelley, T. L. (1935). *Essential traits of mental life.* Cambridge, MA: Harvard University Press.

Kellogg, W. N., & Kellogg, L. A. (1933). *The ape and the child.* New York: Whittlesey House, McGraw-Hill.

Klineberg, D. (1931). A study of psychological differences between "racial" and national groups in Europe. *Archives of Psychology,* No. 132.

Loehlin, J. C. (1987). *Latent variable models: An introduction to factor, path, and structural analysis.* Hillsdale, NJ: Erlbaum.

Luborsky, L., Crits-Christoph, P., Mintz, J., & Auerbach, A. (1988). *Who will benefit from psychotherapy? Predicting therapeutic outcomes.* New York: Basic Books.

Lund, F. H., & Anastasi, A. (1928). An interpretation of aesthetic experience. *American Journal of Psychology, 40,* 434–448.

Meehl, P. E. (1954). *Clinical vs. statistical prediction: A theoretical analysis and a review of the evidence.* Minneapolis: University of Minnesota Press.

Metcalfe, Z., & Burr, E. T. (1936). A practical form of the Girls' Mechanical Assembly Test. *Journal of Applied Psychology, 20,* 672–679.

Miller, G. A. (1969). Psychology as a means of promoting human welfare. *American Psychologist, 24,* 1063–1075.

Miller, N. E. (1958). Liberalization of basic S-R concepts: Extensions to conflict behavior, motivation, and social learning. In S. Koch (Ed.), *Psychology: A study of a science* (Vol. 2, pp. 198–292). New York: McGraw-Hill.

Mischel, W. (1979). On the interface of cognition and personality: Beyond the person-situation debate. *American Psychologist, 34,* 740–754.

Mischel, W., & Peake, P. K. (1982). Beyond de´ ja` vu in the search for cross-situational consistency. *Psychological Review, 89,* 730–755.

Moore, H. T. (1914). The genetic aspect of consonance and dissonance. *Psychological Monographs, 17*(2, whole No. 73).

Norcross, J. C. (Ed.). (1986). *Handbook of eclectic psychotherapy.* New York: Brunner/Mazel.

Pillsbury, W. B. (1921). *Essentials of psychology* (rev. ed.). New York: Macmillan.

Poffenberger, A. T. (1942). *Principles of applied psychology.* New York: Appleton-Century.

Prinzhorn, H. (1923). *Bildnerei der Geisteskranken: ein Beitrag zu¨ r Psychologie und Psychopathologie der Gestaltung* (2nd ed.). Berlin: Springer.

Robertson, G. J. (1987). Anastasi marks 50 years as textbook author: Part I. *The Score, 10*(3), 3, 6, 12.

Robertson, G. J. (1988). Anastasi marks 50 years as textbook author: Part II. *The Score, 10*(4), 8–10.

Schieffelin, B., & Schwesinger, G. C. (1930). Mental tests and heredity, including a survey of non-verbal tests. *Eugenics Research Association Monograph Series,* No. 111.

Seligman, M. E. P. (1975). *Helplessness: On depression, development, and death.* San Francisco: Freeman.

Sexton, V. S. (1987, March). Transcript of interview with Anne Anastasi. *Presidents' Oral History Project.* Washington, DC: American Psychological Association.

Sexton, V. S., & Hogan, J. D., (1990). Anne Anastasi. In A. N. O'Connell & N. F. Russo (Eds.), *Women in psychology* (pp. 13–22). Hillside, NJ: Erlbaum.

Snedecor, G. W. (1934). *Calculation and interpretation of analysis of variance and covariance.* Ames, IA: Collegiate Press.

Snyder, L. H. (1951). *The principles of heredity* (4th ed.). Boston: Heath.

Spearman, C. (1904). "General intelligence" objectively determined and measured. *American Journal of Psychology, 15,* 201–293.

Spearman, C. (1927). *The abilities of man.* New York: Macmillan.

Stern, W. (1900). *Ü ber Psychologie der individuellen differenzen: Ideen zur einen "Differentielle Psychologie."* Leipzig: Barth. (Later editions 1911, 1921)

Suomi, S. J., & Harlow, H. F. (1977). Production and alleviation of depressive behaviors in monkeys. In J. Maser & E. P. Seligman (Eds.), *Psychopathology: Experimental models* (pp. 131–173). San Francisco: Freeman.

Symonds, P. M. (1931). *Diagnosing personality and conduct.* New York: Century.

Thurstone, L. L. (1935). *The vectors of mind.* Chicago: University of Chicago Press.

Thurstone, L. L. (1938). Shifty mathematical components: A critique of Anastasi's monograph on the influence of specific experience upon mental organization. *Psychological Bulletin, 35,* 223–236.

Thurstone, L. L. (1947). *Multiple factor analysis.* Chicago: University of Chicago Press.

Vernon, P. E. (1940). *The measurement of abilities.* London: University of London Press.

Vernon, P. E. (1950). *The structure of human abilities.* London: Methuen.

Vernon, P. E. (1961). *The structure of human abilities* (rev. ed.). London: Methuen.

Watson, J. B. (1913). Psychology as a behaviorist views it. *Psychological Review, 20,* 158–177.

Watson, J. B. (1919). *Psychology from the standpoint of a behaviorist.* Philadelphia: Lippincott.

Watson, J. B. (1924). The unverbalized in human behavior. *Psychological Review, 31,* 273–280.

Watson, J. B., & Lashley, K. S. (1915). *Homing and related activities of birds.* Washington, D.C.: Carnegie Institution of Washington.

Watson, J. B., & Raynor, P. (1920). Conditioned emotional reaction. *Journal of Experimental Psychology, 3,* 1–14.

Woodworth, R. S. (1918). *Personal Data Sheet.* Chicago: Stoelting.

Woodworth, R. S., & Mathews, E. (1923). *Woodworth-Mathews Personal Data Sheet.* Chicago: Stoelting.

Wright, S. (1921). Correlation and causation. *Journal of Agricultural Research, 20,* 557–585.

Wright, S. (1934). The method of path coefficients. *Annals of Mathematical Statistics, 5,* 161–215.

Louise Bates Ames

Associate Director
Gesell Institute of Human Development

◆

Child Development and Clinical Psychology

In the Beginning

I am one of those fortunate individuals who looks back kindly on my childhood. Not only was our household comfortable and safe, it was also intellectually stimulating. Like many children, I suppose, I believed that my father knew *everything*. And my mother, who had given up teaching for mothering, devoted her time and energy to seeing that things went well for us.

While I cannot say that my upbringing steered me directly into the field of clinical psychology, it is fair to say that it was appropriate for any individual who might end up in the field of human behavior. We read in our family, and before we were old enough to read for ourselves, our parents read to us. Winter evenings we sat by the fire with our mother and father, being read to from Dickens, Mark Twain, Poe, or from such poets as Robert Burns, Longfellow, Tennyson, or Walt Whitman.

I myself read very early. In fact, when not quite 6 years of age I started school in second grade because I could already read *The Hen Found a Bag of Flour* (considered in 1911 to be second grade reading material).

And later, as a family, we still read. Especially on Christmas Day, once presents and dinner were out of the way, we all read our Christmas books. New members of the family—my husband, my brother's wife—tried to talk. We would look up from our books, answer their questions, and then go back to reading.

Before being promoted to second grade, I had a week in first and was disappointed because it was not harder. I had brought my ruler, pencil with eraser, and other equipment to school expecting it to be challenging. But it wasn't. Actually, I searched for the anticipated challenge till fifth grade, when decimals challenged me quite adequately, as did algebra and geometry in high school. Otherwise, I did well in school and enjoyed it thoroughly. I was especially excited in the summer before seventh grade at the prospect that we would be learning history.

While growing up, my brothers and I took part in such newspaper contests as "Know Your Own State." We also debated. On at least some Sunday mornings we were collected in our parents' bedroom and given a topic of debate. Whoever won received a prize of five cents. (This was the customary reward for winning whatever contest was afoot—identifying wildflowers or trees—whatever.) Also, our home library was well equipped with reference books, and we were encouraged to use them.

All of this thinking, discussing, and reading inevitably converged much of the time on the foibles of human behavior, the differences in human beings, the whys and intricacies of the ways in which different people responded to life situations. There was always strong emphasis on *not* jumping to conclusions—not accepting people, things, and ideas at surface value. Certainly, our deep immersion in literature, as well as our many discussions and conversations, did lead to a definite interest in human behavior and the intricacies of the differences in individuals themselves and in the society that they created.

In school, though weak in the athletic department, I was strong in debating, public speaking, drama, English literature, writing, and history. And as far as school in general was concerned I was undoubtedly fortunate. Though some today might consider my school situation to have been restricted, public schools in Portland, Maine, when I was growing up were, in retrospect, superior. The student population was highly homogeneous, discipline was excellent, teachers for the most part dedicated and highly qualified. Looking back, I believe that we learned a lot.

Also, home and school were closely related and harmonious. Families routinely invited teachers home to dinner. This was long before the days of teachers' unions. Teachers in those days were an extremely dedicated lot and, for the most part, were respected and admired by students and supported by parents.

Roadblocks

As Dr. Arnold Gesell pointed out in his contribution to *A History of Psychology in Autobiography,* "Choice, free will and necessity—no wise incompatible—all interweavingly work together." Certainly something of this sort was the case—at least to some extent—in my becoming a clinical psychologist. One might have said that the odds were against it.

Having moved on from the original plan I had when I was 7 or 8 to found a school in my grandmother's farmhouse and barn in Penobscot, Maine—she presumably having died and left the farm to me—I decided to become a lawyer. I would have liked to become a secretary—all that typing and filing seemed attractive. But I figured that my parents would be sending me to college and so I had better plan on some profession.

I chose law. My father was an attorney. His work seemed attractive and interesting to me, so I began at an early age to "work" in his office, and by the time I eventually diverged from this course I had come a modest way. I could sue a bill, search a title, and had already come a way in the reading of law. So this was the plan until I married in 1930 and decided to take a different route.

But in the meantime, there occurred another deterrent to my ever becoming a psychologist—even if the idea had occurred to me, which it hadn't. This deterrent was a course in introductory psychology taught by Miss Elizabeth Amen at Wheaton College in Norton, Massachusetts.

Miss Amen not only had a speech impediment—which made it hard to understand what she was saying—but presumably she had some sort of organizational problem as well, because I never knew what she was talking about. I never could figure out why sometimes she talked about people, sometimes about animals, sometimes about the various senses, sometimes about the nervous system. (Our textbook, too, must have been unusually unclear—or else I must have been unusually dense.)

At any rate, I never did understand what this subject—psychology—was all about. Predictably, I received a C in the course. However, at Wheaton, if you infringed any of the rules—came back to campus after 6 PM, rode in a car even in the daytime with a boy, returned late after a holiday—all your grades were reduced by one letter. I did some of these things. So when Miss Amen's endless course was finally finished, as I remember, I received a grade of D and solemnly swore *never* to take a course in psychology again.

There is more. (Two happenings at the University of Maine later turned the tide toward psychology. Since they were of a positive nature I'll describe them later and will continue here with roadblocks to the path that I eventually followed.)

Though both my undergraduate and graduate school experiences at Maine were friendly, useful, and productive, these adjectives could not be applied to my three years of graduate study at Yale. Quite the contrary.

I chose Yale at the instigation of Dr. Charles A. Dickinson, head of the Psychology Department at the University of Maine. It had been his unrealized dream to study with Dr. Gesell. I caught his enthusiasm and when it turned out that in that post-Depression year 1933 neither my husband nor I could obtain a teaching job, I gladly applied to Dr. Gesell for a chance to be on his staff as a research assistant and to enroll in the graduate school at Yale in a doctoral program.

Unfortunately, though it was possible for a student to obtain certain credits for work with Dr. Gesell, any student seeking a doctorate in psychology at Yale was required to major in experimental psychology. That was, in itself, bad enough. The premise behind the program was even worse. The assumption at Yale at that time appeared to be that any respectable psychologist would of course be an experimental psychologist. This individual, the thought seemed to be, would be doing such complicated experiments that equipment for these experiments would not be available for purchase. Rather, he or she would need to make his or her own equipment.

"Shop" was to me a nightmare. Up to that time in my life I had never been without some man—my father, brothers, husband—who could take care of anything mechanical. Having no mechanical ability whatsoever, my idea of a very tricky "experiment" was to screw in an electric light bulb. I loathed, dreaded, and despised my shop course, which taught us how to thread a nut and bolt and other such exquisite achievements. The instructor at one time threatened to charge me a special lab fee if I didn't stop plugging things in incorrectly. (I had never known that there even *was* a right way and a wrong way.)

The one saving grace of this course was the technician, Mr. Peterson. At that time my office, and the adjoining film vault, were below ground. Mr. Peterson assured me that one day I would be through with all this experimental work and would have a big office, above ground, with lots of windows. On occasion he would do my experiments for me.

This and other related courses, especially a course on the conditioned reflex with Clark Hull, were extremely unhappy experiences—and for the most part unrelated to anything of any interest to me. The pro-seminar syllabus (pro-seminar was a course taught by most of the faculty in turn and was expected to take up approximately half of the student's time during the year when he or she was enrolled) definitely gave short shrift to either clinical work or child behavior. According to the syllabus, "The five major fields to be explored are: abnormal, social, genetic, applied and basic concepts."

"Genetic," fortunately for me, featured Dr. Gesell and his staff. Here only was the word *clinical* employed. For three days the outline, under Dr. Gesell's contribution, actually did feature "clinical child development." Also in the pro-seminar, in spite of its off-putting listings, I did enjoy work with Dr. Robert Yerkes and Dr. Walter Miles.

To balance most of the work offered at Yale, I thoroughly appreciated my experiences with Dr. Gesell and his staff at the Yale Clinic of Child Development. Most of these were available to me not through courses in which I was enrolled, but through the fact that my work at Yale, for which I was paid five hundred dollars a year, was as research assistant to Dr. Gesell.

Leaving aside my not entirely happy experiences with the Yale Psychology Department, I was thoroughly satisfied with the working and learning opportunities offered by both Dr. Gesell and his assistant, Dr. Frances L. Ilg. The opportunities were limitless. In retrospect I marvel at the freedom and the inspiration offered to students at the Yale Clinic of Child Development.

Not only did I not appreciate the work offered by the Psychology Department, but the Psychology Department also did not vastly appreciate me. At the end of my first year, Professor Roswell P. Angier, head of the Psychology Department, called me in and said, "Why don't you go away, Mrs. Ames? You will never become a psychologist. And even if you did, nobody would ever hire you."

This sounds rather brutal, and obviously I was not complimented or encouraged. But I did not take it *too* personally. With a few minor exceptions I was not treated in a friendly or supportive way by the Psychology Department at Yale. This partly was my own fault as I was *very* poor at both experimental psychology and statistics. But for the most part I felt that the disdain that some of the faculty showed me was simply part of their dislike of Dr. Gesell, his clinical approach to human behavior, his vast popularity throughout the world, and his success in grant getting.

During the years while I was at Yale, Clark Hull and his students were the dominating force in the Psychology Department. Their contempt for clinical psychology was not hidden. Hull and his students, especially Kenneth Spence and Neal Miller, who with their "neobehavioristic" theories of conditioning and learning viewed the human organism as "a completely self-maintaining robot, constructed of materials as unlike ourselves as may be," dominated psychology at Yale. Hull, who according to Howard Kendler (1989) "equated his own role in Psychology with that of Newton in Physics" had nothing but contempt for Dr. Gesell, his theories, his work, and his students.

Also, Mark May (a short-statured man), head of the Institute of Human Relations, once commented of Dr. Gesell's rather gigantic two-volume *Atlas of Infant Behavior* that it was useful for standing on when he needed to reach a high shelf. Clearly, the Psychology Department and in fact most of the Institute of Human Relations provided an extremely unfriendly and hostile atmosphere for Dr. Gesell's students—and, for that matter, for clinical psychology in general. As Dr. Gesell's research assistant as well as his student, I seemed to be in special disfavor. I did not take it entirely personally. And I became more determined than ever to graduate and to become a successful psychologist.

Some people thought that at that time there was a certain antifemale attitude at Yale, but I never noticed it except from Professor Angier. In fact, at a personal level a number of the faculty were friendly and helpful. And among the students the men, too, were friendly. Hostility to me was shown more by the women.

Ironically, my daughter, Joan Ames Chase, who wished to be and became a clinical psychologist, was also forced, in her case by the University of Maine, to get her doctorate in experimental psychology rather than in clinical as she would have preferred.

One further roadblock, if one could call it that, to the likelihood of my becoming a clinical psychologist was the lure of research. It was in the role of research assistant that Dr. Gesell first cast me, and it was a role that fit me perfectly and one in which I was totally comfortable. Had I and my colleagues not left Yale in 1950, I might never have become a clinical psychologist.

And one final hazard presented itself in a quite unrelated field. Beginning in the 1950s, I had the good fortune to be writing my own daily syndicated newspaper column, syndicated in sixty-five of the major papers in this country. I also on several occasions was featured in a television series of my own. At one point along the way I was offered the tempting possibility of leaving psychology to make my living in the media.

This was a heady and attractive offer, but I felt that I was needed at the Gesell Institute. Also, I appreciated that both television appearances and column writing were tricky areas—with today's success turning into tomorrow's nobody. So I remained with the profession for which I was trained and that safety and common sense suggested.

A Turn Toward Psychology

Now, back to the beginning of my turn *toward* psychology. When I left Wheaton in 1928, the farthest thing from my mind was that I would ever become a psychologist. This was partly because of my unfortunate experience with Miss Amen in her introductory psychology course and partly because my plan and intention to become an attorney was so firmly ingrained.

More by good luck than good judgment, in the fall semester of 1928 I enrolled in a class in child psychology taught by Dr. Dickinson, head of the Department of Psychology at the University of Maine. I took this course mostly because, as I remember, it came at a convenient hour in the afternoon and several of my friends were also taking it. However, I did have misgivings.

Happily, these misgivings were unwarranted. I liked the course immensely and found Dr. Dickinson an enthusiastic and inspiring professor. Having made this fortunate start, in the spring of 1929 I enrolled in a class called "Problems in Psychology"—a sort of independent study course. And I also took a seminar in psychology.

Though I was still majoring in history, as a natural prerequisite to my later expected studies in law, I was so enthusiastic about Dr. Dickinson and his teaching that in my senior year (1929–30) I took all the courses in psychology that I could fit into my schedule. In the fall, mental measurements, problems in psychology, and abnormal psychology. In the spring, experimental psychology (my least favorite of the courses in psychology that I took at Maine), mental hygiene, and another of Dr. Dickinson's problems in psychology courses.

In spite of my enthusiasm for these courses, I doubt that I would have shifted from law to psychology except for an important event in my personal life. In the spring of 1930 I eloped with Smith Whittier Ames, also a student at the university. Since he was at that time planning to go into medicine, we had no idea where we would eventually be located. Now my plan to be an attorney had depended strongly on the expectation that once I had finished college and law school I would end up in Portland, Maine.

Back in those days there were not a great many women lawyers. I felt quite confident that I could do the work. (A number of summers in my father's office had given me a good start on some of the simpler and more practical aspects of practicing law.) But I was not at all sure that I could go into a strange town and find a job as a lawyer. My plan had depended strongly on the expectation that I would join my father's firm.

Thus it seemed reasonable to me to shift my field to something more flexible. Though at that time there were not a great many women involved with experimental or research psychology, it seemed reasonable to me that I could teach psychology or with luck work in a clinic or perhaps a nursery school.

To support the possibility that I might eventually wish to teach psychology, during the time that I was working toward my master's degree, also at the University of Maine and also under the guidance of Dr. Dickinson, I minored in education and did recieve a secondary teacher's certificate. However, as many of my graduate courses as possible were in the Psychology Department. And my master's thesis, for which I used my own daughter as a subject, was titled, "Growth of Motor Coordination in One Child from Birth to Two Years."

It was Dr. Dickinson's enthusiasm for the work of Dr. Gesell that led me to choose Yale as a place to obtain my doctorate, in spite of its emphasis on experimental psychology.

My First Clinical Experience

My first experience, first training, as a clinician, like so many experiences in my life, turned out to be a very fortunate one. It was a four-year assignment (December 1940 to June 1944) in examining preschoolers to determine their suitability for adoption.

In the 1940s the number of illegitimate children available for adoption was large enough that parents could be selective. Also, at that time the Gesell position, shared by many, was that at least a reasonable match between adopting parents and the adopted child was desirable.

Even in those days, environmentalists, like psychologists at the University of Iowa, maintained that in effect the ultimate intelligence of adopted children depended largely on the intellectual level of the family into which they were adopted. That is, they claimed that a highly intelligent family would end up with an intelligent adopted child, regardless of what his or her IQ was to start with (and vice versa). Dr. Gesell characteristically maintained that the level of the family would not substantially influence that of the child.

In the 1940s there was little of today's emphasis on the desirability of adopting the so-called "hard to place" child. In those days the emphasis was on placing each infant or child in a family of suitable, or more or less "matching," background.[1] Dr. Gesell contended that whereas a child of very modest potential might fit very nicely into a family whose expectations were modest, such a child would provide an unnecessary disappointment to a family that planned, and expected, to send their child to college.

---

[1] This notion was later not only disavowed but actually ridiculed by such social activists as Joseph Reid of the Child Welfare League of New York City.

(A brief explanation about the Gesell preschool tests, unrelated to my own professional activities, should perhaps be given here. As early as 1941, in *Developmental Diagnosis* (pp. 114–116), Dr. Gesell emphasized that "developmental diagnosis does not attempt a direct measure of intelligence as such, but should aim at clinical estimation of mentality based upon analysis of maturity status. . . . The D.Q. [Developmental Quotient], unlike the I.Q., is not limited to a single inclusive formula." That is, a child could be somewhat immature but of a presumably normal intelligence. Nevertheless, when behavior was substantially below what could normally be expected for an individual of the child's age, as a rule he or she was not considered to be adoptable. A second examination after perhaps six months was usually recommended, either in the same foster home if that was considered to be favorable, or if that home was considered unfavorable, in a more supportive home.)

Thus my responsibility as an examiner was, with substantial input from my supervisor, Dr. Catherine S. Amatruda, to determine whether each of the children I examined was or was not a suitable adoption candidate. I was also to come to some conclusion as to what kind of home, if any, he or she should be placed in.

We at the Yale Clinic of Child Development worked as consultants to, or examiners for, the Bureau of Child Welfare of the State of Connecticut. Since infant examining was in Dr. Gesell's opinion the province of physicians and not of psychologists, I was not assigned to the examination of infants. My age range in the four years during which I was assigned to this particular service was 18 months to 6 years 3 months.

Of the 192 children whom I examined in this time period, 44 (23 percent) were considered unadoptable, largely on the basis of seeming to be feebleminded. Twenty-one (11 percent) were felt to be in need of a reexamination after they had had some time in a more favorable home environment than the one they had been living in. One hundred twenty-seven (66 percent) were considered adoptable, even though of these 7 were classed as dull-normal and 5 as low average.

The examination that I gave, like the usual Gesell examination, checked behavior in four fields: motor, adaptive, language, and personal-social. Information about the personal-social behavior was obtained through a parent—or usually foster parent—interview, held before the examination proper. When the time came for me to give my first examination, Dr. Amatruda directed me, casually, "Go in and get the parent interview." Though I had felt secure about giving the examination itself, I can remember now how casually she said this and how frightened *I* was. However, all went well.

This total assignment was an extremely rewarding way to begin clinical examining because it was so definite. No mysterious malfunctioning to be diagnosed, as with so many clinical cases. No complex and difficult problems to be solved. No miraculous solution sought by the patient or the patient's parent—just a simple evaluation of the child's status, his or her adoptability or nonadoptability, and the kind of home, if any, into which we thought he or she would fit.

All of this gave me a great feel for clinical psychology. I concluded that I would like to do more of it even though at the time I considered myself primarily a researcher. (And Dr. Gesell so considered me.)

At any rate, for the next few years (1944 to 1950) until I left the university and Dr. Frances L. Ilg, Janet Learned, and I founded the Gesell Institute, my time was spent almost entirely in research, writing, and teaching. However, this experience with adoption cases was, admittedly, rather a heady start in clinical examining. It was, as I remember, quite gratifying to be making these big decisions about children's futures with apparent success and, in my opinion, clarity.

Also, happily, this was a time when the value of testing was not, for the most part, questioned (except by the environmentalists). Most people were willing to admit that some children were relatively more mature, some relatively more intelligent, than others; and that these differences were genetic. The results of such testing were at that time not denigrated as "labeling," "discriminatory," "racist," "tracking" as they tend to be now in the 1990s.

Work at Yale, 1944–50

After finishing the work on adoption I did relatively little clinical work during my remaining years at Yale. I examined a child now and then, and observed many clinical examinations given by Drs. Gesell, Ilg, and Amatruda. I also took part in case conferences that followed these examinations.

However, my work during the years 1944 to 1950 was mostly in research. I also worked extensively in films. I did not do the actual filming. My work had to do with editing and analyzing films and with making both basic unedited films and edited films (and related literature) available to students and professional people.

Also, as (eventually) assistant professor at the Medical School, I did a normal amount of teaching, mostly of medical students and graduate students in education and psychology. And I lectured to parent and professional groups.

A time-consuming but interesting part of my work was entertaining visitors who came in droves from all over the world. Some of these visitors stayed with us for days, weeks, or months. But the majority were seen on the one day a month that I set aside for nothing but visitors. Groups of parents, teachers, and students were scheduled, one group each hour. With these groups our main purpose was to tell them about our work and to answer questions.

The more serious visitors were obviously the most interesting and the most rewarding. Through time we became something of a clearinghouse for what was going on in the field throughout the world, and thus, we believed, served a useful purpose.

For the most part, visitors were enthusiastic about our work and very friendly and appreciative. However, then as always there were many psychologists and others who were strongly environmentally oriented. They believed, then as now, that by doing the "right" things the environment could make almost anybody into almost anything.

Though now that I am older I can accept the fact that there are and always will be people of this persuasion, at the time it upset me greatly. Dr. Gesell, in one of his few personal remarks to me (he was not a chatty man), once advised me, "Mrs. Ames, don't get so angry at these people. If we are right, they'll know it one day. And if we are wrong, you are wasting a great deal of energy."

We Leave the University

In 1948, Dr. Gesell was about to retire from Yale. We at the clinic expected this. It came in the natural course of events. We also expected that his successor would be somebody distinguished, somebody with a good reputation, somebody who liked and admired our own work. Predictably, he or she might lead us in somewhat new directions—even possibly in some we might not have chosen. We might have to accept, and work with, some concepts that had been alien to us. But presumably, the basic Gesell work would go on.

Thus we dismissed as ludicrous rumors spread by secretaries and janitors that Yale was planning to get rid of us. Had not the *American Scientist* in 1949 noted, in describing Dr. Gesell, "In 1915 he was appointed professor of Child Hygiene [at Yale], a field in which he retains undisputed leadership"?

Not only was Dr. Gesell well respected throughout the world, but so also was the work of the clinic. Shortly before we left the university, former Mayor Richard E. Lee (at that time director of public relations for Yale) commented that Dr. Gesell turned down more publicity than he (Lee) could attract for the university. *Life, Time, Readers' Digest, Colliers,* and many other popular magazines (as well, of course, as the scientific journals) featured or included his work.

Thus we as a staff were sanguine about the future. What transpired went far beyond our wildest nightmares. Yale appointed a committee to see "what could and should be done about child development at Yale." On this committee were Clyde Hill, a friend (whose own Department of Education was soon to be demolished), Neal Miller, definitely not a friend, and—either on the committee or acting as consultants and advisors—Mark May, Grover Powers, and others.

Their decision as to what to do about child development at Yale was to engage a new director for our clinic, one Dr. Milton J. E. Senn, who was gradually to dispose of Dr. Gesell's staff, find a staff of his own, and change the emphasis of the work to something with a true Freudian slant.

Dr. Senn first came into our sight on a day when Dr. Gesell was seen to be showing a rather nervous-looking individual around the clinic. This in itself was unusual. Dr. Gesell himself did not show people around. For the most part I did, finally taking only the relatively more distinguished to Dr. Gesell's office. This particular tour, conducted by "The Boss" himself, ended in his office. Dr. Gesell was not one to gossip with the staff, but, somewhat shaken when this particular visit was over, he did share it with us. Once seated in Dr. Gesell's office, Dr. Senn had reportedly said that "They" had told him that the Yale Clinic of Child Development would offer him substantial space in which to do his work, but that "They" had not told him that "all of these people were involved."

Dr. Gesell allegedly replied, "I have a large and distinguished staff, Dr. Senn." Senn then reportedly replied, "Well, when I take over they will have to be loyal to me, not to you, Dr. Gesell." Gesell replied, "The staff is loyal to *the work,* Dr. Senn—not to any one individual." Dr. Gesell at his chilliest could be exceedingly frosty. One can imagine that this particular interview was frosty indeed.

At any rate, Dr. Senn was appointed director of the Yale Clinic of Child Development with, so rumor had it, five years to get rid of Dr. Gesell's staff and five more to establish his own work.

It was only on July 5, 1949, after being for many months in Dr. Senn's employ, that I actually had a conversation with him. He said he would like to have me stay and work in his new Child Guidance Clinic along with his psychiatrist and social worker and with Dr. Katie Wolf, who "would be able to teach you how to do research." I would presumably have a larger salary. I suggested taking one day a week to work on our adolescent study, rather than having a larger salary. He agreed, tentatively.

Shortly thereafter, however, I was dissociated from Dr. Senn's staff on the grounds that I was, with Dr. Gesell, working on a film, *Embryology of Behavior,* sponsored by the American Medical Film Association and supported by government funds. So in the second year of Dr. Senn's directorship I left his group, but continued at Yale as curator of the Yale Films of Child Development. I also worked on the film *Embryology of Behavior* and on our adolescent study.

By this time we as a group were faced with the need to plan our future. The American Optometric grant that had supported Dr. Gesell and Dr. Ilg for these two final years at Yale had run out, along with Yale's willingness to give us house-room. Even if we could attract our own funds, the university assured us that we could not work within its confines. They suggested California as a good place for us to settle.

We did have one or two tentative offers to come, as a group, to other universities. However, aside from individual personal reasons for wishing to remain in New Haven, we had an outstanding professional reason. We had, collaboratively, already published two volumes of what would eventually be known as our trilogy—a comprehensive study in which we followed longitudinally a group of boys and girls from birth through age 16.

We had already examined and interviewed many of our 10 year olds and were approaching the time when many of them would be turning 11. By our figuring, 11 might be expected to be a difficult, disruptive age. If our New Haven subjects, who had (predictably) been in rather good equilibrium at 10 should, indeed, turn disruptive at 11—even though there were no substantial changes in their environment— we would seem justified in considering 11 to be indeed a time of disequilibrium.

If, on the other hand, we moved to an entirely different community and found 11s difficult, we would not be certain whether it was the age or simply their environment that had caused the disruption.

So we stayed in New Haven. Out from under the wing of Mother University we realized there would be a financial problem. But the National Institute of Mental Health assured us that if we would just borrow the money to get started and then apply for a grant to support our adolescent study, adequate funds would in all likelihood be forthcoming. Also, we suspected that foundations and/or baby food companies would very likely supply funds for this or some other aspect of the research we were doing.

Several problems offered themselves immediately. The chief one was to find a place to work. We truly scoured the town and saw many interesting houses. But the moment we saw 310 Prospect Street we all fell in love with it. No matter how many other tempting houses we saw, we always came back to it and finally bought it— thanks to money that Dr. Ilg had inherited from her friend and mentor, Laura Botsford.

Our basic starting group consisted of me, Dr. Ilg, Janet Learned, Richard Apell (as head of our proposed vision department), Ruth Métraux, and Dr. Gesell, who stayed on with us as research associate. We engaged one secretary, Marcella McKeon.

Thus the two first and most important steps had been taken. We had decided to stay in New Haven as a group and we had bought a house. The next step was equally important. We had to set up housekeeping. Though great goodwill, vast energy, and substantial cooperation prevailed, it was not entirely easy for three women of vastly different temperaments and tastes to take this step in perfect harmony. What the actual scientific and professional work should be was never in question. Less important, more domestic issues did cause modest problems.

For instance, what should we name the new venture? Janet Learned and I were 100 percent in favor of calling ourselves the Gesell Institute of Child Development. Dr. Gesell's name and reputation seemed to us virtually our sole equity. Dr. Ilg., however, favored something vaguer and broader, such as Institute for Bio-Research.

Should the basic colors in the living room be green or blue? Should we retain the original grandeur of the large living room, with its two levels, its beautiful pillars, its semicircular window arrangement at one end—graphic reminders of the genius of the architect, R. C. Sturgis? Or should we split the room in two? Should we keep the beautiful floor-to-ceiling mirror in the front hall? Should we, especially since we had virtually no money, furnish the building very cheaply, thus advertising our need for funds? Or should we try to be as elegant as possible in order to give the appearance of stability and success?

Administrative problems, like the actual work itself, presented no difficulty. Dr. Ilg said to me, "Why don't *you* be the director?" I said to her, "No, *you* be the director." Dr. Ilg agreed to try it for a year. She liked it and so did remain as director until her retirement in 1975.

According to our constitution and articles of incorporation we were required to form a board of directors. This was done, with Dr. Ilg for president, me for secretary-treasurer, and Janet Learned and Dr. Gesell as further members. Other members were soon added.

"This isn't an institute, it's a love affair!" exclaimed one of our close friends as we set about with great fervor to create our new institute.

(I have described our transition from Yale to our new Gesell Institute at some length for two reasons. To begin with, to the best of my knowledge it is not described elsewhere in the literature. But mainly because if I and Dr. Senn had been compatible, I would in all likelihood have remained at Yale and would have continued to be primarily a researcher and would not have become a clinical psychologist.)[2]

Research Leads to Clinical Work

My first clinical experience (the testing of adoption candidates) was based on our own research—not mine but that of Dr. Arnold Gesell. Though during my graduate work at the University of Maine I did inevitably learn something about standardized tests, in examining the infant and child subjects of our adoption service I used exclusively the Gesell Infant and Preschool Examinations.

Once that service was concluded (in 1944), I returned almost exclusively (except for a certain amount of teaching and the inevitable entertaining of visitors) to research. Much of this had to do with various aspects of motor and personality development, investigated by means of cinemanalysis.

However, during our final years at Yale came some research that for the next forty years has added immensely to the hoped-for effectiveness of my clinical work. That was our research on the Rorschach.

When the Rorschach test was first introduced in this country, to the best of my knowledge no special distinction was made between responses of children and adults. Thus if a child gave a response that in an adult Rorschach would be considered suspect, the child was considered suspect. This presented us with something of a puzzle, especially when the child in question in all other ways seemed, to us and to his or her parents, to be quite "normal." Many clinicians, however, did seem to consider that if there were adverse signs in the Rorschach response, there was something wrong with the child, who was then given "help."

It seemed to me (and this was one of my few really original ideas—for the most part, inspiration and ideas at the Yale Clinic of Child Development came from Dr. Gesell or Dr. Ilg) that possibly just as more specifically motor behaviors changed from age to age in a patterned way, especially in children, so perhaps those aspects of individuality revealed by the Rorschach also might change from age to age. I hypothesized that behaviors that in the adult would be considered unusual or even pathological, might be quite customary and typical and expected at certain ages in

---

[2] To bring this report up to date, it seems important to note a basic change in the child behavior scene in New Haven. Currently, a "rapprochement" has been arranged between the Child Study Center and the Gesell Institute. Yale University has established an Arnold Gesell professorship at the Child Study Center. One of their staff members, Dr. Linda C. Mayes, has been appointed to this chair. I, myself, am back on the university faculty, and joint research aimed at the restandardization of the Gesell/Yale examinations is being considered.

children. It seemed reasonable to suppose that the individuality of succeeding ages—4, 5, 6, 7, 8, and so on—as revealed by the Rorschach might also in certain ways reveal what we were already determining by other measures and kinds of observation to be the individuality of each age.

Intensive research carried on from approximately 1948 to 1952 supported our hypothesis. As anticipated, the Rorschach response very definitely changed with age, in a patterned and predictable way. And to a substantial extent, the individuality of the age as demonstrated by the Rorschach agreed with what we had earlier, on the basis of other types of observation, determined to be the basic characteristics of each age. One or two examples will suffice:

> *4 years*: The 4 year old is, in his or her Rorschach responses, definitely extra-tensive, egocentric, and unmodulated. Subjects identify concepts very positively—"I know with no doubt." They also seem to believe in the reality of things seen on the cards. The typically unbridled imagination of 4 is expressed in much confabulation, and many objects are seen in an unnatural orientation.
>
> *5 years*: The response of the 5 year old is primarily global and shows a high generalizing ability. Response is relatively more introversive than at surrounding ages, and color responses are fewer than at any succeeding age until 10 years. The child seems to be striving for complete accuracy, and accuracy of form is relatively high. In choice of content, 5 is focal and factual, close to home and close to his or her own body. He or she appears to be in relatively good equilibrium—calm, smooth, and untroubled.
>
> *5½ years*: Here the equilibrium of 5 years is breaking up, resulting in marked disequilibrium and in variability and unpredictability of behavior. The child seems unduly sensitive and vulnerable, and emotions are unduly uncontrolled. There is much emphasis on broken and shattered things. A strong drive to produce combinatory wholes frequently leads to contamination. However, the child is rigid and exact in his or her responses. He or she finds modification and qualification difficult. The child of this age thus shows himself or herself to be sensitive, vulnerable, insecure, unpredictable, and in considerable disequilibrium. He or she is outgoing, excitable, impetuous, and subject to uncontrolled attacks of temper. He or she is also rigid, unmodulated, and poor at interpersonal relations.

These samples should be enough to suggest that the typical Rorschach response of young children changes substantially from age to age and is in many ways quite different from what would be expected of the adult. Especially conspicuous is magic repetition, the fact that animal movement definitely predominates over human movement, that through the first eight years color predominates over movement, and that in the preschool years F percent tends to be higher than F+ percent.

Two examples of our hypothesis that the typical and expected Rorschach response at some ages would in the adult be considered signs of neurotic or even psychotic behavior should suffice.

3½ years: The response at this age has many of the characteristics sometimes found in schizophrenic individuals. The drive toward organization of wholes is considerably greater than the ability to perceive accurately and to coordinate past perceptions into accurate wholes. Animate and inanimate are confused, as are reality and the pictured items. Extraneous objects are introduced into the cards; descriptions are confused and garbled; objects seen appear to be independent of the usual spatial orientations.

7 years: The morbidness and suspiciousness often found at this age is sometimes associated, in adults, with paranoid behavior. At any rate the 7-year-old response tends to emphasize decay, damage, mutilation, and generally gruesome concepts. Things are torn, chopped up, bloody. There is a great deal of confusion and confabulation.

To the best of my knowledge, this general notion—that child Rorschachs quite normally are different from those of the adult and that responses that would be considered undesirable or atypical in the adult can be quite benign in the early years—is currently fairly well accepted. At the time when we first suggested it, it was not accepted and was even denigrated by many Rorschach workers. In a course at Yale taught by Seymour Sarason, a course that I was required to take in order to become a member of the Society for Projective Techniques, Sarason was totally unaccepting of the mere notion, let alone some of the details that I suggested.

Also, Dr. Milton Senn, who came to Yale in 1948 as I have described for the purpose of dismantling the Yale Clinic of Child Development and establishing his own Child Study Center, opposed our work with the Rorschach. I was briefly on his staff at the time I was starting my Rorschach research. When he heard that I was researching the Rorschach he told me that since the Rorschach as a test supposedly measures the unconscious and since I did not "believe in" the unconscious, I had no right to use this instrument. Also, he said that his associate Katie Wolf had pronounced that the Rorschach was not useful under 12 years of age. Thus I should not be studying this test as given to children under 12. I replied that that was what I was hoping to find out—Was the Rorschach indeed useful at the younger ages?

At any rate, these objections did not discourage us. Having published our findings on the first ten years of life (*Child Rorschach Responses*), we proceeded through the adolescent years (*Adolescent Rorschach Responses*). And skipping quite a few years, we also researched and published a book on *Rorschach Responses in Old Age*. This demonstrated, to our satisfaction at least, that just as the Rorschach response develops and builds up in the early years of life, so it diminishes, lessens, and deteriorates in old age in a manner almost the reverse of the way in which it developed. Since this work on old age did not project itself into my clinical work, it need not be elaborated here.

This work on the Rorschach that I and my colleagues carried out has been described in some detail because it has strongly influenced almost all of the clinical work that I have done in the past few decades. Our Rorschach research was supplemented by an investigation of the way in which responses to the Lowenfeld Mosaic

Test changed with age. Though the chief purpose of giving projective techniques is by no means to obtain an age rating, nevertheless I am more comfortable in using any such test if I am well informed about age changes to be expected.

At one time we had considered researching age changes in Burns and Kaufman's Kinetic Family Drawing Test. However, before we could accomplish this, these authors had gone so far with their own investigations that further work by us seemed superfluous. And I personally have never used the Thematic Apperception Test to any extent, even after the Children's Apperception Test was added, simply because to the best of my knowledge no year-by-year study of age changes has been carried out, and we ourselves have not been motivated to conduct such a study.

Research Again Leads to Clinical Work—School Readiness

The Gesell Institute, as long as Dr. Gesell and Dr. Ilg were still active, was indeed a very yeasty place. We did not so much decide what we would do next; rather, one project or interest or idea led to the next. It was a natural rather than a conscious evolution.

And so it was with our (what turned out to be) far-reaching work on school readiness. Our earlier research and interest had been directed primarily toward the child in the home, even though Dr. Gesell's very early work had had to do with children in school. In fact, Dr. Gesell was reputedly the first school psychologist in the United States.

However, it was not until the 1950s that a substantial number of the children whom we saw in our clinical service were children with school problems rather than home problems. In the mid-1950s, it occurred to Dr. Ilg and me that seemingly a majority of the children brought to us because they were having trouble in school— many of whom had been labeled by the school as learning disabled—were simply quite normal children who had started school before they were ready and were thus overplaced.

A check on the one hundred clinical cases seen in sequence just before this notion occurred to us revealed the possibly surprising fact that virtually every one of these children was, in our opinion, overplaced in school. (Some had problems other than this, but overplacement appeared to be a common denominator.)

We then asked ourselves, Was this rather startling amount of overplacement characteristic only of children who were in enough difficulty that their parents brought them to a clinic for help? Or, if one checked in a reasonably typical school district, would we also find that a substantial number of the children were overplaced?

Research carried out in the Hurlbutt School of Weston, Connecticut, supported by the Ford Foundation and reported in the book by Dr. Ilg and me titled *School Readiness: Behavior Tests Used at the Gesell Institute,* was set up to answer three questions: How many, if any, of the children in kindergarten, first grade, and second grade in this school were, in our opinion, overplaced? Did the unready children catch up? And to what extent did our tests, given in the fall of any year but not revealed to the teachers, predict what the teachers would say about each child's success or failure at the end of the year?

Research revealed the following answers to these three questions: In general, at each grade level about one third of the children were fully ready, about one third questionably ready, and one third definitely unready. Very few of the unreadies caught up. And, most telling, there was a high degree of agreement between our predictions of readiness and the teachers' conclusions at the end of the year.

There turned out to be an 83 percent agreement between our predictions and the teachers' findings at the end of the first year for the kindergarten class; 68 percent agreement with the first grade; 59 percent agreement with the second grade. Clearly, the younger the child the closer the agreement between predictions made on the basis of readiness testing and the teacher's judgment at the end of the school year, the time when decisions about promotion or nonpromotion had to be made.

These findings encouraged us to proceed with our major thesis—that children should ideally be entered in school on the basis of their behavior age rather than on the basis of their birthday age or their level of intelligence. Our proposal was that all schools should be run developmentally with this in mind. To make this possible we recommended that all children be given a developmental test before they were entered in school. For those not old enough behaviorally to start kindergarten (even though they were legally old enough to do so) we proposed that each school system provide a prekindergarten.

And for children who had completed a year in kindergarten but were still not ready for first grade, rather than having them repeat this year (though we are by no means as opposed to the general notion of repeating as are many), we proposed a pre–first grade or transition class. It would of course be a rather unusual child who would need three years of school before he or she was ready for first grade, but we would like to see these three levels available.

The idea was that by having this slower course available for those children who needed it, every child could be successful in school right from the time that he or she began, rather than starting in with tasks that were (as is often the case today with kindergarten curriculums being as academic as many are) way over his or her head.

To implement this rather ambitious notion, several steps had to be taken. First of all, we needed to write a book that would present our point of view, our findings, our norms, and instructions for giving and evaluating the tests. Since the children in our research school (the Hurlbutt School in Weston, Connecticut) were somewhat above average socioeconomically, we chose two local schools where, on the basis of the parents' socioeconomic status, the children could be considered to be reasonably "average."

Then came an interesting incident, with what turned out to be far-reaching implications. To gather our norms, it was necessary to train two teachers from the North Haven School System, where we were to work. When word of this training got out, half a dozen other individuals, from schools such as Albertus Magnus College in New Haven and St. Joseph's College in Hartford, asked to be included. And there were others.

And thus was born our first workshop held for the purpose of training educators and psychologists to give those of the Gesell tests that were needed to determine school readiness. Originally these workshops were two weeks in length and were given almost exclusively by Dr. Ilg. As time went on they took different forms and were given not only in more or less all states in the United States but in foreign countries as well.

The minimal offering was a one-day introductory workshop, not to train people in giving the tests but merely to introduce the concept of readiness to school districts that were interested. (I myself gave a few of the one-day presentations though I was not involved in the more comprehensive training.)

In the early years, as noted, Dr. Ilg gave most of the workshops, and in many instances they were held at the Gesell Institute in New Haven and were of two weeks' duration. During the second week the students were given hands-on experience in testing, supervised personally by Dr. Ilg. Gradually, as many of the would-be students were unable to make themselves available for a two-week period, the workshops became of one week's duration or even, sometimes, shorter than that.

Inevitably other staff members were involved in the instruction, and gradually, more by good luck than design, people we had originally trained and who were out in the field (teaching in public or private school systems or in colleges or universities) took over teaching some workshops. This was helpful since there were, at least during some periods and increasingly, more demands than our own Gesell staff could meet. At present (1992) our national lecture staff, under the leadership of Jacqueline Haines, consists of some two dozen trained psychologists or educators who represent us (on a part-time basis since all have their own professional commitments).

We also work in an advisory capacity in various school districts that request this service. The most comprehensive example of this kind of relationship was our several years long consultation in the schools of Brevard County, Florida. Here we trained enough developmental examiners that eventually they themselves, without our continued help, were able to service all the schools of Ft. Lauderdale.

Obviously, not all the individuals trained by us were able to return to their hometown schools and initiate a developmental placement program. But a surprising number were, though it was often uphill work. Today a rough estimate is that more than 15 percent of schools in this country are run developmentally. That is, children are tested for readiness before they begin school.

Our intense interest in school readiness did not, at first, have any substantial influence on my own clinical work. From the time we started the Gesell Institute I did occasionally give preschool examinations, though for the most part my clinical work consisted of giving the various projective techniques. However, by the mid-1980s and increasingly, I have focused substantially on school readiness cases, for the most part questions of readiness for kindergarten and first grade.

Perhaps largely because of our own writings, parents in this country have become much better informed than they were earlier about normal preschool behaviors. We have received many fewer referrals made on the basis that children are not eating, not sleeping, are wetting their beds, sucking their thumbs, behaving in the customarily oppositional way quite characteristic of 2½ year olds or the wild and out-of-bounds manner characteristic of 4 year olds. Probably the majority of referrals of 4 to 6 year olds from 1975 on have had to do with school readiness. (When the problems of preschoolers have had to do with seemingly serious behaviors, for the most part I have seen these children in conjunction with colleagues—usually Jacqueline Haines or Anne Miller.)

Also, from 1975 to 1985 I did, for the first time, a certain amount of infant testing. Dr. Gesell had been adamant that infant testing was best left to physicians, so that while we were at Yale I did not do much if any infant testing, though I was exposed to a great deal of it. After Dr. Sidney M. Baker came to the institute as director and head of our medical department, he expressed an interest in the testing of infants. Thus I did a small amount of this testing on some of his own patients and those of his associate, Dr. Robert McLellan. However, from 1975 to date, for the most part my examining has been largely restricted to school readiness testing.

Interestingly enough, the demand for school readiness testing currently is slightly less than it was even two or three years ago. It is, perhaps, an example of the "giving away" of psychology. Now many schools routinely give readiness tests themselves. Also, many school systems do provide either a prekindergarten class or a pre–first grade class, or both. Thus these problems of placement are often taken care of in the school system itself.

At any rate, this is an easy and very satisfactory kind of service. The parents come to us with a very specific question and for the most part we can, after giving a Gesell Preschool Examination, answer their question easily and, for all concerned, satis-factorily. Though out in the field (that is, in local schools themselves) for the most part readiness programs are well received, in many communities there is one set of parents who take great exception to the fact that their particular child is judged to be not ready for kindergarten. Some become extremely agitated—even suing the school district or taking their problems to the Phil Donahue show. (In most communities it is the parents who have the final say and even should this not be the case, our advice to schools is not to fight the parents. Better that a child be overplaced and suffer than to ruin the entire readiness program in an effort to "save" one child.)

But parents who bring their child to a clinic to find out whether or not he or she is ready to start whatever grade may be in question, usually arrive with a reasonably open mind and with confidence in the specialist and willingness to follow his or her advice. Thus the whole visit tends to be gratifying to all concerned.

Research, Writing, and Filmmaking

Since the major part of my time for the past fifty or so years has been spent not in clinical work but in research and writing, I should perhaps give these activities a special overview.

My first research was conducted almost exclusively by the method of cine-manalysis. Eleven studies were carried out through this method from 1937 to 1944. Perhaps the most significant of these was "The Ontogenetic Organization of Prone Behavior in Human Infancy" in 1940. Six further cinema studies were done in the years that immediately followed. Most of these were published in the *Journal of Genetic Psychology* or the *Genetic Psychology Monographs.*

Other research studies published in the years before 1950 (when we left Yale) covered such topics as "The Gesell Incomplete Man Test," "Variant Behavior as Revealed by the Gesell Developmental Examination," and analysis of imaginary companions in the young child.

A next small group of studies was carried out in our nursery school and focused on observations of smiling behavior, the development of the sense of time and space and the sense of self, and children's stories. And a first paper was published on the special characteristics of the 3½ year old child (not up till then considered an age with special characteristics of its own).

The next group of research papers had to do with the Rorschach test in children. There were five primary reports, published in 1959 and 1960. Rorschach research thereafter was more focused on the elderly or on the Rorschach response throughout the entire life span. These publications continued as late as 1974. A companion projective technique, the Lowenfeld Mosaic, was analyzed and discussed in three monographs published in 1964 and 1968. Research reports on children's academic behavior in school, half a dozen or more, were published from 1964 to 1966. Also, after that date there were several papers on children with learning disabilities or on the general topic of learning disability. Three studies published in 1965, 1966, and 1967 reported our findings when we compared the performance of black primary school children with that of white children from the same community.

There were, of course, many isolated research reports but those noted here were the main groupings.

By 1970 and following, my writing focused decreasingly on research reporting and more on books, book reviews, and what one might describe as "talk pieces." I began my newspaper column in 1952 and am still writing it.

Books, like research studies, tended to fall into groups or clusters, though here, too, a few individual books did not relate to others published. Most of the books were written in collaboration, chiefly with Dr. Gesell and/or Dr. Ilg.

The very first book of which I was a co-author was the first of the Gesell books written partially for parents. It was not an advice book but in parts it was suitable for parent reading. Its title was *The First Five Years of Life.* Then followed in 1943, 1946, and 1956, the so-called trilogy—*Infant and Child in the Culture of Today, The Child from Five to Ten,* and *Youth: The Years from Ten to Sixteen,* all written with Gesell and Ilg.

In 1955, Dr. Ilg and I published a collection of our newspaper columns under the title *Child Behavior.* This moved into paperback and soon became the best selling of all our books.

Then came a series of books dealing with projective techniques. These included *Child Rorschach Responses,* by me, Métraux, and Walker; and *Rorschach*

Responses in Old Age—by me, Learned, Métraux, and Walker; also, in 1962, *"Mosaic Patterns of American Children"* by me and Dr. Ilg.

Our interest in school readiness is reflected in *School Readiness* (with Ilg, 1964); *Is Your Child in the Wrong Grade?* (1966); *Stop School Failure* (with Gillespie and Streff, 1972); *Don't Push Your Preschooler* (with Chase, 1974); and *What Am I Doing in This Grade?* (1985).

Probably our most popular series of books has been one written directly for parents, describing behavior to be expected at the various ages of early childhood— *Your One Year Old, Your Two Year Old, Your Three Year Old, Your Four Year Old, Your Five Year Old, Your Six Year Old, Your Seven Year Old, Your Eight Year Old,* and *Your Nine Year Old,* written with Ilg and/or Haber. These books, published between 1976 and 1990, were inspired by Dr. Ilg's concept that just as every person is an individual, so each of the ages, too, has its own individuality. A 4 year old, for instance, is not just a bigger and better 3 year old, but in many ways a quite different sort of person.

There were also numerous individual books. Among my favorites were a high school textbook, *Child Care and Development,* an "accepted text" in several states until it was lost in the publishers' takeover shuffle of the 1980s. A book written with my granddaughter, Carol Chase Haber, *He Hit Me First,* enjoyed modest success. My latest, and favorite, is *Arnold Gesell: Themes of His Work* (1989).

Filmmaking was quite something else again. It was nothing I would have aspired to, but it came about quite naturally as a result of the studies I carried out by the method of cinemanalysis. It was Dr. Gesell's suggestion that after having analyzed our film, both the 16-mm and the 35-mm films, to find out how some certain behavior developed, it would be useful for me to put selected footage together to demonstrate behavior I had already described in print.

My very first film, published in 1938 by the Encyclopedia Brittanica, had to do with my dissertation topic, prone progression. It was called *How Behavior Grows: The Sequential Patterning of Prone Progression.* The second, *The First Five Years of Life,* was put together in 1940 and covered characteristic behavior in the fields of motor, adaptive, language, and personal-social behavior in the first five years.

The year 1941 showed quite a flurry of filmmaking, with the following titles represented: *Similarities* and (a second film) *Dissimilarities of Behavior in a Pair of Identical Twins.* I edited three more films that year: a film covering the first ten years of life of one of our research subjects, Justine Ford; a film on oral behavior patterns; and a film on visual fixation in early human infancy.

In 1942 there was a further film on vision, *Successive Localizing Visual Fixation in Early Human Infancy.* The year 1943 saw just one film, *Patterning of Leg Behavior in the Supine Infant: A Comparison of Supine and Prone Postures.*

In 1944 I edited a series of films on home behavior: *The Baby's Bath, Bottle and Cup Behavior, The Conquest of the Spoon, Self-Discovery in the Mirror,* and *Early Play.* In 1946 there were two further films: *Laterality I* and *Laterality II.* And in 1948 one more, *Reciprocal Neuromotor Interweaving.* These three marked the end of my editing of films. When we left Yale, we were not permitted to take our films with us, bringing an end to that work.

There was one notable exception, a bit of film history in which I played a minor part. In 1948 the Medical Film Institute of America decided to make a series of medical films that they would publish and make available to medical schools throughout the country. Before that time, numerous good medical films had been for the most part filmed and edited privately and were available only by loan from the authors.

The Medical Film Institute decided to fund and produce films on a major scale, making them available to medical schools that might be interested. To Dr. Gesell's delight, since he had always held that medical students and physicians must, as he put it, "know development as well as disease," this group decided to make their very first film on the development of behavior in fetus and infant. They thus chose Dr. Gesell and his work as the subject of this initial film. I was included as a member of the staff who would produce this film.

It was a long and interesting winter's work. The end result was a 28-minute, 16-mm color film entitled *Embryology of Behavior.* It was a splendid and fitting culmination of Dr. Gesell's lifetime work with the cinema. I include this film in my own story since I did have the privilege of being part of the crew that produced it, though my role was relatively minor.

I have not made films since 1950, though early in the 1980s I appeared as the spokesperson in part 1 of the film *School Readiness,* filmed at the Gesell Institute by Programs for Education of New York City and sold commercially.

My Responsibilities as Historian, Librarian, and Curator of Films

My responsibilities as a librarian began at Yale and have continued through our years at the Gesell Institute of Human Development. The Yale Clinic of Child Development had a substantial library—maybe a thousand books plus many boxes of reprints. It was my responsibility to keep this library in shape. The duties were not arduous.

When we left the university, this position nearly ended, along with the books. *We* held that the books were ours since they had been bought with clinic funds. However, Yale maintained that the books were theirs, and they kept them.

Reestablishing our library was difficult. We had no money, and it was painful to spend money we didn't have to buy books that had originally been ours. However, we stuck with it and eventually reestablished an adequate library, one that was officially registered (and recognized) among libraries in this country.

In addition to our scientific library of books and journals, we had a (much-used) parents' library, made up of popular books for parents. And we also had a good children's library. All of these were my responsibility.

I was also for some years the curator of the Yale Films of Child Development. This position was created by Dr. Gesell sometime around 1945. At the time of our leaving the university there was much discussion as to who *owned* the films. We believed that we owned them since they had been filmed and edited at our expense, with special grant money given for that purpose. Yale believed (hoped) that *they* owned them.

Finally it was agreed (by Dean Long of the Medical School and others in authority) that if we would allow them to keep the films, I could continue to be curator of the Yale Films of Child Development, with a permanent assistant professor rank and all due privileges, though no salary. We accepted this arrangement. However, at the end of the first year, Yale decided that they did not *need* a curator of the Yale Films, and my position was abolished. Fortunately, these films eventually came into the hands of Dr. John A. Popplestone, head of Child Development Film Archives at the University of Akron. And I came back into relationship with them as one of a (rather ephemeral) Board. The films at Akron were our basic file films.

Luckily, we had been able to keep a selection of our edited films. And in 1989, through a fortunate arrangement with Sara Richards of the Historical Audiovisuals Collections, History of Medicine Division of the National Library of Medicine at the National Institutes of Health in Bethesda, Maryland, these edited films have come to a happy ending. The original edited films have been made into videotapes. The films themselves are in a "safe" vault somewhere in Pennsylvania. We have copies of the videotapes, which through the National Library of Medicine are also to be made available to any responsible users because of their historic value.

As to my role as a historian, this is quite unofficial. But since both Drs. Gesell and Ilg have been long deceased and since it has always been my responsibility (beginning with the time in the 1930s when I was Dr. Gesell's research assistant) to keep files and records, this role does seem to have fallen to me. I am getting as much down on paper as possible while I am still available.

A brief history of the Gesell Institute (by me) appeared in the summer 1983 issue of *Update,* the Gesell Institute newsletter. More substantially, my book *Arnold Gesell: Themes of His Work,* mentioned previously, traces in some detail twenty-two of the major themes of Dr. Gesell's work. It also includes evaluations of his work by others; two chapters titled "Dr. Gesell and Others—Historical" and "Dr. Gesell and Others—Contemporary"; and a brief history of the institute. I am at present writing a history of the Gesell Institute in some detail. This may or may not actually ever see the light of day.

I also have turned over to Yale my file containing reprints of every article in Dr. Gesell's bibliography of well over four hundred items. My office file still contains reprints of all of my own articles (also well over four hundred items). And on my shelves are copies of all of Dr. Gesell's books as well as my own (some three dozen).

Experiences with the Media

Though in some ways, looking back, my life seems to have followed a fairly straight course—I was at Yale for seventeen years after getting my master's degree in psychology at the University of Maine and have been working at the Gesell

Institute since 1950—at least several of the paths I have taken have been more by good luck than by intent. Certainly, the last thing I had ever contemplated was to be a media psychologist.

At the time we left the university in 1950, Dr. Gesell, Dr. Ilg, and I had just begun on the research that was eventually published as *Youth: The Years from Ten to Sixteen.* This was to be the third in a triology, as mentioned earlier. The first two of these books had been very well received, both by the public and professional readers, and the third book was awaited by many with reasonable enthusiasm. The National Institute of Mental Health (NIMH) promised support for this research. They advised us to borrow money, set up the Gesell Institute, and apply for a grant to cover this work.

We followed their advice. Thus, needless to say, it was a shock and a disappointment when nine months after the institute's beginning, NIMH turned down our grant application. Our friend Margaret Mead, who was on the grant committee, reported that the meeting about our work was one of the bitterest she had ever encountered. Perhaps 45 percent of the group felt that of course they would honor their commitment and support this work. Perhaps 55 percent of the group voted against our proposal. (By that time we had many of what one might describe as enemies, especially among the Freudians. Dr. Milton Senn was reported to have commented that Mrs. Ames was the most dangerous woman in America because not only was she non-Freudian but people also believed what she said and actually thought it helped them.)

At any rate, the National Institute of Mental Health did say that we could change our proposal slightly and resubmit it. We did so. Nine months later they turned us down again.

Newspaper Column

At this point, it must have been March or April 1952, I gave a lecture in Darien, Connecticut. After the lecture, a man in the audience, Mr. Robert M. Hall, came up to me and said, "I wish I could give you some money." Of course I asked him what he had in mind. He said he was a newspaper syndicator and it had been his dream to have the Gesell Institute (or at least the Gesell people) write a column for him. But, he said, Dr. Gesell would not even give him an interview and he knew that Yale would not permit this kind of activity anyway.

I was able to tell him the news that we were no longer at Yale and that Dr. Gesell was no longer the director. Very quickly, plans were made. We agreed that we would write a daily column *if* he could sign up at least thirty major newspapers to make it worth our while. He did so, and in July 1952 we started our daily newspaper column, "Child Behavior," which soon was being published in sixty-five of the largest papers in the country, spanning the United States from Portland, Maine, to Portland, Oregon.

This column provided us not only with funds to keep the Institute going but also with an unusual opportunity to present to the public our own non-Freudian point of view. Writing the columns was not especially difficult—we had plenty of material to share with the public. Answering the mail was rather demanding. At times I sat at my desk till midnight, responding to the plaintive pleas of parents.

These letters were not entirely easy to answer since many began with the comment, "My pediatrician does not know how to handle this problem, so I am turning to you." So it was not just a matter of acknowledging the mail. It was, in many instances, a question of trying to solve people's real child behavior problems.

Fortunately, not all of the letters were hard to answer. Many of the supposed "problems" that people wrote about were merely behaviors that we considered more or less typical of certain ages, certain personalities, or just of children in general. Some only required referrals to appropriate local resources for help, and some were so routine that they could be answered by a form letter. This was particularly true of bed-wetting problems, which abounded. At any rate, we did answer all mail that came in from both newspaper column readers and viewers or listeners of television or radio programs.

It is probably true that in those more conservative days, Yale would not have allowed us to write a newspaper column. Certainly, had Dr. Gesell still been the director he would not have approved. It was only some years later, after (or so it seemed to us) we had tested the waters, that perfectly "respectable" professional people, including Dr. Spock, began writing in magazines for the general public and/ or appearing on television.

As long as the Hall Syndicate continued under the able leadership of Robert Hall, our column was very secure. However, sometime in the early seventies Robert Hall sold his syndicate to another that unfortunately had its own child behavior writer. A dozen or so of our papers stayed with us, but we lost the majority. Aside from the financial benefits to the institute of having a column, I considered it a privilege to have daily newspaper space available to me for propounding our basic (Gesell) biological point of view. And so we continued with the column, even though the number of papers that carry it has definitely diminished.

Television

At any rate, the column was well received, especially in its first twenty years. One of our most enthusiastic papers was the *Boston Globe*. Though with most papers, the syndicate's and my dealings were with promotion personnel, in the case of the *Globe* I was dealing directly with John I. Taylor, grandson of the founder. He invited me to give a series of lectures in towns around Boston, as a "gift" from the paper. He accompanied me to these lectures. They were successful and as a result, he developed the notion that it might be a good idea for me to undertake a television series.

Television was very new in those days and, of course, just in black and white, and there was no taping. Nearly all shows, as far as I remember, were live. At any rate, Mr. Taylor took me over to WBZ in Boston, where we conferred with John Stilli and others of the management. John Taylor said he thought it would be a good idea for me to have a weekly television program on child behavior. They asked if I had had any experience. He said no, but I could do it all right. They asked what kind of program we envisioned. I responded that since I felt I could go to Boston only once a week, I would not be available for rehearsals and therefore it would have to be a live, unrehearsed show.

They said this was a rather difficult kind of program to do, but John Taylor said I could do it all right. So a week or two later (spring 1953) I gave the first of what were to be thirteen weekly television programs. The format was that WBZ used their Studio A, a small theater. Anyone wishing to be part of the audience met at the *Boston Globe* and was brought out to the studio on a bus. The program consisted of the audience asking me questions and my answering these questions. The MC was a very capable veteran television man, Arthur Amidon.

This trial thirteen-week series was successful enough that it was continued for two years, with a weekly radio show also taped just following the program. (One viewer, who apparently came to television late, once told me, "I used to hate you on radio but then when I saw you on television I realized that your voice went with your face").

After some months of having the program produced in Studio A, we moved to a smaller studio with only four guests for each program. These guests could be mothers, fathers, people from the Scouts, mayors—in fact almost any set of four who volunteered. Arthur Amidon was still the announcer. In this format (which was still a half hour in length) I answered one or two questions from each guest. Then Arthur read three or four selected letters from viewers, which I answered. And then I went back to the studio guests. I was always touched by the fact that these people seemed to feel that if they were fortunate enough to get to ask their questions, their problems would actually be solved. To most of them the program seemed to be no mere exercise in entertainment.

WBZ liked the program because it got good ratings in the New England area, and also because it "did them good" with the FCC, being a program of presumably useful content. At the end of two years, the studio told me that they could not afford the entire program anymore, but for another year I was a guest on a variety program called "Swan Boat." (The performers were introduced to the audience sitting in a boat that resembled the famous swan boats of the Boston Public Garden.)

This project at WBZ was successful, fun to do, and very remunerative. Since that early beginning in Boston in the 1950s, I have done a good deal of radio and television. Among the more rewarding series was one of twenty-six taped programs, taped at WEWS in Cleveland, Ohio, at the instigation of Donald L. Perris, at that time assistant manager of the station. These programs were taped in Cleveland over a series of weekends and then distributed to stations around the country.

My next extended and serious television undertaking was a series of daily half-hour programs, taped again at WBZ in Boston and titled "Playmates/Schoolmates." It was a nursery school on the air. It was initiated by George Moynihan, the original producer of my 1953 Boston series, who by then was a vice-president of Westinghouse Broadcasting Company. The format was that of an actual nursery school. The children played for twenty minutes, with their parents watching the play on a monitor in another part of the studio. In the last ten minutes of the program I appeared on the set with the parents, who asked questions either about what they had just seen or about anything that interested them about their children.

The message of this program was primarily that children do not need to be "taught" or instructed in nursery school, along with our usual message that behavior changes from age to age in a patterned, and to some extent predictable, way. We did a series on each age level from 2 years through 4 years. These programs were aired on all the Westinghouse stations: Boston, Philadelphia, Baltimore, Pittsburgh, and San Francisco.

Through all these years from the early 1960s to date, I have also very frequently appeared as a guest on such popular talk programs as Mike Douglas, Phil Donahue, Oprah Winfrey, Sally Jessy Raphael, AM Chicago, Kennedy and Company, the New York morning talk shows, and many others. I have always found being on television to be a lively, interesting activity and a wonderful way to give our developmental message about children to many people who might not otherwise come in contact with it.

Lecturing

Though this does not exactly come under the heading of "Media," I should mention that I have probably spent as much time in public lecturing, not only in this country and Canada but as far away as Bangkok, Thailand, as I have in clinical work, though less than in research. Through the years 1950 to 1988 I lectured probably once a week, often more than that, to both professional and lay groups. This is a story in itself and I will not elaborate here.

The Louise Bates Ames Parenting Center, 1988–90

My own parenting center has turned out to be an ambitious but, unless someone comes to its rescue, rather short-lived venture, due to substantial changes in the staff and structure of the Gesell Institute that took place in late 1989 and early 1990. This center, for which we had ambitious hopes, started with a series of lectures to parents given by me and other members of the staff. The initial series had to do with parenting the preschooler, helping the child feel more secure in school, and parenting the teenager. These lectures were reasonably well subscribed and seemingly much appreciated by the mothers and fathers who attended. The series was repeated in the spring and fall of 1991.

Administrative Work

One further aspect of what may sound like a rather fractured professional life has been a modest bit of administrative work. When we first left Yale University and started the Gesell Institute, all three founders—Drs. Frances L. Ilg, Janet Learned, and I—did everything. Dr. Ilg was for twenty years or so director and I was associate director. When she retired, Dr. Richard J. Apell and I became co-directors. This continued till 1977, when I was appointed acting executive director until a new director could be found. He *was* found, in the person of Dr. Sidney M. Baker, who took over as director in September 1978. I returned to being associate director, but my administrative responsibilities from then on have been minimal.

People Who Have Influenced Me

Obviously, I have been influenced in the course of a lifetime by a great many people. I'll mention just a few who were outstanding.

To begin with, I have been and still am very much influenced by my father, whom I admired vastly. I still try to do things in a way he would like. I try to work hard, not waste time, not say foolish things, and certainly not put in salt when I am cooking green peas, as it makes them tough.

Next was my University of Maine professor Dr. Charles A. Dickinson, formerly head of the Department of Psychology. It was because of him that I reversed my decision, made after taking one course from Dr. Elizabeth Amen at Wheaton College, *never* to take another course in psychology. He taught me what it was all about and made it seem interesting enough that I chose it as a life's work. Equally important, he encouraged me to study at Yale with Dr. Arnold Gesell, whose work he admired.

Unquestionably the greatest influence in my professional life was Dr. Arnold Gesell. It was indeed a privilege to have worked with him. My first appointment during my graduate school years was as his personal research assistant. I moved on from that to further job titles, but from 1933 when I first went to Yale till 1950 when we left the university, I worked very closely on a daily basis with Arnold Gesell.

He was not the kindest or easiest man to work for. On one occasion, when leaving with Mrs. Gesell for a Florida vacation, he instructed the staff that "there is to be no informality at the clinic while I am gone." "Informality" meant being outside one's office during working hours. He had no patience with mistakes or forgetfulness. Once, having forgotten something, I commented rather brashly that I didn't have a card-catalogue mind. He replied, "You should have, Mrs. Ames."

Some of the staff used to grumble about Dr. Gesell's authoritarian manner. My position was that this same individual who was much of the time so stern with staff was also the one who by his very character could, even without intent, offer us so many advantages. The opportunities were boundless, the working and learning conditions matchless. Almost every day in Dr. Gesell's clinic provided a learning experience. He permitted staff great freedom as to tasks they would work on and ways to approach these tasks. I don't remember his ever saying that an idea was worthless or couldn't be followed up. And he was very quick to incorporate what we thought were our best ideas into the body of the clinic's work.

More than that, because of his prestige we were in touch with scholars not only throughout the country but also throughout the world. It was my responsibility to meet with and "entertain" the many visitors who came to the clinic. In the year 1946–47 we had 1,060 visitors; in 1947–48, we had 1,049. In that latter year people came from, among other countries, South Africa, South America, China, India, Canada, Hawaii, the Phillipines, Austria, Belgium, Czechoslovakia, Denmark, France, Holland, Italy, Poland, Norway, and Sweden. (Our books had been translated into twenty or more languages.)

It was very rewarding throughout these years at the Clinic of Child Development to be in touch with what was going on in the field of child behavior all over the world, and to share our own findings with other scientists and students. (And of course it was rewarding to have the opportunity of arriving at these findings.)

At any rate, Dr. Gesell was an incredibly brilliant leader who offered staff an unparalleled opportunity for working and learning. Although in the years after Yale we went on into fields that he, having grown older, questioned—our studies of adolescent behavior, constitutional psychology, projective techniques—the basic principles that he taught us still ring very true. I cannot think of any of his basic principles that have not, for me at least, stood the test of time.

Next in time, not in order of importance, is Dr. Frances L. Ilg, a cofounder and first director of the Gesell Institute. I met her in 1934 when we were still at the Yale Clinic of Child Development. Dr. Ilg was easily the most creative person I have ever known. She had more new ideas per day than many people have in a lifetime. Not *all* of her ideas seemed sensible to me; but she had enough that it was quite practical to discard the ones that did not seem reasonable.

Following up on Dr. Gesell's basic thesis that human behavior develops in a patterned, largely predictable way, that environmental factors support, inflect, and modify but do not generate the progressions of development, and that each and every human being is a special individual, different from all others—even from his or her identical twin—Dr. Ilg introduced a further basic notion. This was that just as each person has a special individuality, so does each age.

She introduced the idea, fitting in with our concept of reciprocal interweaving, that ages of equilibrium tend to alternate with ages of disequilibirum, ages of internalized behavior with ages of externalized behavior. This idea was a basis for information provided in our trilogy that covered the years from birth through 16 and for my own series of books on the individual ages, largely co-authored by Dr. Ilg.

Omitting the dozens and dozens of useful ideas on which we based numerous research papers as well as our own clinical service, I should mention also Dr. Ilg's basic notion about education, which carried out—even though she was not aware of this fact—Dr. Gesell's own concept introduced in the early part of this century. This was that children should be entered in school and subsequently promoted on the basis of their behavior age, not their age in years or their intellectual level. The instrument by which developmental or behavior age could be determined was, predictably, the Gesell Developmental Examination.

Based on this notion of Dr. Ilg's, we recommended that all schools be run developmentally. This means that before any child starts kindergarten, he or she is examined to determine whether behavior is up to a 5 year old level, which would mean that the child should be able to accomplish the work of kindergarten. If the behavior level is below 5 years, we would recommend a prekindergarten year to precede kindergarten. Similarly, before the child enters first grade we recommend further evaluation, and if the child had not completed kindergarten successfully or if the behavior age is below 6 years, then the child should spend an extra year in a transition class between kindergarten and first grade.

This whole concept, and a description of the tests to be used and how to use them, had been expounded in numerous texts co-authored by Dr. Ilg and me (and in some instances by others). *School Readiness,* published in 1964 and revised in 1978, is the basic original text to describe this whole notion. At this writing more than 15 percent of schools in the United States are said to be run developmentally.

Dr. Ilg also had a major influence on my career in that when we left Yale University, she, together with Janet Learned and me, founded the Gesell Institute of Child Development. Without her strong support we could never have done it.

Another individual who influenced me, not so much by her thinking as by her basic lifestyle, was Margaret Mead. Working as an anthropologist, her interpretation of the role of the environment—that is, society—in determining human behavior was quite the antithesis of my own. But I very much admired her total dedication to her work, her boundless energy, her many accomplishments, and her very clear thinking. In the several instances where we had the privilege of working with her, I admired her vastly.

One further individual of the many who have influenced my thinking was Dr. William H. Sheldon, who helped us start our work on somatotyping. Though Dr. Richard N. Walker of our own staff was the person at the institute who carried out virtually all of our research on body type, or constitutional psychology, I was very much influenced in my thinking about human beings and human behavior by Dr. Sheldon and his work on constitution and behavior. Though consitutional psychology is somewhat out of fashion at the moment, I have found it extremely useful in my own clinical work to think of each child in terms of his or her body type. Dr. Sheldon influenced me not only in what he had to say about constitution and behavior, but also in his general approach to human behavior. The most casual conversation with this remarkable man was always highly instructive.

Dr. Gesell himself was highly influenced by the work of Charles Darwin. I myself have been most influenced not by historic figures but by those living, some of whom—Drs. Gesell and Ilg, Sheldon, Margaret Mead, Margaret Lowenfeld, for example—have now become historic figures.

The Future of Clinical Psychology

I personally am highly concerned about the future of clinical psychology. I think of testing as the main tool of the clinician. Unfortunately, society is at the moment turning vigorously if not viciously against testing. This appears to be on several counts.

To begin with, environmentalists (perhaps not going quite back to Watson, who insisted that you could make any child into anything if only you did the right thing) seem to be moving in that direction. Take education, for instance. The Gesell point of view is that children should be started in school and subsequently promoted on the basis of their behavior age rather than their age in years. We hold that not all 5 year olds are behaving like 5, and thus some though legally old enough to enter kindergarten may not be adequately mature.

We support the notion that once children are correctly placed, we should provide individualized teaching and a developmentally appropriate curriculum. The National Association for the Education of Young Children, under the leadership of David Elkind, Sue Bredenkamp, and Lillian Katz, strongly opposes developmental evaluation. They appear to hold that all 5 year olds should be entered in kindergarten—that it does not matter whether they are mature or immature. They seem to hold that individualized teaching and developmentally appropriate curriculums will take care of everything.

What I view as a misinterpretation of civil rights concepts adds to this environmental approach. Misinterpreting the dictum that all individuals are equal in the eyes of the law, many now seem to hold that all children are equal—or would be if only they had the right environment. Such individuals (as I see it) oppose any sort of testing, since testing might show that some are different from others. Intelligence tests have long been denigrated by many. Other tests are now under fire.

Projective techniques such as the Rorschach have long been opposed by experimental psychologists, who argue long and loud that they are neither reliable nor valid.

One further objection to testing is now being offered by at least some graduate schools in their courses for school psychologists. This is suggested at a practical level but offers a real obstacle to students in training who are interested in learning how to test. This objection, as I interpret it, is that under Public Law 94-142, every school system, once it diagnoses a child as having a certain difficulty—a difficulty that can be labeled—is legally responsible for curing or at least doing something about that difficulty. Testing tends to end up with a label being given. Thus the field of school psychology appears to be turning against testing.

Since in my opinion testing is as important a tool for the clinician if he or she is to understand behavior as medical tests are for the physician if he or she wants to understand a patient's illness, I can only hope that this trend, which is currently taking on all the earmarks of a political movement, will soon be tempered.

Conclusion

I have always found clinical work extremely exciting, stimulating, and satisfactory. I am primarily a researcher and I have enjoyed doing research. But it is *rather* a long, drawn-out process. First we decide what questions we will investigate. Then we gather the data. Then we analyze these data. Then we write them up. Then we send them to an appropriate journal. Then we write our paper over according to the journal's wishes. Then the paper is in press for many months. Finally, often years after its inception, the whole thing sees the light of day.

Clinical work requires much less patience. The results and rewards are much more immediate. I still, after forty years or so, find it very exciting to be faced with a clinical case. One knows at the outset the nature of the parents' complaint about the child. But as in a detective story, this offers only clues. The solution comes, we hope, at the end of the clinical session when we see what our tests, supported by our own insights, come to. Taken together they could lead anywhere.

It is very gratifying to come to our conclusions, to find our solutions, to share them with parents, and to see the extreme acceptance, relief, and even gratitude with which most parents greet what we have to tell them. Even after many years in the field, each case is a rewarding adventure to me.

References

Ames, L. B. (1938). *How behavior grows: The sequential patterning of prone progression.* Film. New York: Encyclopedia Britannica Films.

Ames, L. B. (1940). *The first five years of life.* Film. New York: Encyclopedia Britannica Films.

Ames, L. B. (1941a). *Similarities of behavior in a pair of identical infant twins.* Film. New York: Encyclopedia Britannica Films.

Ames, L. B. (1941b). *Dissimilarities of behavior in a pair of identical infant twins.* Film. New York: Encyclopedia Britannica Films.

Ames, L. B. (1942). *Successive localizing visual fixation in early human infancy.* Film. New Haven: Distributed privately.

Ames, L. B. (1943). *Patterning of leg behavior in the supine infant: A comparison of supine and prone postures.* Film. New Haven: Distributed privately.

Ames, L. B. (1944). Series of films on home behavior: *The baby's bath, Bottle and cup behavior, The conquest of the spoon, Self-discovery in the mirror, Early play.* New Haven: Distributed privately.

Ames, L. B. (1946). *Laterality I* and *Laterality II.* Films. New Haven: Distributed privately.

Ames, L. B. (1948). *Reciprocal neuromotor interweaving.* Film. New Haven: Distributed privately.

Ames, L. B. (1966). *Is your child in the wrong grade?* New York: Harper & Row.

Ames, L. B. (1974). *Child care and development.* Philadelphia: Lippincott.

Ames, L. B. (Commentator for part 1). (1984). *School readiness.* Film. New York: Programs for Education.

Ames, L. B. (1985). *What am I doing in this grade?* New York: Programs for Education.

Ames, L. B. (1989). *Arnold Gesell: Themes of his work.* New York: Human Sciences Press/ Plenum Press.

Ames, L. B., & Chase, J. (1974). *Don't push your preschooler.* New York: Harper & Row.

Ames, L. B., Gillespie, C., & Streff, J. (1972). *Stop school failure.* New York: Harper & Row.

Ames, L. B., & Haber, C. C. (1982). *He hit me first.* New York: Dembner.

Ames, L. B., & Ilg, F. L. (1943). Variant behavior as revealed by the Gesell Developmental Examination. *Journal of Genetic Psychology, 63,* 273–305.

Ames, L. B., & Ilg, F. L. (1955). *Child behavior.* New York: Harper & Row.

Ames, L. B., & Ilg, F. L. (1962). *Parents ask.* New York: Harper & Row.

Ames, L. B., & Ilg, F. L. (1962). *Mosaic patterns of American children.* New York: Hoeber.

Ames, L. B., & Ilg, F. L. (1964). *School readiness: Behavior tests used at the Gesell Institute.* New York: Harper & Row.

Ames, L. B. (with Ilg, F. L. and/or Haber, C. C.). (1976–90). A series: *Your One, Two, Three, Four, Five, Six, Seven, Eight,* and *Nine Year Old.* New York: Delacorte.

Ames, L. B., & Learned, J. (1946). Imaginary companions and related phenomena. *Journal of Genetic Psychology, 69,* 147–167.

Ames, L. B., Learned, J., Métraux, R. W., & Walker, R. N. (1952). *Child Rorschach responses.* New York: Hoeber.

Ames, L. B., Learned, J., Métraux, R. W., & Walker, R. N. (1954). *Rorschach responses in old age.* New York: Hoeber.

Ames, L. B., Métraux, R. W., & Walker, R. N. (1959). *Adolescent Rorschach responses.* New York: Hoeber.

Gesell, A., & Amatruda, C. S. (1941). *Developmental diagnosis.* New York: Hoeber.

Gesell, A., & Ames, L. B. (1952). *Embryology of behavior.* Film. Produced by the Medical Film Institute. Distributed by the International Film Bureau of Chicago.

Gesell, A., Amatruda, C. S., & Ames, L. B., et al. (1940). *The first five years of life.* New York: Harper & Row.

Gesell, A., Ilg, F. L., & Ames, L. B. (1956). *Youth: The years from ten to sixteen.* New York: Harper & Row.

Gesell, A., Ilg, F. L., Ames, L. B., & Bullis, G. (1946). *The child from five to ten.* New York: Harper & Row.

Gesell, A., Ilg, F. L., Learned, J., & Ames, L. B. (1940). *Infant and child in the culture of today.* New York: Harper & Row.

Kendler, H. H. (1989). The Iowa tradition. *American Psychologist, 44,* 1124–1132.

Raymond B. Cattell

Professor of Psychology
University of Hawaii at Manoa

◆

Planning Basic Clinical Research

My first contact with clinical psychology came when I took a position at the newly formed London Child Guidance Clinic in 1927. As a researcher in the fascinating Spearman Laboratory my interests were in the newly developing factor analysis, and I turned to clinical psychology to satisfy a wider conviction that psychology was the answer to the political and social evils then rampant after World War I. In fact my adoption of a career in psychology, after qualifying with a first class B.S. in chemistry, was based on the belief that the rules of thumb by which we conducted social and political affairs needed to be swept away by a radically new set of premises. (It was the heyday of Shaw and Wells, which disturbed conventional thinking in the students of the day.) My friends in chemistry and physics nevertheless thought me crazy for forsaking a good career for the hazy realms of psychology.

I fit immediately into Spearman's laboratory, my school training in the essence of scientific method causing me to appreciate Spearman's profoundly scientific attitude in the otherwise all-too-speculative field of psychology. Though a little aloof in manner he was a man easy to get on with, and he gave me the green light for any progressive suggestions I ultimately made.

I persisted not only in psychology, earning a Ph.D. with Spearman, but also in clinical psychology. For I felt that it was there, and not in the cognitive domains of Wundt, that the provocative questions would be met and the important aspects of human behavior seen. Personality theory, except for Freud and perhaps Jung, was then in chaos, enlarged by the overconfident generalizations of countless exponents. It did not take me long to realize that, as in all sciences, psychology had to begin with a foundation of accurate description and measurement, and that new discoveries by systematic research had to supplant dependence on simple observation and "old wives' tales." This conclusion forced me to set aside most of the talk current among psychologists and start out with an immaculate, independent approach to develop measurement in the personality realm. Some good order had already been set up in the ability area by Spearman, Burt, and later Thurstone; but in personality there was only a succession of paranoid enthusiasms for immediate explanations—as in Kretschmer, Sheldon, the "authoritarian personality," extraversion, Spranger's types (popularized by Allport and Vernon), Herrington's "social type," Osterald's semantic versus classical-expressive versus restrained, and so on indefinitely. These were either pulled out of thin air or supported as correlation clusters but not as factors. I reviewed them all in my 1946 book, *The Description and Measurement of Personality.*

The prospects for a young psychologist in Britain were at that time extremely poor. There were six professorships in the country, occupied for the foreseeable future. By good luck, however, in 1932 the city of Leicester in the Midlands set up a city Child Guidance Clinic, and I was deemed the best psychologist to head it up. An attractive feature was a clear division between the school's medical director and the psychologist. The former was an intelligent medical-psychiatric man who nevertheless expressed no difficulty in leaving all the clinical psychological work and decisions to me. I also had good contacts with the young psychiatrist at the city mental hospital.

This division was found in no other center. Elsewhere the psychologist, usually a woman M.A., was definitely subordinate to the psychiatrist and restricted largely to giving Binet tests. The new service was well received by the city and by teachers (for whom I gave introductory lectures), and I had an assistant psychologist and two good social workers. An innovation was a "hospital school" to which maladjusted children were transferred, staffed by psychologist teachers with whom I had weekly case conferences.

I fell quickly into a mainly Freudian treatment, though a few more superficial cases were handled by Adlerian principles. I became convinced (aided by a teaching analysis with Jennings White in London) of the truth of the basic propositions of the unconscious, child sexuality, repression, and transfer, while at the same time I persevered with developing tests—notably the Projection Test (1936), which preceded Murray's TAT and had an objective scoring design. I used Spearman's excellent little intelligence test, factor validated, instead of the scrambled Binet. The results of my first five years' experience I published in two books, *A Guide to Mental Testing* (1936) and *Crooked Personalities in Childhood and After: An Introduction to Clinical Psychology* (1938a).

Thus I made amends for my absence from a university post. However, my daily contact with a steady stream of "backward child" referrals, who turned out to be largely below an IQ of 80 (in an efficient school system) awoke my interest in a social problem. It had long been known that intelligence was largely hereditary and that the birthrate was higher in families with lower social status. But no one dared reach the conclusion that the latter were in general of lower intelligence and that the consequence must be a declining intelligence level nationally. At that time I had the good fortune to meet, in the Eugenics Society, Major Leonard Darwin, the son of Charles Darwin, who offered to finance a direct study of intelligence and fertility. Though he offered only £250 a year, I undertook to drop my practice for a couple of years to work on it. Aided by my recent construction of Culture Fair Intelligence Tests, I succeeded in testing every 10 year old in the city schools and a balanced sample from the public schools in Oundle and Winchester. The results were startling—a mean family size of 4.21 and 3.72 at IQ 70 and 90 and of 2.31 and 1.80 at 150 and 170. I extrapolated to a downward change in scores in one generation of about 1.0 mean IQ point in my book *The Fight for Our National Intelligence* (1937a). It had good forewords by Darwin, the education officer of Leicester, and the king's physician, Lord Horder.

To my surprise (since like most young men then I was leftist in politics) this book brought down on my head the bludgeoning of a host of leftist politicians and journalists. But I did not worry because the facts spoke for themselves. (Maybe it was my choice of foreword writers that brought down the cry of "old school tie.") I further wrote a more speculative article for the *British Journal of Psychology* entitled "Some Changes in Social Life in a Community with a Falling Intelligence Quotient" (1938b). Most of the predicted changes—declining school performance, increased delinquency—are now at length beginning to show themselves. I have been astonished that for fifty years no social psychologist or sociologist has thought this issue to be of paramount importance in research.

No sooner was this task accomplished than I received a totally unexpected letter from E. L. Thorndike inviting me to be a research associate to him at Teacher's College. Attached though I was to England and Devonshire (my *Under Sail through Red Devon* had just appeared), I decided that an effective career in psychology was more important, and in 1937 I sailed for the United States. Although I found Thorndike all I had hoped for, I found America (at least New York) depressing. It was the heyday of Carnegie's *How to Win Friends and Influence People* (1936), a dastardly misuse of friendship. (One didn't *win* friends. You drifted into lifelong congeniality with them.) I was also disturbed by the too-frank pursuit of the Almighty Dollar. But culture shock eventually gave way to appreciation of the virtues of working-class minds with middle-class incomes.

Psychology departments in Britain were still trying to get out from under the blanket of philosophy. This was evident, for example, in the constant fight for independence Stephenson had to make against the philosophers at Oxford. It showed too in the obeisances a student's essay had normally to make to Stout, Brentano, Locke, Hume, Mill, and, of course, Aquinas, Plato, and Aristotle. The long and painful emergence of psychology as a separate science is described in scholarly terms in Spearman's *Psychology Down the Ages* (1937). The battle, ending with the emergence of Watson, was shorter in America; it did not have to contend with the revered stonework of Oxford and Cambridge.

From Thorndike I went to a professorship—later to be the G. Stanley Hall chair—at Clark University. It was now clear to me that I wanted to devote my life to clinical research rather than clinical practice. Psychology's need in this area was immense, for most practitioners were depending on nothing but intuitive claims for this or that fashionable doctrine—as in Rogers, Skinner, "interaction," and the remains of Freudian, Jungian, and Adlerian doctrines.

I started therefore systematically on my primary "diktat": that one must build a comprehensive understanding of human trait structure. Actually, disturbance at Clark and the world disturbance of Hitler's aggressive acts from 1936–40 forced me to postpone well-planned action until I entered the Harvard department three years later. At Clark, Hunter and Murchison were at loggerheads, communicating with each other only through their secretaries. Meanwhile, the question arose when war was declared by Britain whether I should return to England. Fortunately, authorities gave me a direct no on the latter, but I was called down to Duke University to instruct inductees into the medical program.

Thence I passed into the Adjutant General's Office, where I found the country's chief psychometrists at work on officer selection and the like. It was the most satisfying and stimulating position I had known: to be able to discuss at lunch with Richardson, Rundquist, and other leaders the most advanced questions in psychometry. The basic work on factoring the personality sphere of ratings I had completed at Harvard, recognizing twelve to sixteen factors, some of them known clinical factors like extraversion, ego strength, superego strength, and so on. Now I conceived the idea of doing the same on a wide spread of *objective* personality measures. By objective I did not mean objectively scored (conspective) tests like questionnaires, but objective in the sense that the subject simply behaved in response to a defined stimulus. The management at the AGO saw at once the value of this, for all the AGO's work was based on "fakable" questionnaires (except the ability measures). In three months of solitary invention I produced some three hundred "miniature situations." After the usual bureaucratic delays the battery was administered, prior to factor analysis, to a large sample of recruits in a camp in Georgia. But by then it was the end of the war, and the disturbances upset the experimental dependability of the data. I nevertheless tried to get the data back in order to work the factor analysis myself, but the law said it was government property and as the AGO group was disbanded, the data vanished beyond recall.

From my state of mourning I was recalled to the postwar world by a letter from Herbert Woodrow of the University of Illinois, offering me a research professorship in psychology. It was exactly the kind of position I needed. I spent little time debating the alternative of return to Harvard, versus the Midwest. The former had always struck me as excessively socially competitive. Memories of the lowly position of creative men like Lashley and Murray, compared to the socially competitive, came back to me. I found the University of Illinois, sustained by its farmers, more peacefully democratic and conducive to untrammeled work. The subsequent slow decay of the "top" Harvard and Yale psychology departments supports my observations.

At Illinois I was given the financial support of two research associates, two secretaries, and—as an unexpected bonus—the opportunity of the newly (1947) constructed Illiac computer. I got to work on the definition of personality factors—in ratings, questionnaires and objective tests—without delay. Soon I was aided by graduate students like Saunders, Horn, Gorsuch, Scheier. And to my surprise I had visitors from abroad who stayed a year or two: Pawlik, Tsujioka, Warburton, Radcliffe, Sealy, Schneewind, Schmidt, the Beloffs, Child, and Hundleby. Some from this country—for example, Digman, Sokal, Sweney, Blewett, and Baggaley— came as well to spend a sabbatical year and get into the swing of the new factorial advances.

For the next twenty years my life was that of a humming dynamo—smooth but powerful. I was generally the last out of the parking lot at midnight. There is a story that I arrived at the laboratory one day to find, to my amazement, not a soul there. I phoned and was told, "We are just sitting down to Thanksgiving dinner." All days were the same to me—except that they yielded new findings and new problems. Naturally, constantly using the instrument—multiple factor analysis—we made continued advances in bringing out the neglected powers of factor analysis—a test for number of factors, an automatic oblique rotation program, confactor rotation, the Procrustes program for evaluating the fit of a given solution to a hypothetical solution, and so on. In this I was helped by discussion with the group of top workers in this field—Tucker, Kaiser, Tatsuoka, Cronbach, and Humphreys—that Woodrow had accumulated at Illinois.

One does not enjoy the creative zest of a situation like this without a sound domestic life. And I found the perfectly adaptive wife in Alberta Schuettler, a Harvard graduate student in mathematics, who looked after (while I neglected) our four children. She came of a German family and had the traditional belief in a woman's role of "Kinder, Kirche, Kuche" except that she was a rationalist as to the second. I suppose this makes me a "male chauvinist," but at least I was unconscious of it, and four children now in professions—a surgeon, an artificial intelligence specialist, and two psychologists—are pragmatic proof of how well this traditional arrangement worked. And we enjoyed our children without meeting any of the "problems of adolescence"—except one daughter who chose to march in protest demonstrations on worthwhile issues.

Although most of our findings and theories were published (in more than four hundred articles and forty books), they created no general stir in psychology. I was looked upon as bypassing the "mainstream" in some curious production of trait names and calculations beyond the average psychologist's readiness to follow and learn. I thought that when after twenty years' hard work, I produced an *objective* battery (now known as the O-A battery) of personality factors I should be like the inventor of the better mousetrap to whose door all would make their way. The publications with Warburton (1967), with Hundleby and Pawlik (1965), with Sweney, Horn, and Radcliffe (1963), and others passed with no comment (except Cartwright's witty review, "Up, Up and O-A"). Even to this day the gift to clinical and general psychometry is little used. Clinicians continue to fool with very low validity tests like the Rorschach, the TAT, and other enthusiasms of their graduate days, with little regard for the new evidence.

Until about 1960 I and my colleagues had been so absorbed with finding and measuring the real factor traits in personality that we had done little to integrate the findings in a broader perspective. But I now paused to set out the connections of first-order and second-order traits with the principal states, in the book *Personality and Mood by Questionnaire* (ultimately published in 1973). We had been puzzled for some time by the lack of alignment of the questionnaire's sixteen factors with the objective test factors in the O-A. They should have been merely different clothing for the same essential structures. Suddenly, a couple of joint variable researches showed us the answer in that second-order factors in the questionnaires (anxiety, extraversion) were first-order factors in the O-A. It was apparently a difference in the "closeness of texture" in the variables that had led to our mystification.

Meanwhile, by using R-technique (factoring of differences between persons on single occasions) and P-technique (longitudinal factoring of the single individual) we had located the chief human psychological states or mood factors. It was interesting to find that extraversion (an undoubted trait to Jung) was also a state. Horn was able to show that intelligence—as fluid intelligence, g_f, and crystallized intelligence, g_c— also varied, in the same patterns, slightly from day to day. Izard and others (Spielberger) had made up scales for states ignoring our findings on their number and nature. But this happened all the time around us, with scales for entirely imaginary traits—for example, in the California scales and the MMPI—enjoying popularity. That we were not integrated into the "mainstream" of popular concepts was not our fault. We simply went on discovering and verifying the structures that really exist, and leaving other experimenters to use the scales and batteries we constructed for discovering further relations.

We nevertheless indicated the "grand plan" of research that was becoming necessary for 1960–80. First we had to ask how much heredity and how much environment entered into each trait, before we started theorizing about its nature. In 1963 I published a first article on the MAVA methods due to supplant twin study in human genetics. In this we took as many family constellations as possible (about seven) and wrote out the combination of the two variances producing the experimentally seen variance. For example, for siblings reared apart in different families it was:

$$\sigma_{sa}^2 = \sigma_{wh}^2 + \sigma_{we}^2 + 2r_{whwe}\sigma_{wh}\sigma_{we} + \sigma_{bh}^2 + \sigma_{be}^2 + 2r_{bhbe}\sigma_{bh}\sigma_{be}$$

where *wh, we, bh, be* indicate abstract variances respectively from within-family hereditary differences, within-family environmental variances, between-family (means of children) hereditary variance, and so on. With six unknowns (including the two *r*'s) on the right, and six constellations for which one could measure concrete variances on the left, a solution for the abstract variances on the right was possible by handling six simultaneous equations. R. G. Fisher OK'd the design, but Loehlin (1965) suggested a slight improvement. With this and about two thousand subjects we were able to get nature-nurture ratios for the sixteen primary personality factors and intelligence. In the last-named, the difference of g_f and g_c (0.8 and 0.4) explained the debates among users of mixed $(g_f g_c)$ tests so long plaguing the field.

After fixing the genetics (1977) the next systematic need was to plot the typical life course for each factor (as had long been done for intelligence). This strained our resources, but eventually we were able to show highly characteristic plots for each. For example, surgency, F, climbs to late adolescence and then declines for the rest of life, whereas ego strength, C, follows much the same shape as intelligence, but climbs slowly later, through the whole life span.

These findings, and countless others coming in on occupational and syndrome profiles and prediction equations, permitted fuller theorizing about the nature of primary and secondary (second-order) traits. This has reached readable form in my wife's book, *Psychology in Depth: The 16PF* (1988).

All along I was aware that we were omitting the exploration of purely *motivational* traits. I was detained from investigating them by warnings that factor analysis would not possibly be flexible enough to capture the protean human interest and motivation field structure, the fact that we were too busy to release the high-level researchers that this area required, and the obvious unfitness of a questionnaire validly to estimate motive strengths of variables. However, in 1960 with Sweney and Radcliffe we began by asking which of the fairly numerous devices in the literature used as measures of motivation strength were really valid. We took, then and later, over a hundred into consideration, ranging from GSR and reaction time, to Freudian defense mechanisms such as projection and autism, to memory effects and perceptual distortions.

Our first finding, disturbing to many, was that a single motivation strength does not exist. In every attitude we examined there were seven primary components, which we simply labeled α β γ δ and so on. The only sense we could make of them—though we had begun with no psychoanalytic theories—was that they represented a component from the id (α), from the ego (β), from the superego (γ), and, among others, a purely physiological response component. Fortunately, when the dismaying array of primaries was factored it yielded two interpretable secondaries, which we labeled U (unintegrated) and I (integrated) sources, the former loading projection and autism and the latter, word association and information (on the course of action defined by the attitude). Applying next these objective devices to a wide array of common personal interests, we obtained eight factors that were clearly basic drives and several others that had the very different character of acquired sentiments—for example, to home, to religion, to career. We called these, respectively, *ergs* and *sems.*

Further research showing that ergs change their strength according to stimulation and that all attitudes eventually subsidiated to ergic goals, supported the view that we had found a way to discover the human ergs. Our results differed from those of Freud, Adler, Murray, and others who listed goals subjectively. However, we did verify Freud's view of two forms of sex drive—ordinary heterosexual drive and narcistic sex (autoerotic) behavior. We also showed in married couples a relation of measured sex erg level to copulative times.

Following up the subsidiation chains, which crisscrossed, we arrived at the concept of the *dynamic lattice* (Allport kidded me by asking about "the dynamic lettuce"), the complete exploration of which (by P-technique) gave the dynamic structure of an individual's interests and complexes. To provide nonfactorists with an instrument for research we constructed a ten-factor test—the Motivational Analysis Test (MAT), covering the five ergs most commonly involved in clinical problems and the five sems that were largest (home, career, self-sentiment, super-ego, and sweetheart-wife).

The use of the MAT to get life associations, and work on the profiles of the chief clinical (DSM) syndromes is presently only about twenty years old (Cattell & Child, 1963). But the associations confirm that we have a powerful objective instrument for clinical use. Research can now go in several new directions—conflict analysis, situational effects, genetic differences, prediction of achievement and occupational fitness, prospects in psychotherapy, and so on—not previously systematically explorable. Indeed, I feel that this breakthrough in the dynamic area of personality is the most important finding for the future of clinical psychology. Together with the measurement of personality traits, of states, and of ergs, it completes the round of structured research that we began long ago.

Between what we have accomplished and what psychologists in the "mainstream" think that we have accomplished there is, however, a very large gap. Some seem to know only of the 16PF. And the advent of push-button computer programs has resulted in a weedy growth of other instruments with diverse structures based on various misunderstandings of what sophisticated factor analysis can do. There are, for example, examinations of the factor structure, of the 16PF, of the MMPI, Guilford's questionnaire, Eysenck's trinity, and many other constructions—for example, arbitrary scales of "activity level," locus of control, authoritarianism, sensation seeking, and so on. To be sure, the intention to relate these specialties to basic, real personality dimensions is worthwhile. But the more common alternative of spending much time on using their imaginary scale concepts as themselves important personality dimensions is a sheer waste and distraction.

The extent of appreciation of my work extends from those who know me only as the author of the 16PF to those who understand the whole scheme of structural checkings in ratings, questionnaires, and objective tests. To those who see the importance of the dynamic developments, the long developments of factor analytic methods, the nature of psychological states, the clinical associations, the spectrad model of attribution theory, the formulation of structured learning theory, the MAVA contributions to personality genetics, the invention of the taxonome program for finding types, the numerous specification equations and profiles for use in everyday life in the clinic, and so on, there is an enormous gap in perception.

Every innovator (Freud is a good example) feels his work is unappreciated. Certainly I feel that I do not belong in what is vaguely called "the mainstream of psychology." My track through the voluble "theory" of the thirties to a program of systematic description and measurement left me with few followers. I am inclined finally to put down this neglect to the use of a method, factor analysis, that is too complex for the average psychologist to follow. When challenged, the resistance of many had shown itself in such charges as "factors are mere mathematical abstractions." So they may be in many misuses of the method. Yet it remains true that factor analysis and its child "functional equations" remain the only methods we have to penetrate the underlying causes in a wild jungle of variables, such as few other sciences have had to face.

The concluding point I must now make is that at last, after arduous lonely years of building up knowledge, we are in a position to integrate a system. I have put forward this system in my two-volume work *Personality and Learning Theory* (1979) and in two smaller books, *Human Motivation and the Dynamic Calculus* (1985) and *Psychotherapy by Structured Learning Theory* (1987) (a first full account of the latter).

These present a final integration of my own theories. It begins with the model of the behavioral equation, which insists all behavioral response is a result of the total personality and the total situation, thus:

$$A_{hijk} = b_{hjkl}T_{li} + b_{hjk2}T_{2i} + b_{hjks}S_{ski}$$

where h is the stimulus, j the kind of response, k the ambient situation, T_1, T_2 and so on trait scores of individual i, and S_{ski} the state level of the individual i in situation k. There would of course be several more T's and S's involved in actual work.

From this I terminate with a systems theory in which the usual parts of a system cooperate in an ever-changing series of responses. This system is still to be filled out by quantitative research. It must now be recognized therefore that from the detailed work of the early description and measurement I have reached the point where a complete theory of personality—peculiar in the path I have taken—can be presented. The system is consistent in its early phases with our confirmation of the main psychoanalytic concepts. But it has moved from words to figures. It is, in fact, the inevitable development of the psychometric beginning. Although very few clinicians indeed are presently availing themselves of the synthesis possible, this is not because psychology as a science has not yet availed itself of mathematics but because psychologists have avoided mathematical training.

To describe my unifying theory I will note that its roots are in Freud. It accpets the psychoanalytic concepts of ego (C factor), superego (G factor), and narcism (as I now spell it) in the MAT, of the unconscious as revealed in the U component in MAT measures, of conflict and repression (as shown by negative loadings in the behavioral equation), and of ego defense mechanisms and transferences. All of these concepts are now verified factorially by repeated researches, except that the reality of defense mechanisms has had to rest on a single research. Studying them in misperceptions and misbeliefs, Cattell and Wenig (1952) located four defense mechanisms as showing individual differences in quantity: projection, autism, rationalization, and fantasy. What is more, these were shown to correlate with known personality factors: projection .27 with L factor (protension), rationalization .45 with superego (G); autism .33 with dominance (E); and sex erg .53 with fantasy. These associations make sense, but the whole area would doubtless reveal more defense mechanisms and more associations if followed up in more than a single research.

My theory begins by recognizing and refining to specific measurements the main concepts of Freud (up to 1915). But it then proceeds far beyond, into a list of traits A, B, E, F, H, I, L, M, N, Q_1, Q_2, Q_3, Q_4, which we know modify the action of C, G, and narcism. We also recognize the importance in individual behavior of state liabilities, and the truth of modulation theory. The differences in genetic determination of traits also modify clinical practice. Our understanding of the structure and growth of the ego is also systematized (Cattell, 1987). We realize that the *b* weights (behavioral indices) in factor analysis are actually the sum of two values—a situational index, *s,* saying how much the state (or trait) is modified in its own strength, and a potency index in *b*'s, saying how much this state or trait operates on the dependent variable, a_{hjks}. Finally, the VIDA systems model explains the internal interactions and cognitive resources that determine the final response.

The theory still has gaps, and filling them is a matter of whether psychologists are ready, by training, to attack the complex questions involved. But I have no doubts about the firmness of theory so far built up by the pursuit of measurement of structures and processes. It was a long path, but the only correct one.

References

Carnegie, D. (1936). *How to win friends and influence people.* New York: Simon & Schuster.

Cattell, H. B. (1988). *Psychology in depth: The 16PF.* Champaign, IL: IPAT.

Cattell, R. B. (1936) *A guide to mental testing.* London: London University Press. (2nd ed., 1948; 3rd ed., 1950)

Cattell, R. B. (1937a). *The fight for our national intelligence.* London: King.

Cattell, R. B. (1937b). *Under sail through red Devon.* London: Maclehose.

Cattell, R. B. (1938a). *Crooked personalities in childhood and after: An introduction to clinical psychology.* London: Century.

Cattell, R. B. (1938b). Some changes in social life in a community with a falling intelligence quotient. *British Journal of Psychology, 28,* 430–450.

Cattell, R. B. (1946). *The description and measurement of personality.* New York: Harcourt, Brace & World. (Republished by Johnson Reprint Corp., New York, 1969)

Cattell, R. B. (1973). *Personality and mood by questionnaire.* San Francisco: Jossey-Bass.

Cattell, R. B. (1979). *Personality and learning theory* (2 vols.). New York, Springer.

Cattell, R. B. (1982). *The inheritance of personality and ability: Research methods and findings.* New York: Academic Press.

Cattell, R. B. (1985). *Human motivation and the dynamic calculus.* New York: Praeger.

Cattell, R. B. (1987). *Psychotherapy by structured learning theory.* New York: Springer.

Cattell, R. B., & Child, D. (1963). *Motivation and dynamic structure.* New York: Halstead Press.

Cattell, R. B., Horn, J. G., & Sweney, A. B. (1964). *The Motivation Analysis Test.* Champaign, IL: IPAT.

Cattell, R. B., Hundleby, J. D., & Pawlik, K. (1965). *Personality factors in objective test devices.* San Diego: Knapp.

Cattell, R. B., & Stice, G. (1970). The dimensions of groups and their relations to the behavior of members. Champaign, IL: Institute for Personality and Ability Testing.

Cattell, R. B., Sweney, A. B., Horn, J. G., & Radcliffe, J. (1963). The nature and measurement of components of motivation. *Genetic Psychology Monographs, 68,* 49–211.

Cattell, R. B., & Warburton, F. W. (1967). *Objective personality and motivation tests: A theoretical introduction and practical compendium.* Champaign, IL: University of Illinois Press.

Cattell, R. B., & Wenig, P. (1952). Dynamic and cognitive factors controlling misperception. *Journal of Abnormal and Social Psychology, 47,* 797–809.

Eysenck, H. J. (1973). *The inequality of man.* London: Temple Smith.

Fisher, F. G. (1930). *The Genetical Theory of Natural Selection.* Oxford: Clarendon.

Freud, S. (1934). *New introductory lectures on psychoanalysis.* London: Hogarth Press.

Hundleby, J. D. (1968). Objective performances and indices of emotional disturbance in middle childhood [Special issue]. *Multivariate Behavioral Research.*

Loehlin, J. (1965). Some methodological problems in Cattell's multiple abstract variance analysis. *Psychological Review, 72,* 156–161.

Nesselroade, J., & Cattell, R. B. (1988). *Handbook of multivariate experimental psychology.* New York: Plenum.

Spearman, C. (1937). *Psychology down the ages.* Edinburgh: Clark.

W. Grant Dahlstrom, Ph.D.

Kenan Professor of Psychology
University of North Carolina at Chapel Hill

◆

Psychology from My Point of View

Origins

Two factors contributed to a pattern of major disruptions in my early education: changes in my father's work resulting from the economic depression of the 1930s, and a chronic infection in my eyes that reduced my vision and often kept me from regular class attendance. My visual difficulties dated from before the age of 3 and were severe enough at times to render me totally blind. Persistent problems in seeing clearly enough to do well in various laboratory sciences finally diverted me from my early determination to pursue a career in internal medicine. Medical psychology as structured by Starke Hathaway at the University of Minnesota was an easy second choice.

I was born in Minneapolis, Minnesota, on November 1, 1922, into a family of mostly Scandinavian origin. My father's ancestors were Swedish (but some originated in Scotland, hence my middle name); my mother's family were all Norwegian immigrants. I was the second of three children. My brother Arthur was a little over five years older and my sister Dorothy three years younger. My parents met while he was a medical student in Milwaukee. My mother had received some business school training after high school but she met and married my father before she had taken any position in business.

Although my mother's family was deeply religious (she regularly attended Bible school in Norwegian, German, and English-language churches each Sunday), I do not believe my father had any formal religious training. Like his father he was a Mason and interested in Rosicrucianism. Except for brief prayers before meals and bedtime, religion played a very small part in our family life. As a teenager, I did attend a summer Bible school at a Presbyterian church long enough to learn the names of the books in both testaments, the Beatitudes, and a few other New Testament features.

After completing his medical training at Marquette University, my father had practiced medicine in a small Minnesota town for a few years before joining a group practice at the Sievertson Clinic in Minneapolis. My mother never worked outside the home; she never even learned to drive a car. By the time I was nearly 3 we had moved out of an apartment and into a middle-class neighborhood in south Minneapolis. It is difficult now to realize how far out on the edge of town this development actually was: cows grazed in pastures less than a block from our house; a large barn on a hillside held hay harvested from meadows behind the houses across the street; all deliveries to our home were made by horse-drawn wagons (ice, coal, milk, bakery goods).

In our family, life was peaceful, congenial, and comfortable. My father usually arrived home around five o'clock (although he would occasionally make house calls after supper). The neighborhood was full of children about our same ages and there were plenty of playmates and group games. My mother was always waiting for us children to come in for supper at six.

Two of Minneapolis's large lakes, Nokomis and Hiawatha, as well as the Minnehaha Creek and the Minnehaha Falls, were nearby. Swimming in the summer and ice skating in the winter were easily at hand. My brother and I made many models of World War I airplanes and we, along with several of the other boys on our block, "flew" them in cross-country racing games that we had invented. One summer our neighborhood was in the newspaper headlines when a pilot from nearby Wold-Chamberlin Air Field crash-landed his biplane into the roof of a house across the street from our house. Somehow my father persuaded the owner of the plane to leave the fuselage of this wreck in our backyard. Until it was completely demolished, all of the neighbor kids spent long hours in it with us re-enacting aerial combat. Then it was replaced with the body of my father's old Oldsmobile when he bought his first Elcar (an early predecessor of the Auburn and the Cord automobiles produced by a small firm in Elkhart, Indiana). Our games then changed to cops and robbers or rum runners and Treasury agents like those in the serials we watched on Saturday afternoons at the East Lake movie theater.

Cyrus Northrup Grade School was a little over a block away and I attended school there through the sixth grade. The teachers were amazingly patient with me through my prolonged periods of absence from class. They would frequently stop at our home after school and bring make-up materials for my mother to review with me. In class, they provided me with a movable desk to shift about among the fixed rows so that I could see the assignments on the blackboards or work where the light was better. Somehow I was able to keep up with my class and was regularly promoted.

I learned to read early and spent time when I could see well enough with the Doctor Doolittle or Oz books that filled the shelves in the bookcases on the landing of the stairs to our second floor. I tried reading various volumes of the "Five-Foot Shelf" of the Harvard Classics but they were less interesting than browsing the *Compton's Encyclopedia* or the ten volumes of the Living Library of Classics with *Grimm's Fairy Tales, Pilgrim's Progress, The Water Babies,* and scores of other stories and puzzles. My father had a complete set of the writings of Elbert Hubbard but I could never get very far with these essays, although I thought the leather-bound volumes were the most elegant ones in the bookcases. Later I discovered the wonders of my medical textbooks.

One summer when infection had swollen both of my eyes shut for several months, my cousin Arlene read aloud ten or twelve books in the Horatio Alger series from those same shelves. It took me some time to realize that each one of his books was basically the same story. This was during one of my cousin's many stays in our home. In the early 1930s, we often had relatives living with us for extended periods of time while out of work or needing a refuge to get started on some new job. The practice of medicine was more resistant to economic shifts than most kinds of employment and our home was open to our relatives who were more vulnerable.

By 1935, however, extreme hard times had hit the Twin Cities and my father's group medical practice collapsed. In an effort to keep us going financially, my father tried to establish a business of producing a prescription medication for hypertension of his own devising in a "factory" he set up in our basement. The whole family (and any relatives visiting at the time) had assigned tasks: he mixed the batches, mother filled the small glass vials, my brother sealed the ends of the vials in a Bunsen burner, the rest of us were busy folding boxes, cutting cotton strips to cushion the vials, applying labels after the vials had cooled, and filling and sealing the boxes. It was an enjoyable enterprise but overly optimistic; sales were good but collections were no better than had been true of the group practice. It all ended in gloom and pessimism when some laundry coming down a chute from the second floor dislodged the chimney duct, caught fire, and started a conflagration that could have been fatal to us all. (I was the first to wake up that night at 3:00 AM, disturbed by a dream in which my father's cigarette smoke was choking me as I sat listening to him read to me!) Although we all escaped without injury, the costs of repairs to the house proved to be the final financial blow; we lost our home and moved into a small rental place.

My father tried another avenue. He learned of an available medical practice in Springfield, Missouri, and traveled south to try his hand at general medical practice again. The rest of us stayed on in Minneapolis, hoping that he would soon be able to send for us to join him there. Collections there proved to be no better and he came back broke and discouraged. Only a timely call from the Bureau of Indian Affairs about an opening for a reservation doctor to serve in a remote part of northeastern Montana saved us from further hardships.

My father went to this assignment first. We joined him after he had arranged for housing in the government compound on the edge of town. The families of ten or twelve other officials in the Indian Service lived in adjacent houses; three of them were Indian families and we soon became acquainted with our new set of neighbors. Although it was turning spring back in Minneapolis, it was still harsh winter on the plains. The mile and a half walk to school was a new hardship that united us in the common misery of 50-degree-below-zero temperatures and 40-mile-an-hour winds. We quickly made friends with the kids around us and we all welcomed the appearance of milder weather, with ball games on the open ground in the center of the compound, even tennis in the battered court next to the ballfield.

My seventh, eighth, and ninth grades were spent there in Poplar, Montana, on the Fort Peck Indian Reservation. The town schools and the school previously run by the Indian Service had been integrated (with considerable turmoil) just before we came, but by the time that we arrived, classes were both integrated and segregated. That is, white and Indian students sat in the same classrooms but the Indians, by preference, almost always occupied the back rows, as far from the teacher as possible. Little participation from them was elicited, even by the most skillful instructors. A few did participate, however, and did well; they were the ones who eventually left the reservation and attended college. The more usual pattern was for the boys, particularly, to progress slowly through the grades, arriving in high school at about the age of collegiate athletes. The presence of these older Indian students on our high school football and basketball teams made us likely finalists, year after year, in the state tournaments. Rules of eligibility were only loosely enforced.

In the depths of the Depression, college teaching positions were scarce. Even in this remote spot on the prairie we had teachers with master's or doctoral degrees. Four years of Latin were available and courses in psychology and sociology were senior offerings. It was a real bonus to us students, and a compensation for the other deprivations, that the quality of our school programs benefited greatly from the hard economic times.

As the only physician on the reservation, my father was kept extremely busy, carrying out surgery, attending wards in the small hospital, and making wide-ranging house calls over the miles of dim tracks on the prairie. I would occasionally go with him on these calls, amazed at the diversity of the medical problems he encountered and at the array of medications he carried in his car. Diagnosis was frequently hindered by his limited knowledge of their Dakota Siouxan or Assiniboin languages. However, he must have been quite effective in these interactions because at the end of his stay on the Fort Peck Reservation he was given an Indian name and inducted into the Sioux tribe.

In 1938, my father had formulated a proposal to the Bureau of Indian Affairs for a nationwide tuberculosis control program. When it was finally given official approval after a direct meeting with President Franklin Roosevelt in Rapid City, South Dakota, we moved to Philadelphia so that he could carry out preparatory training and research at the Phipps Institute (the medical equivalent of the psychiatric center of the same name in Baltimore). There he studied the complex interaction of the racial background of the subjects being screened and interpretation of the results of the tuberculin test, a screening device for exposure to tuberculosis. Research was also under way on a potential vaccine against tuberculosis. He let me visit the institute from time to time and meet some of the international visitors who were conducting research there. Particularly intriguing were views of the vaults containing bacteria for Hansen's disease (leprosy), which were structurally allied to the bacteria causing tuberculosis.

After a month or so spent in a "business college" taking high school level courses while my father argued with the Philadelphia school officials against my being placed in a school for the blind, I entered Boys Central High School. The following two years of my education were completed there in an institution with more than 3,000 students drawn from south Philadelphia. (The school enrollment was three times the size of the whole community of Poplar, Montana.) From small-town intimacy, to classes with adult dropouts hoping to complete their schooling, to anonymity within a multicultural, multiracial student body in a first-rate urban high school, the learning I acquired was much more than academic. Occasional fights broke out there involving knives or razors and police appeared frequently, patrolling the hallways. Some faculty members seemed to enjoy tormenting some of their students who were more limited academically, standing them in front of the class and exploring the depths of their ignorance of biology or physics. These victims were often black students; however, other blacks were among the students on the Barnwell Honor Roll. Again, it was the diversity that was impressive to me.

Generally, however, the faculty members were considerate and extremely well educated. All of the instructors were male and most of them held doctoral degrees. (We always addressed them as "Fess" for professor.) I finally learned that there were plans to turn this institution into a city college. Recruiting of the necessary faculty was well under way and the state legislature had already granted Boys Central a charter to confer bachelor's degrees. To keep this charter from lapsing, each year selected students (those who completed the program while on the Barnwell Honor Roll) received both a high school diploma and a B.A. or B.S. degree. My grades were good and I earned the Barnwell pins each term so I looked forward to an early degree. However, I missed that opportunity; we left Philadelphia before my senior year. My mother, who had been ill for some time, died that spring near the end of my father's stay at Phipps.

My last year of high school was spent back in Minneapolis where my father established headquarters for his ambitious program of screening, treatment, and prevention of tuberculosis (at that time the major cause of death on all Indian reservations in the United States). My sister and I enrolled in University High School on the main campus of the University of Minnesota. Once again the classes were about the size of those in Poplar, but the teachers were often graduate students in various academic disciplines on campus who needed some financial support while completing their dissertations. The students were typically children of university faculty members. The talented young instructors usually made these courses highly innovative; the in-class discussions proved to be lively and the material was uniformly challenging.

Psychology graduate students on campus found a ready source of subjects at University High on whom to practice their administration techniques for a variety of psychological tests. We took intelligence batteries and interest inventories. During that year, my sister and I were also among the classes tested by Hathaway in his first efforts to administer the MMPI to teenagers. At graduation in June 1940, I was surprised to find that my fourth-year Latin instructor had nominated me for membership in Eta Sigma Phi, the national classical language honorary fraternity.

College

With my vision restricted to only one eye (and not very good in that one, which had been rather badly distorted by corneal scarring from the unremitting chronic infection), I decided that medicine was out as a career. I determined, instead, to try a prelaw program. I was admitted to both Harvard and UCLA, but without scholarship support from either place, I had to choose California where I could room with an aunt and uncle in nearby Westwood. Academically, the year there was a good one and I made Phi Eta Sigma, the national freshman honorary fraternity. Socially, it was disappointing—everyone interesting lived twenty or thirty miles from campus and commuted to UCLA by bus or car.

During this freshman year I took my first course in psychology. The lectures, class demonstrations, and supplementary readings were effective in offsetting the deadly impact of the primary text, Knight Dunlap's *Elements of Psychology* (1936). (He had recently moved to UCLA from Johns Hopkins University and was apparently successful in getting his book accepted as the basic text in the beginning course.) The outside readings (Crafts and Schneirla's *Recent Experiments in Psychology* in Dashiell's McGraw-Hill Series, 1939) were particularly intriguing in showing what psychologists were doing in the laboratory and the field. Also, we all fulfilled several hours of research credit by participating in experiments conducted by graduate students for their dissertations. These sessions, too, helped us to gain a more modern perspective, in sharp contrast to the dull Wundtian introspective activities and reaction-time studies summarized in Dunlap's text.

On weekends and after classes I often took long hikes through the foothills or spent time at the beach in Santa Monica. My health improved in general and my eye infection stabilized. Once again I was tempted to try medicine rather than law. At the end of the year at UCLA I returned to Minneapolis, and just before the start of World War II, I transferred to the University of Minnesota. After completing most of the premedical program and with wartime acceleration under way, I was actually enrolled in the Medical School before I once again faced reality. It came in the form of a course offered by the Zoology Department on histology and organology. There were too many things I was supposed to see on the slides under the microscope that I was not seeing. It seemed clear that I would make a poor medical practitioner.

The study of psychology, however, did not seem to involve the same degree of visual acuity, at least the behaviorally oriented kind of psychology being taught at Minnesota. I decided to take more psychology courses instead of physics or philosophy, alternatives that were equally tempting in shifting from the premed sequence to an academic major. Before I could do so, however, I had to go through the battery of tests that all psychology majors were required to complete at the

Testing and Counseling Bureau. In addition to further aptitude tests, there were the Strong and Kuder interest tests and the MMPI. The results were reviewed by a counselor in Eddy Hall and by my advisor, Richard Elliott, the chairman of the Psychology Department. I made it.

As part of the premed sequence I had already had courses in abnormal psychology with Charles Bird and physiological psychology with Starke Hathaway (plus a small seminar with him the following quarter). Courses in genetic psychology and animal psychology with William Heron, the psychology of sensation with Miles Tinker, and a senior research project on the effects of insulin comas on recent learning in rats directed by Heron completed my major. I was able to enroll in graduate courses in clinical psychology with Howard Hunt and in human behavior with my advisor, Elliott, while still a senior, giving me some advanced standing when Hathaway admitted me into the medical psychology program. In addition to Phi Beta Kappa, I was admitted to Psi Chi, which the Department of Psychology used as an undergraduate honorary society and a graduate colloquium organization. I took a special oral examination as a candidate for higher honors but failed to achieve magna cum laude.

I always made some contribution to add to the financial support I received from my father. One summer I sold a cleaning service for the Holland Furnace Company. That experience convinced me I was not cut out for sales. Another summer I worked for a short-order restaurant, the Toddle House chain (owned, I believe, by the Greyhound Bus Company), starting as the night dishwasher. I learned to prepare the various items on their limited menu and was night cook and finally night manager before I resigned to go back to the university. Again, this kind of direct service to the public, although less stressful than inspecting furnaces and selling cleaning work, was not the sort of career that I felt suited me either.

After my senior year, the experience I had had in running rats and administering insulin to induce comas or seizures in them qualified me for a summer job in the laboratory of Ernst Gellhorn, professor of neurophysiology. He was conducting similar experiments on rats with both electroconvulsive and insulin shock. A German refugee, Professor Gellhorn ran his studies with an exacting protocol and demanding routines. At the same time each week I was scheduled to meet with him to go over the records of each animal in detail and plan the following week's work. At the end of the training, all of the rats had their heads shaved but only half were given electroconvulsive shock; the others were injected with insulin (the electric shock group got neutral saline solution). Later, I read with interest his hypothalamic-sympathetic theory of emotional balance and the etiology of schizophrenia, based in part on the findings from that summer's investigations.

Graduate School

As I began graduate studies, I was pleased to find that I had gained a position in the Psychology Department as chief teaching assistant. I wanted no more involvement with temperamental rats and chancy insulin dosages! Academic activities of this sort were much more satisfying. For the rest of my graduate training I earned my sole support as a part-time instructor in the introductory laboratory course to accompany the general psychology course, in demonstrations of occupational and vocational tests and procedures, in an evening course on general psychology, and finally in a general psychology course for nursing students.

I also took on a very unusual assignment for John Darley, who was then serving as the dean of the College of Science, Literature, and the Arts. He had formed a committee to try to resolve growing complaints that several different departments on campus were offering essentially the same general course in abnormal psychology. That is, sociology, criminology, anthropology, and psychology all appeared to be giving course offerings in the area of behavioral pathology. The charge to the committee was to assess the extent of this duplication (and the extent to which students were receiving credit hours for completing the same course again and again!). Hathaway was named to this committee and he proposed a novel approach: construct a basic inventory of the core concepts in this field and use it to assess the degree of familiarity with each of these terms as the students entered and left each of the courses under scrutiny. He convinced the committee that this approach was feasible and they cast about for someone to prepare such a listing.

My assignment was to comb the various textbooks available for these courses and abstract a set of core concepts or ideas covering the field of human psychological disorders. All my spare moments were devoted to the compilation of these items, a very enjoyable and enlightening task. Stacks of three-by-five cards grew and filled my desk (very much like the account I read later of James Murray in his efforts to collect citations for the *Oxford English Dictionary*). I conferred frequently with Hathaway and Dean Darley. Just as I completed my task, however, the committee's charge was resolved by more traditional campus politics (additional sections of abnormal psychology were added by the Department of Psychology, and the sociology and anthropology departments withdrew their pathology-oriented offerings). My compilation never saw the research applications that we had anticipated. However, it was a fine resource for me later when I began teaching abnormal psychology myself.

In those days graduate work at Minnesota for those with an undergraduate major from there was primarily composed of a series of seminars. A few courses were required: experimental psychology (Tinker), two years of the history of psychology (Tinker), and the psychology of individual differences (Donald Paterson). The faculty ran a two-year basic seminar; each member covered special topics over successive one-month intervals. Each student had to pick a topic for special research and presentation to the seminar; mine was the history and development of the intelligence test. I also had courses with Paul Meehl on personality and with Richard Elliott on advanced biographical psychology.

For the latter course I carried out an analysis of the content of the letters exchanged between Abélard and Héloïse in Paris early in the twelfth century using a method of co-occurrence of themes proposed by Alfred Baldwin for the psychological analysis of personal documents. I located a volume in the rare book room of the university library that contained the correspondence in original Latin. I worked to translate several different passages from both correspondents to assess the literalness of the available English-language versions. The documents I had seemed acceptable, so I proceeded to tabulate several recurring themes in their letters. The crucial incident upon which these tabulations hinged was the difference in thematic configurations before and after Abélard was castrated by agents of Héloïse's uncle Fulbert, canon of Paris. At the time I was unaware of the controversy concerning this set of letters and the possibility that Abélard had written both the letters attributed to him as well as those of Héloïse. However, in retrospect, the results of the Baldwin method of analysis seemed to support the validity of both sets of letters in this exchange. They seem to have been written by two quite different individuals. Also, Abélard was distinctly more didactic in his religious instructions to her in his letters following the attack!

Several of us graduate students had an opportunity to sit in on a series of lectures on sexual behavior and pathology that Hathaway presented each year to senior medical students. These talks were very wide-ranging in coverage and pioneering in content. Few medical schools offered such material to their graduates. His familiarity with these topics was impressive. This same expertise led to his frequent consultation with the police departments of both Minneapolis and St. Paul on various sex crimes that had proved baffling to them. Many hours in the MMPI office in Millard Hall were devoted to his filling the graduate students in on the issues under consideration in these investigations.

I also had two seminars with Hathaway, one on clinical psychology and the other on psychotherapy. During the course of the latter seminar we tabulated and plotted in detail various quantitative indices of change in the transcripts of Carl Rogers's full recording of the nondirective therapy of a single female client. Toward the end of this project Hathaway brought to class a request that he had received from his old friend George Kelly. Kelly described the circumstances of a woman he was treating and asked Hathaway to have each of the students in the seminar write a letter (theoretically to this woman) outlining our best advice to her on how to solve her problems. We all agreed to draft such letters, with the proviso that we would each read our own letter aloud to the other seminar members before they were assembled and sent to Kelly at Ohio State. It was not until considerably later when I found out about Kelly's fixed-role therapy and his style of prescribing alternative scenarios to his therapy clients that I understood what he was planning to do with these letters.

Statistical coursework was not then offered by the Department of Psychology; students had to shop around for training in this area. I took courses on mathematical statistics and matrix algebra in the Mathematics Department, on biometrics in the Medical School with Alan Treloar (famous for his extensive records on menstrual cycles obtained from women in various cultures), on factor analysis with Merrill Roff in Child Welfare, and on multivariate analysis with Palmer Johnson in Educational Psychology.

The first year I was in the graduate program the war was still on and the number of students enrolled was relatively small. Hunt and Meehl were completing their dissertations, Mary Jeffrey, Elaine Wesley, and Marcella Vig were carrying out research for their master's theses; most of the other students were in either experimental or organizational psychology. However, at the end of the war everything seemed to explode. Funding from the Veterans Administration and the Public Health Service enabled Hathaway to expand enrollments and offer generous fellowships. William Schofield returned with advanced standing in the program. George Welsh (with a master's degree from the University of Pennsylvania and extensive experience in the Army working with Italian prisoners of war in Utah) was named acting chief of the psychological service in the VA Hospital at Fort Snelling while he worked on his doctorate. Even more impressive, Harrison Gough entered the program with several publications on the MMPI to his name and with data for several more! Suddenly, the seminars were larger and even livelier, research discussions ranged widely, and the ratio of men to women assumed more balance.

My first research involvement was a particularly enjoyable collaboration with Hathaway, Meehl, and Edward Borden from the counseling program. The four of us met one evening a week for a couple of months preparing data obtained from a unit of the Army Specialized Training Program (ASTP) then in residence on campus. The students were all undergoing training for assignments as interpreters to deal with prisoners of war during combat or to work with civilians during periods of occupation by our armed forces. They lived together in dormitories, took classes and meals together, and soon got to know each other well. They all agreed to take the MMPI and participate in a matching task for us. Brief personality summaries were to be prepared on each individual solely from his MMPI profile. Then each student was to name the eight individuals in his unit that he believed he knew best. Each person would be provided with the eight personality synopses he had designated and asked to try to match description to name.

My task was to draft a personality synopsis for each of the several hundred profiles. Hathaway and Meehl then went over each of my tentative interpretations and we worked out a consensus version. They were then typed up, given code numbers, and assembled into sets for the ASTP students to read and try to match with the names of their eight nominees; that is, they had to identify the individuals solely from their MMPI interpretations. Borden and Meehl carried out the data tallies and analyses.

The brief personality sketches proved to be quite easily recognizable; the accuracy of their matching was far beyond a chance level. Information captured within the MMPI profile, even from effective, well-functioning individuals whose scores were rarely elevated more than two standard deviations above the general mean, could be translated into identifiable synopses of the person's characteristics. There were other related research questions: Are some profile patterns more readily identifiable by this method? What are the MMPI characteristics of accurate judges (matching all eight names) as contrasted with those who did more poorly than chance? What sorts of MMPI features characterized those individuals who were included in many of the sets of nominations as opposed to those who were not nominated in any set?

This general line of research was very promising, but this particular study was never published. Hathaway and Meehl found encouragement in these data to study the ratings of relatively normal individuals by close acquaintances using adjective checklists. Many of their findings in such investigations added to the early interpretive lore of the scales and patterns of the MMPI. George Welsh and I added their findings to the appropriate sections of the *MMPI Handbook* when we were developing that manuscript in the late 1950s.

During my internship year on the psychiatry service in the University Hospitals, Meehl and I began a long series of efforts to develop objective rules for classifying MMPI profiles. As case after case was presented at the clinical rounds, a routine had developed of drawing the patient's MMPI profile on the grid that Hathaway had had painted on the blackboard. The psychiatric resident, the psychiatric social worker, members of the nursing staff, and the psychology trainees would each in turn present their separate but overlapping findings about the individual under discussion. Those of us in the audience would listen, all the while staring at the pattern of scores in the profile, trying to match clinical observations to aspects of the test configuration. It helped us immensely to build in our heads an interpretive framework of extra-test correlates of the MMPI profiles, particularly diagnostic impressions, but also a wide array of sociocultural background and psychodynamic implications as well. However, these impressions were difficult to systematize and hard to convey to persons beginning their work with the MMPI.

Meehl and I decided to begin such a systematization by developing an explicit set of rules by which various test patterns could be identified as reflecting either a neurotic or a psychotic state. A few simple summary characterizations had already been circulated among staff and students so we began with them using sizable samples of records from the files in the MMPI office. These had to be checked for the reliability of the nosological assignment by obtaining blind judgments of the case summaries. Then we started in with a long series of graphic plots, carried out by research assistants in Hathaway's office. As the first approximation to the rules emerged, we would try them out on the patterns posted at each case conference. We would then await the clinical consensus to emerge on the patient under discussion, hoping to obtain a good match. As the rules grew in complexity, Meehl and I would be spending nearly the whole period of the presentation calculating the necessary profile values and working through the decision points. I had long since left Minnesota and was in my fourth postgraduation position by the time this series of studies was completed and Meehl and I were ready to publish (Meehl & Dahlstrom, 1960). The use of such explicit and detailed rules to assign MMPI patterns to categories contrasts markedly with the scheme devised by Hathaway, and extended by George Welsh, to form such groupings on the basis of a summary code of the clinical profile. The latter method has proven to be far and away the preferred approach to the summarization of individual MMPI patterning data.

Hathaway ran an evening seminar on Thursdays in his home. Its membership was always heterogeneous, including advanced students from several programs and applied psychologists from the Twin Cities area. As a deliberate shift away from a focus on psychopathology, Hathaway decided to devote the seminar time one year to an evaluation of the suitability of our traditional assessment methods to the characterization of normal men and women. It began well: we heard presentations on the use of the MMPI to assess creative talents among the engineers at the Minnesota Mining & Manufacturing and Minneapolis-Honeywell companies. I presented data I had obtained by giving several tests to my aunt (the MMPI, TAT, Rorschach, Wechsler-Bellevue, Kuder, and a sentence completion test). A few others gave presentations on friends or relatives. Then John Black broke the pattern by presenting material on a foreign student with complex sexual problems being seen in the Counseling Center, George Welsh followed by giving a summary of a neo-Nazi he had worked up at the VA, and soon the group was back focusing as usual on the pathological and deviant. It was hard to resist discussing fascinating clinical cases.

Dissertation Research

My minor was a concentration in neuropsychiatry, starting with a course in neuro-anatomy (taken along with freshman medical students) from A. T. Rasmussen. Courses in neurophysiology from Ernst Gellhorn, neuropathology from Abe Baker, neuropsychiatry from Bertrum Schiele, and case conferences with the staff in the Department of Neuropsychiatry completed this work. With this background, it was an easy step to proposing a dissertation topic with Hathaway, working to develop a clinically useful test for aphasia. Hathaway had himself tried to develop a more systematic and practical assessment instrument along the lines of Luria's diagnostic procedures but had not had the opportunity to pursue it fully.

Tradition at Minnesota strongly supported research on the development of useful psychological instruments: for example, for his dissertation, Howard Hunt had just completed his own test for the early detection of brain damage. Two other events combined to direct my attention to the need for a sound assessment device for aphasia: Charnley McKinley, chairman of the Department of Neuropsychiatry and co-author of the MMPI, had recently suffered a stroke that rendered him aphasic, and my own paternal grandfather, Oscar Dahlstrom, had had a similar cerebral vascular accident with the same outcome. Both of these men were willing to serve as subjects in my efforts to screen potential items for such a battery.

A dissertation committee was formed and I began assembling materials. I visited McKinley and my grandfather several times, trying out items and discovering the complexities of their speech problems. In the meantime I was monitoring the flow of cases through the Division of Neurology to determine the numbers of patients that I could expect to study for this work. After some period of piloting this research, it became clear that I would need several years to complete this project based on those individuals receiving a workup in neurology at the University of Minnesota Hospitals. Reluctantly, I gave up this task and at the suggestion of Meehl changed my dissertation to a factor analysis of psychiatric symptoms in a search for statistical support of the classic psychiatric syndromes. However, Hathaway continued his interest in this area of aphasia testing and shortly after this directed the dissertation of Hildred Schuell. She carried out a successful research program to develop an aphasia battery using vastly more generous patient resources from several midwestern Veterans Administration hospitals. This test was later published by the University of Minnesota Press.

In 1946, I joined the American Psychological Association and attended my first convention. It was held in Philadelphia on the campus of the University of Pennsylvania (the last time it could be accommodated at a college or university). I traveled by train, and coming out of Chicago I had the good fortune to be seated across from Ernest Hilgard. (Looking back, I am not sure that he fully appreciated the opportunity to sit and talk psychology endlessly across four states.) Eagerly, as a new member, I attended paper sessions, listened to the classic debate between Thorne and Rogers on directive versus nondirective counseling, and watched Robert Woodworth receive the first Gold Medal in Psychology for the textbooks and writings that I had slaved over during my first two years of graduate work. Alfred Kinsey gave the invited address that year, two years before the publication of his first volume on human sexual behavior in males. All of these exciting offerings were a great way to start attending professional meetings.

The next summer, Paul Meehl and I traveled to Bard College on the Hudson River north of New York City for Bruno Klopfer's two-week workshop on the Rorschach. It was a beautiful setting on a quiet campus. We lived in a student dormitory, emptied of students for the summer. Several well-known psychologists decided to attend that summer, including the Ansbachers, Heinz and Rowena (who helped introduce Alfred Adler to American psychology), and Catherine Cox Miles (co-author with Louis Terman of *Sex and Personality*), together with her husband Walter Miles from Yale. Werner Wolff was there, too, and offered evening sessions on his own psychodiagnostic techniques with handwriting analysis, gestural styles, and body language. He ran film clips of his subjects and pointed out crucial variations in the ways they walked and carried themselves.

Stephanie Dudek was our instructor for the introductory material on administration and scoring. Paul and I had already had a few lectures from Marcella Vig, who had brought back to Minnesota her own experiences from Margarite Hertz's workshop. We found Klopfer's approach less precise and quantitative than what we knew of Hertz and her scoring tables. Gradually, however, we acquired some skill in the judgments needed to complete the scoring and compute the numerous summaries in the psychograph. Sessions lasted all morning and broke into small groups in the early afternoon to practice the inquiry and scoring procedures.

By late afternoon we all (beginners and advanced alike) assembled in a large classroom to watch Klopfer himself do a blind analysis of an individual protocol, response by response, card by card. He was an excellent showman and made many comments and elaborations along the way, ending with a psychodiagnostic and psychodynamic integration of the case under review. Unfortunately, in this way Klopfer also worked to undercut the meticulous approach to scoring that we were hearing from Stephanie. That is, he depended much more on response content, scoring sequence, and evidence of reactions to the cards than he did on either scoring summaries or the various percentages and ratios we were being drilled on. Quite often he was well along in his formulation of the individual's personality and emotional problems by the time he got to Card VIII, long before he had been given any of the usual data included in the psychograph. In this regard he was very much like Margaret Thaler Singer in her emphasis on extra-card commentary, situational attitudes, and stylistic approaches to the task as a basis for personological inferences.

It was an enjoyable and profitable two weeks. On the way back Paul and I stopped off in New York City to show him some of the tourist sights. I was surprised to find that the observation deck of the Empire State Building had been fenced in since I had last visited it with my family in the late thirties. We parted in Chicago, where Paul had also arranged to attend the summer Rorschach workshop offered by Samuel Beck. Since he planned to make up for the lack of teaching of projective techniques at Minnesota by offering a course on the Rorschach, Paul felt he needed to know all three major approaches. I never expected to take on such a teaching assignment, however, so I was comfortable with the Klopfer background for any clinical work. (Later, I had to learn Beck, and eventually Exner as well, when I taught various adult assessment courses.)

Doctoral candidates at Minnesota at that time still had to qualify in a reading knowledge of two foreign languages, only one of which could be a Romance language. I had little difficulty in passing the requirement in French, but my premedical courses in German had not given me an adequate basis for meeting the very demanding standard in that language at Minnesota. (All of us graduate students were dismayed to learn that one of our fellow students had failed this examination despite the fact that she had successfully written her master's thesis on Freud in German!) Recklessly, I decided to start over in Russian since the word was out that it was a much more lenient examination than German and since at the end of the war there was a strong interest in things Russian, especially in psychology. Hathaway himself wanted to add Russian to his reading knowledge of German, French, and Spanish.

Accordingly, we both enrolled in an evening course in scientific Russian offered by Professor Samuel Corson, a Russian émigré then on the faculty in the Department of Physiology. The assistant in that course was an undergraduate psychology major, Leona Erickson. Since Corson was notoriously late in all of his commitments to this course, we frequently saw her rushing into class at the last minute with the materials for his evening presentation.

When I later began coursework with Miles Tinker in experimental psychology, I was delighted to find that Leona was now working as his research assistant. (She was not surprised to learn that neither Hathaway nor I had gotten very far with our Russian, having had similar difficulties. I turned back to another attack on German and finally got by that requirement as well.) Leona and I began dating then and just before I left campus for my first job at Ohio Wesleyan University in the fall of 1948, we were married. Before that time, however, Hathaway had also been impressed with Leona's abilities and had hired her away from Tinker to head up the fieldwork for his ambitious testing program to administer the MMPI to all ninth-grade students in the Minneapolis school system. (Access to this population was eased for Hathaway since his wife, Virginia, was chief clinical psychologist for the

Minneapolis public schools.) Both Hathaway and I occasionally served as proctors on Leona's testing team. At one memorable session, a policeman appeared in the study hall to apprehend a suspect for some delinquency or other. As he was hurriedly removing the young man from the room, Hathaway tried unsuccessfully to have the officer allow the culprit time to complete the inventory. One more subject was lost from the prospective investigation, the first aim of which was the prediction of juvenile delinquency.

Leona had completed a master's degree with Paul Meehl and all of the coursework for a doctorate with Hathaway. She helped me collect data on my sample of psychiatric patients and carry out reliability checks on the process of abstracting information from case records. Packing up these raw data, we traveled to Delaware, Ohio, where we both taught psychology courses and carried out the endless analyses involved in doing a Thurstone-style multiple-group factor analysis on these data with a Friden calculator in precomputer days.

First Psychology Position

It would be hard to imagine a more hectic schedule for us that academic year. The first semester I taught for the first time sections of the psychology of adjustment, statistical methods, physiological psychology, and experimental methods. In addition I co-chaired a senior seminar on clinical psychology with Winifred Horrocks. In the spring, the adjustment course was repeated, but advanced statistics and advanced experimental methods followed the fall's introductory sections, and advanced general psychology replaced physiological psychology. Leona had accepted a half-time appointment to teach introductory psychology (for the first time for her). Weekends we carried out data runs on the primitive IBM equipment made available to us by Professor H. A. Toops at Ohio State University, twenty-five miles away in Columbus. Evenings, after we had worked out our lectures for the next day, Leona and I ran the calculator to compute the basic 110 x 110 variable intercorrelational matrix that constituted our goal for the year. (We were blissfully unaware of the interference we were causing in the reception on all the radios in the apartment building where we lived. Fortunately, our neighbors attributed the annoyance to something mysterious going on in the gas station across the street.)

Somehow, by June 1949 we had managed to fill in all the spaces on the chart we had pinned on the wall. I had even squeezed in a return trip to Minneapolis for a few more cases after discovering some incomplete records from our hurried efforts at last-minute data collection. Along with Ronald Greene, our chairman, I was also able to attend the Second Moose Heart Symposium on Emotion sponsored by the University of Chicago.

Life as a faculty member at a small liberal arts school like Ohio Wesleyan proved to be very appealing: highly selected and well-motivated students, a manageable course load (once one had developed a workable set of lecture notes!), and little pressure to produce on any fixed deadlines. The faculty members were congenial and got on well with one another. However, that year the other members of the Department of Psychology saw little of us socially. We were frequently invited to picnics and bridge sessions but often had to refuse because of the press of time. At the end of the spring semester, I turned down an offer from the dean of a three-year contract with a small raise and began looking for an academic placement at a university with a strong medical school.

We returned to Minneapolis that summer to complete the factor analyses (and an additional Tryon-style cluster search) on the psychiatric symptom patterns while working through final job negotiations. An offer from the State University of Iowa came through and we traveled to Iowa City. Most of the analyses were completed for my dissertation but the rotations continued to be problematic. I was fortunate to find Harold Bechtoldt, a former student of Thurstone's at Chicago, already on the faculty there. In spite of his general dismay with the untidiness of the results from the psychiatric domain, in contrast to the neat rotational fit he was used to obtaining with ability and aptitude data, Harold gave me solid support for my final placements of the axes. A neat additional trick was the use of Dwyer's extension to project into these factor solutions from the symptom lists the variances from the scores on the MMPI basic scales that I had obtained on these patients. Modest support was obtained both for the classic syndromes as symptom clusters and for the inventory measures established on these syndromes. Dimensions could approximate whole syndromes.

The Iowa Years

My position in the clinical program was on "soft money" from the NIMH training grant, but in terms of duties I was to serve as a faculty substitute for Charles Strothers, who had recently left Iowa to assume the directorship of the clinical program at the University of Washington. His departure left a huge hole in the coverage of the assessment offerings and in the supervision of the practicum facilities in Iowa City. I began teaching introductory assessment of intelligence for the graduate students and the psychology of adjustment for undergraduates. I also supervised the teaching assistants in the introductory course taught by Don Lewis, setting up their demonstrations and organizing their discussion sessions.

At Iowa the faculty was close-knit and very socially active. Psychology was discussed night and day by faculty and graduate students alike. Kenneth Spence was the head of the Department of Psychology, and Arthur Benton directed the clinical training program. Like so many other faculty members staffing the newly expanded academic clinical programs, Benton was recruited to Iowa from a clinical position in a psychiatric service (University of Louisville). He brought a wealth of clinical skills with children and with adults as well from his service in the Navy during the war. He soon began to develop his research program in the Department of Neurology on neuropsychological disorders that led to his making a wide array of contributions in that difficult field.

In the early 1950s, the clinical graduate students still tended to be drawn from the ranks of World War II veterans who had returned home to complete their undergraduate studies and were now ready for advanced work. Many were my age or older; some had had considerable clinical experience as technicians in the military. One first-year student taking my course on intelligence testing had administered more than 250 Wechsler-Bellevues—far more than I had given. It was painful to have to point out to him after observing his test administration procedures that there were several things that he had been doing wrong!

There were practicum services for our clinical trainees in the University of Iowa Speech Clinic (directed by Wendell Johnson), in the University Hospitals, and in the Children's Hospital. Until Erving Polster arrived the following year to take over the service in the Children's Hospital, I supervised students in all three locations. I could not have managed that array of clinical activities without the able assistance of advanced clinical students like Margaret Shuttleworth and Patricia Moldawsky. Leona accepted a position as a half-time clinical psychologist in the Otolaryngology Department, supported by funds from a training grant in speech pathology and audiology. Graduate students in that program took seminars with her in the psychological assessment of physically handicapped children. Occasionally we were both present at case presentations at the Speech Clinic and in the hospital, but the otolaryngology service was one of the few that we did not cover with our clinical psychology trainees.

Late in my first semester at Iowa I was finally ready to defend my dissertation. I had sent drafts of the chapters back and forth to Minneapolis for Hathaway's approval. I met with my dissertation committee in early December for the final oral with the sudden realization that the make-up of this committee was the same combination formed for my research on aphasia. The neuroanatomist, the neurologist, and the neurosurgeon who were still members of the committee were likely to be as lost among the centroids, rotations, and loadings of my data plots as I would be in the cerebral cortex exposed by a surgical flap in the cranium of some patient. They were kindly tolerant of the range of discussions carried out among the psychology members in attendance and wished me well at the end of the two hours.

After obtaining my degree I was eligible to serve on dissertation committees. My first committee membership was to replace Strothers on Norman Garmezy's doctoral oral examination. Norman had just returned from his internship at Worchester State Hospital; it was a very lively and engaging session. Soon I was able to direct dissertation research myself, an activity I have always found enjoyable. My first doctoral candidate was Stanley Moldawsky, husband of Patricia. He used a behavioral sample obtained through a role-playing task to evaluate the external validity of the Iowa Rigidity Scale, an instrument developed by Elizabeth Wesley in her dissertation there the year before. Stan obtained good interjudge reliability on the recordings of the subjects' efforts to carry out a role assignment as salesmen but found little support for the use of the scale in predicting task flexibility. Previous sales experience proved to be a better basis for such predictions than scores on the Wesley scale. I directed three more dissertation projects before I left Iowa.

One of the major topics of research, both animal and human, in the department at that time was the clarification of the role of anxiety as a drive within a Hullian behavioral system. Previous studies had demonstrated its enhancing properties on the learning and performance of very simple responses. However, there was growing evidence that the elevated drive state from anxiety could bring about behavioral decrement in more complex response sequences. There was a problem in putting this formulation to a direct test, however, since the targeted responses were so qualitatively different (for example, eyelid blinks versus psychomotor coordination tasks). However, one kind of performance seemed to offer both simple and complex tasks within one general series of responses: the recall of the nine designs of the Bender-Gestalt Test after one short exposure to the test patterns. John Williams and Charles Spielberger, both advanced graduate students in the clinical program, came to me to discuss a plan to try to capture the crossover effect of high anxiety within this kind of performance. We were later joined by Leonard Goodstein, a recent new faculty member in the Counseling Center.

The first step we envisioned was to change the traditional order of presentation of the Bender stimuli to maximize the ease of remembering the simple designs and the difficulty of remembering the complex ones. This involved working out the various orders of presentation to find the easiest and hardest positions, as well as establishing the easiest and hardest designs to recall after a single exposure in an incidental memory paradigm. We also had to establish clearer scoring standards for acceptable productions from our subjects (Goodstein, Spielberger, Williams, & Dahlstrom, 1955). From these various combinations we located the three easiest designs and the three hardest ones. We also demonstrated again the primacy and recency effects in serial learning of these patterns. The results of the analyses dictated the placement in the new series to assure the greatest difference between hard and easy designs for recall.

The four of us had split up by the time we were ready to run the crucial test with high- and low-anxious college undergraduates: Williams and Goodstein at Iowa, Spielberger at his first job at Duke University, and me at the University of North Carolina at Chapel Hill, ten miles from Duke. Accordingly, we were in a position to replicate the study on college men and women at all three institutions. Not many studies can claim results that held up at three different places with clear support for the crossover from different levels of the Taylor Anxiety Scale: high-anxious students recalled the easy designs (in the easy locations) significantly more frequently than low-anxious subjects but did significantly more poorly on the hard designs (in the hard positions) (Spielberger, Goodstein, & Dahlstrom, 1958). There were some interesting interactions as well with gender and institution that we did not pursue any further. Spielberger later used some of the theoretical implications of anxiety as a drive to introduce a brief anti-anxiety intervention at Duke for freshmen who encountered academic difficulties in their first semester of college.

This investigation combined concepts and materials from both experimental and clinical methods. It was in the tradition of research being carried out at Iowa by I. E. Farber and Judson Brown. I learned a great deal about experimental personality research methods from both of them in long conversations and while participating on dissertation committees for their students.

Thanks to Benton's efforts, my closest and most productive ties to the medical faculty were with members of the Departments of Neurology and Neurosurgery. One project involved my carrying out psychological assessments of candidates for surgery on their herniated intervertebral disks and then making blind predictions from the test scores about the extent of their functional recoveries following successful physical repairs. Although several patients on whom I filed predictions did not undergo operations (the neurosurgeons seemed to perceive the same poor prospects from their workups that I had detected on the MMPI profiles), my predictions stood up very well over short periods of postsurgical follow-up. However, we had also planned to keep track of these individuals for a year or more to see if other problems replaced the low back pain syndromes in some of the neurotic individuals. Our research group broke up before more long-term data became available.

At Iowa, my aim had been to work out a pattern of clinical and research involvement similar to the way that Hathaway, Meehl, and Schofield at Minnesota had integrated clinical practice and research in the Medical School with ties to the academic Department of Psychology. It was difficult to make such arrangements at Iowa, since the psychiatric services were located in the Psychopathic Hospitals, a separate clinical facility with only tenuous ties to the other medical and academic facilities. I was not successful in working out the necessary joint appointment in the Medical School. As a result, I was willing to listen to an invitation from Dorothy Adkins, chairwoman of the Department of Psychology at the University of North Carolina, to explore a possible position as director of psychological services in the North Carolina Memorial Hospital, with academic appointments in both the Psychology and Psychiatry departments. In the summer of 1953, I accepted the offer and we moved to Chapel Hill.

The Chapel Hill Years

In those days, Chapel Hill in late summer was virtually deserted. Leona and I arrived there on a humid, hazy afternoon with temperatures in the nineties. Few restaurants and only one motel were open. John Thibaut had arranged for us to rent a small house set deep on a wooded lot that offered some relief from the summer heat, but it was not ready for us yet. Still, it was arguable whether Chapel Hill at that time of year was much worse than the muggy weather we had left back in Iowa.

Two quite different challenges were awaiting me at UNC-CH. In the hospital a new clinical service had to be established. The hospital system itself was very new, part of a large-scale expansion of the Medical School the year before from a two-year program to a full four-year school. Previously, medical students took only their basic work in medical sciences in Chapel Hill, transferring to places like Johns

Hopkins, Pennsylvania, or Harvard for the clinical years. Now the UNC program was to be the third medical school in the state, competing with Duke in Durham and Bowman-Gray in Winston-Salem. All of the clinical departments were in the first stages of getting established. I had my major appointment as associate professor of psychology in Psychiatry. To serve the entire hospital, however, I had to set up referral procedures, purchase equipment, establish record-keeping systems, and, most important, try to recruit additional staff. Soon clinical psychology trainees would be coming over from campus for practicum supervision.

The other challenge was even more daunting. The entire faculty in the clinical psychology training program on campus had been asked to resign and almost all had already left Chapel Hill. As one of his first actions in assuming the chairmanship of the Department of Psychiatry, George Ham had protested the role of various members of the clinical psychology faculty in carrying out clinical practice on UNC-CH undergraduate students through the Student Infirmary. With only one or two psychiatrists in town, the members of the clinical faculty had been offering psychodiagnostic and psychotherapeutic services to help cover the mental health needs of the university community. Ham saw these practitioners as a direct threat to the private practice needs of the psychiatrists he was bringing in as part of the faculty of his new Department of Psychiatry. A confrontation had been staged in the office of the chancellor. In this showdown the psychology faculty had lost and they had been asked to resign. Joseph Dawson went to Louisiana State University, Dorothy Terry took a position with NIMH, and Lloyd Borstelmann moved to Duke. A year later, Irvin Wolf accepted a position at Denison University. Close to retirement, Harry Crane resigned from the staff of the Student Infirmary but stayed on in the Department of Psychology. The clinical training program, established in 1948, was in complete disarray. Our NIMH clinical psychology training grant and the APA accreditation both were in jeopardy.

Dorothy Adkins had negotiated three other appointments: my fellow graduate student at Minnesota, George Welsh, from the VA Hospital in Oakland, California; June Chance, a former student of Julian Rotter's, from the University of Maryland, where she had taken an academic position after finishing her degree at Ohio State; and Earl Baughman, then director of the clinical training program at the University of Wisconsin. (However, Earl did not feel free to join us in Chapel Hill until the following year because of his commitments to the program in Madison. George served as acting director for the first year.)

All four of us met with the visiting committee from the APA and were able to convince them that we could put the program back together. They were particularly concerned, of course, with the fate of the students who were well along in the program and who needed continuity to complete their training. George, Earl, and I had already had appreciable experience in supervising graduate students and directing thesis and dissertation research projects. If the NIMH training grant could be retained, we were convinced we could provide the continuity needed to get these students through on schedule. Fortunately, we kept the grant and the accreditation. Soon I was teaching the assessment course (projective techniques), working with Charles Elliott, Herbert Eber, and Carl Cochrane on their dissertations, and supervising practicum students in the hospital as my part of this new enterprise.

Recruiting additional psychology faculty in the Department of Psychiatry proved to be more difficult. Since I wanted these individuals to hold joint appointments on campus, candidates had to pass screening from both sets of faculty and from the university administration. To my surprise, I encountered prejudices among the administrators at that time of pervasive segregation that extended well beyond the usual one against black candidates. Since that time, of course, attitudes have changed markedly, but these anti-Catholic, anti-Semitic, and antifemale feelings were new to me. I was greatly relieved finally to be able to recruit Milton Rosenbaum for the outpatient service, Dean Clyde for the inpatient service, and Shepherd Liverant for the children's service. It was gratifying to have such capable staff members to share the supervisory and referral responsibilities of our rapidly expanding program.

After Earl Baughman arrived, he took over the course on projective techniques and I reactivated a course on neuropsychology and introduced a new offering in personality research methods. June Chance taught the course on intelligence testing and George Welsh gave the objective personality techniques course. This kind of coverage of various assessment methods has continued to be one of the strengths of the clinical training program at UNC-CH. To acquaint the psychiatric faculty with the potentialities of psychological assessment, George Ham, George Welsh, and I established an informal weekly seminar for interested staff and residents. We met for a year and won several converts to the use of various tests, particularly the MMPI, in both their clinical practice and their various research projects.

One outcome of these meetings was a series of collaborative studies on the new psychoactive drugs with Wilfred Abse, one of the senior psychoanalysts, and with various psychiatric residents. These investigations were some of the first published studies with blind evaluations of comparison drugs and placebos. The patients in these projects came from both Memorial Hospital psychiatric services and state hospital wards (Abse, Curtis, Dahlstrom, Hawkins, & Toops, 1956; Abse & Dahlstrom, 1960; Abse, Dahlstrom, & Tolley, 1960).

As part of my instruction of the third- and fourth-year medical students (coming through in groups of ten on their rotation on the psychiatry service), I began my weekly seminars with each cohort by having each of them take the MMPI. I then met with the students individually and discussed his or her test results. By this means I helped them better understand the psychodiagnostic material that they later saw on their patients, either in the grand rounds or on individual referral. (However, the MMPI was not used in screening these students on admission to medical school the way that it was in other places around the country.)

When I shared these data with Milton Rosenbaum, we became quite interested in knowing the extent to which their profile patterns were an expression of having already completed some years of medical training. We had an opportunity to explore this question when the psychiatry faculty decided to design an evaluation study of the effects of taking the course in human ecology that the faculty of the Department of Psychiatry gave freshman medical students every Saturday morning.

The material in the course covered various ways in which cultural and environmental factors might affect physical and emotional health. In addition to lectures and demonstrations by the psychiatrists in the department, medical sociological topics were covered by Harvey Smith and cultural anthropology was presented by Weston LaBarre. (For these rather hardheaded and fact-oriented first-year students, I think that the physical anthropology offered by George Holcomb as part of the anatomy course came across better than LaBarre's material.) The general research question was: Did this series of presentations early in the medical curriculum work to offset the coldhearted, icy objectivity of the medical sciences and lay the groundwork for more humane and empathic clinical sensitivity on the part of these budding physicians?

We proposed including in the battery of measures to be administered before and after the course both the MMPI and a standard attitude scale toward mental disorders. Milton Rosenbaum and I took responsibility for this part of the investigation. As a form of comparison group, we used the same instruments to study changes on these measures in first-year law students who had no such course in their curriculum. We found little evidence in our measures of appreciable changes in attitude toward individuals with serious emotional problems (in either academic program). Nor did we get much change in the MMPI patterns. The data from these investigations, however, proved to be particularly valuable in following up these men and women later on in the midst of their medical or legal practices. The MMPI records from the students in these professional programs provided the scores on the Cook and Medley Hostility (Ho) scale, which rather neatly captured the hostile and cynical variance elicited by the standard Type A interview procedures (Barefoot, Dahlstrom & Williams, 1983; Barefoot, Dodge, Peterson, Dahlstrom, & Williams, 1989; Barefoot, Smith, Dahlstrom, & Williams, 1989).

Move to the Department of Psychology

In our faculty discussions in the Department of Psychiatry on the strengths and weaknesses of the human ecology course, opinions varied widely and heatedly. Our evidence that the course changed student attitudes only negligibly added fuel to the debates, and student scuttlebutt also indicated widespread dissatisfaction with the course. I believed that psychology staff should be permitted to participate in the lecture series in addition to attending the discussion sections. Others also argued for a stronger coverage of substantive material rather than the focus on feelings and emotional acceptance that the course emphasized.

The exclusion of psychologists from this teaching assignment was just one of the increasing number of problems that I was encountering in the development of clinical psychology in the department. Psychologists were not allowed to carry out psychotherapy or earn private practice supplements to their basic salary. New faculty positions were going to psychiatric staff in preference to psychology or social work. Our recruiting was at a standstill and our salary levels were tied to state pay schedules, rather than to university academic scales. Finally, I reached an impasse in my efforts to develop clinical psychological practice in this setting; I offered my resignation and wondered what my next move should be. The situation was complicated by the birth a few months before of our first child, a daughter we named Amy. (Two years later a boy we named Eric was born to complete our family.)

Earl Baughman was very sympathetic with my circumstances, however, and intervened to negotiate several new arrangements. He proposed that I move to the Department of Psychology on funding from the NIMH training grant but retain a clinical appointment in the Department of Psychiatry. He also offered to help in the recruitment of my replacement if the Department of Psychiatry were willing to consider several changes in salary levels, role assignments, and numbers of staff positions. Skillfully, he managed to get additional positions for clinical psychology, shift the salary scale to an academic base, arrange for private practice income for the new director and his staff, and open the door for psychologists to carry therapy cases. Hans Strupp was brought in as director. He soon established a lively team of investigators of psychotherapy process, including Kenneth Lessler, Ronald Fox, and Martin Wallach. Hans built up a large clinical psychology service before leaving for Vanderbilt University to direct the clinical training program there.

Even before I moved to campus to join Earl and George in the clinical group, George and I had collaborated on our first book on the MMPI. We were well aware of the lack of any organized material with which to teach various aspects of the use of the test. Reprints of the original derivational articles were unobtainable. (When Leona worked in the MMPI office with Hathaway, she had had to bundle up sets of mimeographed versions of these articles to send out to individuals all over the world since supplies of the originals had been exhausted long before.) We decided the quickest way to prepare some comprehensive basis for using the test was to organize a set of readings. With Hathaway's encouragement we contacted the University of Minnesota Press. Fortunately, the director, Helen Clapesattle, was very supportive. Her own book on the two physicians who established the Mayo Clinic in Rochester, Minnesota (*The Doctors Mayo,* 1941), had become a best-seller for the press; they now had the resources to take on a less promising venture like the one we proposed. She encouraged us to broaden the coverage of the material to be included so that we could reach the lucrative medical textbook market.

Accordingly, evenings and weekends, George, Leona, and I sent out requests for reprints and permissions to reproduce articles and assemble materials from investigators in a wide variety of fields in which the MMPI was being used. Before the days of xerography, the best arrangement was to use two copies of the reprint to glue to separate pages in the manuscript, one for the front, the other for the back of each page. Mercifully, the editors at the Minnesota Press were willing to work from such diverse type formats rather than insisting on a complete retyping of the entire set of sixty-six articles. We saved space by cutting out the redundant introductory paragraphs in which each author typically described the instrument and by consolidating all references into a single bibliography at the end of the volume. We were particularly pleased to be able to cajole Hathaway into writing a chapter on the basic derivational material on three scales (Mf, Pa, and Sc) that he had not previously described in the journal literature. The *Basic Readings* appeared in 1956 and contrary to the pessimism of the director of the press, proved to be a strong, steady-selling item on their list for many years.

Before I moved to campus in the fall of 1956, George and I began discussing the writing of an organized presentation of the administration and interpretation of the MMPI that would serve as a more systematic introduction to the test than a collection of diverse articles could provide. We were both familiar with a practical guide to interpretation of the Strong Vocational Interest Battery that John Darley and Ralph Berdie had written. It served as a model for our initial planning. We worked on it off and on for a year or so before George took a year's sabbatical to Florence, Italy, on a Fulbright fellowship. We had assembled various kinds of data for some technical appendixes but had not progressed very far on the main part of the volume. While he was away, however, I taught the course on objective assessment techniques and began serious work on the manuscript. By the time he returned, the book had grown considerably beyond our initial outline and we again sought support from the University of Minnesota Press to publish the manuscript as an MMPI handbook.

The press was willing to take on this publication, but there was one sticking point: we wanted to include as one of the technical appendixes all of the items in the MMPI so that test users and research investigators would not have to seek out a test booklet every time some question of item content arose. The University of Minnesota held the copyright on the test and The Psychological Corporation had exclusive rights to its sales and distribution. There was great reluctance to let us put the complete contents of the inventory into a volume of this sort, which would be on the open shelves of major university libraries. In our efforts to resolve this difference of opinion, George and I met with Hathaway and Harold Seashore of The Psychological Corporation at the APA convention in New York City in 1954. The outcome of this meeting was permission to list the individual items comprising each individual scale but not the test booklet per se. (By the time we revised the *MMPI Handbook* in 1972, the whole test booklet was reproduced in an appendix.)

When I was working on the *MMPI Handbook* during the late 1950s, it was possible with some effort to become familiar with virtually the entire research literature on the test. George and I knew personally many of the investigators who had carried out basic research on the instrument. The test itself typically was the focus of such research: Was the test able to do what was claimed for it? (Later, the focus shifted gradually to the many ways in which the test facilitated the conduct of research on other problems and topics.) We often ordered copies of doctoral dissertations from other universities to see the findings before they appeared in print. We continued to collect data on new research scales devised from the same item pool. Thus, weaving together the findings from this growing research literature, a pattern of assessment uses emerged and the organization followed a natural path. Over the years this volume also proved to be one of the best-selling items in the catalog of the University of Minnesota Press.

One of the technical appendixes in the *Handbook* served to stimulate a lengthy series of controversial studies on the impact of various response sets on the meaning of the scores on scales like those making up the basic MMPI profile. Based in part on the studies that they had carried out at the Menninger Foundation on the ways that different individuals approached the task of completing a psychological test, Douglas Jackson and Samuel Messick offered a distinction between the tendency to respond to the content of test items directly and individual styles of taking tests. These latter individual variations were termed "response sets." One such approach to test taking had been proposed by Allen Edwards in 1953 as a social desirability set in which the individual fails to respond to the items honestly but instead attempts to create the most favorable impression possible in his or her answers. By 1957, Edwards had extended his studies to include data from the MMPI and had derived a new scale (Sd) to assess this response tendency. Jackson and Messick, by then at the Educational Testing Service (ETS) in Princeton, New Jersey, had carried out studies that seemed to confirm Edwards's findings and had added a second major response set, the tendency to acquiesce to the test demands implicit in the reason for administering the test in the first place—that is, acknowledging various kinds of psychopathology. In their view, these two styles of responding to items of the MMPI together would appear to account for major components of variance in the basic scales of the inventory. Since these were seen as sources of test artifact, supporters of the response set interpretations of MMPI scores were contending that there was little left in the basic scales that reflected actual score validity. That is, the only thing that the scales in the MMPI profile reflected were combinations of two different sets to the test, either to go along with the test examiner's demands to reveal indiscriminately one's pathologies, or to make oneself look as socially acceptable as possible. By including data on item favorability in an appendix of the 1960 *Handbook,* we facilitated a new series of studies on this issue.

In 1960, Messick and Jackson held an invitational conference at ETS devoted in part to these issues. In my comments about the papers presented there that summarized both the Edwards and the Messick and Jackson points of view, I tried to relate this work to the well-established validity scales already available on the MMPI, which seemed to me to show that Hathaway and McKinley had actually anticipated both kinds of test distortion and done a good job of providing checks against their potentially adverse effects on test score validity. I was apparently not very persuasive, and a wave of research studies devoted to response sets and related issues continued to appear in the MMPI literature. For a period of time, the editorial policies of some journals were affected by these claims and legitimate empirical studies based in part on the MMPI were systematically rejected. It remained for Jack Block at the University of California at Berkeley, in his book *The Challenge of Response Sets* (1965), to marshal the results of the appropriate psychometric analyses and empirical scale correlates and thus demolish these specious claims. What had been discarded as invalid test variance in the acquiescence and desirability response set measures turned out to be necessary information about important personality attributes. These measures were not error but actually part of the way that the MMPI functioned to provide information about the individuals completing the test.

With the publication of the *MMPI Handbook* in 1960, both George and I earned promotions to full professor in the Department of Psychology. Thus, the time was favorable for a new venture involving collaborative research. Earl had completed his long series of studies on altered forms of the Rorschach, and Halbert Robinson had recently joined our faculty, bringing expertise in child clinical psychology. We had each become puzzled and intrigued with the problems pandemic in the county school system in the rural areas near Chapel Hill. Our first information came from the experiences encountered there by George's wife, Alice Welsh, a speech therapist, in her efforts to work with the pupils in the four grade schools and the two high schools. She found that both the white and the black children were academically delayed and often handicapped by speech disorders. The schools were racially segregated from first grade through high school. Wives of some of our graduate students often found teaching positions in these schools and they, too, reported on the numbers of children with academic and emotional difficulties that they encountered in their classes. More recently, we had had students use some of these classes as sources of research subjects for their thesis or dissertation research. Their reports were consistent with the experiences of the others.

After conferring with the school administrators in the county system and exploring the possibilities with various parent and teacher groups, the four of us organized a research proposal that we submitted to the NIMH covering several aspects of a multifaceted study of the abilities, personalities, and academic achievements of the students in the four grade schools, two serving white children and two serving black. Earl and I wanted to study patterns of intellective abilities and personality characteristics as they interacted in determining school achievement. George was more interested in early antecedents of creativity, and Halbert wanted to introduce an intervention program to try to reduce the high rate of school failures that we already knew to be a problem in these schools. We also envisioned that such a concerted research effort would provide many opportunities for graduate student involvement.

Admittedly, the proposal as submitted was only loosely tied together and lacked the kind of detail that we would soon have after getting under way, but the results of the site visit and our subsequent feedback via the NIMH pink sheet were quite devastating. The site visitor had come to a quick decision that, in his view, the only supportable part of this plan was the intervention effort proposed by Halbert. Long before the end of his visit he had stopped discussing matters with Earl, George, or me, and had focused his attention on Halbert. We were able to anticipate the negative outcome of the review and had already begun seeking alternative avenues of support. George soon made contact with the officials who were operating a summer program for academically and artistically gifted high school students (the North Carolina Governor's School) that drew from school systems throughout the state. Halbert sought support from both the NICHHD and the Kennedy Foundation to launch an abecedarian program in Chapel Hill to prevent mental retardation. These efforts later led to the establishment of the Biological Sciences Research Center and the Frank Porter Graham Child Development Center.

Earl and I resubmitted a more modest request to NIMH for support of the Orange County Child Research Center. This request was successful and we began with a comprehensive survey of all students in the system between first and eighth grade, using both the individually administered Stanford-Binet (S-B) Intelligence Scale and the group-administered Thurstone Primary Mental Abilities (PMA) and Stanford Achievement Test (SAT) batteries. Later, we also launched an intervention program that included the establishment of experimental kindergartens in one white and one black elementary school (the other schools served as controls) and a pilot study of an outreach program to stimulate the intellective development of prekindergarteners in their own homes. The kindergarten program also carried a parallel investigation by Eugene Long to explore the feasibility of using Skinnerian operant conditioning methods to enhance the mastery of verbal and perceptual materials like those incorporated in the Thurstone PMA tests. In addition to collaboration with Professor Long we continued to rely on Halbert Robinson, and his wife Nancy, to monitor our staff in their administering and scoring of the newly published 1961 version of the S-B scale. Both of the Robinsons had worked with Maude Merrill at Stanford University in her efforts to complete the revision of the famous scale. Through their contacts we were able to obtain some of the first test kits available to the field for use in our school surveys.

With only modest financial support, we budgeted time and funds carefully. The research associates we hired for the white schools (Sophie Martin, Musia Lakin, and Anne Spitznagel) and for the black schools (Carol Bowie, Barbara Nixon, Eva Ray, and Rosemary Funderburg) worked very hard to complete the initial surveys and lay the groundwork for our follow-up studies. The appointment of black members of our research staff through the Department of Psychology at the university constituted some of the very first academic appointments for black faculty at UNC-CH. Within the operation of the Child Research Center itself there was, of course, full integration, but any mixing of the racial membership of our staff within the schools was kept to a minimum to reduce the risk of raising antiblack emotional reactions in this rural community during the course of the project. However, we attempted to explore the potentially negative impact on the performance of a child from having a member of the opposite race carry out the administration of the intellective tests. In a master's thesis, Jean Eder LaCrosse completed an asymmetric design in which she retested both white and black children with the S-B scale. (However, no black test administrator was permitted to retest students in either white school.) Both male and female white students showed some slight gain in their IQ scores on retest but the black male and female students showed small losses. This difference could well have been attributed to Jean's race, but her results were equivocal without the rest of the statistical design.

Our follow-up of the effects of introducing a kindergarten year before enrolling in first grade (for the first time in any public school in North Carolina) demonstrated some substantial short-term gains in intellective performance (through the third grade), but the largest effects appeared in the observations of the first-grade teachers. They found the pupils coming out of our kindergartens immediately adapted both behaviorally and emotionally to classroom procedures and routines. Children entering school directly into the first grade only gradually got used to staying in their seats, paying attention to the teacher's instructions, and refraining from idle chatter. Several weeks would pass before they became accustomed to working on some project on their own at their seats. Many did not have any experience with indoor plumbing or the necessary skills for eating in the school cafeteria. Later, when we introduced a set of routine home visits to our white and black preschool subjects, we gained insight into the reasons that these children were encountering such serious difficulties in adapting to schoolroom routines. Clearly, the kindergarten experiences were giving many of these children from both white and black families socializing experiences that their parents were unable to provide for them. Nor were all of the efforts during that kindergarten year ones involving additional controls or increased inhibitions. One of the few complaints that we heard from parents of youngsters coming to these programs was that they felt their children often seemed to be more independent and challenging of parental controls than they were before they started kindergarten!

We came close to having this valuable component in our research program destroyed before we had obtained any of the basic data we needed to evaluate the potential benefits of the kindergartens. In 1963, the Kennedy administration issued a far-reaching policy decision: from that time forward, no federal funds could be used to support programs carried out in racially segregated school systems. This well-intentioned edict was potentially disastrous to our ongoing studies; only some timely financial support from the UNC-CH administration enabled us to carry our project to completion. When we reported some of our positive results, we were gratified to find that officials in the state school system were attentive to these findings and soon launched state-supported kindergartens for the first time in county after county across North Carolina.

Earl carried most of the administrative responsibilities for our program in the Orange County schools. We both were continuing full-time in our roles in the clinical training program; a few of our clinical graduate students (and some from other programs in the department) carried out their thesis and dissertation research in the Child Study Center. For one year, however, Earl obtained federal support for a leave at Stanford University and I served as the director of the center. By that time we had rented three small houses in the Efland community and our operations were spread over the four original schools and a newly established junior high school as well (to follow our students through their seventh and eighth grades).

During that year I arranged for the administration of the MMPI to all our eighth-grade subjects (plus some seventh graders who would have been in eighth grade had it not been for their being held back academically). It was clear from our survey of the general level of reading comprehension of these students (by means of the Stanford Achievement battery) that they would have great difficulty in completing the inventory using the test booklet and answer sheet. The typical reading level of the eighth graders was at the fifth grade; many fell below that level. However, the experience of James Panton at the Classification Center at the North Carolina Central Prison in dealing with incoming prisoners who had serious reading deficits proved to be very helpful. His practice was to have the MMPI items read aloud to the assembled group; with this procedure he was obtaining valid records from most of the prisoners.

I talked one of our advanced students, James Butcher, into preparing a taped version of the text to be played in front of each class; all any student had to do was listen to each item and complete his or her answer sheet as the tape was played. We ran a small-scale study with college undergraduates taking both the booklet and taped versions and obtained reassuring evidence of the comparability of these two forms of MMPI administration. Butcher's soft Southern accent on the tape was probably helpful in obtaining the cooperation and comprehension of the subjects we tested with that version. (The taped version distributed later by The Psychological Corporation employed a neutral, TV-style announcer to provide the voice for their presentation.) The results we obtained from this form of test administration met the usual criteria of protocol validity to a satisfactory degree.

Butcher employed this version later to obtain test records from the parents of eighth-grade boys found to differ in aggressiveness on ratings from their teachers. By this means he was able to compare child and parent patterns within high- and low-aggressive groups for his dissertation research. Ten years later, Joseph Lowman, Bernadette Gray-Little, and David Galinsky carried out a follow-up study of the eighth graders who took the MMPI. These investigators related various kinds of test data, both personality and academic measures, to the postschooling careers of these young men and women. The variables from the S-B, SAT, and MMPI proved to be good predictors of the extent of their additional education, their work histories and marital patterns, as well as their geographic mobility. These MMPI data were also entered into the large data set employed by Philip Marks and Peter Briggs as a composite for the first adolescent norms for the instrument, appearing in several places including the 1972 *MMPI Handbook.*

Earl and I realized that many of the results of our studies could be potentially distressing, even inflammatory, to school officials and community residents in the area in the racially tense climate of the times. The magnitude of the differences on Stanford-Binet and PMA scores between our black and white students was comparable to that of many other reports appearing at that time. (It did not matter that the individual earning the single lowest score on the S-B in our schools was a white boy or that the single highest score was earned by a black girl; the differences in central tendency showed a large black-white gap.) Many of our professional colleagues in the field would also have been highly critical of our results if presented in fragmentary form in a series of small studies. Deliberately, we waited until we could report our findings in book form within an organized and coherent account of the project and its cultural and geographic context.

One unfortunate consequence of this strategy was that we did not at first generate the usual flow of research publications and conference presentations expected from a major research program. Accordingly, funding agencies to which Earl later appealed for further support of his home outreach program apparently came to the opinion that we were a nonproductive group of investigators who were of questionable competence in conducting basic research of this kind. He was not successful in finding financial support for what could have been a very early demonstration of the value of preschool enrichment of children's intellective and motivational experiences.

In 1963, I accepted an invitation to join a study section for the National Institutes of Health (Mental Health B). The NIMH was still part of NIH at that time so most of the research proposals we reviewed were destined for that agency, but any proposal having to do with psychiatric, psychological, or behavioral topics came to either the A or B sections. Arthur Benton was chairman of A and Alfred Baldwin chaired B. (I was delighted finally to meet and work with the psychologist who had devised the techniques that I had used much earlier in analyzing the correspondence of Abélard and Héloïse.) As virtually all who have served in such a capacity for the federal funding agencies will attest, the concentrated immersion in discussion after discussion of the pressing intellectual and methodological issues of the day in one's own field constitutes a rare privilege. The three- or four-day sessions of ten or twelve hours at a stretch that we had on Mental Health Section B were both stimulating and challenging, as were many of the site visits. Many of these visits provided us with an opportunity to meet and discuss research with the leaders in American psychology and psychiatry.

During the last year of my service on the NIH panel I followed Baldwin as chairman of the section. It was a year of transition during which NIMH was separated from NIH and combined with new agencies for drug and alcohol research under ADAMHA. The new institute needed to establish a peer review system, and both Sections A and B were co-opted to form a nucleus of their review mechanism. It was also the year in which major concerns were raised about the potential misuse of human subjects in behavioral research studies. The particular instances that brought attention to these issues were actually biomedical projects, and the extension of these concerns to behavioral investigations struck me as hasty and excessive. I still am convinced that the heavy-handed application of these oversight mechanisms in our area has caused more damage to our research efforts by way of the chill on research initiatives devoted to urgent mental health problems than good in preventing inhumane investigative methods. This proved to be particularly the case when federal agencies forced every institution receiving federal funds of any kind to apply the same stringent review mechanisms on *all* behavioral projects carried out within that institution regardless of any specific dependence on federal support. There were several hours, formal and informal, devoted to discussion of these issues in our study section during the last days of my chairmanship.

On campus at UNC-CH the administration was becoming increasingly concerned about the rapid rise in student drug involvement, mental health crises, suicides, and violence. The dean of the College of Arts and Sciences formed a committee, headed by the director of the mental health section of the Student Infirmary, Clifford Reifler, to consider steps to try to anticipate such problems and if possible to intervene to prevent them. George Welsh and I both worked with Reifler to consider the best strategies by which to attack these problems. Better training and increased staffing of the residence hall advisory system was a natural first step, and some of our clinical graduate students were recruited as trainers (and as research investigators as well since they were able to use these settings for community mental health research projects).

However, the most promising long-term outcome of this committee's efforts was gaining the administration's support for a program of routine screening of incoming freshmen by means of the MMPI. A crucial aspect of the plan as executed was that the test results on any particular student would remain inaccessible to others on campus for as long as the student was enrolled. (The only exception to this "locked file" procedure would be the appearance of the student at the mental health section in the infirmary, when he or she would take a second MMPI; then the results for that student could be claimed by the clinician and compared to the more recent profile.) There was a strong interest on the part of Reifler, George Welsh, and myself in many aspects of student adjustment to university life and in their subsequent careers. We were able to obtain excellent cooperation from the incoming students with the assurance that nothing they reported on their answer sheets could adversely affect their period of stay on campus or beyond.

The testing of successive cohorts began in 1964 and continued until general student agitation on our campus during the late 1960s stemming from the Vietnam War protests seriously disrupted our testing efforts along with many other university activities. I still have copies of the the flyers handed out during Freshman Orientation Week: "Wreck The MMPI! Answer Randomly!" Prior to such anti-intellectual and highly charged emotional efforts, however, we obtained valid and useful data from several cohorts of incoming students. The incoming class in 1964, for example, was one of the first at UNC-CH to include a substantial number of women students. (Before this time, most women students attended the Women's College in Greensboro [later called UNC-G]; only the nursing students and a few townswomen were among the incoming classes.) Leona and I used the data from the 1964 entering class to compute the college norms for the MMPI that were included in the 1972 revision of the *Handbook*.

Reifler left UNC-CH for a position in the New York State University system and turned these files over to me. Since some of the cohorts were still on campus, I kept the files secured and waited for the appropriate time (and financial support) to explore the questions that we had in mind when the data were collected. That time proved to be longer than I thought, and it was not until the 1980s that I was finally able to obtain the support, both financial and collegial, to follow these young men and women to discover their subsequent careers, at UNC-CH and beyond, and relate the outcomes to the information we obtained from them as entering students (Siegler et al., 1989).

Earl Baughman, in his capacity as director of the clinical program, was approached by administrators of the Umstead State Hospital and the Murdoch Training School, both located thirty miles from Chapel Hill in the small community of Butner, to work out some joint staffing arrangement whereby these institutions could recruit and retain more qualified psychologists. In a proposal that worked out extremely well for both hospitals and our clinical psychology training program, Earl negotiated a contract that enabled us to hire staff psychologists through UNC-CH and share their time and talents between Butner and Chapel Hill. George Baroff was hired to head the service at Murdoch and two additional staff members there also held academic appointments with us. Similarly, William Eichman (who had been a student in the clinical program at Iowa while I was there) was brought in from the Veterans Administration Hospital at Salem, Virginia, to direct the service at Umstead Hospital. One of Eichman's first staff appointments was Paul Fiddleman, a dissertation student of mine who had just left the Army and was looking for a place to settle. Later Eichman brought in Lynn Lubker, also from the staff at Salem VAH, and a former undergraduate advisee of mine at Iowa who had obtained his clinical training at the University of Kentucky. The contributions of the various clinicians recruited to our area then and later by these means have been an important factor in the growth of the UNC-CH clinical program to its present national stature. Their classroom teaching and their field supervision for our clinical trainees over the years have provided our students with real-world skills and acumen. They have also provided access to research populations that we would not otherwise have been able to give our students.

In 1965 a maverick United States congressman from New Jersey, Cornelius Gallagher, started a witch-hunt against the use of personality tests in screening applicants for various federal agencies, on the basis that the tests constituted an unwarranted invasion of privacy and were probably unconstitutional. He held headline-grabbing hearings and caught the attention of television network news-casters. Quickly, our senator from North Carolina, Sam Ervin, countered with a subcommittee of his own and scheduled a similar series of hearings in Washington. George Welsh, Earl Baughman, and I prepared a statement for the Ervin Committee. We were asked to send someone to appear before the Senate hearings, and I agreed to go to Washington in June 1965 to present our position in defense of the appropriate use of these procedures in screening for emotional fitness for positions with special duties involving high levels of stress or risk. At first, we were apprehensive that our North Carolina senator had joined forces with those attacking the professional use of such psychological instruments, but it gradually became clear that Senator Ervin had moved to limit Representative Gallagher's damage to these methods of screening and evaluation. In the end, no restrictive legislation was enacted; various national security agencies, the State Department, the Peace Corps, NASA, and the military were able to continue to employ the MMPI in their programs. It was an interesting and informative lesson in the complexities of the legislative process (Brayfield, 1965).

A Year at the Menninger Foundation

While on the Mental Health Study Section, I had become close friends with many of its members. One was Philip Holzman, at that time on the staff of the Menninger Foundation. From him, I learned a great deal about the various training, treatment, and research programs there and at the associated hospitals and clinics. During that period we reviewed a research proposal from Menninger designed to complete their long-running research project comparing psychoanalytic treatment with dynamic psychotherapy. After participating in that site visit to Topeka, I realized that it would be an ideal place to spend a sabbatical year. Although UNC-CH had always had very limited funds to provide leaves for its faculty, I was able to get support through a senior postdoctoral fellowship from NIMH and could accept an invitation from Holzman to spend the academic year 1967–68 there.

By this time, George Welsh had little interest any longer in continuing to work on a revision of the *MMPI Handbook*; his research had shifted almost entirely to the assessment of creative potentiality. (In this area, of course, he did continue to employ the MMPI and later developed research scales not only for the MMPI but for the CPI, SVIB, and ACL as well, all measuring the attributes of intellectence and origence.) Therefore, it fell to Leona and me to update this book (and later the *Basic Readings* volume as well) and try to cover the ever-expanding literature on the MMPI. Since this was to be our primary involvement while on leave at the Menninger Foundation, we took our growing collection of reprints with us to Topeka.

Although it was not an ideal time for Amy and Eric to change schools (she was about to enter junior high school and he was starting the fifth grade), they reluctantly agreed that it might be an interesting challenge for a while. Both fared well in the Topeka school system and made many friends in the neighborhood, although as the year went by they talked with increasing frequency about getting back to Chapel Hill and their old friends. Their teachers commented to us on their glowing descriptions of our southern paradise, and told us that many of their other students were ready to move back with us.

In addition to the MMPI materials, we brought with us to Topeka the page proofs of the volume that Earl and I were completing on the Orange County school project. Indexing that book took our first few weeks at the foundation but it was soon off to the printer. An interesting problem was posed for Earl and me in deciding on its title: the term *Negro* had assumed quite general usage at that time in scientific writings about individuals in our country who have African-American origins, but the term *black* was rapidly gaining greater acceptance. We decided to stay with the older terminology (*Negro and White School Children: A Psychological Study in the Rural South*, 1968), but the cultural changes in the United States soon made our title outdated. This work covered a wide variety of topics on the abilities and personalities of the children we had studied. When it appeared from the Academic Press, it won the Anisfield-Wolfe Award for the best contribution of the year to race relations.

At the foundation, we were provided a very comfortable office in the research laboratory building (later named in honor of Gardner Murphy) and were soon at work rewriting the *MMPI Handbook*. Covering the recent literature was facilitated by the detailed discussions we had with staff members and postdoctoral fellows in a special MMPI seminar that Phil Holzman organized for us. (The proximity of the laboratory building to the excellent library maintained by the foundation also helped immensely.) Many of the other offices in our building were occupied by research psychologists and psychiatrists. Midmorning refreshments were delivered to the building every day, and lively ongoing discussions with the other investigators soon developed over coffee. It was in many respects an ideal intellectual environment; only the absence of graduate students and the lack of weekend research activities kept it from reflecting a truly university atmosphere. We made a good start on the revision of the *Handbook,* which eventually filled two volumes.

The NIMH fellowship was adequate to provide support for the summer of 1968 and we moved from Topeka to Berkeley over the protests of two homesick children. I hoped to become familiar with the procedures of both an intensive clinical assessment like that at Menninger and an extensive research assessment like the one employed by the staff at the Institute of Personality Assessment and Research (IPAR). The former procedures involved a fixed battery of tests and observations that had been introduced by David Rapaport in the 1940s, and by the time we observed them, an impressive clinical lore had grown around them. Every year postdoctoral fellows in psychology were brought in to master these techniques and absorb the lore. Little individual variation was permitted; even the original forms of the Wechsler-Bellevue were retained to preserve the material, despite the appearance of two revisions of the scale in the intervening years. We found that there was little room for anything new like the MMPI in this battery at Menninger.

The methods of assessment there were in sharp contrast with the procedures we studied at IPAR. At that time, little had been written about the history of this research enterprise and its highly specialized techniques. Many of their investigations, however, had made significant contributions to the interpretive literature of the MMPI, as well as other test instruments. It was good to have the opportunity to learn more about their methods of interviewing, their formal and informal observational procedures, and the ways in which findings on each individual under study were codified and recorded. No new assessments were under way that summer, but the director, Donald MacKinnon, invited us back to participate in a series when we were able to get the necessary funding. (It was not until the academic year 1976–77 that we were able to return to IPAR.)

In December 1967 Raymond Cattell organized a conference at the University of Illinois at Urbana on various personality typologies. We stayed on a country estate just outside town that the university owned. Participants came from around the United States, Europe, and Asia; I roomed for three days with Jeffrey Gray from Oxford. We discussed at length his efforts to combine the growing body of information about the components of the central nervous system and the processes involved in the dynamics of anxiety and conflict. My own paper was later expanded into a chapter for a proposed handbook of personality research methods that Cattell was organizing. Eventually, however, I withdrew it from his volume (after several publication delays) and published it in 1972 as a separate module, with the General Learning Press (Dahlstrom, 1972). In this module, I outlined my views about a neglected area of personality investigations: personality systematics. I believe that this kind of theorizing is basic to all well-developed biological sciences and undergirds their taxonomies and nosologies. As psychologists, I feel we have neglected this kind of endeavor to our detriment. Typologies are still quite out of favor; empirically derived MMPI-based code groups continue to demonstrate the potentialities inherent in these formulations. Paul Meehl's taxon search procedures provide sound ways of starting this sort of investigation.

We returned to Chapel Hill in 1968 to a new building for the Department of Psychology and further writing on the revision of the *Handbook*. Work had been completed on the first volume when in July of 1971 I accepted an invitation to serve as chairman of the department. The work load was heavy: I continued to teach my regular courses, the manuscript for Volume II was demanding long hours of writing and bibliographic organization, and the departmental problems were insistent. We still had some faculty positions on outside funding; university-based support had to be sought to underwrite these staff members. The university had also launched an affirmative action plan and we were eager to obtain some of the new positions made available through minority recruiting. In addition, the mental health services in the state were undergoing reorganization in ways that affected the training arrangements that Earl Baughman had articulated with the administrators at Umstead State Hospital and Murdoch Training School. Careful negotiations were needed to preserve the integrity of the staffing and services that were so integral a part of our clinical training program. Some of these components were relocated intact to other state facilities; for example, George Baroff's Mental Retardation Training Unit was moved to the campus of UNC-CH, along with his part of the state budget. All of these maneuvers helped preserve valuable assets for these hospitals and for our training program; all took time.

For relaxation during these years, I turned to a completely different kind of activity, inspired by what we had seen at auto shows in California during our summer there in 1968: the assembly of a dune buggy. Leona and I took a course in auto mechanics, bought a kit and an old Volkswagen chassis, and began to haunt the local wrecking yards for component parts. Following through the complexities of a wiring net or putting together a roll-bar assembly provided some necessary relief from the administrative headaches of the Psychology Department. The car finally reached a streetworthy level and was licensed for the use of our teenagers.

In the mid-1970s, David Lachar asked Malcolm Gynther and me to serve as consultants to a research project in which he was involved, studying individuals who were found by their physicians to be abusing various prescription drugs. The MMPI had been included in the assessment battery to evaluate the psychological adjustment of these patients. Preliminary analyses had been carried out and consistent differences between white and black abusers had been found. Gynther had begun a series of investigations into the nature of black and white differences on the MMPI, and our data on the eighth-grade students in the Orange County schools had shown patterns similar to those reported by Gynther on high school students in Columbia, South Carolina. After discussions with Lachar, the three of us proposed carrying out a study of community adults of both ethnic backgrounds in order to clarify the implications of racial differences encountered in the polydrug abuse data.

With funding from the larger project, Lachar provided support for three parallel testing efforts to obtain MMPI records from black adult men and women: from central Alabama, from the Piedmont area of North Carolina, and from the metropolitan area of Detroit, Michigan. We were not able to fund a similar effort to obtain data from white community adults. However, James Webb and his student Luther Diehl had conducted a similar testing program in Ohio and West Virginia about the same time that had sampled primarily white adults. Graciously, they permitted us to use their records as a basis for contrasting two contemporary ethnic groups. By means of the two data sets, Lachar and I were able to carry out a number of comparisons involving time changes and cohort differences at the item, scale, and configural level of MMPI analyses. Malcolm Gynther had by this time withdrawn from the project, although he and I wrote a chapter together covering previous MMPI studies on black and white differences and the three of us contributed a second chapter on the general test survey we had conducted. In addition to a review of the relevant literature on black and white differences on the MMPI, a chapter by Leona was included summarizing the available findings on other ethnic minorities in the United States. Kevin Moreland, an advanced clinical graduate student at UNC-CH, carried out many of the analyses for this volume. He also used our findings on the community adults in his own dissertation based on MMPI records from black and white psychiatric patients in Cleveland State Hospital. Those records were part of the data gathered in a large-scale study carried out with the support of federal funds by John Graham (another former student of mine) at Kent State University.

After a long series of delays, the results of these investigations were published in 1986, in a volume from the University of Minnesota Press (*MMPI Patterns of American Minorities*). In a series of multivariate analyses of these data, we were able to demonstrate that the differences we obtained between black and white adult men and women more clearly reflected socioeconomic differences (with black subjects more heavily concentrated in the lower socioeconomic levels) than ethnic or subcultural differences per se. Furthermore, when different sets of norms were used for black and white psychiatric patients, their MMPI scores as bases for diagnosis or personality assessment lost accuracy when compared to the profiles based on the standard (largely white) norms collected by Hathaway and McKinley in the 1930s.

A Year at IPAR

My appointment as chairman had been for a term of five years. At the end of that time I was ready to pass on the responsibilities of that office to John Schopler, a member of the social psychology faculty, and take another leave. I sought support from the Kenan Fund on campus and from the James McKeen Cattell Foundation; both sources enabled me to return to IPAR in Berkeley as a visiting scholar during the academic year 1976–77. IPAR had weathered the period of radical student activism that saw physical confrontations between staff members like Wallace Hall and invading groups of protesters in the halls and offices of the institute. As a result, entrances to IPAR were kept securely locked and all visitors were carefully monitored.

This time Leona and I anticipated serving as interviewers and judges in one or more of their assessment sessions. Again we were disappointed; funding cuts had crippled the operation of the institute. (The year after our stay there, IPAR also lost the building that had been so conducive to their assessment procedures and moved into smaller quarters adjacent to the Psychology Department in Tolman Hall.) I was able to spend time working on their large data archives and preparing for the new courses on adult psychopathology and personality research methods that I was scheduled to teach back at UNC-CH under a reorganized curriculum of the clinical training program. (David Galinsky had taken over direction of our program and we had modified the course offerings to fit into a developmental sequence: child psychopathology, child assessment, and psychotherapy were to be offered to beginning students in the program, followed by adult psychopathology, adult assessment, and research methods in the spring semester.)

The new director at IPAR, Kenneth Craik, instituted in addition to the traditional weekly noontime research colloquia, an informal afternoon session each week during which the staff would take turns discussing their current research ideas and problems. In such contacts, I acquired a new appreciation of Jungian concepts and methods from Ravenna Helson, an introduction to environmental psychology from Craik, and further insights into psychobiographical methods and issues from McKinley Runyan and Gerald Mendelsohn. The latter psychologist had been developing a psychological analysis of Giuseppe Verdi's personality, tying his conclusions to the major operatic themes. Harrison Gough was extending his assessment methods to the study of various population issues such as birth-control practices by couples with different personality patterns. Even without assessment sessions, the year was a busy and productive one. During the holiday break, we had a welcome visit from our son and daughter, both college students, now more eager to revisit Berkeley and San Francisco and the many attractions of the Bay Area.

While I was still at IPAR the issue of invasion of privacy surrounding the use of the MMPI arose once again, this time in a federal suit brought against city officials in Jersey City, New Jersey, for basing appraisal of fitness for jobs on the city fire brigades in part on answers to the MMPI. The plaintiffs were supported by the local chapter of the American Civil Liberties Union. (This was one of the few times I did not agree with the stand of this admirable organization, which I had joined in the 1950s.) I agreed to serve as a witness during the trial in support of the use of the inventory for these purposes, given proper safeguards for the rights of the job applicants. Fire officials gave vivid testimony about the stresses involved in duty in these brigades (particularly during large-scale riots, during which the firemen were exposed to gunfire as well as the usual conflagrations). They also documented instances in which recruits panicked and froze tightly to their ladders twelve or fifteen stories up. They believed that susceptibility to emotional breakdowns under circumstances of this kind should disqualify applicants for these jobs. The city officials seemed to me to be seeking appropriate help in such screening when they employed an independent agency to administer a battery of psychological instruments, including the MMPI, to their trainees and job applicants, from which they would make individual recommendations about their emotional stability and freedom from psychopathology. No city official saw any of the individual answers to the MMPI items or specific responses to the Rorschach or other tests. This agency also included an appeal mechanism by means of which an unsuccessful candidate could request a review of the test findings and further screening by a qualified psychiatrist. The trial was held during the summer of 1977. The outcome was favorable to this circumspect use of the MMPI. The judge ruled in favor of the Jersey City officials: no violation of the constitutional rights of the applicants was involved.

New Interests

In 1980, Pieter Bierkens, a Dutch psychologist we had come to know through the MMPI seminar at the Menninger Foundation, invited us to attend a conference on psychosomatic disorders he was planning, to be held in the spring of 1981 in Nijmegen at the Catholic University. Our plans for the meetings, and for travel in Europe afterward, were well under way when we learned that the conference had had to be canceled. Leona and I decided to go to Europe as planned to try to locate and visit sites where meaningful MMPI research was being carried out. Our travels turned out to be extensive and our views of MMPI-based work broadened immeasurably. We visited centers and talked informally with psychologists in Brussels, Groningen, Glostrup (near Copenhagen), Oslo, Bergen, Uppsala, and Turku. I was invited to give colloquia at the Universities of Nijmegen in the Netherlands, Copenhagen in Denmark, Louvain in Belgium, and Helsinki in Finland. Everywhere, the MMPI (in translation) was in use, usually based on Minnesota norms and employing the standard profile scales. However, it was rare that psychologists in one area were familiar with similar efforts in other countries, even though many of their publications were in English. (In this respect, research in Europe resembled the situation that we found in Japan in 1979 while at a conference held in Kyoto: investigators working in isolation from one another in different university centers without significant sharing or communication with one another. In some ways the situation in Japan was worse, since each major professor had typically carried out independent translations of the MMPI without comparing their versions. In 1979, Leona and I had also attended a conference in Krakow, Poland, on the assessment of suicidal risk. There, too, psychologists from around Europe working on problems within this one area of concentration were just starting to share experiences with the application of the MMPI.)

In my presentations in Europe I focused on the use of the test as a means of evaluating the outcomes of various kinds of treatment interventions. I had organized this literature for a chapter in a publication edited by M. B. Parloff and Irene Waskow (published by NIMH in 1975) that was intended to bring a consensus to the test batteries employed in outcome research by investigators funded by that agency. It was enlightening to me to realize how often European users of the test had restricted their MMPI applications to intake assessments only. The data I presented on the kinds and amount of change reflected in MMPI scores seemed quite surprising to many of the investigators.

At these meetings we spent much time telling research workers in one place about findings from other centers. We also talked about the possibility of a European conference on the MMPI to take place soon. In the summer of 1983, when such a conference was held in Glostrup, Denmark, many of the psychologists we had met in 1981 attended and made presentations of their work.

Early in the 1980s I began a collaboration with John Barefoot, then a part-time faculty member in our social psychology program, and Redford Williams, a cardiologist in the Department of Psychiatry at Duke University. Using first the MMPI records from the various classes of medical students at UNC-CH that I had tested in the mid-1950s, and later the law student cohort as well, we worked out a method of locating these physicians and lawyers, all of whom were male, to discover their current health status, if still alive, or the cause of their deaths, if deceased. Based on earlier studies at Duke of MMPI records from patients with coronary artery disease (CAD), Barefoot and Williams had identified the Cook and Medley Hostility (Ho) scale from the MMPI as a sensitive measure of the anger and hostility component in the classic Type A personality pattern. Accordingly, the Ho scale was expected to be a predictor of CAD or other cardiovascular diseases as causes of premature death in these professional men, who would be by that time in their mid-forties or older.

The results were quite startling. The men who scored high on Ho when they were students in medical or law school were more likely either to have died of some circulatory disorder or to be currently suffering from such a condition. Generally, the higher their Ho score, the higher the probability of their premature death from any cause, but particularly from CAD. That is, a personality measure derived by Walter Cook and his student D. M. Medley at the University of Minnesota School of Education, based on observations of the performance of student teachers in their first efforts at classroom teaching, turned out to be related to the kinds of hostile reactions physicians and lawyers may show that can damage their circulatory systems.

The consistency of these results encouraged Redford Williams and his colleagues to include a project on the implications of the Ho scale in a large program grant proposal that was submitted to the National Institute of Heart and Lung Diseases, based on data from the mid-1960s testing of entering freshmen at UNC-CH initiated by the Reifler Committee. At last we would be able to fulfill many of the ambitions of the committee by locating these former students and studying their careers both while at Chapel Hill and after they left campus. These investigations are still under way and are called the UNC Alumni Heart Study. Under the direction of Ilene Siegler at Duke University, a series of efforts to find these men and women was instigated. We have been successful in enrolling more than 5,000 of the approximately 7,000 originally tested, and we are still searching. One of the inducements that we were able to employ was the promise of a donation to the Carolina Alumni Association in the name of the graduating class with the largest percentage enrollment in the follow-up study. Another was a drawing from the names of those enrolled to determine the winner of a trip for two to Hawaii (or a comparable trip if the winner was already living in Hawaii!). Both of these awards were funded from private sources in the Behavioral Medicine Research Center (BMRC) at Duke under the control of Redford Williams.

Other research investigators at the BMRC have also been following up the implications of the Ho scale scores by designing studies to try to establish the linkages between personality style and cardiovascular physiology, biochemistry, and vascular pathology. Still others have been designing and testing intervention programs to try to alter the psychodynamics of anger and hostility. The consistency of the patterns of response over time has proven to be impressive and a real challenge to efforts to reduce risk of these disorders through behavioral change. At the interpersonal level, research is under way to further our understanding of the relation of Ho scores to life stresses and to any deleterious effect hostility patterns may have on an individual's social relationships.

The Restandardization of the MMPI

In a preface written for the 1972 *MMPI Handbook,* as well as in a paper given at a conference organized in 1971 by James Butcher on the future of the MMPI, Starke Hathaway noted the lack of substantial progress in the field of assessment of psychopathology and in the MMPI itself. He had just retired from the faculty of the University of Minnesota and was quite pessimistic that nearly forty years had passed without substantial change in assessment methods. Others at the conference debated the virtues of a total revision of the MMPI versus a restandardization of the norms on which the component scales had been based. (My own suggestions there focused on the desirability of separating measures of personological predisposition to various forms of psychopathology from measures of the pathological states an individual may be manifesting at any given time.)

After that conference, proposals for updating the inventory were debated at other meetings and conferences. However, it was not until the contractural agreements between the copyright holder (the University of Minnesota) and the test publisher and distributor (The Psychologcial Corporation) were canceled and the university made new and more favorable arrangements for distribution with National Computer Systems (NCS) that more concrete plans could be made. The University of Minnesota Press was named to act for the university, and John Ervin, director of the press, formed a committee of those interested in and knowledgeable about the MMPI to discuss its future. In addition to Hathaway, two of his longtime colleagues, Paul Meehl and William Schofield, were added to this group. Two others from the University of Minnesota, Norman Garmezy, professor of psychology, and Beverly Kaemmer, senior editor at the press, were also on this committee. Leona and I were asked to participate.

At a meeting called by Ervin in the summer of 1981 it was quickly conceded that The Psychological Corporation had delayed far too long in initiating any effort to update the instrument. It was less apparent, however, just how extensive the repairs should be. New diagnostic standards for psychiatric nosology had been introduced into psychiatric practice with the publication of the American Psychiatric Association's *Diagnostic and Statistical Manual—III.* However, there were still serious reservations about the reliability with which this nosological schema would actually be employed in psychiatric services around the country. Finally, it was proposed that an effort to restandardize and modernize the MMPI short of a total revision be carried out through the University of Minnesota Press. Beverly Kaemmer was given the responsibility of organizing a working committee for the restandardization project and of negotiating the needed contributions for this work from NCS.

Initially, the Restandardization Committee was comprised of James Butcher at Minnesota, John Graham at Kent State University, Beverly Kaemmer, and me. Somewhat later, Auke Tellegen, a psychometric specialist at the University of Minnesota, was added to this group. We issued appeals to individuals around the country who were knowledgeable about the MMPI to offer suggestions about the work to be done, as well as about any alterations or additions to the test items. At working sessions in Minneapolis, all members of the committee contributed to the changes needed in the test items and to additions to the item pool, resulting in two experimental test booklets: the AX (adult experimental) version and the TX (teenage experimental) booklet. We also designed research forms to obtain background information on the subjects to be drawn from communities around the country, as well as to gather data on any life changes or other experiences that might have affected their emotional status during the six months prior to their being tested. We established the levels of fees to be offered to the participants and added a sampling feature to include couples, married (or living together) for at least a year. Each member of a couple would take the MMPI and provide us with information about the personality characteristics of his or her partner and about the nature of their relationship and degree of satisfaction experienced from it. All of the forms for the restandardization project were designed to be machine-read and recorded by computers.

With so much of the data processing automated, we anticipated a rather short interval between our data-gathering efforts and the publication of the new norms. Our early optimism was quickly dashed. Due to glitches in the various testing efforts around the country, the information from the test forms and answer sheets had to be very carefully scrutinized and painstakingly corrected. Tedious work with the help of graduate research assistants at Chapel Hill was required to iron out inconsistencies and omissions that could have been largely avoided by more careful examination of the materials at the time of the original testing sessions. Some omissions or contradictions could occasionally be reconciled by comparisons across forms or from data provided by a rating partner, but in some cases the whole array of data on a subject was lost through such crucial oversights. In addition, some MMPI records were apparently answered on a completely random basis in callous disregard for the purposes of the investigation. From the approximately 2,900 people tested nationwide, 2,600 valid records with adequate background information were obtained. These data formed the normative base for MMPI-2.

In addition to these delays, there were occasional disagreements about substantive issues in regard to the inventory itself. While most of these differences in point of view were worked through under the cool and steady guidance of Beverly Kaemmer, a few were never resolved to any satisfactory degree. One of these was the decision to include data on the subtle and obvious components of scales 2 (D), 3 (Hy), 4 (Pd), 6 (Pa), and 9 (Ma). Daniel Wiener and Lindsey Harmon had introduced these subscales back in the 1940s; many clinicians using the MMPI had built up a great store of clinical lore about these components in their practices. However, relatively little material had been published about extra-test correlates of the subscales on which to base an evaluation of their clinical utility. Nevertheless, it seemed to me that it would be a disservice to longtime users of the MMPI if they could not obtain scoring materials, norms, and profiles for use with these subscales. The decision was made to provide these materials to MMPI users but not to include the components in the routine scoring service for the MMPI-2.

However, during the discussions of the committee, it became clear that the major reservations about interpretive reliance on subtle subscales were the doubts their use cast on content interpretation of the test. Based as they are on the assumption that by means of subtle scales, test subjects are very indirectly revealing some quite significant aspects of their personalities and emotional states, their use runs counter to reliance on critical items and content scales. If the actual psychological significance of some endorsement of an item, or set of items, lies well outside the specific content of the statements themselves, then serious doubt is cast on the ability of the psychologist to determine what is actually going on with the client or patient from an examination of the content of the items that he or she answers when completing the test. Hathaway's empirical scale construction approach had been based on his serious skepticism about the capabilities of clinicians to do this kind of content interpretation. As indicated in the *MMPI-2 Manual,* the issue about subtle and obvious subscale scores was never fully resolved within the committee.

After most of the disagreements among the committee members had been worked through, it was with great relief that the work of the group finally appeared in the form of the restandardized MMPI-2 at the APA convention in New Orleans in the summer of 1989. Further work on the data from the restandardization has been published separately as monographs and supplements to the *MMPI-2 Manual.* There have been continuing efforts to gain some degree of unanimity from the group in these various publications. Some of the same members of the original Restandardization Committee have continued to work on the teenage version (MMPI-A).

Later Developments

In 1987, I was promoted to Kenan Professor of Psychology at UNC-CH, an honor that carried with it the advantage of additional research funds. That year I was also given the Eugene Hargrove Award by the North Carolina Mental Health Foundation for advancing the cause of mental health practice in the state. Many of my sixty dissertation students had taken positions in state mental health agencies as well as in the Departments of Psychology and Psychiatry. It was a particular pleasure to receive this honor in Eugene Hargrove's name. He was an early member of the faculty of the Department of Psychiatry at UNC-CH while I was still director of psychological services there. He had introduced training in short-term psychotherapy by medical students who were on rotation through the psychiatry service, and we had collaborated in the use of the MMPI to assess the outcomes from the student treatment efforts. He had continued to introduce a variety of innovative procedures in mental health services around the state after he became commissioner of mental health for North Carolina.

In 1991, I was named a co-winner (with Joseph Matarazzo) of an award from the Board of Professional Affairs of the APA for distinguished professional contributions to knowledge. I am now close to retirement but I plan to continue teaching until 1993. However, after that time I will be working on a manuscript on personality systematics and taking more time for travel. We will also be visiting more frequently with Amy, who has become a linguist specializing in American Indian languages, and Eric, who is an aerospace engineer.

Some Final Thoughts

While in Uppsala in 1981, I made a special point of visiting the university library's memorial to Carolus Linnaeus, the famous systematist. His heroic efforts to develop a taxonomy provided a preliminary biological framework within which the research efforts of thousands of separate investigators in botany and zoology could be brought into a collaborative synthesis. Their work, in turn, has made it possible for microbiologists and biochemists to elaborate the unifying details of genetic structures and processes that are bringing a rush of advances to many different fields, including neurobiology. Ever since I read Ross Ashby's *Design for a Brain* (1952), around which I built my course in neuropsychology, I have had a growing appreciation for the role of taxonomies and systematics in furthering a given scientific endeavor, or in impeding progress when they have been lacking.

Psychologists have struggled to obtain basic consistencies and replicable findings without first establishing such a foundation in their study of human behavior. Methods of studying fully functioning, intact systems, like those of the human personality, are quite different from the ways that easily disassembled structures are investigated. As I tried to make clear in a chapter for the *Festschrift* volume in honor of Paul Meehl (1991), early efforts in psychology have tried to emulate methods in the ahistorical sciences (physics and chemistry) rather than in the less prestigious but more comparable sciences (astronomy, geology, evolutionary biology) that focus on historical, divergent processes and outcomes. When psychological research has finally generated its own area of systematics, and erected a framework of comparable elegance, our field will be ready to profit from these biological advances as well. Nosologies of emotional disorders, new methods of personological assessment, as well as more effective techniques of ameliorative intervention will all follow. Lacking such overarching schemas to integrate our diverse lines of research, workers in our field will continue to struggle to make sense out of a welter of separate endeavors.

Organizing the discrete findings in the rapidly expanding MMPI research literature over several decades into our *MMPI Handbooks* was an absorbing task. (My dune buggy was the largest three-dimensional jigsaw puzzle I had ever attempted; assembly of the MMPI literature was a cognitive jigsaw puzzle of comparable complexity.) It seems clear now, however, that the end results of such a synthesis would have been infinitely more consequential had an underlying research structure been in place when these diverse lines of investigation were carried out. Psychologists in the future should face the challenge of developing our own systematics and the taxonomic framework on which it can rest. Meehl's recent publications in which he has devised the strategies and methodologies needed for such research have paved the way for those psychologists who are mathematically and statistically sophisticated enough to capitalize on his efforts. I believe that such work would soon reveal that human personalities fall into quite diverse typological groups, each with its own characteristic modes of responding to particular circumstances. Study of representatives of each taxon might well yield response consistencies when approached from the perspective of Ashby's fully joined systems. In anticipation of these exciting payoffs, I am convinced that I entered psychology fifty years too soon.

References

Abse, D. W., Curtis, T. E., Dahlstrom, W. G., Hawkins, D. R., & Toops, T. C. (1956). The use of reserpine in the management of acute mental disturbance on an in-patient service: Preliminary report. *Journal of Nervous and Mental Disease, 124,* 239–247.

Abse, D. W., & Dahlstrom, W. G. (1960). The value of chemotherapy in senile mental disturbance: A controlled comparison of chlopromazine, reserpine-pipradrol, and opium. *Journal of the American Medical Association, 174,* 2036–2042.

Abse, D. W., Dahlstrom, W. G., & Tolley, A. G., (1960). Evaluation of tranquilizing drugs in the management of acute mental disturbance. *American Journal of Psychiatry, 116,* 973–980.

Ashby, W. R. (1952). *Design for a brain.* New York: Wiley.

Barefoot, J. C., Dahlstrom, W. G., & Williams, R. B. (1983). Hostility, CHD incidence, and total morality: A 25-year follow-up study of 255 physicians. *Psychosomatic Medicine, 45,* 59–63.

Barefoot, J. C., Dodge, K. A., Peterson, B. L., Dahlstrom, W. G., & Williams, R. B. (1989). The Cook-Medley Hostility scale: Item content and ability to predict survival. *Psychosomatic Medicine, 51,* 46–57.

Barefoot, J. C., Smith, R. H., Dahlstrom, W. G., & Williams, R. B. (1989). Personality predictors of smoking behavior in a sample of physicians. *Psychology and Health, 3,* 37–43.

Baughman, E. E., & Dahlstrom, W. G. (1968). *Negro and white school children: A psychological study in the rural South.* New York: Academic Press.

Block, J. (1965). *The challenge of response sets.* New York: Appleton-Century-Crofts.

Brayfield, A. H. (Ed.). (1965). Testing and public policy [Special issue]. *American Psychologist, 20,* 857–1005.

Butcher, J. N., Dahlstrom, W. G., Graham, J. R., Tellegen, A., & Kaemmer, B. (1989). *Manual for MMPI-2.* Minneapolis: University of Minnesota Press.

Clapesattle, H. (1941). *The Doctors Mayo.* Minneapolis: University of Minnesota Press.

Crafts, L. W., & Schneirla, T. C. (1938). *Recent experiments in psychology.* New York: McGraw-Hill.

Dahlstrom, W. G. (1960).The roles of social desirability and acquiescence in responses to the MMPI. In S. Messick & J. Ross (Eds.), *Measurement in personality and cognition* (pp. 157–168). New York: Wiley.

Dahlstrom, W. G. (1972). *Personality systematics and the problem of types.* Morristown, NJ: General Learning Press.

Dahlstrom, W. G. (1975). Recommendations for patient measures in evaluating psychotherapy: Test batteries and inventories. In M. B. Parloff & I. E. Waskow (Eds.), *Psychotherapy change measures: Report of Clinical Research Branch, NIMH Outcome Measures Project* (pp. 14–31). Washington, DC: U.S. Government Printing Office.

Dahlstrom, W. G. (1991). Psychology as an historical science: Meehl's efforts to disentangle science B from science A. In D. Ciccheti & W. M. Grove (Eds.), *Thinking clearly about psychology.* (Vol. 1) Essays in honor of Paul. E. Meehl (pp. 40–60). Minneapolis: University of Minnesota Press.

Dahlstrom, W. G., & Dahlstrom, L. E. (Eds.). (1980). *Basic readings on the MMPI: A new selection on personality measurement.* Minneapolis: University of Minnesota Press.

Dahlstrom, W. G., Lachar, D., & Dahlstrom, L. E. (1986). *MMPI patterns of American minorities.* Minneapolis: University of Minnesota Press.

Dahlstrom, W. G., & Welsh, G. S. (1960). *An MMPI handbook: A guide to use in clinical practice and research.* Minneapolis: University of Minnesota Press.

Dahlstrom, W. G., Welsh, G. S., & Dahlstrom, L. E. (1972). *An MMPI handbook.* Volume I: *Clinical interpretation.* Minneapolis: University of Minnesota Press.

Dahlstrom, W. G., Welsh, G. S., & Dahlstrom, L. E. (1975). *An MMPI handbook.* Volume II: *Research applications.* Minneapolis: University of Minnesota Press.

Dunlap, Knight. (1936). *Elements of psychology.* St. Louis: Mosby.

Goodstein, L. D., Spielberger, C. D., Williams, J. E., & Dahlstrom, W. G. (1955). The effects of serial position and design difficulty on recall of the Bender-Gestalt test designs. *Journal of Consulting Psychology, 19,* 230–234.

Meehl, P. E., & Dahlstrom, W. G. (1960). Objective configural rules for discriminating psychotic from neurotic MMPI profiles. *Journal of Consulting Psychology, 24,* 375–387.

Siegler, I.C., Peterson, B. L., Kaplan, B. H., Dahlstrom, W. G., Harvin, S. H., Barefoot, J. C., Wing, S. B., & Williams, R. B. (1989). Hostility as a predictor of findability, locatability, and participation in the UNC Alumni Heart Study. *American Journal of Epidemiology, 130,* 802–803.

Spielberger, C. D., Goodstein, L. D., & Dahlstrom, W. G. (1958). Complex incidental learning as a function of anxiety and task difficulty. *Journal of Experimental Psychology, 56,* 58–61.

Welsh, G. S., & Dahlstrom, W. G. (Eds.). (1956). *Basic readings on the MMPI in psychology and medicine.* Minneapolis: University of Minnesota Press.

Robert R. Holt

Professor of Psychology Emeritus
New York University

◆

An Exploratory Study of Life: Progress Report

Childhood

With the help of one of my psychoanalysts, I figured out that I became a psychologist in the hope of understanding my mother and my difficult relationship with her. A talented singer with an extraordinary, three-octave (soprano *and* alto) voice, she also had the good looks and acting ability to have become an opera singer. In her early twenties, she won a national singing contest with a trip to New York to try out for a Broadway musical, but had to return crestfallen to her native city, Jacksonville, Florida, because of uncontrolled epileptic seizures. There she followed a much more modest musical career for much of the rest of her life.

Gracie (as people called my mother) had a histrionic, gaudy sort of personal style, which many people—especially men—found charming. To me and my beloved sister, Dorothy, a year and a half my elder, it was extremely trying. Despite her gushing, exaggerated declarations that she adored us, we never felt that she really cared very deeply for her children or anyone else. Here is the first and central one of many paradoxes that made her so hard to understand. Frequently sick with various psychosomatic afflictions, Mother appeared fragile, yet survived her second and third husbands and lived to her early eighties. She often drove us wild with naive and apparently stupid declarations (Mother rarely just *said* anything), yet she proved herself capable of managing a household of five efficiently and of doubling her inheritance by shrewd investments when she was first widowed.

She married shortly after dropping out of college and the singing contest fiasco. My parents were temperamentally quite unsuited to one another. Walter J. Watson, my father, an easygoing man just a few years older than she, came to Jacksonville with his mother and photographer-father from Illinois at an early age and went no further than through high school. (I never met either of his parents and know very little of his family.) He entered his father-in-law's laundry business, which he continued to run most of the rest of his life. Mother had ambitions to rise in the class hierarchy; she found Daddy somewhat coarse and uneducated, satisfied just to read his paper, listen to the radio, and go to bed early after dinner, while she longed for travel, romance, and the "finer things" of life—music, the theater, and art.

So the marriage failed, but not until she had given birth to Dorothy, to me (on December 27, 1917), and then to a stillborn brother. Despite heavy doses of barbiturates, her seizures became uncontrollable, and when I was about 3 she had what was discreetly called a nervous breakdown and went north to Johns Hopkins for treatment. That did succeed in getting her out of the marriage. While she was away, and until she remarried, we lived in the house of my paternal grandparents, Thomas and Elizabeth Hilditch.

My earliest memories are of life with my sister in that house. There seems to have been very little rivalry between us; at least, all my memories of playing with her are pleasant. I recall ecstatic feelings of joy in riding my tricycle, in exploring a volunteer tomato plant under an ornamental palm in our front yard, and on finding snowbanks of white lilies growing in a burnt-over field accompanied by my beloved black nurse, Sharlie. Actually, she took care of me as only one of many duties, which included cooking, cleaning, and laundry.

Two unpleasant memories also stand out. For a while, I had a little garden of my own in our back yard, where I grew radishes and carrots for Mother. Then one day some city workers came, tore down our side fence, dug up my garden, and proceeded to construct a sidewalk where it had been. I was so outraged that I furiously attacked them, and Momma (my grandmother) made me stand in a corner with my face to the wall as punishment. I had other playmates besides my sister, including a little neighbor girl named Marie. One day, she and I were discovered in a dirty-clothes hamper busily exploring one another's genitals. I was dragged out and made to feel guilty. Shortly thereafter, Mother and a local doctor agreed that this abnormal and disgusting behavior must have been caused by penile irritation, and so I was circumcised. Mother assuaged my crying on the car ride home by giving me a new book. This "therapy" worked: for many years afterward, I was very shy with girls, sexually inhibited, and took refuge in books.

I can still feel a somewhat ego-alien identification with my strong-minded, prim, and proper grandmother. Born and raised in New Jersey, she never adopted southern ways of speech, and I can only conclude that her influence (and that of her mother) may be responsible for the fact that after I left Jacksonville I retained few traces of a southern accent. She had a strong interest in language, which she probably transmitted to me; she paid particular attention to the proper pronunciation and spelling of words, as Mother did also to a lesser extent.

In the Jacksonville of my childhood, even lower middle class families could afford a servant like Sharlie, since Negro women would work long hours for extremely little money. It was a time of total segregation, of an extreme racism taken wholly for granted. Once, when I was about 6, I made some comment about "that lady," pointing to a black woman on the street, and was verbally chastised for using the work *lady* in reference to a "Nigra woman." By doing so, my stepfather sternly told me, I had insulted my mother. That seemed almost as absurd to me then as it does now. The only reason I and my sister could ever discover for our failure to absorb our parents' prejudices is that Sharlie and other black women who took care of us were genuinely and directly affectionate and warmly accepted our love, while Mother was often away or locked up in what today I would call narcissistic emotional unavailability. For whatever reason, we were at odds with our family about the injustices routinely meted out to blacks and the constant indignities to which they were subjected.

When I was 5, Mother married again. I was initially opposed, but soon came to like my new father. A bachelor well over 40, he was the son of a railway clerk who had run away in his youth with the daughter of an affluent Georgia plantation owner. Dad (as I called him to distinguish him from my father, Daddy) had dropped out of high school before graduating to help support the family. As a young man, he read law at night, passed the bar examination, and became a lawyer. Despite his lack of formal education, he read a lot, had an impressive store of all kinds of information, and respected intellectual achievement. He was an active citizen who became president of the Kiwanis Club and devoted a good deal of time to philanthropic activity. He formally adopted me and had my name legally changed from Watson to Holt. I have no memory of any particular reaction to that event.

Because of a divorce settlement that today seems extraordinary, I had remained with Mother while Daddy got custody of my sister, who went to live with an aunt until he found a second wife. For about ten years, I would go perhaps once or twice a month to visit them and play with her. He was emotionally remote enough so that I remained in contact primarily with Dorothy.

In 1923, then, we moved to a three-story white frame house where Francis Michael (Frank) Holt lived with his mother, father (Pop), and older sister, who became my Aunt Fannie. I became good friends with a boy who lived next door, and at one time we had a string telephone between our bedrooms, with tin cans for receiver/transmitters. The best thing about the house was its large side yard with flowering shrubs and big back yard with a climbable and deliciously bearing fig tree, scrawny peach trees, and Pop's flower and vegetable garden. There was also a garage and a small woodshed, where I cut kindling from fatwood for the big old woodstove on which my new Grandma did the family cooking.

It was during this period of my childhood that I first became aware of entoptic and similar phenomena. Once, sitting on the toilet in an unlighted closetlike room, I noticed that the crack of light by the door was doubled if I looked in a certain way.

Playing with that discovery, I learned to diverge and converge my eyes at will and to notice double images. From that I proceeded to pay attention to floaters when looking at the sky, to pressure phosphenes, and other visual oddities. Only years later, when I turned my research attention to forms of imagery, did I think to mention these experiences to anyone (Holt 1964; 1972a).

Mother's parents were Episcopalians, but she was never a devout believer and was happy enough to switch to Frank's church, the Presbyterian, when she married him. I was therefore sent to the Sunday school of the First Presbyterian Church, right next to the public library. I went pretty regularly every Sunday, learning a good many of the Bible stories and some of the elements of Presbyterian dogma. I recall being particularly fascinated by the notion of predestination, which seemed so much at odds with the free will we were otherwise assured we have and which therefore puts on us the burden of choice between good and evil. (That is doubtless the source of my continuing interest in the problem of free will; Holt, 1967a, 1984a.) Doubts about such doctrinal contradictions drove me, by the time of puberty, to a brief flirtation with the Episcopal church, to which my Aunt Fannie belonged. The more confirmation classes I attended, the more preposterous the dogma unfolded there seemed to me, and shortly after being admitted to membership, I gave up religion entirely.

The greatest event of this period of my life took place near its end, in 1926. That summer, Mother, Dad, Grandma Holt, and I went on an extended train trip north. First stop was Philadelphia, where I attended the sesquicentennial exposition while Dad underwent a successful operation for bladder cancer. Then we went on to New York, Boston, and (by ship) to Nova Scotia, where we stayed for several weeks. Much of it was in a country inn in Smith's Cove, right by the shore where I could observe the extraordinary tides coming in. Mother, Dad, and I also took a week's canoe trip into the unspoiled wild interior with two half-Indian guides. That was the high point not only of the summer but my entire childhood. I had learned to paddle at Aunt Fannie's camp; now I was entrusted with the bow paddle of one birchbark canoe. Our guides taught me all kinds of woodlore; we ate fish we had caught and cooked over a campfire, picked wild blueberries, saw moose and other wild animals, slept in bedrolls on balsam boughs, and were immersed in an unforgettably beautiful wilderness.

The big event of the next year, 1927, was building our new house and moving. Dad, by now a partner in the successful law firm of Marks, Marks, and Holt, hired an architect who produced a prizewinning design. I didn't realize it at the time, but the move gave concrete evidence of the fact that the family was moving up in the socioeconomic scale. The old neighborhood was lower middle class, this one (called Avondale) was distinctly upper. Now we lived closer to Dad's business friends, some of whom were wealthy. Dad joined the country club and the yacht club, eventually attaining leadership positions in them.

Yet a couple of years after our move the Great Depression hit; for a while Dad feared that he would not be able to make payments on the house and would lose it. Those were anxious times. Generally Dad would come home quite late, tired and looking tense, after putting in long hours at the office. I knew that I had to do my part by taking over the effort to build a lawn so that we could give up our yard man; I was paid ten cents an hour.

We still had one servant, a dear black woman named Ella Mack. She did everything for us except the grocery shopping, for Mother couldn't cook and was too busy with her musical career to do housework or hand laundry. Ella was paid only a little more than I was: $10 per week plus carfare for about 75 hours of work. She is another of the black women to whom I feel I owe a great deal. Sometimes, when I was hanging around the kitchen, she would tell me stories of how she was mistreated by police or bus drivers, her voice full of righteous indignation. She did a lot to instill in me a passion for social justice and an empathy for the oppressed.

In the summer, we always visited Aunt Fannie's camp for girls in Brevard, North Carolina, among the cool Blue Ridge Mountains. I spent anywhere from a weekend to a full summer there over a decade, ending up as nature counselor when I was 15. I got to know every part of the woodland acres belonging to Camp Keystone, specializing in trees and nonflowering plants (for example, ferns and mushrooms). That summer of 1932 I tried to learn to smoke a pipe, ending up so violently sick that I easily gave tobacco up for life. In the Boy Scouts, I had learned how to cook over a campfire and had had my first nights of sleeping in a tent in the wild. Now I polished my skills; amazed to find on one overnight hike that not one of the girls knew how to make a meal, I took over with success and began a lifelong hobby.

Aunt Fannie, who never married, lived for that camp and made a modest success of it. Now that I was a six-foot teenager, she arranged a trade with another camp owner in western North Carolina: she took in his daughter for the cash-scarce summer of 1933 and I had the full season at Camp Mondamin. There I found the first of a series of father substitutes in the nature counselor; I learned wood carving and photography, which became my hobbies; I went on overnight horseback trips; and I got an intoxicating taste of a counterphobic sport, body-surfing in the chilly waters of a rushing mountain river. A sound drubbing in a boxing match made me swear off all contact sports from then on, but I became a confirmed lover of the outdoors, hiking, and wilderness camping. At Keystone and Mondamin I also learned tennis and horseback riding and became a good swimmer, modest skills that gave me a lot of pleasure thereafter.

When I look back on my early years from a clinician's perspective, something strikes me that I never thought about before: they presented me with a constant series of "object losses." Mostly they were deaths, but the most poignant of all was losing my father. A couple of years after the divorce, before she remarried, Mother gave me a couple of children's song books, one Dutch and one Chinese; I can still sing some of those songs, almost seventy years later. One in particular was illustrated by a picture of a Dutch boy sitting on a piling looking wistfully out to sea; the song is his lament that his father has gone off on a voyage. It seemed inexpressibly sad to me, and would bring tears to my eyes whenever I heard or saw it though I have no direct memories of being saddened by the divorce. I believe I was 3 when it occurred.

The deaths started at about the same time: first my great-grandfather, Goldsmith Presberry Hall. He had gone to the Yukon in the Alaskan gold rush, and left us various mementoes of that time—some scrimshaw, a double-barrelled shotgun with a beautifully engraved stock, and letters to Granny telling of his adventures. Alas, all these have disappeared. Then Thomas Hilditch (Poppa), Mother's father, a Liverpudlian who had emigrated as a young man to Florida. I have his spare frame, long neck, and sloping shoulders, and a shadow of his voice, which Mother more fully inherited. He began as a tenor and ended up a bass, singing in many a church choir and barbershop quartet. Mother adored him, and though I have a sense of having loved him, too, I was too young to have known him well before he died. Shortly after, my dear Granny (Hall), a sweet old woman who was devoted to her great-grandchildren, died. When Mother and I moved to the Holt house, I effectively lost Sharlie, though I did see her occasionally. Daddy gave her a job at the laundry, which he took over when Poppa died, and on occasions when I would go to visit him at his office he would take me into the huge steaming room full of mysterious machinery to the sheet-ironing machine she operated. She would give me a hug, pull back to survey me, and slap her thigh while she went in to one of her choked guffaws: "Laws, boy, how you done growed!"

No sooner had I gotten to know Pop Holt, my new Dad's father, and become rather fond of him, but he died too. I was much impressed by his white goatee; he had a moustache too, like Poppa, but he was the first man I knew who had a beard. I decided that when I got to be old—say, 70—I would grow a white beard too, as in fact I have done.

At about the time of Pop's death, my Uncle Tommy died also. He came between Mother's two younger sisters and was her only surviving brother. I didn't know Uncle Tommy very well; I believe that by the time Mother went home to Momma at the breakup of her marriage, he had struck out on his own and had moved to Sarasota. For a short time after Poppa's death, Momma moved to Sarasota too, and I spent at least one summer vacation there with them.

Those few months in Sarasota were repeated a few years later, so again it is hard to sort out the memories. The second time, surprisingly enough, Mother sent me off by myself on the train. I had to change trains in Tampa and could not have been much more than 7. I often had the feeling that she overprotected (or babied) me, but it seems that she was able to let me discover some modicum of self-reliance.

The next death must have come about five years later, after we had already moved to Avondale. There, in our fine new house, Dad's Aunt Mamie spent her last days with us, succumbing to cancer in the bedroom just across the upstairs hall from mine. She had been a sweet, passive, rather ineffectual spinster with whom I had no important relationship. But I still recall the stench of her fatal disease and the uneasiness I felt at having a slow death occur so near to me.

Come to think of it, moving to that house was itself a kind of object loss. I left behind a familiar neighborhood, all of my (few) friends, the big back yard with its garden and fig tree—many things I didn't realize that I loved. It took a while to get used to a brand new house, with no grass or flowers, and a new set of neighbors not all of whom were welcoming. The boy next door promptly beat me up, and I was in some fear of him for a long time afterward.

At first, reflecting on this history, I couldn't see any ways in which I had been scarred. I am surely not a depressive; I don't think I have ever been depressed and don't have very good empathy for those who suffer this common affliction. Indeed, I have been generally pretty healthy. But it may be that these repeated losses are partly responsible for one of my less desirable characteristics: I do not form as close and intense attachments as many other people. I have a strong tendency not to think about people I love when separated from them, and though I have grieved every time a good friend has died (something that has happened all too often), it does not take me long to get over it. Perhaps this emotional shallowness is based on identification with Mother, too. It may be partly responsible for my disinclination to do therapeutic work.

My grandfather loved books; at least, he was a sucker for every itinerant bookseller who came to the door, buying many a set of beautifully bound volumes for a growing library. Mother inherited many of them, and about the time we moved to Avondale I began to read in earnest. The leather bindings and exotic pictures in a set of sacred books of the East fascinated me, but I found that the pages were still uncut. Eventually I read some of the Book of the Dead, the Koran, and the Apocrypha in various of those volumes in our "study," one wall of which was well-filled bookshelves. Our family was not strong on formal education (I was the first one in any of the three branches to graduate from college), but books were held in high esteem by the Holts as well as the Hilditches. Since I was not strong or athletically gifted, tall but thin (Sheldon later somatotyped me as a 3-3-5, a predominant ectomorph), I was usually one of the last chosen for team sports. Still vivid in mind is the occasion when the captain of a pick-up football team decided to let me try carrying the ball, resulting in a several-yard loss. Humiliated, I quit the game for good and retreated to the safe haven of books.

In adolescence, I began to interact intellectually with Dad, to his considerable pleasure. As I became more politically aware, he and I began an ongoing series of debates about issues and policies. They upset Mother, but we enjoyed them thoroughly. Dad had the unusual capacity to treat me as an equal, even conceding on one memorable occasion—a debate over Roosevelt's destroyers-for-bases deal with Britain—that I was right! That experience left me with a sense of intellectual competence that has served me well, and lasting feelings of respect and loving gratitude to him.

I went regularly to the public library, always having several books going. Dinosaurs fascinated me; I read every book on them I could find. Indians and their woodlore were another of my favorite topics; my blood boiled when I discovered how unjustly they had been treated. As I grew older, I ranged up and down the stacks of the library, having a great time dipping into all sorts of books.

The first enthusiasm for a school subject I can recall is my fascination with geography and maps, which I collected. Later, stamp collecting reinforced my interest in world geography. In grammar school and junior high I was a good student but not at the very top of my class. Nevertheless, I became aware that I understood and learned things more easily than others and was quite ready to correct them when they were wrong. One day near the end of grammar school the teacher sent me out to walk the halls until I could stop critcizing other students. Since then I have tried to become more tactful, but in editorial work, teaching, and scholarship (for example, Holt, 1989b) I have recurrently taken the role of critic. I skipped a half year in grammar school and then attended summer school to graduate in June, so I was a full year ahead of my age-mates. That made my social life even more difficult.

During junior high school years, my favorite subject was ancient history. I was not strong in algebra, perhaps not unrelated to the fact that I cut up in that class enough so that at one point the teacher broke a yardstick across my back. That got my attention but not my genuine interest. The only math I excelled at was geometry, in senior high. There I was fascinated with chemistry and biology, but also fell under the influence of Miss Peek, a devoted teacher of Latin who was overjoyed to find a student who seemed to like the stuff. After several years of study, we were now reading Virgil, and she made the poetry of it come alive for me. At home, I set up a chemistry lab during junior high years and devoted many hours to it. A few years later, I joined a telescope club and often worked half an afternoon on grinding and polishing a mirror. One by one, every member of the club dropped out except Bradshaw Wood, who completed the instrument and eventually became a professor of astronomy at Princeton.

In the public library, I came across a translation of Binet and Simon's monograph on intelligence testing near the end of high school. I had already dipped into one other psychological book: Karl Menninger's (1920) *The Human Mind,* for my parents had received it from a book club to which they belonged. I can't recall just why I never read much of it. Oddly enough, the French classic held my attention and seemed just right for a report to the Science Club, of which I had recently become president. I decided then and there to take a course in psychology when I got to college.

That was delayed a year, for when I graduated in 1934 I was a rather immature 16 year old, full of social anxiety. If I had had to apply then, I would have chosen Harvard because it was the only northern college I had heard of. One of my first friends when we moved to the new house my parents had built, in 1927, had gone to a prep school in Pennsylvania, the Hill School. Since he and his parents spoke highly of it and I managed to get a scholarship, I went there for a year of getting used to the north and living away from home before tackling college. There I discovered the pleasures of writing for publication. Essays and verse printed in the school magazine won me the poetry and prose prizes at graduation and confirmed a developing literary bent; working on the magazine gave me my first editorial experience.

College

Following the lead of a couple of friends, I applied to Princeton, though I knew so little about it that I addressed my letter to New Haven. It eventually got there, and so did I. On the whole, I liked it: at last, I found a number of peers who shared my bookish and intellectual interests, even though we were distinctly outsiders in the rah-rah culture of the eating clubs (Princeton's substitute for fraternities). Freshman year, I did take introductory psychology and found it somewhat disappointing. There were a number of good guest lecturers, but it was presided over by Herbert Langfeld, a genial old stuffed shirt who had studied with Stumpf and whose own favorite subject was esthetics. Literature courses interested me much more, and I briefly toyed with the idea of someday becoming a literary critic. Nevertheless, I decided to give psychology one more try: I took social psychology with Hadley Cantril my sophomore year and was hooked.

The tall, boyish, informal Cantril immediately attracted me with his shy warmth, his winning grin, and his capacity to make the topic immediately relevant to the real concerns of life. I was soon ready to transfer my hero-worshiping search for an ideal father to him. (I had already idolized a nature counselor at Camp Mondamin and my biology teacher in high school, both somewhat charismatic men who encouraged my budding interest in science.) But most important was the fact that in that course for the first time I was able to learn a fresh vantage point from which to view the world and at last knew the intellectual excitement of possessing a set of categories and a frame of reference that made many ordinary matters seem freshly significant and meaningful. With growing eagerness, I chose psychology as my major and took virtually all of the courses offered, always getting top grades.

The department had a conservative, stodgy outlook in those days, and I don't have the feeling that I learned anything much in most of the courses. The team of hearing experts, Wever and Bray, were considered the faculty's stars, but Wever was a poor teacher and Bray, though more informal and approachable, never aroused my interest. Cantril was the only person in the department who seemed interested in the most exciting contemporary work in psychology. The best course I had other than Hadley's two was called "Philosophy of Mind," given in the philosophy department: we read nothing but William James's (1890) *Principles* but got through most of the two volumes—a marvelous experience.

The introductory course had given me a distaste for experimental psychology, confirmed by the fact that Cantril evidently did not think much of it. The lab course was required of all majors, but with his intervention I was able to get permission to substitute a special course with him, in which I did "experiments" in social psychology. He suggested one study, which was the effect of manipulating the name of the performer on ratings of how much one enjoyed a musical performance. Another topic I picked myself, obviously from personal experience: I was curious to learn how other people reacted to the experience of having one's name changed, and so I simply interviewed everyone I could find who had had that experience, mostly married women.

These little studies were fun, but I learned very little about research methods. (As a matter of fact, I was later to regret having been excused from the requirement of taking not only experimental psychology but a few other undergraduate courses that would have been helpful to me.) Moreover, the statistics course I took was given in the Economics Department and all of the examples were from business applications, so I didn't grasp its transfer to the sorts of problems that interested me. As a result, when I did a series of little studies as part of my senior thesis, I had no idea how to analyze the data and was reduced to presenting mean differences that looked substantial but without any tests of significance.

The thesis was on the psychology of personal names, a considerable enlargement of my earlier study on name change. Its lack of statistical sophistication didn't matter to Hadley; he liked its combination of library research into history and anthropology, personal interviewing, and experimental studies of the possible effects a person's name has on others. He gave it the highest possible grade (1+) and wrote an appreciative note saying that a teacher's greatest pleasure was to have a good student capable of independent work. I have said the same to a number of my own favorite pupils, each time thinking of Hadley.

It seems to me pretty clear that Hadley Cantril was responsible for my becoming a psychologist. He influenced me in several ways besides those mentioned. In another course, he introduced me to Gestalt psychology, psychoanalysis, and the work of Henry A. Murray; he assigned both Allport's (1937) *Personality* and Murray's (1938) *Explorations.* In the true sense of the word, he was a mentor who took me under his wing, gave me lots of advice about my education and what it was like to be a professor of psychology, steered me toward Harvard for graduate work and to Gordon Allport in particular, and served as an all-around role model. He often had me out to his home, an eighteenth-century farmhouse a mile or so outside of Princeton. There I, and perhaps another undergraduate or two, would help him with the yard work, have dinner with him and Mavis, his wife, and listen to Bach on his old phonograph as well as talking about psychology. He clearly had a lot of faith in me, which helped me have faith in myself. Our relationship continued for several years after my graduation; I visited him at least once during my graduate years, in addition to keeping in touch by letter.

There is one odd footnote to this friendship. In 1947, Cantril published (with Muzafer Sherif) *The Psychology of Ego Involvements,* a concept I used a good deal in those days. I was delighted to have a chance to review it. To my astonishment, however, I found in it a section on the psychology of personal names, with a footnote acknowledging that in it he had drawn heavily on my senior thesis. I never published on the topic myself, and his reference served to get the work into the literature. A good many years later, I was surprised to find that the psychology of names had grown into a substantial subspecialty within psychology, with its own journal. One issue of the journal was dedicated to me as a pioneer in the field; years earlier, the psychologist who was to become its editor had read Cantril's book and had sent for my thesis on interlibrary loan.

There was more to my Princeton experience than psychology, of course. I loved one peculiar course, consisting of the history of India and China, climatology, and a bit of anthropology. I worked on the *Nassau Lit* and wrote a fair amount of verse, but my main extracurricular activities were musical: singing in the choir and glee club and getting to know a marvelous repertory of motets, madrigals, and masses.

Two summers of my college years were devoted to travel: in 1937, Mother used a small inheritance to send Dorothy and me to Europe on a conducted tour, and the following year the whole family took the train to California where we stayed with

Mother's sister Anna and her husband, then an executive with Walt Disney. My love of travel, already strong, was heightened.

I graduated from Princeton in 1939, with highest honors; the year before I had made Phi Beta Kappa. (The only grade I got less than a 1 was in creative writing. In that course I learned the hard way that I have no talent for writing fiction.) In my senior year I was on the "no course plan," which enabled a few lucky fellows to bypass taking any formal courses—though we could audit whatever we liked, getting all the fun of learning without the pain of exams—and devote as much time to a thesis as we wanted. At Princeton, every senior writes a thesis, not just those who are going for honors. Cantril gave me my head: I cleared the general idea with him and then was able to work quite independently. It was such great fun that I decided for certain that I wanted a career of this kind. I had done some tutoring to earn a bit of money and thought that I could manage the teaching side of it, but research was what really excited me. It still does!

Graduate Study

So I applied to Harvard and got in. It was as simple as my entering Princeton had been; years later, it took me a long time to be able to empathize with students who had such great anxiety about getting into the university of their choice. It was all much less competitive and pressured then. I arranged to room with Kent Cooper, a friend and singing companion who was going to Harvard Law School. In the same rooming house on Oxford Street we discovered a couple of ex-Yalies, a baritone and a bass with whom we quickly formed a barbershop quartet. The Oxford Four had a couple of years of modest success at parties and Radcliffe teas, and a tremendous lot of fun. Later, I also sang in the Harvard choir and glee club, getting to appear on the stage of Symphony Hall under Koussevitsky's baton a few times.

In September 1939, I found my way up to the top floor of Emerson Hall, past sociology and philosophy to psychology's domain, ruled over by Edwin Garrigues (much later, Garry) Boring. There I found the office to which I had been assigned, which I shared with Robert H. Knapp, and learned that my old rolltop desk had once belonged to William James. That impressed me as Princeton never had. Bob and I got along well enough so that we decided to share an apartment the next year (Cooper having decided that the law was not for him) with a friend of his, Robert Freed Bales, and Bill Vickery, a graduate student of education. We had two years of good fellowship there, culminating in Freed's marriage. The fun at our parties was provided much less by alcohol than by games, notably The Game (charades).

Cantril had sent me to work with Gordon Allport, who had been his mentor and close friend. So I expected to slip into the same kind of relationship and was unpleasantly surprised to find that it just didn't work out that way. Gordon was a polite, emotionally distant, rather shy man with whom I never felt really comfortable. He was nice to me, invited me to his home a few times, and made an effort, but nothing clicked between us.

Luckily, however, I found many friends among the graduate students and young faculty. There was a group who hung out in the lab, bringing lunches there and having lots of informal conversation. For decades, a gag picture has hung on my wall, which we set up using my camera, with Ralph Gerbrands releasing the shutter. Inspired by a wonderfully stuffy and posed picture of his laboratory sent by Muensterberg before he came to Harvard, it portrays Jerry Bruner, Doc Cartwright, Mason Haire, John Harding, Jack French, Al Baldwin, Johnny Arsenian, Flash (Arthur) Bernstone, and me hamming it up with various pieces of lab equipment. (Bill Prentice and Bob Knapp weren't there that day.) Other members of the crowd, which included many advanced students as well as us beginners, were Leo Hurvich and Irv Child, both young faculty members. Most of us have kept in touch during many of the subsequent years.

Several of this group had been to Swarthmore and had studied with none less than Köhler. Their easy familiarity with Gestalt psychology, Marxism, psychoanalysis, and other sophisticated topics about which I knew next to nothing left me feeling desperately naive, and I learned a great deal from our conversations. Thanks to their influence, I joined the APA and SPSSI in 1941.

In my first year, when World War II was beginning far away in Europe, Boring inaugurated a proseminar, required of all first-year students. We had enormous assignments (for example, we read his entire *History of Experimental Psychology* in two weeks) and had a chance to see all of the major faculty in action. Jack Beebe-Center was the best teacher of the lot. Karl Lashley was pretty impressive, though at the other end of the approachability continuum. In the spring we covered soft psychology, Allport leading off. It was a brutal course, but it prepared us well for prelims, which I took at the end of the spring. Again, I learned a lot from peer interaction, for a group of us graduate students (including Babette Samelson [Whipple] and Olof Johnson) formed a study group and drilled one another intensively. Quite a good deal of what I learned stuck with me for years afterward.

During my second year, there was an ingathering of alumni of the graduate department. For it, the current student group prepared a set of skits and songs in which we mercilessly lampooned our professors—their characteristic phrases, gestures, and foibles. A group-composed sample ditty remains with me; here's the first verse:

> I began with Aristotle,
> Locke and Berkeley held my bottle;
> Thus began my oral stage,
> Sucking wisdom from a sage.
> Ta-ra-ra Boom! de-ay,
> Our work is so much play,
> We're at it every day;
> We hope it's here to stay.

After my first year, I had teaching assistantships to help finance my graduate work, the costs of which were otherwise paid by my family for three years. After that,

I had a research assistantship at the Harvard Psychological Clinic, which paid my living expenses, academic expenses, and most of my analysis (all out of $500 a year!).

As Boring's assistant in the introductory course, I had two main duties: to show slides and movies or make sure that equipment needed for demonstrations was on hand, and to teach sections, sometimes called recitations. One of the fringe benefits was getting to know Garry Boring well and eventually becoming quite fond of him. He was a fussy, demanding, obsessive-compulsive personality who nevertheless had considerable warmth and charm.

Boring was a remarkable lecturer. One day he was to take it easy while I showed a film on hypnosis for most of the lecture, but I couldn't get it going. First it was upside down, then backward, then jammed. Finally Boring told me to stop trying and launched into an impromptu lecture on hypnotic phenomena, which had the students enthralled, without text, notes, or anything.

To get to his small, book-lined office you walked through a much larger room completely lined with his huge reprint collection, neatly boxed; there his secretary sat. Inside, he chain-smoked cigarettes, never noticing how long the ash would grow until it fell on his vest. He took his duties as director of the laboratory very seriously, firing off memos to one and all about matters he thought we should consider. For example, one addressed to everyone took up the meaning and proper use of *parameter,* already becoming a vogue word in the early 1940s. To make sure that the clocks on the floor were all on time, he would listen for the radio signal of the hour with stopwatch in hand, and then go around resetting each clock to the second. But he also took a genuine personal interest in his students, who remained his friends long after leaving Harvard.

Most of my professors at Harvard were good writers, some of them superb. And many of them handed back term papers and even exam papers with grammatical mistakes corrected, plus stylistic suggestions. Allport circled every nonspecific *this* in my thesis draft, making me specify "this *what.*" Murray freely scattered metaphoric gems through its first few chapters. For example, I had commented that an early piece of work (probably on level of aspiration) had contained no statistics. He crossed out my prosaic words and wrote in that it was "unredeemed by the divine strategies of mathematics."

Having passed prelims, I had only one requirement besides language exams and the thesis: a second year of course work. In all, my courses included a seminar on history with Boring, a rather odd one on higher mathematics and logical positivism taught by S. S. Stevens, an advanced statistics course, seminars with Kurt Goldstein, Kurt Lewin, Bill Sheldon, and the team of Harry Murray and Clyde Kluckhohn covering culture and personality. I was able to fit in courses in modern schools of philosophy, one with Talcott Parsons on sociological theory, and introductory physics with a grand old man, Saunders—the undergraduate course premed students took, which was the hardest course I ever had. In a seminar on the psychology of personality, Gordon Allport gave us a peculiar hodgepodge of leftover topics rejected from his recently published book. But it is specially memorable because Freed Bales and I decided to do a joint paper. One assignment for the course had been Dollard's (1935) *Criteria for the Life History,* of which we did not have a high opinion. So we decided to prepare a better, more comprehensive set of criteria and—almost as an afterthought—to illustrate their use by a case study.

A friend of another Princeton friend of mine volunteered at just the right moment, having picked up some personality test forms lying on the piano in our apartment and confessing that such things always fascinated him. We got him to write an autobiography, interviewed him extensively, put him on a couch for a couple of free association sessions, gave him all the paper-and-pencil tests we could lay hands on, and (clumsily) administered a TAT. He turned over to us files of letters, clippings, his baby book, and miscellaneous documents. Freed got a map of his hometown and did a sociological study of the neighborhoods where he had grown up. A couple of friends helped out: Marianne Weil (Lester) gave him a Rorschach, and Ruth Markmann (Murphy) administered the Wechsler-Bellevue, which she was learning in the course in clinical psychology. (I didn't take that course because there was nothing to it but learning intelligence testing; and hadn't I already read Binet?)

We were a bit startled to learn that our subject had had a lot more homosexual than heterosexual experience, for he was a big beefy fellow who fit none of our stereotypes about "fairies." Piecing his life together and trying to make sense out of the test data was a challenge for which none of our courses had prepared us, but an important learning experience. After I learned diagnostic testing, I reanalyzed his data and used them in my course on personality at the Menninger Foundation School of Clinical Psychology, assigning each pair of students the task of making sense of selected chunks from the standpoint of a different theory. And since I had kept in touch with the man over the subsequent years, I was able to get him to come to the Research Center for Mental Health twenty-six years later for a follow-up reassessment at age 52. The results were incorporated in my book *Assessing Personality* (Holt, 1971b).

One morning in the spring of my first graduate year, I awoke feeling sore and seeing my roommate bending over me with concern; my tongue was bleeding. I had had a grand mal seizure, my first, though I had been having minor petit mals since early adolescence. I never witnessed one of Mother's major seizures, but frequently saw her lose consciousness and crumple with a petit mal. Mine were not so incapacitating and usually were not apparent to others; they consisted mainly of a strange alteration in my state of consciousness during which I could not speak coherently or understand language. They must have contributed to my introspectiveness and interest in the subjective world.

I went to Massachusetts General Hospital and found myself in the expert (though arthritically crippled) hands of Stanley Cobb. After a thorough neurological workup, including an EEG, he told me that I seemed biologically OK though my brain was a bit undersized, but the EEG had clearly indicated idiopathic epilepsy. Phenobarbital would prevent further seizures, and I took small daily doses for many years. For less symptomatic treatment, he recommended psychoanalysis, saying that his patients had had relatively good results from it.

In the fall of 1940, I began treatment with a recent graduate of the Boston Psychoanalytic Institute, Nils Antonisen. Like many other young analysts, he was cautious, neutral, and rather passive. Not a lot happened. So when he told me in the spring of 1941 that he was moving out of Boston and offered to refer me to Felix Deutsch, I had no regrets. A single interview with Deutsch convinced me that he would be a better analyst for me, as indeed he was: active, provocative, and insightful, but steady and warm. It was a pretty classical analysis, focusing on oedipal problems. In the winter of 1943–44, things came to a head: for a couple of days, I had petit mal experiences almost continuously, but came out of it feeling that I understood a lot and had probably licked it. The petit mals ceased, never to return.

Just to finish this clinical story let me jump ahead a bit. Shortly after terminating the analysis, I decided that I was cured and went off my medication. Within a week, I had another grand mal seizure. That was a bitter disappointment; but I resumed the phenobarb. After two more years, I again stopped taking my nightly pill and soon had my third (and last) seizure. This time, it was at least five years until I began to grow careless, forgetting occasionally and finally stopping the nightly ritual entirely. I still had the nuisance of a restricted driver's license until after I moved to New York. There an internist said that he doubted that I had ever had epilepsy and suggested that I get a new EEG. I did, and the old spike-and-dome pattern had disappeared, even with such vigorous hyperventilation that I tetanized myself briefly. With my doctor's written opinion and the normal EEG to back it up, I was able to get a regular driver's license. My neurological diagnosis did, however, put me firmly in 4-F (medically deferred) for the draft during the war years.

During the fall of my second year at Harvard, following the scenario Hadley had laid out, I thought that I ought to get started on a thesis topic. "You don't want to spend a lot of time in graduate school," he had once told me. "Graduate students are a dull lot. You should be able to pass your prelims at the end of the first year, start on a thesis after that while you take the rest of the courses they require, and finish it off your third year. Then you can get out, get a job, and start having some real fun in psychology."

So far I was on schedule. But somehow, I couldn't seem to find a topic as easily as I had for my undergraduate thesis. After a few months of floundering, embarrassed and ashamed, I confessed to Gordon Allport that I was getting nowhere. "Well," he said, "in a recent conversation I had with Hadley, an interesting idea came up which you might want to pursue: a psychophysics of aspiration. Maybe there is something like a Weber-Fechner ratio between what a person has achieved and what he aims for. Why don't you look into it?"

That grabbed me. I had learned from a memorable seminar with Kurt Lewin about the work of his student F. Hoppe on levels of aspiration, and people like Jerome Frank and Rosalind Gould were currently doing interesting work on the problem, so I plunged into the literature. After a while, I saw a number of gaps that needed filling, which seemed to me more promising than the original suggestion.

In the fall of 1941, I took my new ideas to Gordon. He looked them over, sighed, and suggested that I try another topic. I was crushed. Meanwhile, however, I had been hearing rumors about an exciting new enterprise at the Harvard Psychological Clinic: Henry A. Murray was back, had assembled a new team of collaborators, and was beginning a second set of "explorations in personality." Though I was one of the denizens of Emerson Hall, I had followed some of the older graduate students to the clinic the year before to a voluntary evening seminar given by Robert W. White, then its acting director. He would present extensive biographical materials on an anonymous student he had studied, then distribute TAT stories. After we had had a chance to see what we could make of them, he would go over them line by line, pointing out implications and verifying them from independent data. Heady stuff!

I made an appointment with Murray, already a legendary figure, and laid out my thesis idea to him. "Great, marvelous!" he exclaimed. "Come join our group and do your research on our common pool of subjects." It was a dream come true. The great man himself would be my sponsor, and I would be on the inside of the most exciting research enterprise I knew of. The only problem was, what could I say to Allport? I took the coward's way of procrastination and avoidance. Many months later, he finally cornered me and told me that he had heard I was now working with Murray: fine, feel no obligation, full speed ahead. Such a kind and empathic person, uptight though he was!

So now I had an office at 64 Plympton Street, the old frame dwelling turned into a research clinic. (Very few, if any, patients were ever seen there; any therapeutic work was done so discreetly that most of us were quite unaware of it.) A rambling structure with several additions, it contained lots of little rooms suitable for staff offices, plus a big living room turned into a combination conference room, library, and lunchroom. The atmosphere was a unique mixture of genteel, slightly shabby elegance, informality, intense intellectual interchange and excitement over ideas, and the sense of being part of a historic enterprise. Here the big names that were dropped in conversation were not just the experimental or social psychologists you heard about at Emerson Hall, but psychoanalysts as well. I felt at home, being in psychoanalytic treatment, though I chafed at my analyst's rule that I was not to read in the field (except for specific assignments).

The central figures of the original band of explorers were there—ebullient, charismatic Harry Murray; the cool, enigmatically beautiful Christiana Morgan (whispered to be his mistress); and gentlemanly, reserved, patrician Bob White. Occasionally one of their first crew, such as Saul Rosenzweig or Nevitt Sanford, would come for a visit; but notable scientists like David Rapaport, Gregory Bateson, or Julian Huxley would come also, or figures from the arts like Paul Robeson. Harry, it seemed, knew just about everybody, charmed them all, and gave even lowly graduate students a chance to meet them informally over lunch.

Lunch at the Harvard Psychological Clinic was an experience never to be forgotten. Harry knew the deep magic of breaking bread together as a way of uniting a group. Every afternoon, just before staff meeting, we would have afternoon tea (Christiana pouring) and cookies, and every day lunch was served at a big round table seating perhaps a dozen. Since there were a good many more than that on staff, we had to take turns, but I was able to eat there at least a couple of times a week. Very often there would be someone notable from outside, often enough people who disagreed strongly with Harry on some theoretical point. Then there would be great discussions; but the general level of conversation was usually high.

The people Murray attracted as his staff were a rather extraordinary lot. Jurgen Ruesch and Fred Wyatt had full-time, paid staff positions. Elliot Jaques was the Rantoul Fellow, fresh from working with Adolf Meyer after getting his M.D. at Johns Hopkins. The other staff member with a doctoral degree was Silvan Tomkins (about whom more shortly). Then there was a group of people who did not have offices at the clinic and probably weren't paid, but who participated in the research and in many of the staff meetings: of these, James Grier Miller and Hobart Mowrer stand out in my mind.

During that first fall, we were planning and tooling up for the gathering of data, which took place mainly in 1942. Every day there would be a staff meeting, at which someone would present either some theoretical ideas or a research proposal. My turn came before long, and I talked about level of aspiration and my idea that publicly committing oneself to a goal in an ongoing endeavor was a kind of self-evaluation, to be understood in the context of other such appraisals of self. The reception was friendly but serious; various people offered theoretical and practical suggestions, which I found stimulating and useful.

At a series of these meetings, Murray set forth his new conceptual scheme, a revision of the one presented in *Explorations.* The central focus was to be on the understanding of a person's *sentiments,* a term he and Christiana Morgan used to comprise attitude, belief, and value. But first he laid out for us the revised list of overt needs, expanded to a Mendeleevian ninety-two traits and structural variables; facts of past history; characteristics of sentiments; abilities; defense mechanisms; and imaginal press and needs. We became skilled in using these concepts to discuss just about anything. Using the clinic's jargon was a badge of in-group membership, a statement of identity that meant a lot to us.

Joining the clinic group got me acquainted with a remarkable man, who became my best friend: Silvan S. Tomkins. He had a sociable side of great warmth, ebullience, humor, and good fellowship, but also a serious side of intellectual depth, subtlety, and commitment. Silvan had received his Ph.D. in philosophy at the bottom of the Depression, when the only academic jobs available paid no salary. For a while, he supported himself by gambling at racetracks, but decided to go into psychology, having had a long Kleinian analysis. With his usual good nose for talent, Murray took him in, giving him barely enough money to live on while he intensively educated himself. At almost any hour of the day or night he was in his little office, always interruptable but always working, usually with a book or journal open and pecking away at his typewriter, making notes. In this way, he was working his way through a major part of the psychiatric and psychoanalytic literatures. With characteristic generosity, he let me borrow and read these notes. I profited so much that I thought others would like to also, and I proposed to Silvan that he start taking his notes on mimeograph stencils. I would run off copies and peddle them, and we would split the (very meager) profits. The success of this small joint venture encouraged him to put together the first of his successful psychopathological anthologies (Tomkins, 1943).

Intensive analysis of personality by multiform assessment was the slogan of the clinic. We trained the diverse talents and instruments of about thirty people on ten undergraduates who were willing to be studied, for pay. They had been subjects in the Harvard Growth Study, which turned over to us its files (of predominantly anthropometric and physiological data) on each of them.

The doctoral thesis research of Daniel Horn (1943) required that the staff be divided into two diagnostic councils of five each, and a remainder who did not participate directly in the thesis. The subjects were split into subgroups of five also; each council member became official biographer of one of them. It was his or her task to assemble and digest all the information gathered by his own council, plus selected data from the larger pool (for example, autobiographies and standardized inventories). Bob White chaired our council and administered the TAT; I put each of the five young men through my level-of-aspiration procedure and obtained several other kinds of self-evaluations. Each of us was paired with a member of the other council; thus, I also worked on Dan Horn's Repeated Questionnaire, while he collected the data I needed from the other half of the subject sample. Thus the members of each team remained blind to information about half of the subjects.

An expert statistician, Dan had decided to see if the unreliability of self-administered inventories could be put to use. His questionnaire (measuring a group of the main needs) was designed to be as unreliable as possible, with a twenty-point rating scale for each item. Subjects took it once a week for the ten-week period of our intensive assessment, and their self-ratings did indeed vary over time. Dan's method was to correlate pairs of items across occasions and then apply a crude form of cluster analysis. I was delighted to find, for example, that one subject's ratings of overt n Aggression had a significant negative correlation with his covert n Aggression (expressions in fantasy). A few years later, I successfully used this technique to show that the notorious fluctuations in choices of liked and disliked faces of the Szondi test were meaningfully related to changes in self-ratings on an adaptation of the same Repeated Questionnaire (Holt, 1950).

Dan's thesis was a pioneering study of the contribution of each test, interview, and the like (alone and in combination with others) to the assessment of various areas of personality—motives, abilities, traits, and so on. Each member of Council A worked through the anonymous dossier of a subject from Council B, whom he had never seen. The first stage might be the autobiography for one subject, the Rorschach for another, or an interview and self-ratings about abilities for a third. (Since most of us had had no training in the Rorschach, Jurgen Ruesch gave us all a quick crash course.) After absorbing that much information, the council member made quantitative ratings on all of Murray's variables, then repeated the process for the next stage. The criterion was the set of ratings provided by the other council, all of whom had analyzed the same dossier in any order they liked, but one of whom (the biographer) had also digested all the additional information collected by non–council members. For example, Thelma G. Alper was such a staff member, who used the pool of subjects in her dissertation research (Alper, 1946, 1948) and contributed the data she obtained to the collection available to biographers. Another was a novelist, Mrs. Harriet Robey, a motherly middle-aged woman whose role was to be unobtrusively knitting in the waiting room, where she could observe each subject before and after each appointment and converse sympathetically with them. Transcripts of her shrewd observations and conversations were valuable additions to the pool of data.

Being a biographer was an important learning experience for me. I immediately formed a strong identification with the young man I was assigned and gave him a set of projective ratings noticeably discrepant from those of my fellow council members (White, Fred Wyatt, Elliot Jaques, and Leo Bellak, at the time a fellow graduate student). Unfortunately, I was able to argue them into accepting my general view of the man, introducing a bias that was corrected only at the final phase, after Horn's thesis was completed. We had ten meetings of the entire staff, one for each subject, when all of the ratings given in the experiment were presented, variable by variable, discussed, and corrected. Staff members who had not been on one of the councils could bring in relevant data from their observations or other data, and we all had the advantage of familiarity with the entire group. Those final "official" ratings were made available to everyone for whatever light they might throw on experimental or test data. I was able to use them as criterion data against which to evaluate the subjects' self-ratings of the principal manifest needs, in a little study of insight (Holt, 1951a).

That two-year period of gathering and analyzing data, with the unique opportunity to validate one's hunches and inferences against both independent data and the consensus of a large group of experts, was an invaluable learning experience. It thoroughly hooked me on the fascination of studying personalities by clinical methods, but also taught me how vulnerable one's ratings were to a variety of errors. By doing, I learned a lot about what could be inferred from clinical data but never developed the blind faith or sense of mystique about pet procedures that I observed in colleagues who had been trained in more conventional ways.

Life at the clinic was by no means all research and intellectual discussion. Working closely together, we became good friends and had many memorable parties. A highlight of clinic staff parties was often Bob White's delightful character portraits improvised on the piano.

Some of us decided to live together: Silvan Tomkins found a small, six-room, three-story house on Cowperthwaite Street (which we called Cockroach Manor) and took the risk of signing a lease for it. A number of graduate students—John Harding, Ernest Haggard, Dalton Vernon, Brewster Smith, and I—shared the space and rent. There was no central heating, only a big kerosene-burning stove in the kitchen, and no insulation. Despite the space heater we bought for the dining room, we had to *put on* extra clothes to go to bed in midwinter and gave it up after one academic year.

But we had great fun and companionship. Tired of eating in restaurants, we hired a cook and enlarged our group with boarders. It never was quite a financial success, but those uproarious communal meals were well worth a few extra cents. And our parties were the talk of the department.

The next year, a nucleus of us (Silvan, Olie Johnson, Stu Kirby, Dalton, and I) found a nearby vacant apartment above a cleanser (Bostonian for dry cleaner) and the Harvard literary magazine's offices. Its main attraction, however, was the fact that the floor just below us was let by a group of female graduate students, some of whom had been part of the eating club: Louisa Pinkham (now Howe), Babbie Samelson (Whipple), Ai-li Sung (Chin), and Suzanne Noble (Gordon). Again we hired a cook and ran another private restaurant for an extended group and occasional distinguished guests, among whom I recall Ashley Montague and Milton Erickson. In an effort to stretch the food budget, a couple of the guys once brought home a beautiful big roast—something usually way beyond our means in those war years. They didn't reveal that it was horse meat until partway through the dinner, one that several guests didn't finish.

In retrospect, the war had surprisingly few memorable impacts on my life. I was somewhat ambivalent about being exempt from the draft, though mostly quite grateful. After the shock of Pearl Harbor, Murray, Allport, and a few others formed a volunteer morale seminar, for faculty members and graduate students. I took on an assignment to develop a code for critics of the national administration, balancing patriotism against the need for democratic dissent and feedback. I was delighted when the document produced for the seminar found its way to the hands of a congressman, who put it into the *Congressional Record:* my first (albeit anonymous) publication! It was subsequently incorporated in the seminar's chief product, the paperback book *Psychology for the Fighting Man* (Boring & Van de Water, 1943). My first real publication (Sanford & Holt, 1943) came out of that seminar, too.

The worst thing about the war, for me, was the fact that when I was only a couple of chapters into the writing of my thesis, Harry Murray left on a secret mission. The always reliable Bob White took over the clinic's direction; but I had to go sheepishly back to Allport and ask him to sponsor my thesis again. He did so graciously and generously, with never a chiding word, and was a great help to me. To my considerable surprise, he counseled me to omit one long chapter, a case history in which I tried to make sense of one subject's experimental performance in light of his personality. "It's a nomothetic thesis," he said, "and this idiographic chapter just doesn't fit in." I completed the draft in November 1943, but the thing was so long that the final defense took place only in February of 1944 (see Holt, 1945, 1946). I made use of the deleted chapter, first as my contribution to an unpublished Festschrift for Harry put together by Bob White under the title *Random Harpoonings*—an echo of Harry's well-known obsession with Melville and *Moby Dick.* Later I boiled it down into a paper (Holt, 1951d).

My oral exam took place during one notable, hypomanic week, when I also finished my psychoanalysis and got married. My bride was Louisa Pinkham, whom I had met in the Murray-Kluckhohn seminar; the minister was her father; the best man was Silvan; and it took place in our apartment. Propinquity and mutual interests had done it, plus the fact that in the cooperative labors of cleaning up after our joint dinners, Louisa and I often found that we were the only ones available to do the dirty work.

Through her, I had become part of an extracurricular faculty-student seminar on psychoanalysis and the social sciences, which met occasional evenings at Talcott Parsons's house. As one of his favorite students, she was of course invited; Freed Bales was the only other graduate student in it. Both Florence and Clyde Kluckhohn were members, as were Ives Hendrick and Edward Bibring. Talcott's ambivalence about psychoanalysis showed from time to time, and there were at times heated discussions between him and Ives, but Bibring seemed almost Olympian, so unpretentious, courteous, and profound was he. Louisa was in a training analysis with him, as one of the first three Sigmund Freud Memorial Fellows in the Boston Institute and the only social scientist, and I wondered that they could be in this kind of nonclinical contact concurrently. Nevertheless, she told me that she had no trouble forming a strong transference. At the end, however, Bibring told her that she should have more analysis someday with someone else.

First Job

Ph.D. in hand, I now needed a job and was strongly tempted to heed Harry Murray's call to join his supersecret enterprise at OSS (Office of Strategic Services). The work would be a kind of continuation of what we had done at the clinic and a contribution to the war effort, but I would have to live on the post somewhere in Virginia and could be with my new wife only on weekends. That was too much; so instead I took a job at the Division of Program Surveys, Bureau of Agricultural Economics, in the Department of Agriculture.

This division was the forerunner of the Center for Survey Research at the University of Michigan. Headed by Rensis Likert, it had been founded by Henry Wallace when he was Secretary of Agriculture to find out how New Deal programs were being received by farmers. By the time World War II came along, it was one of only two federal agencies with experience in public opinion survey work and was quickly pressed into service by other departments. I was hired mainly to work on surveys for the Treasury Department, which needed to know how to persuade more Americans to buy war bonds. The true motivation was anti-inflationary (to soak up excess purchasing power at a time of full employment and little civilian production), but all kinds of other arguments and devices were used to promote them. What we found, in short, was that far more effective than anything else—advertising, marathons, promotional hoop-la of all kinds—was personal solicitation: having someone ask you personally and directly to buy them.

I was able to start as a study director because of some part-time experiences I had had during the previous few years. First, I had responded to an advertisement for interviewers to work on a Roper survey. In that, I was taught how to do survey interviews, following specific sampling instructions, and had a few weeks of eye-opening experience talking to people from all socioeconomic strata in many parts of greater Boston I had never visited. It brought vividly to life what I had learned in an undergraduate course on public opinion.

Second, my old roommate Bob Knapp had parlayed a thesis project on the process of rumor into a job with Civilian Defense. Through that, he came into contact with many of Boston's politically influential people, one of whom told him about a dilemma faced by the United War Fund. It was just after the heroic defense of Stalingrad, where the tide of Nazi advance into the USSR was turned back, and a contingent was lobbying to get Russian War Relief included in the fund drive, while others had grave doubts: maybe Boston's Catholic majority would give less to the fund if some of the money went to communists. So Bob volunteered that a public opinion survey was needed and even offered to do one. He remembered my interest and experience and offered me partnership: I would do the technical work, he would be the front man, getting us the contract and reporting the findings, and we would split the take. I agreed and set about drawing a sample, using census publications in Widener Library. Then I hired and trained interviewers, wrote the questionnaire with Bob's collaboration, pretested it, and supervised the field work. We then coded the results, had them punched on Hollerith cards, and I ran them off on an old sorter in a university building. The result was pretty unambiguous: except for a die-hard minority, Bostonians were strongly impressed by our new ally and eager to help cope with the Nazi-caused devastation. The money we got did little more than meet our expenses (for once, I met a payroll), but the experience was invaluable.

At Program Surveys, there were state-of-the-art experts doing the sampling and interviewing, and a body of already trained and experienced staff to do the content analysis. Open-ended interviewing and quantitative content analysis of the verbatim protocols formed an established tradition at Program Surveys, and I quickly learned these procedures from older hands there, like Angus Campbell, Dorwin (Doc) Cartwright, and Eleanor Maccoby. The value of probability sampling was vividly demonstrated in each of our Treasury studies, done after every one of the periodical national drives to sell war bonds. We would ask respondents how many they had bought in the recent drive and what their total holdings were, then multiply the totals by the sampling ratio. Each time, we came within a small percentage of the true figures, which were known to the Treasury but not to us.

The spring of 1944 was a hard time for me. Louisa had stayed in Cambridge to try to finish her dissertation (which was to have been on the role of women in modern society) and her analysis, though she had a job waiting for her in Washington. So we had no honeymoon and I rented a furnished room in a dreary area near Dupont Circle. New in town, I had no friends, and went from being a respected senior figure among a graduate student crowd to being a sort of freshman again. I began to have bad stomachaches at night and between meals. On one of my rare visits to Louisa, I went to see Felix Deutsch to tell him about it. He suggested that I see an internist because I probably had an ulcer, but he didn't seem at all taken aback that the symptoms had begun the year before, literally on his couch. I did get medical treatment, which helped.

Finally, Louisa gave up on both of her struggles and joined me. She had a staff job at the National Institute of Public Affairs supervising recent college graduates who had internships in governmental agencies (having been one herself some years before). Life improved; before long, we had our first child, Dorothy, an apartment in

Southeast Washington, and a growing circle of friends. Louisa tried to keep her thesis effort alive between changing diapers and helping interns, but it was too hard. Thanks to her job, I had a chance to visit the White House with a group of interns and have tea with the first lady, Eleanor Roosevelt. I never got closer to her husband, whom I revered, than tearfully standing on a Washington sidewalk watching his funeral procession the next year.

For some extra intellectual stimulation, we attended evening seminars at the Washington School of Psychiatry, with Harry Stack Sullivan, David Rioch, Clara Thompson, Erich Fromm, and Ernst Schachtel. We were quite turned off by Sullivan's narcissism and the adulation of so many of the students, who would write down his pompous pronouncements with little murmurs of ecstasy. The others were good teachers, especially the eloquent Fromm and the scholarly Rioch. Thompson was open and informal, Schachtel distant but impressive; he convinced me, at last, that there really was something to the Rorschach.

To supplement my slender governmental salary, I taught evenings at the Department of Agriculture's graduate school and at American University. It was my first stab at teaching courses of my own, and though I didn't do very well I enjoyed it. Our old friend Leopold Bellak, then a psychiatric resident at St. Elizabeth's, gave me a chance to do some research on the side. He discovered a set of nude photographs of psychotic patients left over from another study, and remembering our common experience of learning to do somatotyping in Sheldon's seminar, invited me to join him in investigating the relation between physique and psychotic diagnosis (Bellak & Holt, 1948).

My coworkers at Program Surveys were a talented and friendly lot. Eleanor Maccoby and I soon found that we had musical interests in common and sang a lot of duets together at parties. It was a special pleasure to get to know brilliant, genial Jim Bayton, who was the first black friend of my adulthood. Doc Cartwright, my kind and helpful immediate supervisor, provided me with a useful antidote to my youthful arrogance: a feeling of genuine intellectual inferiority. Other lasting impressions from those days: Angus Campbell's quizzical dry humor; Ren Likert's warm, open style of truly democratic leadership; and working on the first study of economic behavior with the Hungarian economist-psychologist George Katona. There were almost as many talented women as men in the outfit, too—Marcia Nielsen, Frieda Sarbin, and Frieda Tryon, in addition to Eleanor, with whom I wrote a little paper (Maccoby & Holt, 1946).

The war came to an end, however, and though I wanted to stay in survey research in order to contribute something to the pressing problem of race relations, I also yearned for the old days at the Harvard Psychological Clinic. So when David Rapaport came to town on a recruiting mission, having looked me up on Harry Murray's recommendation, I jumped at the chance to go to Topeka and learn diagnostic testing. Louisa, then pregnant with our second child, was ready to move on, too, since Rapaport promised her an opportunity to do her thesis research.

So almost exactly two years after arriving in Washington, we left it. That brief time at the Division of Program Surveys taught me a great deal that was to prove lastingly valuable for my subsequent research. First, I learned the importance of sampling and the difficulty of getting a representative sample of any population; second, how to do content analysis—a vital skill for anyone who wants to do quantitative research on verbal texts such as those of projective tests or interviews. But perhaps most important, Doc Cartwright taught me that a research problem, as formulated by the consumer, was almost never in usable form. To do a satisfactory job, one had to talk for a while to the person who wanted a survey to find out what the real problem was. Then it was possible to formulate objectives, and research strategies flowed naturally from a clear statement of what was really needed. Years later, I experienced a shock of recognition of the same basic idea when I learned that patients are almost never able to tell you their most important problems, which are rarely the presenting symptoms. When research threatens to bog down, I have found it unfailingly helpful to sit back and ask, What are our ultimate objectives here? What are we really trying to find out, and why?

Topeka Years

We arrived in Topeka in February 1946, when I was 28. My job, staff psychologist at Winter VA Hospital, entitled us to a small apartment at the hospital until we could find permanent housing. The VA hospital occupied a few acres of flat land next to a dairy farm in one corner of this midsized Kansas city. Built during the war as an Army general hospital, it comprised a series of temporary one-story cinder-block buildings, a few of which began collapsing in the next year or so. They were uninsulated, drafty in winter and so hot in summer that patients (almost two thirds of whom were psychiatric) often had to be taken out to stand in their meager shade. Some buildings, over to one side, were used as housing for new staff, chiefly psychiatric residents who had come to study at the Menninger Foundation School of Psychiatry. There were absolutely no apartments for rent in Topeka, and very few houses on the market; most people had to build. We were lucky to find and buy an old house within walking distance, with a huge yard and plenty of room for the kitchen garden for which I had longed ever since early boyhood.

In Winter's unprepossessing physical plant was located as yeasty, exciting an institution as I have ever known. The year before, Karl A. Menninger (always called Dr. Karl) had offered himself as the VA hospital's director, with the avowed intent of making it into an exemplary medical institution. He did so, partly by charismatic leadership and partly by the device of making it an educational center. First established was the School of Psychiatry, just getting under way as I arrived; then came the Menninger Foundation School of Clinical Psychology, in mid-1946, and schools for social workers, pastoral counselors, psychiatric aides, nurses, and perhaps others.

Right after the war an outburst of investigative journalism revealed disgraceful conditions in the country's mental hospitals. Not only did the inmates suffer from dirt, poor nutrition, and general neglect, but they received virtually no therapy— only custodial care, and that of miserable quality. The hospitals of the Veterans

Administration were among the worst, not to mention the fact that their level of ordinary medical care was abysmal. Wide publicity given to these shocking conditions created a public demand for reform, and awakened people in all walks of life to the huge need and latent demand for mental health services.

At the same time, many members of the health professions were being released from the armed services, after having had hands-on experience with mental patients. There were so many psychiatric casualties during the war that many physicians, psychologists, and social workers with no previous experience or inclination were pressed into attempting to diagnose and treat emotional disturbances of men and women in the armed forces. Not surprisingly, large numbers of them became motivated to learn how to do the jobs right and to enter mental health professions.

Consequently, psychiatric training centers were besieged with large numbers of people seeking residencies, especially those with a psychoanalytic orientation. For the heyday of psychoanalysis in America was just beginning, its prestige growing and its reputation unchallenged as the treatment of choice for most difficulties in living. Because of the reputation of the Menninger Clinic and Dr. Karl himself, the new school had its pick of the most talented doctors as its trainees.

An institution that is a-building has an inimitable atmosphere of optimism and excitement, which makes it an exhilarating place in which to work. That had been true of the rejuvenated Harvard Clinic, and it characterized the Menninger School of Psychiatry to an even greater extent. In such a milieu of hope and high morale, difficulties of the physical plant and our relative isolation seemed minor. Dr. Karl had a reputation for getting on the phone to Washington and raising hell to get red tape cut, even to obtain extra appropriations. No wonder he was able to assemble a first-rate staff to help with the teaching and to set high standards of care for patients.

To counter Topeka's distance from notable contributors to psychiatry, psychoanalysis, and the social sciences, he brought scores of them to speak to us. All the trainees and staff would attend, and such brilliant local talent as Margaret Brenman, Sybille Escalona, David Rapaport, Roy Schafer, Merton Gill, and Robert Knight would speak up in the discussions, puncturing any pretense and probing any weakness of reasoning or research design. A young man could also put in his two cents and try to compete with his elders.

What Dr. Karl was to the psychiatrists, David Rapaport was to the psychological staff. Even though nominally only a consultant, he effectively ran the psychological service. Its chief, Bob Challman, though a bright, pleasant, and competent person, was in no way his match and went along with whatever Rapaport wanted. A good staff was quickly assembled; it included, at its height, Maryline Barnard, John Chotlos, Michael Dunn, Martin Mayman, Milton Wexler, and (for a short time) Roy Schafer. Later, Helen Sargent became Challman's successor. No matter what each new recruit's previous level of experience, however, Rapaport put everyone through the same rigorous training, from the ground up. My experience was typical.

On arrival, I was immediately sent to the Menninger Clinic for a few weeks, to observe expert psychologists at work and to study. *Diagnostic Psychological*

Testing (Rapaport, Gill, & Schafer, 1945–46) had just been published; it was our bible, along with the briefer *Manual* (Rapaport, Schafer, & Gill, 1944–46). We were expected to read not only both big volumes but all the references in them as well in only a couple of weeks. Several times a day, I would observe Rapaport, or Sybille Escalona, or Margaret Brenman giving the tests of the standard battery; Rapaport himself always gave the Rorschach. Afterward, I would have a session with him to describe what I had observed and to ask any questions. After several days of this kind, I was sent to the Topeka State Hospital to administer first the Wechsler-Bellevue (W-B), then "the Babcock" (actually just a story recall test), the Sorting Test, the Word Association and Szondi tests, the TAT, and finally the Rorschach. I had to submit my verbatim protocols and incidental observations for close super-vision and correction, until I had mastered the local style of administering them and scoring the simpler ones.

Then I began my duties at the VA hospital, testing ward patients. Every morning, we (the new staff) would meet with Dr. Rapaport (as he insisted on being called, even by Mike Dunn, who had known and helped him when he first arrived from Budapest). One of us would present a case, beginning with the profile or scatter pattern of the W-B and then reading every response. He would draw out all our interpretive hunches, make us explain and justify them, and then present his own with full rationale and often citations of relevant research. As we went through the tests, a number of diagnostic hypotheses would be developed, and gradually each would be either sustained by new evidence, modified, or discarded.

I had about six months of this superb learning experience, importantly supple-mented thereafter by my contacts with people Rapaport had already trained, notably Marty Mayman and Roy Schafer, who became my close friends, and by presenting test reports at the frequent case conferences, chaired by such excellent psychiatrists as Lewis L. Robbins and Robert P. Knight. They pressed me to follow Rapaport's example of brief reports, to the point and free from unnecessary jargon and in-tellectualized obfuscation.

When I had barely mastered the rudiments, I suddenly found myself pushed into the role of supervisor for a new crop of recruits: the students of the newly founded School of Clinical Psychology, headed by Rapaport. It was a joint enterprise of the Menninger Clinic, the VA hospital, and Kansas University in nearby Lawrence. For a while, we even talked about trying to make it a degree program in medical psychology, a la Kubie (1954), combining medical, psychological, and social work training. Rapaport recruited an outstanding bunch of students, who included Philip Holzman, Herbert Schlesinger, Harry Levinson, Arthur Kobler, Riley Gardner, and Gerald Ehrenreich (as well as others who seemed equally talented but whose names are not as likely to be recognized). All were set to work immediately on a version of the training regimen I had just finished, while I and other members of the staff did our best to imitate Rapaport. Of course I wasn't ready for it, but having to teach is undeniably an excellent way to learn. It also brought me an appointment as clinical assistant professor at Kansas University (without compensation).

There were opportunities for classroom teaching, too. Both Louisa and I gave courses to the psychiatric residents (on sociology and personality theory, respectively); and for a while we ran a joint experiential seminar on group dynamics, trying out W. R. Bion's techniques and others that were emanating from some of Kurt Lewin's former students. I had kept in touch with them, being for a couple of years a member of the informal small society of topological psychologists that formed right after his death.

In the fall of 1946, I took over Louisa's class one morning, first announcing that she had just given birth to our second daughter, Catherine Frances Holt. As soon as possible, I flew to Jacksonville for a last visit with my beloved stepfather, who was dying of cancer.

At Winter VA Hospital, I had a few years of immersion in diagnostic testing with a rich variety of patients of all kinds. In those days, psychologists did only testing, teaching, and research, and though many of my colleagues longed to find a way to do psychotherapy, my wish was to get back into research. Meanwhile, these clinical years and the less intensive ones that followed were invaluable. There was plenty of time to talk to patients as well as to test them and even some opportunity to follow their course in the hospital. Because of Rapaport's enormous prestige and very real clinical accomplishments, psychologists and their craft of testing commanded more respect than in most other places at that time. When residents often showed such obvious anxiety that their diagnoses not differ from mine, even though I was professionally so green, I could hardly feel like much of a second-class citizen. My forte was always the TAT, on which I had cut my clinical baby teeth, but one of the strengths of Rapaport's approach was to apply thematic analysis wherever possible, even to a patient's incidental remarks while taking an intelligence test. He also taught us to apply formal and structural analysis to all forms of data, too, so I began to find and exploit new sources of information within the TAT itself. (See Holt, 1951b & c, 1952, 1958b, 1978a [Vol. 1].)

Despite his formidable persona and his old-world formality, Rapaport was a person of great warmth, humor, and charm. I was enormously flattered when he invited me to get on a first-name basis, and our real friendship began. He filled all of the aspects of a mentor's role to the utmost: demanding and disciplined teacher, supportive and affectionate friend, insider who opened many doors for me, and believer in my ability who shored up my always fragile self-esteem and gave me faith in myself. It is difficult to express how much he helped my career, guided and shaped my thinking about psychology, and inspired imitation and identification. I have tried to say more about him and our relationship in the memoir I wrote right after his death (Holt, 1967c).

Here I want to emphasize that he taught me what he called the structural point of view. From my present vantage point, I would say that it went much further, being an approximation of the systems outlook. It encompassed not only an analytic awareness of configural aspects of test performances, but also an approach to the understanding of persons that complemented what most clinicians call dynamics (motives, significant life events, and patterns of content in fantasy, symptoms, and so on) by a study of organizational aspects of adaptive behavior in nonstressful situations. He would point out how certain kinds of effective problem-solving strategies were structurally identical to defensive maneuvers for dealing with anxiety and conflict. And despite his formidable mastery of the most abstract theories, he scorned empty intellectualizing, always emphasizing a first approach to a case in commonsense terms, starting with the most basic objective facts. All of that fit in well with Murray's and Bob White's general theories and also their clinical approach to the study of lives, so I had little difficulty making it my own.

The fall of 1946 brought me an experience of considerable professional importance: my first APA meeting. The first convention following the war, it was heavily attended by the Big Names of psychology, and Rapaport introduced me to many of them. For example, so eager was he to enlarge my circle that when he spotted Hans Eysenck making a phone call as we walked down a corridor that he interrupted him to present me, to the Englishman's evident annoyance. I also met again a number of old friends—Princeton faculty members, teachers and fellow graduate students from Harvard, and old colleagues from Program Surveys, now moved to Michigan. It became a kind of delirious high, an experience I was determined to repeat. David helped by getting me involved in Division 12, of which he was secretary. I quickly was appointed to various committees and became active in division affairs.

APA's clinical division was just beginning its exponential growth under the impetus of the postwar boom in the mental health professions. The revitalized VA played a considerable part, with its clinical psychology branch under the decisive leadership of an old clinic friend, Jim Miller. At that APA meeting, there was special excitement because of the just-completed merger of APA with the American Association of Applied Psychology. Many of the latter's members were clinicians, and the political temperature of Division 12 was hot. At the business meeting, in the middle of a stormy debate, Laurence Shaffer stood up and passionately declared, "Mr. Chairman, I want to make an emotion!" His slip was a great tension-breaker as the hall exploded with laughter.

I attended a meeting of TAT workers there, at which I met old friends and made new ones. In those days, projective techniques had a great vogue, and there were lots of sessions about them in professional meetings. We found it so stimulating to learn what everyone else was doing that someone suggested that we should have a newsletter to keep those of us who were devoted to the test in touch. There being no other volunteers, I took it on and had a lot of fun for several years putting out the *TAT Newsletter* quarterly and seeing it grow and have some influence. It lasted from September 1946 (Vol. 1, No. 1) to Spring 1952 (Vol. V, No. 4). Beginning in 1949, it appeared in the *Journal of Projective Techniques,* and was continued there briefly by Ed Shneidman.

When the Menninger Foundation School of Psychiatry was being planned the year before I came, Rapaport had proposed that the opportunity to do research on it should not be missed and had begun a project on the selection of physicians for psychiatric training. He set up a procedure of systematically gathering the following data. Every applicant whose credentials looked promising came to Topeka where he or she was interviewed by two or three psychiatrists and was given the standard battery of psychodiagnostic tests by a psychologist (usually David himself). Each of the assessors also independently made a rating on the same scale, attempting to predict how good a psychiatrist the applicant would make. The data were then used to help make the decision, and most of those who were invited to come accepted.

In the summer of 1947, David decided that the research should be expanded, with more of a staff. He proposed that I come to work with him on it, going to half-time at Winter and being a half-time member of his Research Department at the Menninger Foundation (as it began to be called). He was also hiring Lester Luborsky, a promising young fellow from the University of Illinois. I eagerly accepted and began my first big research endeavor. It was funded at first by the VA, but in a couple of years I also had my initiation into raising grant funds to continue it.

Before telling the story of the selection project, which occupied most of the rest of the Topeka years, I should briefly fill in the other events. Only a year after I arrived, Rapaport—who was a power in the Topeka Psychoanalytic Society and Institute, where he taught—got Louisa and me admitted as research members. I could attend all scientific and business meetings, even chaired a committee that rewrote the society's bylaws, and after a couple of years became a lecturer on the institute's faculty, although I never gave a full course.

Partly as a result of my efforts, but much more because of the lingering influence of Rapaport, the Topeka Institute took the unprecedented step of admitting a few research psychologists (all of them George Klein's and my students, including Phil Holzman and Herb Schlesinger) to full clinical training. It was one of the beginnings of a long process that has finally opened all institutes of the American Psychoanalytic Association to psychologists.

Best of all, I had the privilege of attending (free) the institute's seminars. So I took advantage of this splendid opportunity to continue my psychoanalytic education and attended seminars fairly regularly, in sequence. Luckily, I was able to drop quietly out of any from which I felt I was getting nothing. Though I attended a couple of continuous case seminars, I made no move to get clinical training.

Actually, one of the best psychoanalytic training experiences I had was not in the institute but in a course Rapaport gave in our School of Clinical Psychology on the seventh chapter of *The Interpretation of Dreams* (Freud, 1900/1953), which enabled me to begin to understand that remarkable document in some depth. After David left to join the staff of the Austen Riggs Center in Stockbridge, Massachusetts, I kept in close touch with him, visited him several times in Stockbridge, and studied every one of the transcripts of his legendary seminars on ego psychology and metapsychology at the Western New England Institute as they were privately circulated.

Topeka was a wonderful place to meet people, and I quickly made some dear friends, several of whom I have already mentioned. In Rapaport's Research Department I found Paul Bergman, a transplanted Viennese psychoanalyst of great warmth, humor, and depth. Each of us liked the other's wife and daughters, and the two families became close. Soon Louisa and I found other highly congenial couples: Lester and Ruth Luborsky, Ben and Dinah Rubinstein (see Holt, 1990), Don and Ruth Watterson, George and Bessie Boris Klein, Milton and Marge Lozoff; and we were just starting to get to know Bill and Margaret Brenman Gibson well when they left. That was the trouble: Topeka did not hold many people for long. Delightful, fascinating people came, stayed long enough for you to get close to them, and then moved on.

The Research Department was full of good friends: Bille Escalona, Mert Gill (for more on him, see Holt, 1984d), and Milt Wexler, in addition to Paul, Lester, Ben, and George. The staff also included Mary Leitch, a psychiatric co-worker of Bille's, and Louisa, who had launched a new thesis topic, an integration of psychoanalytic and sociological theory. We did not meet much as a group. Rapaport's style of leadership was to have an intense relationship with each member or team, keeping in close touch with all projects and giving a great deal of himself and his wisdom. When he left, Bille Escalona took over until she fell ill in 1952; I served as acting director for the summer of that year and the next. Gardner Murphy succeeded me, and he and Lois had been in Topeka for only a year when I finally left Topeka. But this new friendship, like many of the others, survived the move.

In mid-1947, Bob Knight left to head up the Austen Riggs Center, taking Roy Schafer with him as his chief psychologist, and Allen Wheelis. A year later, David Rapaport, Margaret Brenman, and Merton Gill followed. I didn't know Knight well enough then to call him by his first name, but the others were all valued friends. Knight also brought in Erik Erikson, whom I had gotten to know (through his good friend David, of course) during a week when he came to Topeka to teach. It was a great experience to attend, as I occasionally did a few years later, staff conferences at Riggs, where this enormously talented staff brought together their various contributions to discussions of case presentations. It helped crystallize a growing conviction that understanding psychopathology required a multidisciplinary and integrative outlook, organismic but also psychosociocultural.

I believe that it was in the summer of 1950 that George and Bessie Klein went to Mexico for a vacation. He brought back a bad case of hepatitis and was hospitalized for more than a week in Winter Hospital. Since I lived so near, I went over almost every day to see him. In a series of long conversations, we found one another personally and intellectually so congenial that we not only became close friends, but also decided that when we left we would try to go to the same place and work together.

George had set up a laboratory in the basement of the Menninger Clinic's new office building, where he and his assistants—Herb Schlesinger, Phil Holzman, and Riley Gardner, all of whom were doing dissertations under his sponsorship— developed measures of cognitive styles, an original conceptual contribution of his. His reputation began to grow, and shortly Jerry Bruner got him invited to go to Harvard as a visiting professor. He never returned, except periodically as a consultant, to keep the lab work going.

For two hectic years, I held two half-time jobs, continuing my clinical work at the VA and carrying on the research at the Menninger Foundation. That way, I lost out on fringe benefits at both places, getting no vacation, and ended up with more than full-time responsibilities. At last, in 1949, I became a full-time senior psychologist at Menninger. But my old duodenal ulcer had returned, and my marriage was suffering also. I went into analysis with William Pious during 1950 and 1951.

Louisa sought psychoanalytic help, too. We tried various things to save the marriage, if only for our two little girls. We took dancing lessons together; we tried writing a joint paper; we got marriage counseling; we tried a separation. Finally, in 1952, we were divorced; even our joint paper eventually split (Holt, 1955). Louisa remarried, taking the name of Howe, and went off to California with the girls. Losing them was the worst experience I had ever had.

Professionally speaking, I gained a good deal from my years with Louisa. She taught me a lot about sociology and helped me mature my theoretical thinking more rapidly than I could have done otherwise. Her Ph.D. thesis was far ahead of its time. Its integrative theory contained a strong developmental emphasis which later was to make me greet the cognitive-developmental conceptions of Jane Loevinger (1976) with a sense of recognition.

The Menninger Foundation School of Clinical Psychology never fully recovered from the loss of its founder, David Rapaport, though it continued to exist during the rest of my seven years in Topeka. It took in only three classes of students, but we saw them through. After I stopped classroom teaching, I had my first experience in supervising a doctoral dissertation, that of William H. Brown, who got his Ph.D. from Kansas University in 1951.

That year, the psychological staff of the Menninger Foundation chose me as its new director, a position I held until I left. That got me involved in the foundation's intricate internal politics, for which I had little taste or talent. Meanwhile, for several years I had been keeping my clinical hand in by serving as the main psychologist for the Neurology Department of the foundation. That afforded me a good deal of interesting and useful experience with "organic" cases, in which psychological and characterological factors always played a discernible role. It also gave me a chance to serve on multidisciplinary clinical teams, following the progress of cases I had evaluated and contributing to management and therapeutic decisions about them. In addition, I did research testing for Paul Bergman's experiments with various forms of psychotherapy, following their progress and being able to discuss with him what the tests seemed to show in light of his clinical observations.

That led naturally to my participation in the early planning and developmental phases of a large cooperative study, the Menninger Psychotherapy Project (Kernberg et al., 1972; Sargent, Horwitz, Wallerstein, & Appelbaum, 1968; Wallerstein, 1986). At first the project was in the hands of a committee chaired by Benjamin B. Rubinstein; it included Gerald Aronson, Paul Bergman, Michalina Fabian, me, Hellmuth Kaiser, Lester Luborsky, Gardner Murphy, and Donald Watterson. One of our early joint tasks was to develop the Health-Sickness Rating Scale (Luborsky, 1962). I helped to interview some of the (nominally classical) psychoanalysts at the completion of treatment and learned what extraordinary variation there was in the actual behavior of people who used the same word for what they were doing.

Now for the selection project, as we called it: an attempt to learn how to pick good psychiatric residents. Lester Luborsky and I started work at about the same time, having frequent conferences with David Rapaport. We surveyed and organized the files, which contained application forms, letters of recommendation, and the test batteries as well as reports and ratings from interviewers and psychologists. The process of adding to them continued while we began to lay new plans. We were soon joined by William C. Morrow, who had worked on the Authoritarian Personality Project in Berkeley, and then by C. V. Ramana, a young Indian psychologist-psychoanalyst from Calcutta. At first, we concentrated on collecting data on how well the residents were doing during their three years of training. Every six months, we interviewed each supervisor in the School of Psychiatry about all of the residents he or she knew well, also getting ratings on various rating scales. We asked each resident to nominate the three best all-around psychiatrists among their fellow students, the best psychotherapists, research psychiatrists, and administrators. We used these supervisors' and peers' evaluations to validate the predictive ratings given by interviewers and testers at the time of admission.

At the same time, we were trying to develop new selection devices. Ramana furnished some sequences of dreams from his former patients; we presented them, asking for interpretations. We tried the same thing with a small group of TAT stories. Remembering a brief spin-off from the TAT that Murray had developed (called the Mind Reading Test), I put together a Picture Reaction Test (PRT) containing various pictures of people, singly and in groups; each was shown to a subject for approximately two seconds and was then taken away. The experimenter then merely asked, "What was that a picture of?" And Ramana tried out a single hour of free association as a selection device, recruiting volunteer subjects among the psychiatric residents on whom to try it out. As an unexpected result, Ramana soon had a full-time practice and had to withdraw from the project!

Our main subjects for these tryouts, however, were small samples of residents. We used the first set of evaluations (by supervisors and by the residents themselves) to choose the sixteen best and thirteen worst residents, plus three from the middle. All of those we selected volunteered to take our special new procedures. Bill Morrow set up a structured interview based on his previous work; Lester gave the TAT, to which I suggested that he add a Self-Interpretation in which each subject was asked to think back on a selected few stories and say what they showed about himself and his personality. I used the PRT, and we also employed several other possible instruments including those mentioned above.

Most of our brainstorms didn't seem to discriminate the better from the poorer residents, but the interview, TAT, Self-Interpretation, and PRT all seemed quite promising. We therefore developed scoring manuals for each procedure, specifying what features of performance distinguished the two extreme groups and attempting to specify the aspects of personality presumably being measured by each such indicator. It seemed to us an important step to insert these intervening variables between assessment data and ratings of future behavior, since aspects of personality must mediate good or poor performance of the various aspects of the psychiatrist's job.

The next logical step was to plan a predictive study, in which we would cross-validate the manuals for analysis of credentials, Rorschach, TAT, Self-Interpretation, Picture Reaction Test, and interview. During the first few years of the study, we were in frequent touch with Lowell Kelly and Don Fiske of the Michigan project on the selection of clinical psychologists, in a kind of cooperative, friendly rivalry. The design of our predictive study (which I won't try to describe here; see Holt & Luborsky, 1958) owed much to Dan Horn's (1943) thesis project. It aimed to validate our whole method, and since the applicants for two successive classes who were our subjects also went through the old ("rule-of-thumb") selection procedures as well, we could compare the intuitive and traditional method of selection with our more rigorously planned approach. To Bill Morrow, who left us after a year and a half, we owed the idea of developing scoring manuals to guide and objectify the process of clinical analysis of complex materials. Though the scores yielded by the manuals did not do well as predictors of psychiatric competence, this effort helped convince me that a good deal more could and should be done to help objectify the mysterious processes of clinical inference and judgment.

We finished the task of gathering the data for the predictive study in 1951; then began the long, slow process of working through the experimentally subdivided and arranged dossiers on the 64 men and women who had been accepted and had come to Topeka. We had to arrange our social lives so that we had as little contact with the new residents as humanly possible, to cut down the possibility of contamination. At the same time, we were continuing to gather criterion data on earlier classes and were planning our mail follow-up of all subjects outside of Topeka. That included those who had been assessed and rated but who had not come to the MFSP.

By 1953, the main tasks of the selection research were complete when the processes of gathering final criterion data became going concerns, and I decided to move to New York. Lester remained in Topeka for the five years it took to complete the analysis of the data and the writing of our book, while I made four visits a year to work with him. When I told this plan to one couple of dear friends whom I hated to leave behind, Fritz and Grace Heider, Fritz said with his usual twinkle, "Oh, you're becoming a quarterly—I'll subscribe to you!" And I did manage to see them in Lawrence on nearly every visit.

For my first five years in New York, I had to devote a good deal of time to finishing up the selection project. During that time, Paul Meehl's (1954) *Clinical vs. Statistical Prediction* made me realize that Lester's and my work could be relevant to the controversy ignited by that book. True, the overwhelmingly clinical atmosphere of Topeka had made us pay little attention to statistical prediction as an alternative, and the project was in no way set up to make such comparisons, but we had given the Strong Vocational Interest Inventory to most of our applicants. None of its keys, including a special new key based on responses from several thousand diplomates in psychiatry, yielded significant correlations with any of our criteria. Our main findings, however, were that the clinical judgments made by two judges (Lester and me) in our final predictive study after going over all data on each applicant not only had high validities but were significantly superior to the ratings made on the same physicians by the interviewers and testers using the old rule-of-thumb methods. A few other findings are noteworthy: predictive ratings by one initial interviewer were only slightly correlated with supervisors' evaluations ($r = .19$), but the mean of three interviewers' predictive ratings was significantly better ($r = .27$). Surprisingly, the verbal IQ from the Wechsler Adult Intelligence Scale (WAIS) did equally well: $r = .27$, $N = 219$.

I wrote up an epitome of our main findings, which appeared (Holt, 1958a) at about the same time as our book (Holt & Luborsky, 1958). The paper contains an analysis of Meehl's argument and an attempt to shift the focus from what Lee Cronbach called "horse-race designs" to the question of the proper place for clinical judgment in a predictive enterprise. It struck me that in most of the research reviewed by Meehl, rather sophisticated statistical systems were set up to find and cross-validate test scores that successfully predicted various behavioral criteria, but the clinical ratings were always made without the benefit of prior study of the possible relations between their data and the criterion. I therefore proposed that clinical predictions of this kind be called "naive" as compared to "sophisticated" ones, which followed the logic and basic procedures of statistical predictive systems while using such data as interviews and projective techniques and analyzing them clinically. The data of our own study showed how clinical judgment, appropriately disciplined and given a fair chance, could predict meaningful criteria quite well and much better than naive clinical predictions.

The paper attracted so much favorable attention from clinical psychologists that before long I found myself nominated for president of the Division of Clinical Psychology of the APA. Meehl was also nominated, and I won that particular race, but he became president of the whole APA. To my personal frustration, I did not at all succeed in changing the terms of the controversy. It continued to rage for years, while I stood on the sidelines and published a series of papers trying to explain why I thought this research was getting nowhere and what the real issues were (Holt, 1961b, 1970, 1975a; these were collected, with a new essay, in 1978a [Vol. 2] and were followed by two recent retrospective papers, 1986, 1988a).

I have never claimed that clinicians have mystical powers, nor that they must necessarily do better than statistically programmed computers in all predictive enterprises. It is obvious today that computers can function more reliably and indefatigably than human beings, especially in routine computational work. Therefore, if a formula can predict something as well as most clinicians functioning at their best, it is obvious that the machine is preferable for that specific job. My complaint has been about the wild overgeneralizing from more or less inadequate studies in a few predictive realms to assertions that the problem has been solved and there is nothing by way of clinical prediction that an actuarial system cannot do better. I have been troubled by the way such collections of evidence as Meehl's (1954) and Sawyer's (1966) have been used to justify abandoning the teaching of diagnostic testing by means of projective and similarly complex tests, and by the way the outcome of a few "horse-race" designs has been used to proclaim the triumph of mechanism in modern psychology. I have been at some pains, therefore, to point out the many ways in which we continue to rely on human judgment not only in clinical practice but in the everyday work of scientists (Holt, 1961b) and to warn that those who so enthusiastically proclaim their despisal of clinical judgment are poorly qualified to teach new members of a profession who must practice a healing art, in which the wise exercise of judgment is called for every day in situations incapable of being reduced to formulas.

The Research Center for Mental Health at NYU (1953–71)

I left Topeka primarily because I felt that a big city would be a better place to find another wife, but also to seek new professional horizons. Though Topeka had taught me an enormous lot, the point of diminishing returns was at hand. George Klein and I kept in close touch in our job search, and narrowed it down to two places, both of which wanted both of us. We were tempted by the western medical center of the University of Pittsburgh Medical School, where the money and the facilities were most attractive. In the end, we turned it down because the available jobs were as chief psychologists in the personal domains of the two leading psychiatrists there. We learned on visits to the site that they were locked in a bitter rivalry, and we feared that the structure of the situation would make it impossible for us to maintain our friendship.

At the APA meetings in 1952, George introduced me to Stuart W. Cook, head of the Department of Psychology in the Graduate School of Arts and Science, New York University, who offered us jobs. I liked him immediately, and the subsequent years have made my fondness and respect for him steadily increase. A gentle but strong person, he proved to be an almost ideal democratic leader: devoted to getting everyone's input and participation in group decisions and skilled in doing so, but also tough and effective in dealing with deans and fighting for our rights. He was trying to build up a first-rate psychology department at a then rather poor private university by the device of setting up a series of research centers for several of the major divisions of the discipline. He himself had founded one for social psychology, the Research Center for Human Relations, and staffed it with a brilliant and outstanding group of colleagues. The idea was that the leaders of these centers would get grant money to support the research work of bright young Ph.D.'s, who could teach part-time and create a setting in which graduate students would be drawn into ongoing projects. Working as research assistants, they would get investigative training, could get started on dissertation projects, and might find some needed financial support.

George and I decided to run the Research Center for Mental Health jointly. He took the title of director of research, and I had the administrative job of director. We began in the fall of 1953.

The Psychology Department and its first two research centers were located in an ancient brick structure on Astor Square, the Bible House, directly across from Wanamaker's venerable department store. Our building got its name when it was built by the American Bible Society, which still had offices there. After only a few years, we had to move out because it was to be torn down to make way for an expansion of Cooper Union. Wanamaker's closed down in the mid-fifties, too, after a big fire. Indeed, the whole face of the Greenwich Village has changed rather drastically in the past thirty-five years; it has become more dangerous and has less of a community atmosphere.

Despite our dingy quarters, the Graduate Department of Psychology was an enterprising, friendly, busy place to work. We had a good deal of contact with students and faculty alike, in informal coffee hours every afternoon. There we became acquainted with Isidor Chein, a fatherly scholar who always had a group of students gathered around as much for his measured and wise comments on scientific issues as for his endless store of anecdotes. And Marie (Mitzi) Jahoda: a vibrant, witty, brilliant, attractive woman with whom I would have fallen in love immediately if she had been younger. They were on the staff of Stuart's Research Center for Human Relations, along with some gifted younger people: Dick Christie, Mort Deutsch, John Harding, and Murray Horwitz. (Unfortunately for our growing friendship, all of them except Is Chein left NYU after a few years.)

From the Bible House the whole department moved in 1956 to occupy a small building at 21 Washington Place, which was converted from a hatband factory to be the new home of psychology. Our Research Center for Mental Health had the entire fifth floor, which soon began to be too small. We took over part of the basement and began a search for more adequate space elsewhere in the neighborhood. Finally, George and I got a research space construction grant from NIH, after a site visit headed by Harry Harlow. That enabled us to reconstruct another former factory's quarters into a fine new set of offices and laboratories in a building at 707 Broadway. There was a gala opening celebration in March 1965. With our foot in the door, the rest of the department gradually acquired the rest of the twelve floors of what is now known as the Psychology Building, at 6 Washington Place.

Personal Life

I will briefly describe my personal life during these years, and then take up more professional matters. Immediately on coming to New York, I joined the Dessoff Choirs and enjoyed singing with them for several years. Several friends and I broke away to form a smaller, more intimate group, the Canby Singers (led by Edward Tatnall Canby). We had great fun for several years, but the pressure of work on *Personality Patterns of Psychiatrists* finally made me drop out early in 1958. I still sang a bit from time to time, until I had to quit when I developed nodes on my vocal cords around 1970 and had to be entirely silent for two weeks. That taught me how intensely interactive verbal communication is: the fact that I could not respond except in writing struck many interlocutors dumb or made them whisper or shout.

Before leaving Topeka, I had interviewed an unusually attractive prospect for an internship, Crusa Adelman; she didn't take it. To my surprise, I ran into her in New York about a year after my arrival. I asked her out but nothing clicked. Then, just after having broken up with someone else in 1955, I looked her up again. This time it worked: we fell in love. Before we could marry, however, I had to overcome some neurotic problems in my relationships with women. Fortunately, I was able to do so with the skilled help of a fine psychoanalyst, Charlotte Feibel, and Crusa and I were married on my fortieth birthday. We had a wonderful year and a half together. Then, on the second of our trips to Europe, while she was driving us she misjudged a curve and turned the car over. She died shortly afterward. I was uninjured but emotionally devastated.

It helped a good deal that David Rapaport decided to spend a sabbatical year at NYU just then, coinciding with George's taking a year off. David was not only emotionally supportive to me, but also contributed a great deal intellectually to the research center. Notably, he offered another seminar on the seventh chapter of *The Interpretation of Dreams,* hardly repeating at all what he had said a decade earlier in Topeka.

The next year (1960–61), I took advantage of an opportunity (and a fellowship from the National Institute of Mental Health) to spend a year at the Center for Advanced Study in the Behavioral Sciences in Palo Alto, which was then headed by Ralph Tyler. I had gotten to know Ralph well by serving with him (and Neal Miller, Ted Magoun, Douglas Bond, and George Engel) on the Fellowship Committee of the Foundations Fund for Research in Psychiatry (1956–1961). It was a great year in many ways, considerably enlarging my intellectual horizons. I learned some linguistics in contacts with Morris Halle and Roman Jakobson; some philosophy from Abraham Kaplan; anthropology from Edmund Leach; political science from Ray Wolfinger; literary criticism from Henry Nash Smith. I loved living in the redwoods at the crest of the mountains between Stanford and the Pacific; I had an emotionally restorative love affair; I made many friends among the fellows and renewed old friendships with Silvan Tomkins, Nevitt Sanford, and Doc Cartwright; at last I had time to read and reflect, even write some poetry; and Mert Gill was right across the bay in Berkeley. During the year, David Rapaport died suddenly, so I spent some time in Stockbridge with his widow and his secretary, Sue Annin, going over his files and getting his *Nachlass* (literary legacy) in order. That helped bring Merton Gill and me closer together. We met frequently, exchanged manuscripts we were working on, and planned the memorial volume that appeared a few years later, *Motives and Thought* (Holt, 1967b).

During that year I was president-elect of the Division of Clinical Psychology (APA) and gave some thought to what I should try to accomplish in my incumbency. It struck me that the time had come to mount an interdisciplinary effort to give serious consideration to Lawrence Kubie's dream of a new mental health profession. I got some help from friends in the area, notably Milt Wexler, set up a planning committee, and raised grant money. The conference brought together a couple of dozen outstanding people from psychiatry, social work, psychoanalysis, and clinical psychology at NYU's Gould House conference center in Hastings, New York, for a long weekend in 1963. We discussed working papers that had been distributed in advance and reached pretty good consensus: the project was feasible and intellectually convincing, needing only someone with the courage and institutional backing to try it out. These papers became the nexus of a book (Holt, 1971a; see also 1963b, 1965b, 1967e, 1969, & 1972b).

One of the participants, Robert S. Wallerstein, had been one of the subjects in our final predictive study in Topeka. Now he became head of psychiatry at the University of California Medical School in San Francisco. Being a man of courage, initiative, and strong leadership, he took the plunge and founded the first school to offer an integrated interdisciplinary curriculum and a new degree, Doctor of Mental Health. He assembled a first-rate faculty (including Erik Erikson) and attracted a superb student body. I had the pleasure of observing at close hand from time to time as an outside consultant and evaluator. The program fully realized Kubie's dream and my faith that this rational approach would produce better clinicians than any of the traditional disciplines. In one objective evaluation of the work of a group of trainees including psychiatric residents and clinical psychology interns, advanced students for the D.M.H. significantly outperformed all the others. Yet in the end the program had to be abandoned because the threatened established disciplines formed a political alliance that killed it.

On moving to New York, I had decided to get active in politics and had joined the Village Independent Democrats, a reform club in the Village. In California, several of us fellows worked in Kennedy's election campaign and had the rare experience of winning. Over the years, VID gave me experiences in poll watching, canvassing, collecting signatures for petitions, and other basic forms of political activism.

On returning from my year at the CASBS, I immediately got involved in the peace movement. Shaving off my California-grown beard to look as respectable as possible, I addressed a peace rally for the first of what was to be about a half dozen times. Back in 1948–50, I had been a member of SPSSI's Committee on Atomic Education; now I joined the New York State Psychological Association's Committee on Peace (1961–62) and the SPSSI Committee on Arms Control and Disarmament (1961–64). As luck would have it, I was invited to give a paper in the Great Hall of the Cooper Union two days after President Kennedy's address to the nation that precipitated the Cuban missile crisis of October 1961. At a hurried meeting of the SPSSI committee, we decided that I must take advantage of the opportunity to speak out against his one-sided presentation, for my speech was to be broadcast. So I quickly rewrote and called on the president to negotiate a trade under which the Soviets would remove their missiles from Cuba and we ours from Turkey.

At about this time, Leo Szilard was forming the Council for a Livable World, which I learned about through my old friend Margaret Brenman. I seem to have a weakness for Hungarian geniuses; Szilard fired me with enthusiasm, and before long I was heading a New York chapter of the new organization. We held some public meetings and recruited a good many members until the national board decided to terminate the experiment of having local chapters.

Soon I was invited to be on the council of a new organization, the Congress of Scientists on Survival, with my old friend Gardner Murphy and such interesting new acquaintances as Albert Szent-Gyorgy and Harlow Shapley. At one of our first council meetings, very early in the academic year 1962–63, we decided to hold a national meeting in the spring and needed some graduate student assistants to help with a planning session.

One of those who answered my call was an attractive student in our clinical program, Joan Esterowitz, whom I had not previously met. I took the precaution of getting her telephone number and after the meeting asked her for a date. She was a bit reluctant to get involved with a professor sixteen years her senior, but I persisted. In brief, we were married the next summer, August 1963, on Cape Cod. In 1965, our son Danny was born, after which Joan decided to give up the attempt to complete her doctoral studies, choosing instead to be an at-home mother.

She had introduced me to Truro, where we spent our honeymoon, and we eagerly seized the chance to buy a house there. Much enlarged and renovated over the years, it has been our summer refuge ever since. Here I garden, swim, take long walks, and generally live a life that is gratifyingly close to nature. Having this yearly escape made it possible for me to tolerate spending most of thirty-seven years in New York City.

It is difficult to decenter enough to come to an estimate of Joan's impact on my professional life. Despite her having lost interest in becoming a clinical psychologist, she has always had a strong aptitude for psychotherapy and for human relations generally. When I tend to soar into abstractions and cloudy conceptual regions, she pulls me back to the earth of real and suffering people. It was of course her strong commitment to peace and to political activism that brought us together; ever since, she has supported and encouraged my involvement in work of that kind. She also exerts steady pressure on me not to work so hard.

In 1967, Dave McClelland invited me to come to Harvard for a year as visiting professor in their ailing clinical program. Unhappily, Gordon Allport died just before we arrived, and Garry Boring was quite ill. I did have a chance to spend some time with him before he passed away; but in many ways the best thing about the year was the chance to renew and deepen my friendship with Harry Murray. Now retired and a widower, Harry was working on no less than ten books and eager for companionship. We had a regular lunch date once a week, which usually stretched far into the afternoon with great wide-ranging conversations. How happy for him we were the following year when he told Joan and me that he was getting married again, to a psychologist of great intelligence, charm, and warmth, Nina Fish, who proved altogether worthy of him!

Among the new friends of that year were my very helpful teaching assistant, Bert Cohler, and the sociologist Gary Marx and his wife Phyllis, who had the apartment right underneath ours on the old arboretum grounds across from Radcliffe. Happily, Babbie and Fred Whipple, Ai-li and Bob Chin, and Johnny and Jean Arsenian were still around to renew old ties. And by another fortunate coincidence, my year at Harvard was my daughter Cathy's senior year at Radcliffe, so we saw a good deal of her. In that same year, my older daughter, Dorothy, a graduate of Brown, married and received an M.A. from the University of Indiana. The happiest event of the year was the arrival of our second son, Michael. Raising my two boys has been one of the most deeply rewarding experiences of my life and surely not irrelevant to my career in clinical psychology. I am sure that I have been a more humanistic and empathic teacher and researcher because of a warm and happy family life.

In the summer of 1979, shortly after the accident at Three Mile Island, Joan and I joined a Cape Cod attempt (ultimately successful) to block the construction of a second nuclear power plant in Plymouth, directly across the bay. On returning to New York, Joan began doing antinuclear work with the New York Public Interest Research Group. She established NYPIRG's Indian Point project, a multifaceted campaign to close down the nuclear plant in nearby Westchester County. Soon she was working up to eighty hours a week, and our adolescent sons and I had to take over the housework. Fortunately, we all like to cook, and though none of us likes cleaning, we managed.

Meanwhile, I was serving as Joan's scientific consultant, reading the technical stuff and trying to translate it for her. Naturally, I got quite interested in the problem of the biological and medical effects of radiation, and the psychological aspects of trying to run this kind of industry. I even wrote a paper on the latter topic, which I presented in Rome but haven't revised for publication.

Joan worked closely with the Union of Concerned Scientists and other environmental groups. They succeeded in getting the Nuclear Regulatory Commission to hold hearings on closing down the plant—the first time that had been done for an operating reactor. I took a semester off to help her recruit a team of experts from the social sciences to testify (Holt & Holt, 1982). The unsuccessful end of the project in the late eighties at least brought our home life back to normal.

Clinical Practice: Diagnostic Testing

At first when I came to New York, I strongly missed being in a hospital setting in constant contact with patients. George and I did our first research at Kings County Hospital in an effort not to lose touch, and I began to find opportunities to do diagnostic testing as a private practitioner. I kept my hand in it until I went to California in 1960, but never went back after that interruption.

For several years, David Wechsler and I were part of an unusual team of psychiatrists (mostly psychoanalysts) and psychologists engaged by a large international corporation to launch a program of assessing executives. Ostensibly, we were to interview and test them all to establish benchmarks that might be useful in case of future problems. The "Old Man," the president, volunteered to kick it off. When I gave him the WAIS, I was astonished to see an organically devastated picture, which was confirmed by the Rorschach. I at once spoke to the psychiatrist who had interviewed him, who hadn't picked up any signs of brain damage, and urged him to do a neurological exam. My diagnosis was verified; then evidences began to emerge of unexplained temper tantrums and erratic behavior. He was persuaded to accept early retirement and died very soon thereafter. My in-house reputation, and that of psychological tests, was made by that lucky strike. Ironically, the original plan had to be abandoned since our small system was promptly swamped by executives with pressing immediate problems. It gave me a good deal of interesting clinical experience with a population relatively new to me.

Shortly before he died, David Rapaport told me that his main clinical publication (Rapaport, Gill, & Schafer, 1945–46) had been out of print for a while and was much in demand. He wanted to be able to leave its royalties to his two daughters, since he had not been able to save much. Would I undertake its condensation and updating? I agreed to do so and finally got it out (Holt, 1968b). A few years later, I accepted an invitation from Irving Janis to write a quarter of a big volume on personality (Janis, Mahl, Kagan, & Holt, 1969); my section appeared as the little book *Assessing Personality* shortly afterward (Holt, 1971b). Most of my other papers on diagnostic testing have been collected in Volume 1 of my book on methods (Holt, 1978a).

Organizations

The mention of David's death reminds me that shortly after it, several of us who had worked closely with him decided to get together in Stockbridge and organize some kind of continuing though informal association of those who had been influenced by this extraordinary man. Austen Riggs Center, then headed by Bob Knight, kindly gave us a place to meet, and his successors have been equally hospitable. Every June, several dozen of us gather for a weekend of good fellowship and spirited discussion of one another's presentations of current work. The group has slowly enlarged (by invitation, largely to the students and co-workers of the original old Topeka and Stockbridge hands) but remains stubbornly informal and reliably stimulating.

I have of course been a member of numerous professional and scientific organizations, and during the first few decades of my career I found attendance at their annual conventions enjoyable and useful. Doubtless the people I have met there and the discussions I have had—even the papers heard!—have had important impacts on my thinking and work. But in the past thirty years or so, APA meetings have become so enormous and hectic that I don't enjoy them any more. When I became actively interested in systems theory, I joined the Society for General Systems Research but have felt something of an outsider there. I was surely an insider in the Society for Projective Techniques (now, for Personality Assessment) and was active on its committees for a few years in the fifties. But when I was offered the presidency I had to face the fact that I didn't really believe in psychological testing or assessment except as part of clinical or personality psychology; so instead, I resigned my membership.

Another informal grouping has meant a lot to me, though it is so unlike most professional associations that it doesn't have any definite membership. That is the group of friends who gather every summer at the Wellfleet home of Robert J. Lifton to discuss some aspect of psychohistory. I believe I was first invited in 1973 and have attended regularly ever since. The group had begun as an expansion of discussions between Bob Lifton and Erik Erikson, whom I had always admired and respected, so I was happy to have a chance to prolong and deepen my friendship with him. Some of the gifted and stimulating people I have met there are Norman Birnbaum, Harvey Cox, Daniel Ellsberg, Kai Erikson, Dick Falk, Steven Jay Gould, Gerald Holton, Rosabeth Kantor, Ken Keniston, John Mack, Philip Morrison, Dick Sennett, and Chuck Strozier. A few I had known before, such as Margaret Brenman, Carol Cohn, Chuck Fisher, and Dan Yankelovich, whom I brought in. I must resist the temptation to go on listing remarkable people who have been brought together by Bob Lifton, who has a great gift for finding, attracting, and rewarding them by facilitating marvelous shoptalk in a beautiful setting.

During the past half dozen years, I have found another organization of congenial colleagues, the International Society of Political Psychology. Under the heading Teaching and Research Concerning Peace I relate how my work has veered in this direction; I have become active enough in the society to have been elected to a term on its board of governors (1988–90) and greatly enjoy its annual meetings.

Teaching

So that George and I could devote ourselves to building up our new center, our associate professorships carried light teaching loads—one or two seminars and courses per semester, all for graduate students. I have been lucky enough to make most of my teaching relevant to my main interests. At first I gave the clinical students a course on research methods and in subsequent years one on the design and evaluation of clinical research; that led to several publications (Holt, 1962a & b, 1965a, 1973, 1978a [Vol. 2], 1982c). For years, I gave a course in the interpretation of the TAT, the part of diagnostic testing I enjoyed the most, and thought about writing a book on it. The closest I came was a group of chapters (Holt, 1951b & c, 1952, 1958b, 1961a, 1978a [Vol. 1]). As I got well into measuring manifestations of the primary process in the Rorschach (see next section), I occasionally gave seminars on the scoring method I had developed. In 1970, I was invited to give a week's workshop on the scoring at the University of Bergen (Norway) and in 1980 a similar one at the University of Rome.

At APA meetings, I had become friendly with Jane Loevinger and learned that she too was working on a scoring manual that, like mine, attempted to objectify some of the processes of clinical analysis of qualitative verbal data. When hers appeared (Loevinger, Wessler, & Redmore, 1970), I found it so interesting and stimulating that I organized a group of colleagues to motivate one another to work through the self-training exercises she provided. Then, for several years, I gave a course in ego development, treating the theory of personal maturity, reviewing the research on related methods (such as that of Kohlberg, 1984, and Douglas Heath, 1965) and hers, and training students in the scoring. That in turn led to some research, discussed later.

The student rebellions of the mid-sixties had a salutary effect on my teaching. NYU undergraduates demanded that the senior members of the only recently unified faculty cease their exclusive preoccupation with graduate students and offer undergraduate courses. The department agreed, and I gave one of the courses they wanted, on the psychology of alienation. Two of my brightest undergraduate students (Susan Frank [Breitzer] and Barbara Sayres [Ducey]) got so interested in doing research on the topic that we formed mentorial relationships that lasted many years.

In this and other ways, I found undergraduate teaching at least as gratifying as classroom work with graduate students. Over the years, I gave a fair number of other kinds of courses at both levels, notably including psychoanalytic theory, but I never developed into a first-rate lecturer. Occasionally I could do a good job, but the next day I might verbally stumble and wander. I have always been a better writer than talker. When in 1985 I received NYU's Great Teacher Award, I felt that if deserved at all it was for the kind of teaching I always enjoyed most: the one-to-one, collaborative work of supervising research.

Editorial Work

In 1949, soon after beginning the *TAT Newsletter,* I was invited to join the editorial advisory boards of the *Journal of Social Issues* and the *Journal of*

Projective Techniques. Since then I have never been on fewer editorial boards than that, with a steady flow of manuscripts for my blue pencil. Maybe I have learned to sublimate the impulse that caused me to cool my heels in that grammar-school hall; anyway, I have always enjoyed evaluating research and making suggestions for the improvement of papers.

Among the score of journals I have helped edit, three stand out. I have refereed the most papers and for the longest time—35 years—as a board member of the *Journal of Nervous and Mental Disease,* working with some splendid colleagues. For almost as long, I have been with *Psychological Issues,* of which George Klein was founding editor. David Rapaport had had the brainstorm of creating a monograph series with high editorial standards to help develop a new kind of scientific psychoanalysis. George took the idea and ran with it, ably succeeded on his death by his old student Herb Schlesinger. The other members of the editorial board have all been good old friends, many dating back to Topeka days, and our annual editorial meetings over lunch during the December meetings of the American Psychoanalytic Association have been reunions as well as working sessions.

Finally, I want to mention *Psychoanalysis and Contemporary Science.* Benjamin Rubinstein had the idea of a psychoanalytic journal for papers of conventional (nonmonographic) length with truly scientific standards, to raise the level of the discipline. He approached George and me; we were enthusiastic and brought in other friends and colleagues—Leo Goldberger, Lester Luborsky, Don Spence, and Peter Wolff. We were also joined by Emanuel Peterfreund (he and I edited the first volume together), Victor Rosen, Daniel Shapiro, and Theodore Shapiro. Our publisher persuaded us to make it a hardcover annual. For several years we (and some other editors) recruited good papers, edited them carefully, and made a go of it, rotating principal editorship of the volumes. After the sixth volume, however, it seemed prudent to go to a regular quarterly journal format. Leo Goldberger took over the chief editorship of the retitled *Psychoanalysis and Contemporary Thought,* with which I have continued to be associated.

My relationship to another journal, *Mental Health Book Review Index,* is rather different but also memorable. Its guiding spirit was an unusual and gifted woman, Ilse Bry. I had met her when she was librarian of the New York Psychoanalytic Association, whence she went to be the psychiatric librarian at the NYU Medical School. One day in the early 1960s she came to me in a highly agitated state: she had just been fired and was in a mildly paranoid panic. She did not need a salary, since she had a pension from the German government (she had lost her librarian's job in Berlin when the Nazis took over), but she did need an institutional auspice to continue her pet project, the *Mental Health Book Review Index.* So I took her in as a staff member of the Research Center for Mental Health and became in return the chair of the committee of consultants to the index and then (1965–73) president of the Council on Research in Bibliography, which she created and incorporated as publisher of the index. That journal was a useful bibliographic aid which Dr. Bry converted into an instrument of research (see Afflerbach & Franck, 1977). I learned a good deal about many aspects of publication and the functioning of libraries from my years of association with Ilse until her death in 1974.

Administration

My main achievement during the first two decades at NYU was building the Research Center for Mental Health, in close collaboration with George S. Klein. George and I had such good luck with our research grant requests that we began to have a high opinion of our grantsmanship; only later did I realize that the fifties and sixties were the time of huge expansion in the research budget of the National Institute of Mental Health: Congress constantly pressed more money on the institutes of health than they asked for. In one dizzy moment of early success, our requests to both NIMH and the Ford Foundation for several years of program support were simultaneously granted. Since each gave us half of what we had asked for, at first we thought we could accept both, but then we settled for Ford. When that was over, NIMH gave us a couple of multiyear program grants; and though we had one dry year when the university had to carry our operation with little help, we also got substantial grants from several other sources. When the National Institutes of Health announced its program of Research Career Awards, which in effect created a research professorship for the recipient at his or her university, we both applied and got them. Thanks to this unusual grant, the first $25,000 of my salary was paid by NIMH from 1962 to 1988 and I was free to take the equivalent of a sabbatical at full pay whenever it seemed desirable for my research. Awardees were expected to be good citizens of their home departments but were supposed to devote themselves primarily to research. Hence, I rarely ever taught more than one course a semester thereafter and several times only one an entire academic year. It also protected me against any temptation to do more administration than that of the research center.

We had laid out ambitious plans to build up a center for research on the psychoanalytic theory of thinking. Our proposal was to carry on theoretical and empirical studies simultaneously. It was just the right time in history to make such a proposal. The prestige of psychoanalysis was high enough so that foundations and the Institutes of Health were eager to support attempts to make it more scientific. And with funding for a program of interlinked studies, we were able to build up a first-rate staff fairly rapidly. We took in several postdocs from other universities— Irving Paul, Fred Pine, Donald Spence, Paul Wachtel, and David Wolitzky. Since our main teaching assignments were to sponsor doctoral thesis research, we could pick out our most talented students and give them staff jobs: Morris Eagle, Leo Goldberger, Nancy Goldberger, and others. We could even make a place in this nonmedical setting for psychiatric psychoanalysts: Robert J. Langs, Hartvig Dahl, Walter Boernstein, and Merton Gill (not all of them at once!). On a number of occasions, we were joined for a year by distinguished foreign colleagues, such as Gudmund Smith, Pinchas Noy, and Douglas Kirchner.

In the 1950s and 1960s, I again experienced the hypomanic excitement of being part of a new institution in its initial growth spurt. Morale was excellent; excitement often ran high at our regular staff meetings, where students and staff alike could present work in progress for critique or make suggestions about the research of others. At one time, we were affluent enough to afford to hire Melanie Chussid to combine the disparate roles of librarian and cook. Once again I saw the old solidarity-making magic of breaking bread together at work as we had staff lunches daily, where the conversation was at times as good as I remembered it at the Harvard Clinic.

We could also afford to hire Suzette Annin as a part-time editorial assistant for our many publications. Sue had been David Rapaport's personal secretary until he discovered her editorial genius. With us, she spent the other half of her time as managing editor of *Psychological Issues* until her tragic and premature death from cancer.

After about a decade, George and I decided to let our titles (co-director) reflect the actual state of affairs, and we took on my former student and collaborator Leo Goldberger as associate director. It pains me to report that as the years went by, my friendship with George deteriorated somewhat. The main problem was rivalry. We both discovered that we were more competitive than we had realized, and each of us had a tendency to draw to ourselves our own circle of students and junior staff members. Repeatedly, we tried to talk it out, frankly verbalizing our feelings of jealousy and wishes to predominate, but it never really worked. Neither of us took criticism gracefully or gratefully, and for each self-esteem was more fragile than outsiders suspected. I envied George his charisma and his fertility of research ideas; he envied my greater ease in writing and perhaps other things I have forgotten.

In 1969, my periodic impulse to leave New York, a city I never learned to love, got so strong that I resigned the co-directorship in favor of Leo Goldberger and began looking for job possibilities elsewhere. Though I turned up a few, in the end it was too hard to leave the East Coast where my family and Joan's were principally located, so I stayed on but did not resume administrative work. I also declined when colleagues urged me to run for chairman of the Psychology Department, having discovered that life was sweeter without executive responsibility.

In any event, George's sudden and wholly unexpected death in the spring of 1971 threw the Research Center into a crisis. Coincidentally, Merton Gill and Hartvig Dahl had both decided, for different reasons, to leave at the end of the semester. Paul Wachtel and one or two others of the junior staff received good job offers elsewhere. A year earlier, when it was time to submit an application to NIMH for another five-year program grant, I had resigned the co-directorship as just explained, so for the first time the principal investigators were George and Leo Goldberger. When news of George Klein's death reached NIMH, they requested a reapplication, and granted it but at a lower level of funding and for a shorter time. During the next couple of years, the staff—its senior members now decimated—drifted away. Funding, once so easy to obtain, was now very difficult to find. The Research Center for Mental Health died a slow, anticlimactic, and hardly noticed death.

If I ask myself now what the main contribution of RCMH was, I believe that I must answer that it was a training ground for a generation of researchers in psychoanalysis and clinical psychology. At first, our contribution in clarifying psychoanalytic theory and subjecting some of its propositions to empirical testing seemed of paramount importance. By now, however, I feel a bit disillusioned: the principal result of the theoretical work was a series of papers by George, me, and other staff members in which we exposed a variety of severe deficiencies in metapsychology (and, to some extent, the clinical theory). The empirical research, while always informed with a kind of psychoanalytic sensibility, only rarely tested propositions that many psychoanalysts would recognize as part of their theory. I cannot even point to any final reformulation of the psychoanalytic theory of thinking. Nevertheless, the effort was definitely worthwhile, a rich learning experience for many of us.

And now for the main activity of my New York years: research!

Research

MEASURING PRIMARY PROCESS THINKING.   Before I left Topeka, I met Bruno Klopfer at an APA conference. As the leading exponent of a rival school of Rorschach work, his name was virtually anathema among Rapaport's students, but he proved to be a dear old fellow, quite unpretentious and jolly. I was surprised to learn two things about him: that he was a Jungian analyst and that he had a severe visual defect with a rather distracting constant nystagmus. He invited me to write a chapter in a Rorschach book he and a couple of colleagues were writing (Klopfer, Ainsworth, Klopfer, & Holt, 1954): an attempt to consider the test from the standpoint of personality theories.

I decided to approach this interesting challenge not by considering Rorschach phenomena or scores and asking what they might be measuring in terms of various theories, but the other way around: taking up a series of theories and asking what they might contribute to an understanding of Rorschach responding. An unexpected consequence of this decision was that I realized how well Freud's theory of primary and secondary processes conceptualized a good deal that Rapaport had taught me to see in the test, most of it not captured in conventional scores. That was the beginning of a still-unfinished line of work.

One major focus was developing a measuring instrument, a technique of scoring the Rorschach for manifestations of primary process thinking and of a person's means of controlling and defending against it. I scoured Freud's writings for hints about concrete operational indicators of the primary process as well as studying his theoretical remarks about it and the secondary process, and I looked for ways to concretize them, usually with the aid of a body of experimental data. The result was a scoring manual, which went through ten mimeographed editions and which I made available to any interested researcher at cost.

Very briefly, the manual describes 22 categories of content—various manifestations of libidinal and aggressive wishes (and fears)—and 36 formal categories—types of condensation, displacement, symbolization, autistic reasoning, and so on. Then, I noticed quite early that the same kinds of primary process occurred in the Rorschachs of psychotic patients and of normal college students, but with qualitative differences. Studying those, I felt that the normal subjects managed to control the material and defend themselves against its possibly disrupting or disturbing implications by a variety of means. With the aid of Joan Havel, I listed 53 types of such Controls and Defenses, classifying them as types of Distance, Context, Delaying Tactics, Overtness, and (mostly pathological) classical defenses (Holt & Havel, 1960). I had found clinically useful Martin Mayman's (1970) adaptation of Rapaport's form-level scores. Rorschach had originally just divided responses into those with good, convincing form accuracy (F+) and those with unconvincing forms (F−). This dichotomy had now grown into a differentiated scheme of 9 categories. Once I began to think about responses in terms of the respondent's efforts to control his or her perceptual-associative processes, it seemed that Mayman's measures of the fit between concept and the area of the inkblot to which it was coordinated could become a vital part of the Control and Defense scoring. With his permission, I incorporated it, elaborating somewhat on his scoring manual. Adopting a suggestion by Fred Pine, when he was a postdoc at the research center, I added to the standard technique of administering the Rorschach a special "affect inquiry," in which the respondent is asked what emotions (if any) he or she felt while giving each response. It then seemed necessary to summarize all of this detail by means of overall ratings of Defensive Effectiveness and of the response's implicit demand for defense.

The scoring manual lists each category with a general description and then examples of scorable responses. It is supplemented by a section in which Carol Eagle describes methods by which the scoring can be adapted to TAT stories and dreams (see Eagle, 1964), and by scored examples of complete protocols. I have published papers and book chapters on this method ever since 1956, four of which I assembled in Volume 1 of my *Methods in Clinical Psychology* (Holt, 1978a), and a good many of my students have done dissertations using the method and have gone on to publish relevant research findings.

Oddly enough, the two main centers of research using my primary-process manual were in Montreal and Rome. For years, my early publications about the method stimulated inquiries from colleagues in many places, to whom I sent copies of the manual. A fair amount of published research appeared, which I have not yet collected and evaluated. Early on, a Francophone colleague at the Université de Montréal, Germain Lavoie, obtained a copy of the manual and translated it into French. He then interested no less than half a dozen students in doing doctoral dissertations using it, as well as publishing a good deal of such research on his own. A few years later, in the mid-seventies, I had a visit from a pair of psychologists from the University of Rome, Gian Vittorio Caprara and Nino Dazzi. They had heard about the method and were acquainted with some of my publications. After a few hours of stimulating talk, we became good friends and have had a great deal of intellectual exchange ever since, on both sides of the Atlantic. First they returned a year later to participate in one of the informal training seminars I often staged to train students in the scoring. Then they took the manual back to Italy and had it translated. Caprara trained a large group of doctoral students and involved them in dissertation research. (See, for example, Caprara et al., 1977.) A few years ago, he and Dazzi published their translation of the scoring manual (Holt, 1983b). Caprara and I also collaborated on a developmental study of primary process manifestations in Italian children's Rorschachs (Caprara, Holt, Pazielli, & Giannotti, 1986).

There are two main reasons for this much interest in yet another scheme for scoring the oldest projective technique, now discredited in the eyes of many psychologists. First, it offered a face-valid (theoretically plausible), operational, and reliable method of measuring an important psychoanalytic concept. That fact appealed to many who were looking for a way to do controlled and quantitative research on psychoanalysis. Second, as the work progressed, some of the findings offered promise that important constructs were being measured. In particular, what I called a measure of adaptive versus maladaptive regression yielded frequently replicated correlations with creativity and resistance to stress. That is, in male subjects, adaptive regression is a positive predictor of creativity, and maladaptive regression is negatively correlated with tolerance for extended periods of perceptual isolation (sensory deprivation) and other stressful experiences. Despite a few efforts to solve the puzzle empirically, it still remains a mystery why a measure that has given repeatedly replicated results with males fails with females.

In the mid-1970s, it began to look as if the scoring manual had reached fairly definitive shape, and a good deal of research had been done with it. I decided, therefore, to make one final revision and to publish it, with normative data. The strategy was to gather collections of scored Rorschachs that had been used in various research studies where good measures of external criteria were available, put them all into one big computer file, and then tally the frequencies with which each scoring category appeared in relevant subgroups: by sex, age, educational level, diagnostic grouping, and so on. For each protocol, all of the summary scores proposed by various authors (as well as others I confected) would be computed, and the results would be correlated with the available external criteria. I drew up elaborate specifications for the software that would accomplish all this and hired a computer programmer to execute it. Meanwhile, my assistants and I collected over a thousand Rorschachs, all scored by the latest edition of my manual, and coded them, along with the supplementary data on each case.

More than a dozen years later, the task is not yet completed. The whole story is too tedious to tell here; in brief, the programming task was much more complicated than I had realized and had to be done and redone several times by different programmers before the resulting program would produce halfway acceptable output. Repeatedly, I raised more funds (each time with more difficulty), hired a new programmer, and hoped it would be done in a few months. Every time, unexpected ambiguities in the data, bugs in the program, or various types of noise in the system exhausted everyone's patience and the available money before complete and usable data on each case could be produced. Now that I have retired and no longer have a university computer center to work with, it may be necessary to abandon this long effort and merely publish the scoring manual without benefit of norms or the results of statistical processing of a large body of data.

SUBLIMINAL INFLUENCES ON COGNITION.   George Klein and I began the research center with a small grant from the National Institute of Mental Health, to pursue a lead George had turned up at Harvard. Working with Gudmund Smith, he had rediscovered metacontrast: the fact that when a short flash of a visual figure is immediately followed by a longer exposure of another one, the first one is not reportable though it can be seen if presented alone. The grant enabled us to hire a junior staff person, Harriet Linton (later Barr) and two graduate student research assistants: Susannah Gourevitch and Donald P. Spence. Substantively, it launched our center on a program of research on the effects (on various kinds of cognition) of perceptual inputs that were below the threshold of conscious recognition. Our first study had a complex design and somewhat puzzling results, which took us several years to analyze and publish (Klein, Spence, Holt, & Gourevitch, 1958). We were looking for direct effects of crude drawings of male or female genitals on judgments about the supraliminal ambiguous or androgynous figure. Instead, we found that some subjects gave paradoxical contrast effects, apparently as a result of defensive processes. That was followed by a considerable series of other related studies in which I did not participate. I always felt less at home with laboratory projects using equipment like tachistoscopes than I did in the other, psychometric tradition of psychological research (see Cronbach, 1957).

PERCEPTUAL ISOLATION (SENSORY DEPRIVATION).   In the early days of the Research Center for Mental Health, one of the most exciting new developments in psychology was the work done independently by John Lilly and by Donald Hebb and his group at McGill on what became known as sensory deprivation. It seemed as though remarkable regressive effects on cognitive processes could be achieved by keeping subjects in as totally bland and undifferentiated an environment as possible. When a graduate student who had transferred from McGill, Leo Goldberger, approached me about sponsoring dissertation research in this area, I enthusiastically agreed.

Consistent with our overall conception of the research center's work as an exploration of the psychoanalytic theory of thinking, I thought of this special type of experimental situation as an interference with reality contact and reasoned that the strange phenomena reported by prior researchers could best be understood as intrusions of primary process thinking. It was a short step to the hypothesis that the nature of a person's response to being deprived of ordinary reality's support for secondary process (rational, realistic) thinking could be predicted by his or her handling of primary process material in taking the Rorschach test. Leo Goldberger worked out the first technique of combining the scores to generate a measure of adaptive versus maladaptive regression. He predicted that those who were comfortable with wish-fulfilling or autistic modes of thinking in the Rorschach situation would withstand a period of perceptual isolation (as he preferred to call it) better than those whose primary-process responses were distorted and were accompanied by unpleasant affect or pathogenic defenses, all of which was summarized by negative ratings of defensive effectiveness. The results supported all hypotheses.

In Leo's dissertation study, the first of several on which we collaborated, subjects lay on a couch in a soundproof room with halved Ping-Pong balls fastened over their open eyes for 8 hours (or less, if they asked to be released—as a minority did). To our surprise, the changes in cognitive processes expressed in their tape-recorded verbalizations during this ordeal by insipidity only partly seemed well characterized as intrusions of primary process. Instead, much of the thinking was free of wishful content or the classical distortions of the dream work; yet it was fuzzy, or full of errors, or loosely wandering, or the like. So we found that we could reliably rate (in addition to good secondary process thinking, adaptive, and maladaptive primary process) what we called *regressed secondary process* (Goldberger, 1961; Goldberger & Holt, 1958).

During the next few years, Leo Goldberger stayed as a post doctoral fellow, and he and I followed up various leads in his thesis study, mostly supported by Air Force money. We replicated the first study by using quite a different sample of subjects— no longer college students but unemployed members of Actors' Equity—with many of the same results but with some interesting differences, somewhat too complicated to go into here in full detail. In both samples, however, we found two contrasting patterns of reaction, which we called adaptive and maladaptive; though they were related to different personality traits in the two samples, indicators of ego strength were positively correlated with the adaptive pattern and measures of hypochondriasis were negatively correlated in both samples. One that did not hold up was the Rorschach measure of adaptive regression, which had worked well in the original sample but trended in the opposite direction with the actors. It did, however, prove a sturdy predictor in several studies of sensory deprivation conducted outside our own laboratory (Wright & Abbey, 1965; Zubek, 1969; Zuckerman et al., 1966).

EFFECTS OF A PSYCHEDELIC DRUG ON COGNITION.   Our original expectations, that interfering with reality contact would give ready access to primary process thinking, thus proved a disappointment, as had the device of using subliminal inputs to force cognitive processes to go on without awareness. In our initial plan for a concerted effort to study the primary process in all its variants, however, we were banking on two other approaches: the "royal road to the unconscious," dreaming, and consciousness-altering drugs.

For several years, a substantial part of the RCMH's program was devoted to research on dreams. Our new laboratory contained two soundproof rooms specifically designed for this work, with beds, self-contained bathrooms, and built-in wiring to convey many channels of data to an external EEG (electroencephalographic) machine. I was in on the planning of a fair amount of the work, sponsored a few doctoral dissertations in the field, and learned some of the basic research techniques, but did not publish any completed studies. For a couple of years, William Dement worked with Chuck Fisher at Mt. Sinai, developing this technology and innovating several important new lines of work; we were in close touch and I served as a pilot subject for them once. Much of that time, an informal evening seminar on dream research met in my living room. That was where Bill Dement reported his first ideas about dream deprivation and his first findings. George Klein took major responsibility for this aspect of our work, hiring a number of gifted assistants to do the exhausting night work. From the data of my doctoral students, however, principally the dreams collected by Carol Eagle, I learned how disappointingly prosaic most manifest dream texts are. Even dreams from the night following LSD were far from pervaded with signs of the primary process at work.

In the earliest days of our collaboration, George and I worked together on a pilot study of mescaline. My analyst vetoed my taking any, so George was one trial subject and the novelist Waldo Frank a second. The results were a bit disappointing, so we decided to shift to a newer drug about which a small literature was already accumulating: lysergic acid diethylamide (LSD). We obtained a supply of 100-microgram doses from the manufacturer, and a couple of junior staff members tried it out, with promising results. So we got a grant and set up a rather elaborate study, one that involved every member of what was by then a rather large staff of the research center. Since the drug's effects lasted for at least a full working day, it was possible for many simultaneous experiments and exploratory studies to go on. We gathered data for the entire academic year 1958–59, which happened to be shortly before the general public learned about LSD and before the era of its street use. Only a couple of years later, our study would have been impossible.

For subjects, we had to use mature adults instead of the usual college students, and we hit upon a ready source of underemployed people: the theatrical union, Actors' Equity. We screened them carefully, rejecting any who seemed as if they might be too upset by the experience, and obtained their informed consent. Accepted subjects first underwent a day of personality assessment and pretesting. On the experimental day they were randomly assigned experimental or control status by a staff member who administered the drug or placebo and otherwise had no contact; the rest of us were blind. Testing began early in the morning and continued all day, ending with a night spent in the dream laboratory of Donald Goodenough and David Schapiro at the Downstate Medical Center in Brooklyn. There the subject was festooned with scalp electrodes and awakened by Carol Eagle or Helene Kafka when there was EEG evidence of dreaming so that they could get the data for their dissertation researches. Finally, subjects came back to the lab for retrospective discussions and post-testing.

Sixteen of the twenty LSD subjects were later recruited for a day's stay in the perceptual isolation room, for the earlier-mentioned replication of Leo Goldberger's first experiment. That made it possible for us to make direct comparisons between LSD and isolation for their potency in disrupting secondary process thought. LSD won hands down, and there was very little similarity in the effects of the two conditions (Goldberger & Holt, 1961b).

The two or three years during which we prepared for the LSD work, gathered data, and completed the personality assessments were the high points of my experience at the Research Center for Mental Health. For once, everyone was working together on interlinked projects, using the same subjects and studying fascinating phenomena. Every staff member was assigned as biographer for one of the thirty subjects, being in principal charge of assembling, analyzing, and integrating the various available materials for personality assessment. Every subject wrote a short autobiography, was interviewed several times, and took the WAIS, the Rorschach, the TAT, and various other projective tests and structured inventories. Following the model of the Harvard Psychological Clinic's procedures, we agreed on a set of personality variables to be rated in a series of Q-sorts and then went over the distributions of scores across subjects and made final consensual judgments. The result was a rich body of test scores and rated traits; many of us made good use of them in exploring the personological correlates of variables that interested us (see, for example, Goldberger & Holt, 1961a; Holt, 1966).

There is an odd contrast between the sense of having had a great experience of joint work on a problem of great practical as well as theoretical interest, and the meager output of publications that resulted. For a few years, we all worked intensively on the analysis of the huge mass of data; several dissertations were completed, but it took a long time to get out a slim book on the overall findings (Barr, Langs, Holt, Goldberger, & Klein, 1972). By then, LSD was old hat, and doses of 100 micrograms were considered small. So it goes.

IMAGERY. One thing that virtually all of our attempts to study the primary process had in common was a concern with mental imagery. That prompted me to choose as the topic of my presidential address to the APA Division of Clinical Psychology a historical survey of the literature on imagery with some comments about its then-current renaissance. Along with my oral presentation I showed a slide, showing the numbers of papers in the world literature devoted primarily to one or another aspect of imagery—that is, that portion of the literature represented in the *Psychological Abstracts* and the *Psychological Index* preceding it. It took me a full month of haunting the library to get through all those volumes, during which time I coincidentally first experienced scintillating scotomata. (I recognized what they were from my contacts with Lashley and Rapaport, both of whom had them.)

Though the curves in my slide strikingly visualized my argument that a lively topic had been virtually ostracized for generations with the rise of behaviorism and was now making a strong comeback, my friend Ilse Bry persuaded me to omit the figure from the published version (Holt, 1964). Her argument (based on experience in working for the *Abstracts*) was that there are a lot of unknowns about the sampling of the literature, changing from year to year, so that it is very difficult to know what are real changes and what merely reflect fluctuations of editorial policy, budgets, and similar irrelevancies. In retrospect, I feel that the argument is more theoretical than practical and that the general shape of the curves—which is all that concerns most readers—conveyed valid information.

One of the things I did with the LSD subjects was to administer a test of deliberate imaging, with the interesting finding that the drug didn't help much: the imaging process under LSD is out of the subject's conscious control. A little later, I had a chance to pursue my interest further with a part of the subject pool: I interviewed them about their experience of many types of imagery, intercorrelated the results, and found that there was very little generality. Knowing that a person had had eidetic imagery as a child, for example, said nothing about how vividly he experienced pressure phosphenes or how well he could summon up a picture of a car and make it move down an imaginary street. In the paper reporting these findings, I tried to develop some bits of theory about imaging processes (Holt, 1972a).

EGO DEVELOPMENT. When I got interested in Jane Loevinger's Sentence Completion Test (SCT) and her ingenious scoring system (Loevinger, Wessler, & Redmore, 1970) which for the first time made a projective technique into a psychometrically respectable instrument, I not only held that as a kind of model for what I wanted to do for the Rorschach, but I also got into some research with it. As usual, much of it took the form of interesting students in the theory and method and suggesting problems; but I got my own hands into it somewhat also. The story involves a digression back to the topic of teaching.

In the 1960s, my good friend and colleague Bernie Kalinkowitz, who had directed the doctoral program in clinical psychology ever since I turned the job down on coming to NYU, started a postdoctoral training program that soon turned into a psychoanalytic institute—the first run by and for psychologists under university auspices. At first, I did some teaching in this institute, hoping to find students who already knew the basics and who would be interested in a more probing analysis of Freud's ideas. To my disappointment, though the students all had doctorates in clinical psychology, they were no more sophisticated about psychoanalysis than our own graduate students. When I found myself repeating in the evening what I was teaching during the day (and for no additional compensation), I bowed out. But around 1970, I accepted a request to take part in a panel discussion of Freud one evening with another psychologist of whom I had only vaguely heard, Daniel Yankelovich. Dan had just written *Ego and Instinct* (Yankelovich & Barrett, 1970) and I was just turning over in my head the idea that part of what made it confusing to read Freud was that he was working with two quite incompatible images of man (Holt, 1972c). Each of us was surprised to find that the other was thinking along very similar lines, and that was the beginning of a long friendship.

A few years later, Dan and I decided to give a graduate seminar together on the new field of political psychology. Jeanne Knutson's *Handbook* (1973) had come out just in time to be our text, and Dan introduced me to a number of relevant classics in political science. The main thing in psychology I wanted to talk about of which he then knew nothing was Loevinger's work. We gave a pretty good seminar—at least, both of us learned a good deal—and decided to work together on a project if we could. He had been doing a series of studies of the values and beliefs of Americans of college age (for example, Yankelovich, 1974); now funding came through for another, and he asked if I would like to piggyback Loevinger's SCT on it. I was delighted at this opportunity to get a representative national sample of about a thousand—great for norms—and more important, to study the relationship between this measure of personal maturity and political/social thinking.

In the event, we quickly learned that there would not be time to include all thirty-six items, so I chose a rather random sample of eighteen items. But then when the data came back from the field, it turned out that during the pretest, the field supervisor had felt that the test was still taking too much time and on his own had cut it down further to twelve items! At first, I thought that it would be impossible to get a usable measure from them but on trying it out found that it was just barely doable. By then I had given my course on ego development a couple of times and had built up a group of graduate students who knew how to score. I hired a bunch of them, gave them some more intensive training, and we launched on a process that took an entire semester. The job was complicated by the fact that the published manual (Loevinger, Wessler, & Redmore, 1970) treated only the female form, and half our subjects were males. True, the group at Washington University had begun developing manuals for males, but there were about a third of the total group of items for which no specific scoring manual existed. We managed by dint of doing first what was easiest, and then as our group got thoroughly familiar with the test and the theory, they found it possible to score items for which no manuals existed, with almost as good rater reliability (Holt, 1980).

One of the most gifted of the group of scorers, Debbie Browning, took on the challenge of exploring the link between ego developmental level and political ideology in her dissertation (Browning, 1983, 1987), so that a good deal of that did get done despite the fact that I failed to follow through with more publications on a very rich body of data. Several other students did dissertations using Loevinger's scale, up to the most recent by Christopher MacDonald (1990), but I copublished with only one of them (Jurich & Holt, 1987).

In the late 1970s, when a number of people in the research center were getting excited about computers and what could be done with them, George Klein arranged for our staff to be given a brief course in PL-1, then the most promising programming language for manipulating verbal texts. George had in mind the possibility of working on dreams or the full texts of psychoanalytic sessions in this way; but I had the fantasy that it might be possible to write a computer program that would approximate my primary process scoring of the text of Rorschach protocols.

As I learned more about what could actually be done, I gave up this idea but decided that I should learn more about psychometrics to help me do a responsible job of writing up my scoring method. Auditing a course on the subject being offered by a bright new member of our faculty, Marc Fulcomer, I met a woman who introduced herself as a clinical graduate student in search of answers to a series of difficult statistical problems in the analysis of her dissertation data. Irene Kaus and I became friends and discovered that we had several interests in common, including the automation of projective test scoring. She had had a great deal of experience with computers and had a sophisticated grasp of multivariate statistics far exceeding mine. When I told her about Loevinger's test and scoring method, she became fascinated with the possibility of writing a computer program that would assign sentence completions to levels of development.

We decided to work together on it, though my part was to serve mainly as a source of data and a sympathetic sounding board. Despite being plagued by various illnesses, Irene proceeded to devise an ingenious statistical scheme, based on the differential frequency with which specific words occurred in the completions of a specific sentence stem at different developmental levels. After a year or so of work on the scored data of one stem from the national sample, she came up with an algorithm that reproduced the original scoring with an error of less than 10 percent. To be sure, it was not cross-validated, but then it was only one stem out of a potential thirty-six. A few years later, when she had extended the work to a couple of other stems with equally promising findings, I reported on it informally at one of Jane Loevinger's scoring workshops in St. Louis. Another attendant at the workshop, Donald Quinlan of Yale, got excited about the possibilities and joined our team. He and Irene made some improvements in the system so that it was virtually all programmed from the input of data to the output of scoring, and he and I wrote a couple of grant requests to get funding to hurry up the job. No luck. About this time, a cancer was found to be the source of Irene Kaus's recurrent ill health, and she died.

Since then, Don Quinlan has continued the work, insisting on putting my name on a joint paper he presented at a professional meeting and managing not only to extend the findings to several more stems but to cross-validate the system against the data (scored examples) in Loevinger's published manual as well. There was a lot of shrinkage, but enough valid residue to encourage the belief that an automated system could be useful, at least for large-scale research.

As often happened in this New York phase of my career, my interests and ideas outran what I could realistically accomplish. In a way, I find that reflection grimly amusing, for in my interaction with George Klein, I usually played the role of the one who tried to restrain his easily kindled new enthusiasms, reminding him that we had lots of data on hand that weren't properly analyzed and leads that really needed to be followed up. Maybe he was a little worse than I at not finishing things before getting excited about a new topic, but not much. I still don't know whether to advise young researchers to follow their impulses when that leads them to hot topics, or instead to develop a systematic program of research and stick to it. On the whole, I'd say follow your own bent: find your own style and work in the way that seems most congenial and productive for you. Looking back, it seems that I have jumped around a great deal and could surely have accomplished more with, let's say, the primary process scoring method if I had resisted the temptation to pursue other interests. Yet on balance I am glad I did it the way I did.

STRESS. It was through Dan Yankelovich that I got into a field I would never have predicted I would enter, occupational stress. After the earlier-sketched collaboration, we looked for other ways we could team up and wrote a number of fruitless grant requests for a variety of projects. He introduced me to the topic of job enrichment—making work more challenging and interesting by partly reversing the trend toward the division of labor and the simplification of tasks. It struck me that workers at higher levels of maturity would probably respond better to job enrichment than those stuck at the Conformist or lower levels, and for a while it looked as if a foundation liked the idea, too. Indeed, at the beginning of one fall semester, Dan told me that it was in the bag and that I could go ahead and hire a graduate assistant for the project. I did so and then learned that at the last minute the grant had fallen through. To bail us out, the foundation gave me the money for the student (whom I put to work on another project) on the understanding that at some future date I would do a little job for them.

About a year later, they found a way to get me to work out my obligation: I should spend a couple of weeks doing a review of the literature on occupational stress. The fact that I knew nothing about the field didn't bother them; it might help me come up with some fresh insights. With many misgivings, I plunged in. Not surprisingly, I soon found myself fascinated and wrote up the report with gusto. They thought they might publish it, but about the time they decided not to, my old student and colleague Leo Goldberger told me that he and his cousin Schlomo Breznitz were editing a handbook of theory and research on stress. It happened that they needed a chapter on occupational stress; so I revised and updated my report for their book (Holt, 1982a).

For quite different reasons I became interested in another aspect of stress at about this same time. My wife Joan's work in opposing nuclear energy had taken me to the scene of the Three Mile Island accident, where I had a chance to meet and talk with a number of people who had been through that harrowing experience. My friends Bob Lifton and Kai Erikson were involved, too, and we all served as consultants to People Against Nuclear Energy, an organization of citizens in the region of Harrisburg, Pennsylvania. I studied all the relevant literature I could lay my hands on and got to know a number of researchers, notably Henry Vyner, who had studied the aftereffects on the stressed population near Three Mile Island. Joan and I had first met Hank when he presented a paper at the first national conference of radiation victims in Washington. Soon I began with him one of those relationships that are so awkwardly called being a mentor. Terminology aside, I do love making a friendship with a gifted younger person to whom I can offer guidance and transmit some of the lore I have learned doing a variety of kinds of research over many years.

So although I ended up publishing little about the stressful effects of being a victim of a nuclear disaster (Holt, 1982b; Holt & Holt, 1982) and never got funding for any of the projects I conceived, it was an exciting chapter of my professional life and one with some vicarious achievement.

PSYCHOANALYTIC THEORY.   I am writing these words less than a year after publishing a book in which I have collected, revised, and updated my papers on psychoanalysis that seem to me of relatively lasting value (1989b). They date as far back as 1962 and contain a fair amount of material not previously published, including a somewhat autobiographical introduction. There I tell the story of my contact with psychoanalytic theory, how it fascinated but puzzled me, with the result that I spent a substantial part of my working life studying Freud's works and trying to make sense out of them. The fact that I had a total of about eight years of personal psychoanalysis (spread over two decades and with three principal analysts) with marked symptomatic relief and ability to withstand a good deal of personal stress clearly contributes to my conviction that Freud's core ideas have tremendous value. Yet his theories contain so much that is vulnerable even to vulgar and relatively uninformed critics that I have felt that the best way to preserve what is lastingly valuable would be to purge the theory of its errors and fallacies.

David Rapaport of course provided me with a model and a method, and though I doubt that he would be happy with all that I have done following the path on which he started me, my debt to him is enormous. He is such a living presence in my theoretical work that it startles me to realize that I wrote virtually everything in my recent book since his death in late 1960. The next year, on my return to New York, I began teaching a graduate course in Freud's thought, from which emerged many of my biographical and critical papers (Holt, 1963a; 1965c, d, e; 1967a, b, d, f; 1968a; 1972c).

By the early 1970s I had begun to think of collecting and expanding this growing body of work into a book. A publisher persuaded me to put several of the papers together into an introduction to the *Abstracts of the Standard Edition* (Holt, 1974). Though I continued to publish further critiques and historical studies, usually as a result of invitations and requests (Holt, 1975b; 1976a & b), I got sidetracked by an opportunity to collect my various papers on method into a book (1978a) and by the pressures of other work.

A larger design started to take shape in my mind (see 1978b). What had impressed me as two images of man, one mechanistic and one humanistic, now appeared as part of two larger configurations of hard and soft conceptions with deep roots in Freud's intellectual heritage. About a decade ago, I began work on a new book in which I am tracing the antecedents of these two configurations back to the early Greek authors Freud had studied in his Gymnasium years. So far I have published only one piece (1988b) of this manuscript, which now runs to about 400 pages. I put it aside when I got excited about starting a new program on Peace and Global Policy Studies (see the next section), though I continued to use invitations to give lectures or contribute to books as a way of keeping up the work on metapsychology (1981; 1983a; 1984a & b). Finally, when I was asked to address the APA Division on Psychoanalysis with a paper on the present status of psychoanalytic theory (1985), I realized that it was an opportunity to supply the last missing chapter of my critique. That spurred me to finish off the work on the collection of papers, which by then had covered most aspects of metapsychology and found it grievously wanting.

In summarizing the current status of the theory, I found myself leaning heavily on the work of two friends: Adolf Grünbaum and Benjamin Rubinstein. The latter's thought in particular impressed me as vital to an understanding of the contemporary predicaments of psychoanalytic theory, and I undertook to edit a collection of his papers for publication. Beni, who was 12 years my elder, was one of my oldest and dearest friends; the collection was originally to have been presented to him as an eightieth birthday present. As so often happens in this story, however, my estimates of how much I could get done at any one time proved far too optimistic. Beni died in 1989; shortly before, I was at least able to show him the dedication to him I had written for my book. Now my first priority is the completion—with the help of another dear friend, Morris Eagle—of the book of Rubinstein's contributions to psychoanalytic theory (to appear in *Psychological Issues*), which I hope will have the widest possible readership.

Freud's metapsychology was his ambitious attempt to make his theory more scientific by translating his clinical insights into a sort of model based on his understanding of nineteenth-century mechanistic science (especially physics). To have contributed to its demise does not feel like something a person should look back on with satisfaction as a career achievement—not without having provided an adequate substitute, at least. And though I have made a number of suggestions and have pointed a way that seems promising, all of that does not add up to a usable substitute for what I have helped to demolish. At the moment, I feel quite uncertain whether I will ever make much progress on the more constructive job.

Teaching and Research Concerning Peace

Two decades ago, an issue of *Science* contained a momentous article by John Platt (1969) which shook me up. After a synoptic survey of the principal problems facing humankind, graded according to estimated severity, Platt then estimated the amount of scientific effort going into the solution of these problems, reporting a marked negative correlation. Most scientists were spending most of their time and resources on the least pressing and dangerous of problems, while the threats of global disaster—military, demographic, and environmental—were being largely ignored.

I was so struck by this point and so moved by the author's powerful call to scientists of all kinds to awaken to the need and change researches that I made copies for all the staff of the Research Center for Mental Health and near the end of the year called a special staff meeting to discuss it. A remarkably glum session it was! No one disputed the basic facts; no one claimed that clarifying the psychoanalytic theory of thinking and testing it empirically was high in the hierarchy of world problems. Yet we all felt that it would be terribly difficult to make a substantial change in our ways. As is usual with institutions, we met the challenge by appointing a committee to study it and then went about business as usual. If the committee ever reported, I don't recall it.

All that happened was that the consciences of several of us were lastingly troubled. I wrote a paper exhorting psychologists to awake from their slumbers and take up the challenge, which I gave at several universities but never published. For more than a decade, I continued to wrestle with the issue in a number of ineffective ways: I corresponded with Platt and met with him once, offering my services if he wanted to organize an interdisciplinary effort to address the worst problems. I drew up plans for a new research center within the NYU department and tried in vain to interest other faculty members in helping to fund it. And I thought of various schemes to bring my current lines of work to some decent termination so that I could make a fresh start.

Finally, two influences tipped the balance. During the later seventies and early eighties at Bob Lifton's annual psychohistorical meetings in Wellfleet I heard and met such powerful advocates of activism as Philip Morrison and Dan Ellsberg, but also a modest, soft-spoken young man named Eric Markusen who showed me a concrete way to get started. With a colleague, J. B. Harris, he had innovated a course on nuclear war at the University of Minnesota (Harris & Markusen, 1986), and he gave me a copy of their syllabus. Also, Jonathan Schell's *The Fate of the Earth* (1982) made a profound impact upon me.

In the spring of 1982, I joined a student-faculty group at NYU that organized an antiwar demonstration, at which I spoke. That brought me into contact again with Daniel Zwanziger, a physicist with whom I had become acquainted a few years earlier when I was trying to do some political organizing on campus for the McGovern presidential campaign. We decided to find as many like-minded colleagues as we could and to start a faculty seminar for self-education on the complex issues of war and peace. With the help of a sympathetic university administrator, we issued a call to an organizing meeting at the beginning of the fall semester. About 30 people showed up, many of whom thanked us for taking the initiative and enthusiastically joined our seminar. Notable among them was an assistant professor of economics, Dietrich Fischer, an invaluable source of ideas, connections, and general helpfulness.

It quickly became apparent that we had enough people in the group with some relevant expertise to put together our own version of Eric Markusen's course. Dan and I threw together a course proposal and got it through the necessary clearances in time to announce it for the spring semester at the time of student registration. Seven other members of the faculty agreed to give guest lectures, including a few like McGeorge Bundy who had not been part of the faculty seminar; and ten students signed up for the initial offering of "Nuclear War and Its Prevention," an interdepartmental course sponsored by the Physics and Psychology departments.

Meanwhile, the faculty seminar (with the same name) had a successful series of meetings for the entire year, hearing not only from many of its participants (I presented the first draft of what became my paper "Can Psychology Meet Einstein's Challenge?" [1984c]) but from distinguished outside speakers as well. A few colleagues from other nearby universities heard about the seminar and joined us, among them Robert Manley from Seton Hall. He broached the idea of a doctoral program in peace studies, to be offered by a consortium of universities in the area. Shortly afterward, the group responded enthusiastically to my suggestion that we could put together an undergraduate minor simply by assembling courses already in NUS's curriculum. Six other people volunteered to be part of the planning committee, which I chaired: James T. Crown (politics), Faye Duchin (economics), Dietrich Fischer (economics), Michael Lutzker (history), Miroslav Nincic (politics), and Dan Zwanziger (physics).

During the next two years, the planning committee drew up an ambitious plan for a center of research on problems of war and peace, for which we were unable to get enough permission from the university administration to seek funding, and concrete plans for the minor in Peace and Global Policy Studies, which were approved by the faculty of Arts and Science in the spring semester 1985 with only one dissenting vote. Shortly afterward, the *New York Times* printed an op-ed piece by one of the NYU deans, Herbert London, attacking the minor and me personally as politically motivated. Its main apparent effect was to rally the other deans to my support and to put our effort on the map. That spring, the Faculty Colloquium (as it was now known) presented its first public lecture series, " . . . But What About the Russians?" in which five NYU faculty experts on the USSR (including Wassily Leontief) were joined by a Polish scholar, Longin Pastusiak. The growing program received its first external support, a grant of $1,500 from the World Policy Institute, and added several new courses especially planned for the minor.

In the fall of 1985, we began recruiting students for the minor. By now the course on nuclear war (included as the only required course) had grown to an enrollment of over 50. The group of undergraduates working for the minor gradually increased to a high point of 30 at the time of my retirement. I tried many devices to get the program noticed by NYU's huge urban student body, most of whom live off campus. It was a frustrating effort, since the student newspaper consistently judged our yearly public lecture series unworthy of journalistic notice, even when (in 1986–87) it included such outstanding speakers as George Rathjens, Robert C. Tucker, Robert Borosage, A. W. Singham, Robert C. Johansen, Marcus G. Raskin, and Kenneth E. Boulding.

This last group, who spoke on "Steps Toward Stable Peace: Policies for the Next Two Decades to Replace the War System with a Peace System," were all members of ExPro, the Exploratory Project on the Conditions of Peace. Through the good offices of one of that group's founding members, Dietrich Fischer, I had been invited to join at the beginning of 1984, which I did with great joy. A few years earlier, Dan Yankelovich and I had unsuccessfully tried to persuade our friend Richard Sennett to orient NYU's nascent Institute for the Humanities toward the giant task of planning the needed social and cultural changes to bring about a world at peace. Now I found myself part of a group of about two dozen academics and activists with just that mission. ExPro contained delightful people of remarkable intellect from a great variety of disciplines (I was the only psychologist), many of whom had devoted their careers to peace studies and peace research, areas in which I was an eager but ignorant newcomer. We met three times a year for long weekends, during which there were presentations (sometimes by such invited outsiders as Noam Chomsky) and probing discussions. I not only made a number of good friends and invaluable contacts but was helped in the process I had undertaken of quickly retraining myself in a complex interdisciplinary field.

My department and its understanding chairmen, Dick Koppenaal and then Marty Hoffman, helped greatly by allowing me to stop teaching psychology entirely for a few years (as I focused on organizing and chairing the team-taught course on nuclear war, and the minor). For my last four years at NYU, I taught psychology of war and peace, in collaboration with James Uleman and James Sidanius.

The climax of my participation in ExPro came in the spring of 1987, when it fell to me to organize one of the meetings, on the contributions of the social sciences to the transition from a war system to a peace system. I managed to assemble a good group of speakers and papers, and I contributed one myself entitled "Converting the War System to a Peace System: Some Contributions from Psychology and Other Social Sciences" (as yet unpublished). In it I urged that we make explicit the founding of our work in the general systems outlook. Everything I had been learning about the world's current plight pointed to the necessity of considering solutions from a global perspective, not the parochial one of conventional nationalism, and it also became evident that the major problems are indeed intertwined in what the Club of Rome calls the "world problematique." (Hence the emphasis in the NYU program on *global policy* studies.)

In my paper, then, I tried to show how the system underlying war is bigger and much more pervasive than the military-industrial complex. War is integrated, I argued, into an entire psychosociocultural as well as economic and political system within our nation, which in turn is intimately involved with the rest of the nations in a complex world system. I cannot undertake a précis of the whole 70-page paper here. It does, however, summarize the evidence for innate biological bases of aggressive behavior and also of its control, and anthropological evidence that human societies have existed for many generations with no participation in warfare. So, despite the ample evidence of human potentiality for the worst kinds of violence, there is nothing in human nature that precludes the possibility of a world without war. I went on to discuss the psychological barriers to attaining it and some suggestions about how to overcome them.

Since the beginning of 1988, my participation in ExPro has been minimal. Like several others, I moved to inactive status because I became convinced that we had gone about as far as we could with the structure we were working in. To go beyond an initial survey and sketches in broad outline of needed policies, I believe that there will have to be endowed institutions staffed with full-time researchers to do the necessary, hard, sustained intellectual work. Nothing would please me more than to be able to participate in the work of such a center.

Meanwhile, the NYU program began to take on some added dimensions. In the same year when we began the minor, we started planning for graduate studies also. Within an existing program that offered a master of arts in liberal studies, we began offering graduate courses in peace studies in the fall of 1986. I also joined a group under the leadership of Betty Lall, planning a doctoral program. In the spring of 1987, the first two undergraduates who had completed the minor received their degrees, and the program received a grant of $15,000 through Rockefeller Family and Associates.

By then, I had a little program of peace research under way, involving a score of graduate and undergraduate students. One paper (Locatelli & Holt, 1986), on the determinants of antinuclear activism, had been published, based on a completed doctoral dissertations, and another—on the attitudes of adolescent Soviet emigrés toward nuclear war—was in press (Galperin, Holt, & Howells, 1988). Another published study (Holt, Barrengos, Vitalino, & Webb, 1984) brought together two lines of work I had been developing for a few years. My studies of Freud's theoretical difficulties had led me to study metaphysics, especially with the help of Pepper (1942), and then to develop a World View Inventory, a method of measuring people's commitments to each of four major contemporary metaphysical systems or (in Pepper's phrase) world hypotheses. Elsewhere (Holt, 1984c) I had argued that to transcend the pervasive assumptions of the arms race our policy framers needed to be capable of systems thinking, which would constitute a stage of cognitive development beyond the stage of formal operations, where Piaget had left it. The new paper extended the conception, presented a tentative measure of one aspect of systems thinking, and showed that it was significantly correlated with endorsement of systems philosophy. These are topics on which I am continuing to work.

Shortly after Reagan's speech in which he characterized the Soviet Union as an "evil empire," I began a study of stereotyped images of the enemy and their correlates among college students (Holt, 1989a). That brought me into contact with Brett Silverstein, with whom I co-edited a special issue of the *Journal of Social Issues* devoted to the topic of enemy images (Holt & Silverstein, 1989a & b; Silverstein & Holt, 1989). One of my doctoral students did a dissertation in the same area. The research of two others was also part of this program of research on the psychology of peace: a cross-cultural study of patterns of aggression and reactions to it in the dreams of preliterate peoples (Spitzer, 1991); and a successful test of the hypothesis that cooperative (as against competitive) policy preferences in the international realm are correlated with level of ego development and world view (MacDonald, 1990). Three masters students' projects fit in also: a study of Lifton's concept of "psychic numbing," which found that the degree to which people think about the danger of nuclear extinction is significantly correlated with the amount of emotion they claim to experience when doing so but is ambiguously and not clearly related to the degree to which they experience and express emotions in other contexts; a study of temporal (secular) changes in the psychological impact of violent images, which found (counter to expectation) no consistent pattern of difference in two generations of college students' emotional reactions to such images; and a test of the hypothesis that experts with divergent views on nuclear arms policy would have different metaphysical commitments. In addition, I gathered several sets of data on thoughts and feelings about nuclear war, attitudes toward the Soviet Union and security policies—notably that of so-called "political realism"—and related matters, together with various data on aspects of personality, most of which await that mythical time in retirement when I will have a chance to analyze them.

During my final years at NYU, I tried to find someone to take my place as director of the Program on Peace and Global Policy Studies, not wholly successfully. (It is currently being managed by a committee.) I organized one more public lecture series, on "Low-Intensity Conflict in the Third World," during the spring of 1988, this one highly successful. And I put on a conference between Soviet and American psychologists on "Psychological Implications of the 'New Thinking' in International Relations," on June 30, 1988. A year's effort culminated in the unexpected arrival of ten Soviet colleagues, after I had given up the whole thing because I could get no response from Moscow. The full story of how that happened and how I was able to bring off a successful conference at the last minute is amusing, but too long to tell here. It was a rich lesson on the difficulties of cross-cultural communication, as well as a delightful contact with unusually adaptable and agreeable colleagues.

After my formal retirement I was appointed to emeritus status and continued for one more (slightly anticlimatic) academic year, giving my course on psychology and peace for the last time and trying to help my graduate students finish up their dissertations. In the summer of 1989 we celebrated the appearance of my book on Freud by winterizing our summer house in Truro on Cape Cod. As I write now, we are completing the process of moving to it as our permanent residence. In the nice little office my son Danny constructed for me in a basement room, I can look out over the dunes and my vegetable garden and write to my heart's content. (At least, theoretically I can; in practice, there almost always seem to be other, more pressing matters to attend to!)

Afterword: Reflections on Clinical Psychology's Future

At the editor's request, I append this final section with a good deal of diffidence. I don't feel that I have a great deal of right to speak about where clinical psychology is going, since I have been out of its mainstream for so long. Indeed, to most members of the profession today I must seem an odd maverick. Not only have I never learned to do psychotherapy, I haven't seen a patient or client in *any* clinical capacity for three decades. The one form of professional practice at which I was ever any good, diagnostic testing, has been in decline for some time, and though I am told that in some quarters it is alive and well, I have had no personal experience of any renaissance.

Long ago, I came to the conclusion that testing skills alone were not a sufficient basis for a sound profession. Diagnostic testing as I learned it from David Rapaport required a special kind of institutional setting to flourish. It was part of a very expensive, labor-intensive approach to care for the mental health of those few very affluent persons who could afford it. There was never any chance that our society would develop enough highly trained professionals to assess *every* person suffering from difficulties in living, determine what form of treatment would be most helpful, and then offer each sufferer the appropriate therapy.

During the years when I was working to help launch a new interdisciplinary profession of psychotherapy, I learned a good deal about the shocking state of America's health care system, perhaps better called a nonsystem so chaotic is it. The more I have learned about systems theory and its use in planning social reforms (Ackoff, 1974), the more convinced I have become that it is futile to extract an institution from its context and try to reform it and it alone. Of course, it is difficult to know how large a system needs to be taken into consideration. Surely clinical psychology cannot be rationally reorganized without concern for society's total ways of coping with the problems of health and disease. It may be that we will not be able to give the latter the thorough reorganization that it needs before there are larger and more fundamental political changes.

Nevertheless, let me reiterate (see also Holt, 1971a) what seem to be a desirable set of changes, sometime in the next century. I believe that health is a fundamental human right and that the system for its promotion and maintenance should be socially financed so that adequate care is available for all. Granted the limited size of the pool of persons with the necessary abilities to become Ph.D.'s in clinical psychology, psychiatrists, and psychoanalysts, it seems obvious that there will never be enough of them to do the main tasks of mental health care, nor do I believe that society will ever pay for the expensive overtraining that members of these professions now receive, not in the great numbers that will be needed. Most likely, to carry the main caseload we will have to rely on more narrowly trained people, without as many educational prerequisites. Margaret Rioch (1971) and others have already shown that mature people with the right personal qualifications can be rather quickly trained to be good psychotherapists.

To be sure, a good deal depends on the outcome of research in the neurosciences, on the one hand, and in psychotherapy on the other. It is just possible that those who, like Carl Rogers, believe that essentially the same form of therapy is good for everyone will prove right. In that case, the need for expert psychodiagnosis will diminish. My hunch is that it will turn out that different techniques are suitable for people with different diagnoses. But such a result cannot come about unless there are enough researchers with first-rate diagnostic training, using the most suitable techniques, to help do the basic research. For the immediately foreseeable future, therefore, I hope that there will be clinical psychologists with excellent preparation to do psychodiagnosis as well as research. They will have to collaborate with colleagues who combine expertise in psychotherapy with good investigative skills, and many of those may well be clinical psychologists also.

Will the clinical psychology of the future be grounded in psychoanalytic theory? Not likely, I believe, unless that theory receives the thorough, fundamental revision and reorganization that it needs. If we can assume that such work actually takes place, my bet is that the outcome will not be recognizably psychoanalytic. In the long run, we should be able to transcend the present situation of competing schools of thought or theories, as other sciences have done. What is lastingly valid will be retained, what is not will be discarded. To hope for more than that is sentimental.

I will close with some more personal reflections on my own career. It has been a constant struggle between broad and diverse interests and a desire to get it all together, to achieve an overarching synthesis. About 15 years ago, reading Lewis Mumford (1970) catalyzed a first synthesis. My interests in peace, politics, environmental problems, alternative technology, solar versus nuclear energy, philosophy, psychoanalysis, and many of the research topics that had fascinated me all came together with the help of cognitive-affective developmental theory. I saw much of intellectual history as influenced by successive world hypotheses, which I felt could be seen as a developmental series: animism, mechanism, pragmatism, and systems philosophy (sometimes called organicism). Each appears to be congenial to various forms of politicosocial organization, and each has had a strong influence on schools of psychology. As my work has turned to elucidating the metaphysical undergirding of such diverse matters as psychoanalytic theories, types of predictive systems, social policies (including energy and peace/security issues), and political theories, I have felt that my branching out into political and peace psychology was organically connected with my previous, more traditionally clinical interests. Most of the time, I have been striving not to see one of two contending sides win, but to find a synthetic ("win/win") means of resolving the conflict. I regret that I learned about the emerging field of conflict resolution so late; it could have helped me a lot in earlier years if I had realized that was what I was trying to do and if I had had access to techniques others were developing.

In my most recent book (Holt, 1989b), I have tried to show some of the ways psychoanalysis could profit by recognizing that it has—must have—metaphysical foundations. It should supply good ones, I argue, by adopting systems philosophy. That same basis is needed by contemporary clinical psychology and by its foreseeable heirs. No room here to explain how and why, but I hope that the curiosity of some readers may be sufficiently piqued to lead them to become acquainted with the systems view of the world in its philosophical as well as scientific guise. It provides a position on the mind-body problem which, I believe, gives the best basis for understanding such intricate problems as those of psychosomatics and psychoneuroimmunology, which became of fresh interest to me in 1990 and 1991 as I struggled with and overcame a life-threatening illness. Now I feel that I am truly beginning a new life, in which music, poetry, nature, loving relations with friends and family, and participation in a real community will offer new sources of gratification.

References

Ackoff, R. L. (1974). *Redesigning the future: A systems approach to societal problems.* New York: Wiley.

Afflerbach, L., & Franck, M. (Eds.). (1977). *The emerging field of sociobibliography: The collected essays of Ilse Bry.* Westport, CT: Greenwood Press.

Allport, G. W. (1937). *Personality: A psychological interpretation.* New York: Holt.

Alper, T. G. (1946). Memory for completed and incompleted tasks as a function of personality: Analysis of group data. *Journal of Abnormal and Social Psychology, 41,* 403–420.

Alper, T. G. (1948). Memory for completed and incompleted tasks as a function of personality: Correlates between experimental and personality data. *Journal of Personality, 17,* 109–137.

Barr, H. B., Langs, R. J., Holt, R. R., Goldberger, L., & Klein, G. S. (1972). *LSD: Personality and experience.* New York: Wiley.

Bellak, L., & Holt, R. R. (1948). Somatotypes in relation to dementia praecox. *American Journal of Psychiatry, 104,* 713–724.

Boring, E. G., (1929). *A history of experimental psychology.* New York: Appleton-Century-Crofts.

Boring, E. G., & Van de Water, M. (Eds.). (1943). *Psychology for the fighting man.* Washington, DC: The Infantry Journal.

Browning, D. (1983). Aspects of authoritarian attitudes in ego development. *Journal of Personality and Social Psychology, 45,* 137–144.

Browning, D. (1987). Ego development, authoritarianism, and social status: An investigation of the incremental validity of Loevinger's Sentence Completion Test (short form). *Journal of Personality and Social Psychology, 53,* 113–118.

Caprara, G. V., Ferrucci, F., Jacob, C., Maggi, V., Torre, F. M., & Quinti, O. (1977). *Studi sulla personalità: Quattro ricerche con il metodo di R. Holt* [Studies in personality: Four researches with the method of R. Holt]. Rome: Boringhieri.

Caprara, G. V., Holt, R. R., Pazielli, M. F., & Giannotti, A. (1986). The development of primary process in children's Rorschachs. *Journal of Personality Assessment, 50,* 149–170.

Cronbach, L. J. (1957). The two disciplines of scientific psychology. *American Psychologist, 7,* 173–196.

Dollard, J. (1935). *Criteria for the life history.* New Haven: Yale University Press.

Eagle, C. J. (1964). *An investigation of individual consistencies in the manifestations of primary processes.* Unpublished doctoral dissertation, New York University.

Freud, S. (1953). The interpretation of dreams. In J. Strachey (Ed. and Trans.), *The standard edition of the complete psychological works of Sigmund Freud* (Vols. 4 and 5). London: Hogarth Press. (Original work published 1900)

Galperin, M., Holt, R. R., & Howells, P. (1988). What Soviet emigré adolescents think about nuclear war. *Political Psychology, 9,* 1–12.

Goldberger, L. (1961). Reactions to perceptual isolation and Rorschach manifestations of the primary process. *Journal of Projective Techniques, 25,* 287–302.

Goldberger, L., & Holt, R. R. (1958). Experimental interference with reality contact (perceptual isolation): I. Method and group results. *Journal of Nervous and Mental Disease, 127,* 99–112.

Goldberger, L., & Holt, R. R. (1961a). Studies on the effects of perceptual alteration. *USAF ASD Technical Reports,* No. 61–416, 20 pp.

Goldberger, L., & Holt, R. R. (1961b). A comparison of isolation effects and their personality correlates in two divergent samples. *USAF WADC Technical Reports,* No. 61–417, 46 pp.

Harris, J. B., & Markusen, E. (Eds.). (1986). *Nuclear weapons and the threat of nuclear war.* New York: Harcourt Brace Jovanovich.

Heath, D. H. (1965). *Explorations of maturity.* New York: Appleton-Century-Crofts.

Holt, R. R. (1945). Effects of ego-involvement upon levels of aspiration. *Psychiatry, 8,* 299–317.

Holt, R. R. (1946). Level of aspiration: Ambition or defense? *Journal of Experimental Psychology, 36,* 398–416.

Holt, R. R. (1950). An approach to the validation of the Szondi test through a systematic study of unreliability. *Journal of Projective Techniques, 14,* 435–444.

Holt, R. R. (1951a). The accuracy of self-evaluations: Its measurement and some of its personological correlates. *Journal of Consulting Psychology, 15,* 95–101.

Holt, R. R. (1951b). The Thematic Apperception Test. In H. H. & G. L. Anderson (Eds.), *An introduction to projective techniques* (pp. 181–229). New York: Prentice-Hall.

Holt, R. R. (1951c). Chapter 10 [untitled; an analysis of TAT and MAPS test]. In E. Shneidman (Ed.), *Thematic test analysis* (pp. 101–118). New York: Grune & Stratton.

Holt, R. R. (1951d). An inductive method of analyzing defense of self-esteem. *Bulletin of the Menninger Clinic, 15,* 6–15.

Holt, R. R. (1952). The case of Jay: Interpretation of Jay's Thematic Apperception Test. *Journal of Projective Techniques, 16,* 457–461.

Holt, R. R. (1955). Problems in the use of sample surveys. In R. Kotinsky & H. L. Witmer (Eds.), *Community programs for mental health* (pp. 325–358). Cambridge: Harvard University Press, 1955.

Holt, R. R. (1958a). Clinical *and* statistical prediction: A reformulation and some new data. *Journal of Abnormal and Social Psychology, 56,* 1–12.

Holt, R. R. (1958b). Formal aspects of the TAT—A neglected resource. *Journal of Projective Techniques, 22,* 163–172.

Holt, R. R. (1961a). The nature of the TAT stories as cognitive products: A psychoanalytic approach. In J. Kagan & G. Lesser (Eds.), *Contemporary issues in thematic apperceptive methods* (pp. 3–43). Springfield, IL: Charles C Thomas.

Holt, R. R. (1961b). Clinical judgment as a disciplined inquiry. *Journal of Nervous and Mental Disease, 133,* 369–382.

Holt, R. R. (1962a). Individuality and generalization in the psychology of personality. *Journal of Personality, 30,* 377–404.

Holt, R. R. (1962b). A clinical-experimental strategy for research in personality. In S. Messick & J. Ross (Eds.), *Measurement in personality and cognition* (pp. 269–283). New York: Wiley.

Holt, R. R. (1963a). Two influences on Freud's scientific thought: A fragment of intellectual biography. In R. W. White (Ed.), *The study of lives* (pp. 364–387). New York: Atherton Press.

Holt, R. R. (1963b). New directions in the training of psychotherapists. *Journal of Nervous and Mental Disease, 137,* 413–416.

Holt, R. R. (1964). Imagery: The return of the ostracized. *American Psychologist, 19,* 254–264.

Holt, R. R. (1965a). Experimental methods in clinical psychology. In B. Wolman (Ed.), *Handbook of clinical psychology* (pp. 40–77). New York: McGraw-Hill.

Holt, R. R. (1965b). Psychotherapy as an autonomous profession: An alternative to the Clark Committee's proposal. In E. L. Hoch, A. O. Ross, & C. L. Winder (Eds.), *Professional preparation of clinical psychologists.* Washington, DC: American Psychological Association, 1966.

Holt, R. R. (1965c). A review of some of Freud's biological assumptions and their influence on his theories. In N. S. Greenfield & W. C. Lewis (Eds.), *Psychoanalysis and current biological thought* (pp. 93–124). Madison: University of Wisconsin Press.

Holt, R. R. (1965d). Ego autonomy re-evaluated. *International Journal of Psycho-Analysis, 46,* 151–167. Reprinted with critical evaluations by S. C. Miller, A. Namnum, B. B. Rubinstein, J. Sandler & W. G. Joffe, R. Schafer, H. Wiener, and with the author's rejoinder, *International Journal of Psychiatry,* 1967, *3,* 481–536.

Holt, R. R. (1965e). Freud's cognitive style. *American Imago, 22,* 163–179.

Holt, R. R. (1966). Measuring libidinal and aggressive motives and their controls by means of the Rorschach test. In D. Levine (Ed.), *Nebraska symposium on motivation, 1966* (pp. 1–47). Lincoln: University of Nebraska Press.

Holt, R. R. (1967a). On freedom, autonomy, and the redirection of psychoanalytic theory: A rejoinder. *International Journal of Psychiatry, 3,* 524–536.

Holt, R. R. (Ed.). (1967b). Motives and thought: Psychoanalytic essays in memory of David Rapaport. *Psychological Issues,* Monograph 18/19. New York: International Universities Press.

Holt, R. R. (1967c). David Rapaport: A memoir (September 30, 1911–December 14, 1960). In *Motives and thought* (*see* Holt 1967b) (pp. 7–17).

Holt, R. R. (1967d). The development of the primary process: A structural view. In *Motives and thought* (*see* Holt 1967b) (pp. 345–383).

Holt, R. R. (1967e). Discussion: On using experiential data in personality assessment. (Symposium: The role of experiential data in personality assessment.) *Journal of Projective Techniques and Personality Assessment, 31*(4), 25–30.

Holt, R. R. (1967f). Beyond vitalism and mechanism: Freud's concept of psychic energy. In J. H. Masserman (Ed.), *Science and psychoanalysis: Vol. 11. Concepts of ego* (pp. 1–41). New York: Grune & Stratton.

Holt, R. R. (1968a). Freud, Sigmund. *International encyclopedia of the social sciences* (Vol. 6, pp. 1–12). New York: Macmillan/The Free Press.

Holt, R. R. (Ed.). (1968b). Revised edition of *Diagnostic psychological testing*, by D. Rapaport, M. M. Gill, & R. Schafer. New York: International Universities Press.

Holt, R. R. (1969). Kubie's dream and its impact upon reality: Psychotherapy as an autonomous profession. *Journal of Nervous and Mental Disease, 149,* 186–207.

Holt, R. R. (1970). Yet another look at clinical and statistical prediction: Or, is clinical psychology worthwhile? *American Psychologist, 25,* 337–349.

Holt, R. R. (Ed.). (1971a). *New horizon for psychotherapy: Autonomy as a profession.* New York: International Universities Press.

Holt, R. R. (1971b). *Assessing personality.* New York: Harcourt Brace Jovanovich.

Holt, R. R. (1972a). On the nature and generality of mental imagery. In P. E. Sheehan (Ed.), *The function and nature of imagery.* New York: Academic Press.

Holt, R. R. (1972b). Should the psychotherapist prescribe the pills? Preferably not! *International Journal of Psychiatry, 10*(4), 82–86.

Holt, R. R. (1972c). Freud's mechanistic and humanistic images of man. *Psychoanalysis and Contemporary Science, 1,* 3–24.

Holt, R. R. (1973). *Methods of research in clinical psychology.* Morristown, NJ: General Learning Press.

Holt, R. R. (1974). On reading Freud. Introduction to *Abstracts of the standard edition of Freud* (pp. 3–79). New York: Jason Aronson.

Holt, R. R. (1975a). Clinical and statistical measurement and prediction: How *not* to survey the literature. *JSAS Catalog of Selected Documents in Psychology, 5,* 178. MS No. 837.

Holt, R. R. (1975b). The past and future of ego psychology. *Psychoanalytic Quarterly, 44,* 550–576.

Holt, R. R. (1976a). Drive or wish? A reconsideration of the psychoanalytic theory of motivation. *Psychological Issues, 9*(4, Whole No. 36), 158–197.

Holt, R. R. (1976b). Freud's theory of the primary process—Present status. *Psychoanalysis and Contemporary Science, 5,* 61–99.

Holt, R. R. (1978a). *Methods in clinical psychology: Assessment, prediction, and research* (Vols. 1 & 2). New York: Plenum.

Holt, R. R. (1978b). Ideological and thematic conflicts in the structure of Freud's thought. In S. Smith (Ed.), *The human mind revisited: Essays in honor of Karl A. Menninger* (pp. 51–98). New York: International Universities Press.

Holt, R. R. (1980). Loevinger's measure of ego development: Reliability and national norms for short male and female forms. *Journal of Personality and Social Psychology, 39,* 909–920.

Holt, R. R. (1981). The death and transfiguration of metapsychology. *International Review of Psycho-Analysis, 8*(Part 2), 129–143.

Holt, R. R. (1982a). Occupational stress. In L. Goldberger & S. Breznitz (Eds.), *Handbook of stress* (pp. 419–444). New York: Macmillan/Free Press.

Holt, R. R. (1982b). Comment on psychological stress workshop. In P. Walker, W. E. Fraise, J. J. Gordon, & R. C. Johnson (Eds.), *Workshop on psychological stress associated with the proposed restart of Three Mile Island, Unit 1* (pp. 76–89). NUREG/CP-0026 MTR-82W26. Washington, DC: U.S. Nuclear Regulatory Commission.

Holt, R. R. (1982c). Come migliorare la ricerca descrittiva in psicologia clinica [Improving descriptive research in clinical psychology]. *Psicologia Clinica* (Rome), *1*(1).

Holt, R. R. (1983a). The manifest and latent meanings of metapsychology. *The Annual of Psychoanalysis, 10,* 233–255.

Holt, R. R. (1983b). *Il processo primario nel Rorschach e nel materiale tematico* [The primary process in the Rorschach and in thematic materials]. Translated by Alessandra De Coro; edited by G. V. Caprara & N. Dazzi. Rome: Borla.

Holt, R. R. (1984a). Freud, the free will controversy, and prediction in personology. In R. A. Zucker, J. Aronoff, & A. I. Rabin (Eds.), *Personality and the prediction of behavior* (pp. 179–208). New York: Academic Press.

Holt, R. R. (1984b). Freud's impact upon modern morality and our world view. In A. L. Caplan & Bruce Jennings (Eds.), *Darwin, Marx, and Freud: Their influence on moral theory* (pp. 147–200). New York: Plenum.

Holt, R. R. (1984c). Can psychology meet Einstein's challenge? *Political Psychology, 5,* 199–225.

Holt, R. R. (1984d). Merton M. Gill. A biographical sketch. *Psychoanalytic Inquiry, 4,* 315–323.

Holt, R. R. (1985). The current status of psychoanalytic theory. *Psychoanalytic Psychology, 2,* 289–315.

Holt, R. R. (1986). Clinical and statistical prediction: A retrospective and would-be integrative perspective. *Journal of Personality Assessment, 50,* 376–386.

Holt, R. R. (1988a). Judgment, inference, and reasoning in clinical perspective. In D. C. Turk & P. Salovey (Eds.), *Reasoning, inference, and judgment in clinical psychology* (pp. 233–250). New York: Free Press.

Holt, R. R. (1988b). Freud's adolescent reading: Some possible effects on his work. In P. E. Stepansky (Ed.), *Contributions to Freud studies: Vol. 3. Freud: Appraisals and reappraisals.* Hillside, NJ: Analytic Press.

Holt, R. R. (1989a). College students' definitions and images of enemies. *Journal of Social Issues, 45*(2), 33–50.

Holt, R. R. (1989b). *Freud reappraised: A fresh look at psychoanalytic theory.* New York: Guilford.

Holt, R. R. (1990). Benjamin Bjorn Rubinstein, M.D., 1905–1989. *Psychoanalysis and Contemporary Thought, 13,* 173–182.

Holt, R. R., Barrengos, A., Vitalino, A., & Webb, K. (1984). Measuring systems thinking and belief in systems philosophy. In A. W. Smith (Ed.), *Proceedings, Society for General Systems Research: Vol. 1. Systems methodologies and isomorphies.* Seaside, CA: Intersystems Publications.

Holt, R. R., & Havel, J. (1960). A method for assessing primary and secondary process in the Rorschach. In M. A. Rickers-Ovsiankina (Ed.), *Rorschach psychology* (pp. 263–315). New York: Wiley.

Holt, R. R., & Holt, J. (1982). Introduction: An overview of the intervenors' case. In B. Cohen-DeGrasse & J. Gilroy (Eds.), *The Indian Point book: A briefing on the safety investigation of the Indian Point nuclear power plants* (pp. 34–39). New York: Union of Concerned Scientists and New York Public Interest Research Group.

Holt, R. R., & Luborsky, L. (1958). *Personality patterns of psychiatrists* (Vols. 1 & 2). New York: Basic Books.

Holt, R. R., & Silverstein, B. (Eds.). (1989a). The image of the enemy: U.S. views of the Soviet Union. *Journal of Social Issues, 45*(2).

Holt, R. R., & Silverstein, B. (1989b). On the psychology of enemy images: Introduction and overview. *Journal of Social Issues, 45*(2), 1–16.

Horn, D. (1943). *An experimental study of the diagnostic process in the clinical investigation of personality.* Unpublished doctoral dissertation, Harvard University.

James, W. (1890). *Principles of psychology* (Vols. 1 & 2). New York: Holt.

Janis, I. L., Mahl, G. F., Kagan, J., & Holt, R. R. (1969). *Personality: Dynamics, development, and assessment.* New York: Harcourt, Brace & World.

Jurich, J. & Holt, R. R. (1987). Effects of modified instructions on the Washington University Sentence Completion Test of Ego Development. *Journal of Personality Assessment, 51,* 186–193.

Kernberg, O. F., Burstein, E. D., Coyne, L., et al. (1972). Psychotherapy and psycho-analysis: Final report of the Menninger Foundation's Psychotherapy Research Project. *Bulletin of the Menninger Clinic, 36,* 1–275.

Klein, G. S., Spence D. P., Holt, R. R., & Gourevitch, S. (1958). Cognition without awareness: Subliminal influences upon conscious thought. *Journal of Abnormal and Social Psychology, 57,* 255–266.

Klopfer, B., Ainsworth, M. D., Klopfer, W., & Holt, R. R. (1954). *Developments in the Rorschach technique: Vol. 1. Technique and theory.* New York: World Book.

Knutson, J. N. (Ed.). (1973). *Handbook of political psychology.* San Francisco: Jossey-Bass.

Kohlberg, L. (1984). *Essays on moral development: Vol. 2. The psychology of moral development.* San Francisco: Harper & Row.

Kubie, L. (1954). The pros and cons of a new profession: A doctorate in medical psychology. *Texas Reports in Biology and Medicine, 12,* 692–737.

Locatelli, M. G., & Holt, R. R. (1986). Antinuclear activism, psychic numbing, and mental health. *International Journal of Mental Health, 15,* 143–161.

Loevinger, J. (1976). *Ego development: Conceptions and theories.* San Francisco: Jossey-Bass.

Loevinger, J., Wessler, R., & Redmore, C. (1970). *Measuring ego development* (Vols. 1 & 2). San Francisco: Jossey-Bass.

Luborsky, L. (1962). Clinicians' judgments of mental health: A proposed scale. *Archives of General Psychiatry, 17,* 407–417.

Maccoby, E. E., & Holt, R. R. (1946). How surveys are made. *Journal of Social Issues, 2,* 45–57.

MacDonald, C. (1990). *Ego development, basic trust, and political world view in relation to cooperative/competitive political orientation and political trust/mistrust.* Unpublished doctoral dissertation, New York University.

Mayman, M. (1970). Reality contact, defense effectiveness, and psychopathology in Rorschach form-level scores. In B. Klopfer, M. M. Meyer, & F. B. Brawer (Eds.), *Developments in the Rorschach technique: Vol. 3. Aspects of personality structure* (pp. 11–46). New York: Harcourt Brace Jovanovich.

Meehl, P. E. (1954). *Clinical versus statistical prediction: A theoretical analysis and a review of the evidence.* Minneapolis: University of Minnesota Press.

Menninger, K. A. (1920). *The human mind.* New York: Knopf.

Mumford, L. (1970). *The myth of the machine: Vol. 2. The pentagon of power.* New York: Harcourt Brace Jovanovich.

Murray, H. A. (1938). *Explorations in personality.* New York: Oxford University Press.

Pepper, S. C. (1942). *World hypotheses.* Berkeley: University of California Press.

Platt, J. (1969). What we must do. *Science, 166,* 1115–1121.

Rapaport, D., Gill, M. M., & Schafer, R. (1945–1946). *Diagnostic psychological testing* (Vols. 1 & 2). Chicago: Yearbook Publishers.

Rapaport, D., Schafer, R., & Gill, M. M. (1944–1946). *Manual of diagnostic psychological testing* (Vols. 1 & 2). New York: Josiah Macy, Jr., Foundation.

Rioch, M. J. (1971). Two pilot projects in training mental health counselors. In R. R. Holt (Ed.), *New horizon for psychotherapy* (pp. 294–311). New York: International Universities Press.

Sanford, F. H., & Holt, R. R. (1943). Psychological determinants of morale. *Journal of Abnormal and Social Psychology, 38,* 93–95.

Sargent, H. D., Horwitz, L., Wallerstein, R. S., & Appelbaum, A. (1968). Prediction in psychotherapy research: A method for the transformation of clinical judgments into testable hypotheses. *Psychological Issues, 6,* Monograph 21.

Sawyer, J. (1966). Measurement *and* prediction, clinical *and* statistical. *Psychological Bulletin, 66,* 178–200.

Schell, J. (1982). *The fate of the earth.* New York: Knopf.

Sherif, M., & Cantril, H. (1947). *The psychology of ego involvements.* New York: Wiley.

Silverstein, B., & Holt, R. R. (1989). Research on enemy images: Present status and future prospects. *Journal of Social Issues, 45*(2), 159–175.

Spitzer, B. (1991). *Aggression in dreams: A cross-cultural study.* Unpublished doctoral dissertation, New York University.

Tomkins, S. S. (1943). *Contemporary psychopathology.* Cambridge, MA: Harvard University Press.

Wallerstein, R. S. (1986). *Forty-two lives in treatment.* New York: Guilford.

Wright, N. A., & Abbey, D. S. (1965). Perceptual deprivation tolerance and adequacy of defense. *Perceptual and Motor Skills, 20,* 35–38.

Yankelovich, D. (1974). *The new morality: A profile of American youth in the seventies.* New York: McGraw-Hill.

Yankelovich, D., & Barrett, W. (1970). *Ego and instinct.* New York: Random House.

Zubek, J. (1969). *Sensory deprivation: Fifteen years of research.* New York: Appleton-Century-Crofts.

Zuckerman, M., Persky, H., Hopkins, T. R., et al. (1966). Comparison of stress effects of perceptual and social isolation. *Archives of General Psychiatry, 14,* 356–365.

John Money

Professor of Medical Psychology and
Professor of Pediatrics Emeritus
The Johns Hopkins University and Hospital

◆

Explorations in Human Behavior

Mirrors of Childhood

How should I know who I am? I have as many biographies as there are people who have ever known me. Ask all of them for their versions of me if you would know all of who I am. They are the mirrors in which I also must see myself.

In the mirrors of childhood I see a boy whose memories are classified as either Morrinsville or Lower Hutt, before and after age 5 respectively. Morrinsville is still a small town. It is situated south of Auckland, the largest metropolitan center of New Zealand. Morrinsville is very close to Hamilton, the Waikato River city, in which the new Waikato University is located. Nearby is Ngaruawahia, a Polynesian cultural center and residence of the Maori "king," who is presently a woman, Te Arikinue Dame Te Atairangikaahu.

Two of my cousins still live there in Morrinsville, in the same house as they did when I was born next door on July 8, 1921. I was delivered at home with a midwife, not an obstetrician, in attendance. So I was not circumcised. By age 5 I would be

This essay was supported by USPHS Grant HC00325-34.

envious of the large mushroom-shaped, circumcised, and exposed glans penis of my same-age playmate. I was an early beginner in the cosmetics of sex, for I wanted my own glans penis to be like it.

Lower Hutt is named for a surveyor of the New Zealand Company, which colonized the Wellington area in 1840. It is situated in the lower reaches of the valley of the Hutt River. When my father moved there in 1927, it was to take advantage of the pre-Depression building boom that was converting the valley from farmland into suburbia, an expansion of Wellington, the capital city, itself perched on the slopes of an earthquake fault.

My father built a house for his family and put up a sign at the front gate: Frank Money, Builder and Contractor. He was in poor health with what proved to be the early symptoms of glomerulonephritis, a kidney infection, then known as Bright's disease. It was twenty years before antibiotics would be on the medical market and before the disease would be curable. My father was 44 years old when he died in 1929, and I was 8.

It was customary at that time, and in my family, to exclude children from participating in the trauma of dying, death, and burial at first hand. Instead of sparing me, exclusion traumatized me more. Becoming a half-orphan is a legacy that is still with me. "Now you will have to be the man of the house," my father's oldest brother declared, when the assembled relatives broke the news to me that I was fatherless— quite an assignment for an 8-year-old boy. I was left to figure out the duties and responsibilities for myself. I was an early beginner in the psychology of duties and responsibilities. There were many crises of relationship at home and at school, with adults and age-mates. The promise of being able to explain them is what would attract me to psychology when, for the first time, I discovered it existed as an academic study. That would not happen until age 17, when I became a freshman university student.

It had always been easy for me to achieve approval in scholarship. It was a way of circumventing the system of competitive sports and fighting for status in the dominance hierarchy of boyhood. On my first day at school, it was evident that I was not a fighter.

In New Zealand, in 1926, one's first day in school was the day after one's fifth birthday. In July, when I was 5, the school year was already half completed. There I was, a stranger in the midst of the Lords of the Flies, some of them the grandsons of British immigrants and others the grandsons of fierce Maori warriors who had fought the British in the Maori wars.

I went off to school that day enthralled by the prospect of learning, not fighting. In no way had I prepared myself for a replay of the Waikato Maori wars. At mid-morning "playtime," unsure of the routine, I sought the help of my older cousin and found her in the "girls' shed." The girls would have nothing to do with a boy in their sanctuary. They abandoned me to the attacking warriors. Catastrophe! I retreated. I was saved only by the ringing of the bell, calling everyone back into the classroom.

When lunchtime came, instead of eating my sandwiches, I joined the exodus of kids who went home for lunch. My alibi was that I thought the school day was over. I revealed nothing of my monstrous panic and failure as a warrior. I was on the way to becoming a psychological exile who, excluded from the establishment, would survive by getting to investigate it, challenge it, and outwit it. Investigating, challenging, and outwitting—these also apply to my professional research activities in psychoendocrinology, sexology, and psychopathology in general.

My research has taken advantage of a disposition that first showed itself in the play of very early childhood, namely retrieving, collecting, and arranging things. There is a family story that even before my second birthday, my grandmother Money, at the conclusion of a play session with me, was impressed with my orderliness in stacking into their box the various sizes and shapes of wooden blocks my carpenter father had made for me. My own memory has preserved for me, since age 4, the activity of collecting dried worm casts from the lawn after a rainfall and arranging them as miniature sculptures on the cross beams of the water-tank stand.

I am still a collector of art and artifacts, books, sculptures, and paintings. But, above all, I am a collector of research data, some generated directly in clinical inquiries and tests, and some retrieved from earlier sources. I am a developmental archeologist of mind and behavior, in search of sources, sequences, and outcomes in psychoendocrinology and sexological psychology. I find satisfaction in pursuing the conceptual connectedness where it is usually overlooked. I'm not much given to tinkering with instruments or designing apparatuses. I do not have an encyclopedic memory for lists, dates, names, instrumental music, or numbers. Mathematically I was malnourished by an excess of rote instruction in the early grades, and again at high school. To thrive academically I needed to be able to explain.

By around age 12, I needed to explain various of the fundamentalist religious precepts with which I had been reared, but I could not. Nor could anyone else. Belief, I was told, is based on faith, not fact. That did not sit well in a mind that even in infancy had annoyed adults by forever asking What? and Why? It took me another twelve years or more to escape from the philosophy of hellfire and damnation to the philosophy of scientific skepticism. The escape was not final until, at the age of 25, already a junior lecturer in psychology (at the University of Otago in New Zealand), I wrote "Delusion, Belief, and Fact." It was published in *Psychiatry* in 1948.

Having been freed from the metaphysical bondage of faith as applied to religion, I was not about to be metaphysically entrapped in the bondage of faith as applied to psychology. Different schools and traditions of psychology were vying for my faith. As an undergraduate in psychology, I had been reared in the experimental tradition of Wundt, transmitted from Leipzig through Titchener at Cornell to Wellington by Thomas Hunter.

As a graduate student in psychology, I had been powerfully influenced by Ernest Beaglehole, who had returned to Wellington after obtaining a Ph.D. in anthropology from Yale, imbued with the cross-cultural psychology of Franz Boas, Ruth Benedict, Margaret Mead, and others of that era. It was Beaglehole's influence that steered me toward American, not British, psychology for a Ph.D. that at the time was not offered in New Zealand.

Cross-cultural psychology has an affinity for learning-theory determinism rather than physiological or biological determinism. In learning theory, there is a disparity between, on the one hand, behavioristic determinism derived from Pavlov and Watson; and on the other hand, teleological determinism derived from an entire menu of instinct and motivational theorists, including various schools of dynamic and psychoanalytic psychology.

Becoming an adherent of a particular school of psychology for me was too much like becoming an adherent of a religious cult. So it became incumbent on me to find a theoretical escape from exclusive allegiance to either behavioral determinism or teleological determinism. Otherwise I would have no theoretical foundation on which to build a career in psychology.

The foundation stone had been set in place by May 22, 1947, when the British Association for the Advancement of Science held its annual meeting in Wellington. There I presented a paper, "Basic Concepts in the Study of Personality," which began as follows:

The existence of personality maladjustment indicates that there are some basic factors which limit the capacity of the organism to make change in the face of changed conditions. Otherwise there would always be sufficient accommodation to prevent breakdown. It has been customary to consider these basic factors either as inborn (e.g. instincts) or learned (e.g. attitudes). For us as scientists concerned with the dynamics of personality this issue is actually irrelevant. It is sufficient to know that there are certain basic factors in personality, or as I prefer to call them basic inevitabilities of being human, which are stable focus points about which conflict may develop, so making accommodation to changed circumstances difficult.

It is also irrelevant, for our adequate study of personality, whether these basic inevitabilities are either solely organic and constitutional or solely psychological in nature. This dichotomy, however interesting for the ruminations of the philosopher, is not an essential one for the scientific study of personality. Nor is it important to be concerned with the nature of the possible relationship between these two in the human organism. It is enough to know that some of our problems will best be solved if, like the physiologist, we orientate ourselves to the organic viewpoint; whereas others will best be solved if we disregard physiology and become oriented to the psychological viewpoint. There is no doubt that psychological experience is mediated by an organic substrate, as, for example, the nervous system and the endocrine system, but the scientific study of psychological experience is not limited to, not identical with, a study of the organic substrate. Any attempt to make this identity is not only quite outside the boundary of present day knowledge, but is an unnecessary embarrassment and will always be so. There are many problems, especially in the field of personality adjustment, which can be solved without reference to the physiology involved. For this reason it is not necessary to consider the basic factors or variables of personality as essentially physiological, nor, on the contrary, as wholly learned. It is enough to consider them as characterised by functional stability and as being difficult to change.

The phrase "inevitabilities of being human" constitutes the conceptual nucleus of these two paragraphs. In recent writing, I have used the expression "universal exigencies of being human" as a more accurate conveyance of the same meaning. Since 1947 the exigencies themselves also have been renamed and refined (Money, 1957). In 1947 they appeared as follows:

1. Helplessness and the need for security. The complete helplessness of the human baby means that it needs tactile and kinaesthetic stimulation not only in connection with feeding, but also, as Margaret Ribble's observations have shown, for efficient respiratory and circulatory functioning. All three, respiration, circulation and digestion, are beneficially affected by the sound of the mother's voice. Adequate amounts of tactile, kinaesthetic and auditory stimulation are therefore necessary for, at first, the healthy physiological development and functioning of the baby, and later on for the feeling of security which is the psychological counterpart of such healthy functioning. As the baby grows up, feelings of security will become less intimately attached to tactile sensations, and the presence of the mother or other significant adult will be a sufficient stimulus and guarantee. At adolescence, with the maturity of sexuality, the significance of intimate tactile sensations will once again assume a more important role.

2. Separateness and the need for adequacy. The reverse of the need for security which is satisfied by contact with other human beings is the need to accept one's separateness as an individual. Throughout life it is necessary to work out a delicate balance between these two needs. For example, at adolescence it may express itself as a conflict between mating and career. The balance may very easily be upset in a child by the parents' differential treatment of an older or younger sibling.

3. Appetites related to body metabolism, such as hunger, thirst, oxygen and carbon dioxide balance, mineral balance, sleep and elimination. Under ordinary circumstances in our society these appetitive factors are not the focus points of conflict. Their true importance is more obvious in animal experimentations, and in unusual circumstances such as prisoner of war camps where hunger was perpetually present.

4. Sexual status, male or female. With the exception of a few hermaphrodites, every individual has to learn a sexual role for which he is biologically suited in the process of reproduction. In a society which does not have the sexual roles clearly differentiated from infancy onwards and which equivocates in its attitude toward sex in the way that ours does, it is a little wonder that sexual status is, in our cultural pattern, the most significant focal point for personality maladjustment.

5. Death and injury. Ordinarily the anticipation of death or injury is not a focal point for personality adjustment, but in experimental animals and in human beings in war, their potential importance is evident.

6. Physiological characteristics, such as weight, age, effects of disease, and organ inferiorities. It is well known that Adler gave special emphasis to these characteristics in his theory.

Today, the exigencies numbered 1 and 4 have been combined as two manifestations of pairbondship; and number 2 has been merged into the exigency of troopbondship. The names of the exigencies, now five in number, and their definitions are as follows (Money, 1986, Ch. 8):

Pairbondship or pairbondage: Pairbondage means being bonded together in pairs, as in the parent-child pairbond, or the pairbond of those who are lovers or breeding partners. In everyday usage, *bondage* implies servitude or enforced submission. Though *pairbondage* is defined so as not to exclude this restrictive connotation, it has a larger meaning that encompasses also mutual dependency and cooperation, and affectional attachment. Pairbondage has a twofold phyletic origin in mammals. One is mutual attachment between a nursing mother and her feeding baby, without which the young fail to survive. The other is mutual attraction between males and females and their accommodation to one another in mating, without which a diecious species fails to reproduce itself.

Male-female pairbonding is species specific and individually variable with respect to its duration and the proximity of the pair. In human beings, the two extremes are represented by anonymous donor fertilization versus lifelong allegiance and copulatory fidelity.

Troopbondship or troopbondage: Troopbondage means bondedness together among individuals so that they become members of a family or troop that continues its long-term existence despite the loss or departure of any one member. Human troopbondage has its primate phyletic origin in the fact that members of the troop breed not in unison but asynchronously, with transgenerational overlap and with age-related interdependency. In newborn mammals, the troopbonding of a baby begins with its pairbonding with its mother as the phyletically ordained minimum unit for its survival and health. After weaning, it is also phyletically ordained for herding and troopbonding species that isolation and deprivation of the company of other members of the species or their surrogate replacements is incompatible with health and survival. Nonhuman primate species are, in the majority of instances, troopbonders like ourselves.

Abidance: Abidance means continuing to remain, be sustained, or survive in the same condition or circumstances of living or dwelling. It is a noun formed from the verb *to abide* (from the Anglo-Saxon root *bidan,* to bide). There are three forms of the past participle: *abode, abided,* and *abidden.*

In its present usage, *abidance* means to be sustained in one's ecological niche or dwelling place in inanimate nature in cooperation or competition with others of one's own species, amongst other species of fauna and flora. Abidance has its phyletic origin in the fact that human primates are mammalian omnivores ecologically dependent on air, water, earth, and fire, and on the products of these four, particularly in the form of nourishment, shelter, and clothing, for survival. Human troops or individuals with an impoverished ecological niche that fails to provide sufficient food, water, shelter, and clothing do not survive.

Ycleptance: Yclept is an Elizabethan word, one form of the past participle of *to clepe,* meaning to name, to call, or to style. *Ycleped* and *cleped* are two alternative participles. *Ycleptance* means the condition or experience of being classified, branded, labeled, or typecast. It has its phyletic basis in likeness and unlikeness between individual and group attributes. Human beings have had names and have typecast each other since before recorded time. The terms range from the haphazard informality of nicknames that recognize personal idiosyncracies, to the highly organized formality of scientific classifications or medical diagnoses that prognosticate our futures. The categories of ycleptance are many and diverse: sex, age, family, physique, looks, temperament, and so on. We all live typecast under the imprimatur of our fellow human beings. We are either stigmatized or idolized by the brand names or labels under which we are yclept. They shape our destinies.

Foredoomance: Doom, in Anglo-Saxon and Middle English usage, meant what is laid down, a judgment or decree. In today's usage it also means destiny or fate, especially if the predicted outcome is adverse, as in being doomed to suffer harm, sickness, or death. A foredoom is a doom ordained beforehand. *Foredoomance* is the collective noun that, as here defined, denotes the condition of being preordained to die and of being vulnerable to injury, defect, and disease. Foredoomance has its phyletic origins in the principle of infirmity and the mortality of all life forms. Some individuals are at greater risk than others because of imperfections or exposure to more dangerous places or things. All life forms, however, from viruses and bacteria to insects and vertebrates, are exposed to the risk, phyletically ordained, of being displaced and preyed upon by other life forms. Foredoomance applies to each one of us at first hand, in a primary way, and also in a derivative way insofar as it applies also to those we know. Their suffering grieves us; their dying is our bereavement.

Although not signifying causality, exigency theory is able to accommodate a wide range of causal explanations in psychology, taken from, for example, evolution, genetics, phylogenetics, ontogenetics, neurochemistry, neuroendocrinology, neuro-immunology, and so on. Already in 1947 I needed a theory in which explanations in terms of brain functions would be compatible with psychology, for as a junior lecturer I had audited the course in physiology under John Eccles, who subsequently became a Nobel laureate for his work in brain research and whom I would meet again in 1982 as a copanelist at an international meeting on psychoneuro-endocrinology in Tübingen, Germany. At that time, I did not know, of course, that I would spend a large part of my life working with endocrinologists, but was already becoming prepared to communicate with them not in psychobabble, but conceptually in terms that were mutually comprehensible as psychoendocrinology.

Exigency theory allows psychoendocrine explanations and contingencies to be compatible with psychodynamic explanations and hypotheses. In New Zealand in 1947, only a handful of European immigrants, refugees from Hitler, had firsthand training in psychoanalytic psychodynamics. For professional as well as personal sexological advancement, it was on my agenda to obtain experience in psycho-analysis as a graduate student in America. From Pittsburgh in 1948, while making plans for graduate education at Harvard, I wrote enquiring about training and scholarship at the Boston Psychoanalytic Institute. I was advised that applicants without an M.D. were not acceptable and that the only available financial help would be the reduced rate of a personal analysis with a student analyst. My response to this monopolistic exclusion was a tacit resolve that if psychoanalysis would not accept me as a scholar, then eventually my nonanalytic scholarship would require psychoanalysis to yield to its pressure. To some extent that resolve has materialized as a sequel to my writings on hermaphroditism, and the promulgation in 1955 of the concept of gender role and subsequently of gender-identity/role.

Serendipity

The very idiom of our language requires us to talk about wishing, wanting, volunteering, choosing, deciding, and agreeing on courses of action. More than we realize, however, it is serendipity that shapes the courses of our lives.

The abusive interrogation and whipping that my father gave me when I was 4 had the serendipitous effect of confronting me with a lifetime's rejection of even the type of workman's clothing he wore that day, while demonstrating the brutality of manhood and the moral self-righteousness of authority. My father harassed me until I said yes, that I and not my playmate had broken a glass pane in his new garden frame. In fact it was an accident of two boys' horseplay and I did not know who was the one responsible. My father died without my being able to forget or forgive his unfair cruelty.

He died, as aforesaid, when I was 8, and that probably had a serendipitous effect on my education. Had he lived, it is likely that I would have been the oldest of more than three siblings (I have a younger brother still in New Zealand and a still younger sister in Canada). In that case I may have been obliged at the legal school-leaving age of 16 to begin learning a trade and earning full-time wages.

I did, in fact, leave high school at age 16, not as a dropout but as a graduate with a certificate of matriculation, ready to enter the university. By the serendipity of history, I was living in a social democracy in which, for the academically qualified, university tuition was without fees. There were no scholarships or student loans, however, to cover living costs. Even though I would be living at home, that would necessitate my being only a part-time student at the university, taking evening courses. During the daytime, I would receive instruction at the nearby teachers' training college, which paid its students a small stipend. There was one obstacle: I was too young. Seventeen was the lower age limit for admission to the training college. So I took advantage of an opportunity to be the uncertified teacher of six children in a one-room state school in the mountainous back country of provincial Marlborough in the South Island. In the examination for this job, I had succeeded in part by giving a ham-actor's rendition of Hamlet in the soliloquy "To be or not to be."

In Wellington the university is perched on a steep slope commanding a spectacular view of the hilltops of the city and its harbor. Walking fast, it was possible to get from the training college to the university in time for 4 PM lectures, at the earliest. Lectures in the natural sciences were all scheduled for earlier in the day. Thus, I was obliged to exclude the natural sciences from my degree. Psychology was more or less derided as a science, for it still had not gained independence from the Philosophy Department. Nonetheless, it was the only science I could study as an undergraduate. Thus, serendipitously, my future career had its beginning.

There were more serendipitous contingencies to which the development of my career as a psychologist might be attributed. One was that the government's Department of Education, after it had certified me as a schoolteacher, banished me from its schoolrooms when, in 1942, I was officially accorded status as a conscientious objector in World War II. There was a strong pacifist tradition in my family. My mother's three eldest brothers and my father had been imprisoned as conscientious objectors in World War I.

In the years of childhood I did not know that my father and my uncles had been prisoners in internment camps instead of being soldiers. Nonetheless, from age 4 or 5, I grew up to have an absolute aversion to shooting and killing. It must have begun with the gun-killing of birds. I have a very early memory, as vivid as a Dutch still life, of iridescent, multicolored pukekos, New Zealand's indigenous swamp hens, that my father had shot in the wetlands on his way home from work. My mother undermined his prowess as a hunter, for she knew that pukekos were all feather and bone, and no meat. She would have nothing to do with plucking or cooking them.

My mother had been a New Zealander all of her life, except for the first three years in England, where she was born, near London. She knew more about pukekos than did my father. He was an Australian. Both of his parents were Londoners by birth and marriage. He was born in Bundaberg, Queensland, where he had lived in the sugarcane plantation country until he was 18. Then he and his year-older brother, my Uncle Harry, led the exodus of the entire family to New Zealand. Tropical Queensland and temperate New Zealand had entirely different flora and fauna.

I had seen live pukekos in the wetlands, and I was their ally. Like peacocks, which I had never seen, they were colored to be the live inhabitants of a celestial paradise, not of a butcher's block, dead on the kitchen table.

After the shooting of the pukekos, came the shooting of my friends the blackbirds. My unending questioning (which years later, I learned had unendingly annoyed my elders) had allowed me to recognize that the rarest sculptures in my worm cast museum, and the only colored ones, were in fact blackbird droppings. They were the sculptures of my feathered friends, topped with white and berry-blue, like a multicolored ice cream cone.

My father had a vendetta against blackbirds, for they ate all the fruits of his berry bushes and orchard trees in the back garden as soon as they ripened. So there I was on the day when through the opened kitchen window he targeted the fruit-eating thieves, my feathered sculptors and my friends, and shot them dead, one by one. My entreaties on their behalf were to no avail.

As a conscientious objector, I was required to be either working or studying at the university and working during vacations. After I had graduated with a double master's degree at the end of 1944, a vacancy in psychology opened up at the University of Otago in the southern city of Dunedin. My appointment as a junior lecturer began at the commencement of the academic year in March 1945. I gave lectures in undergraduate psychology, supervised one of the two sections of the undergraduate laboratory course, and gave what amounted to personal counseling to students who applied for what was officially listed as "vocational guidance."

My colleague in psychology at Otago, also a junior lecturer, was Peter McKellar. He was less into the pragmatics and more into the esoterics of psychology than I was. Through him I took up an interest in hypnotism. I gave upwards of half a dozen demonstrations of hypnotic trance for psychology students. On one occasion, I gave at his own request a posthypnotic instruction to a young poet, a heavy-drinking admirer of Dylan Thomas, that he would not be able to lift a mug of beer from the bar counter. For two weeks in his young adult life, the subsequently famous New Zealand poet James K. Baxter did not drink. Then the effect wore off. So also did my interest in hypnotism as a therapeutic trance, though not as a phenomenon of leader-follower bonding that for me still remains unexplained. I had a similar response to the therapeutic trance induced by sodium amytal when, in 1953, I participated in its use on a CVAH (congenital virilizing adrenal hyperplasia) hermaphroditic patient at Johns Hopkins. When under the influence of the drug, as when not, he was completely amnesiac about the early years of his life lived as a girl.

The disruptions of war left New Zealand with no commercial overseas passenger travel by ship, and overseas air connections had not come into existence. Currency restrictions made it impossible to import American psychology publications on the open market. Even if I had had the wealth, I would not have been able to convert it to dollars to pay for the graduate school fees for a Ph.D. in an American university instead of a British university. It was, therefore, serendipity of the highest order that, having borrowed an American psychiatric journal from the university library, I should with idle curiosity scan the back pages and there find a notice saying that the newly opened Western State Psychiatric Institute in Pittsburgh solicited foreign graduates in psychology to apply for residency training. Room and board was provided and a yearly stipend of twelve hundred dollars (an amount sufficient to finance an extra year in graduate school). The chief psychologist was Saul Rosenzweig, whose graduate training had been at the Harvard Psychological Clinic under Henry A. Murray.

The University of Otago declined to give me a leave of absence to obtain a Ph.D. So without an obligation to return, I packed a large crate with essential books, writings, and treasures that give continuity to my existence, hammered it closed, and carried the hammer in my luggage, prepared for customs inspection in New York.

Northward from Dunedin I traveled by train, overnight ferry, and train via Christchurch to Wellington and then Auckland, the overseas departure port. In

Christchurch, I had a special mission in the name of psychological rehabilitation and literature. I sought out Denis Glover, the poet, editor, and founder of the small but most prestigious publishing house in New Zealand letters, the Caxton Press. I handed him a manuscript of short stories and verses that I thought were among the highest achievements of New Zealand literature and asked him to consider publishing them. They had been written by a student while she was consulting me for guidance and counseling in the course of what became a severely morbid, suicidal panic state that eventually destined her to prolonged hospitalization. The collection of short stories, typeset by hand, eventually saw the light of day in 1951: *The Lagoon and Other Stories* by Janet Frame. The author has since established the reputation, both at home and abroad, of being in the forefront of New Zealand literature, for which she has received prestigious national and international awards. Jane Campion's 1990 film, *An Angel at My Table,* based on Janet's three-volume autobiography, met with immense critical acclaim worldwide.

It was music, not literature, that first engaged me in the psychology of the creative process. My M.A. thesis in psychology was on "Creativity in Musical Composition." In childhood, music had been my first career choice. Before I left Dunedin in 1947, I had arrived at the sorry conclusion that I was not endowed with the prodigies of aural, kinesthetic, and notational memory with which the virtuosos among my musician friends had begun their training. I traded music for psychology, in my hopes for accomplishment. I am not by inclination a gambler, except on those occasions when I've had to lay a wager on my career.

The *Rangitiki,* the first ship to carry passengers overseas from New Zealand after World War II, was the one I boarded in Auckland after a brief farewell visit with my family in Lower Hutt in mid-July 1947. It was still fitted out as a converted troopship and densely overcrowded. Until you have crossed the Pacific Ocean, you have no idea of the magnitude of the moon. After five weeks and going through the Panama Canal, at last I was on the docks of New York, culture-shocked by even the mechanics of using an American pay phone, not to mention freighting luggage on the Pennsylvania Railroad to Pittsburgh. It was the weekend of Labor Day, and to report to my new job on time, I would need to get the next night train to Pittsburgh. No way! I had not crossed the Pacific in order to bypass New York. That would be like bypassing Cairo without seeing the pyramids. Even though my total worldly wealth was two hundred dollars, I stayed a day in New York. Then, one day late, early in the morning, I made my way with two pieces of handbaggage and a backpack, from the railway station to my new address on De Soto Street in Pittsburgh, to begin my American career as a psychologist. My new boss was none too pleased that I had arrived from New Zealand a day late.

A Ph.D. Takes Shape

One of my assignments in Pittsburgh was to design an experimental test of a proposition in personality theory. So I proposed and carried out the experimental production of inhibition in a frustrating, conflict-producing situation. The students who, with painted blocks, copied complex geometric designs exposed in a tachistoscope showed no signs of either inhibition or facilitation whether or not they were electrically shocked while copying. This negative conclusion to so many hours of work diminished my confidence in the social-causality theory of psychopathology— or at least in the feasibility of its experimental investigation. It was not likely that I would dedicate an entire postdoctoral career to this type of psychology.

During the year in Pittsburgh, I became adept in the clinical art of psychological testing. I wrote reports worthy of a phrenologist or palm reader. They were cunningly spliced together with likelihoods, provisos, the conditional tense, and the passive voice, not to mention abstruse mental terminology like "rich inner life." I became a master of the psychodynamics of projective tests, and divined Rorschach inkblots with the propriety of a priest reading the auguries from the entrails of a bird. Already I half knew that this also was a type of psychology to which I would not be dedicating an entire postdoctoral career.

While still in New Zealand, I had applied to several American graduate schools. New York was on the top of my list of cities to live in, but Harvard had Henry Murray's psychological clinic and the graduate program that appealed to me most. Columbia had accepted me. Harvard had not, but I was eligible to reapply after having taken the Graduate Record Examinations in Pittsburgh. I have always assumed that I was accepted on the strength of a recommendation of a Harvard Psychological Clinic alumnus, Saul Rosenzweig, my boss in Pittsburgh.

I became a graduate student in the then-new (no longer existing) Department of Social Relations in September 1948. The department had four divisions. The psychological clinic, situated on Plympton Street in Cambridge, is where I majored under Robert White, Henry Murray, and others. The other three divisions were in Emerson Hall, one of the edifices of Harvard Yard: social psychology (Richard Soloman, Leo Postman, Jerry Bruner, and Gordon Allport), cultural anthropology (Clyde Kluckhohn), and sociology (Talcott Parsons and Samuel Stouffer). I took courses also with Frederick Mosteller (statistics) and Percy Bridgman (logic of agreement).

I was 27 when I finally became registered as a Ph.D. student. Since high school days, I had always anticipated that I would be one. In that way, I would override the inferiority of not measuring up to the schoolboy macho ideal. I would change my name from Mr. to Dr. I had planted the idea in my mind from the example of my oldest cousin, Herbert Money. He had left New Zealand for Peru and had graduated from San Marcos University in Lima. As a boy he had been very close to his youngest uncle, my father, and would visit my family on his return visits to New Zealand. He was the first person on either side of my colonial immigrant family to get a university education. I was the second.

At 27 I was in a hurry to get finished with going to school, while having to work to earn a living at the same time. Harvard was generous with scholarships, but they covered only part of the tuition fees. On the basis of my grades, I was selected for a big scholarship endowed by Senator Saltonstall in memory of his son, killed in the war in the Pacific, but my status as a wartime conscientious objector meant that I did not get it.

I was in a hurry also to be independent and to make my own achievements. It was good luck for me that Harvard accepted my New Zealand degrees and the residency year in Pittsburgh. That enabled me to concentrate on senior seminars only. They interested me immensely. The mind-expanding joy of being a student was again as great as when I had first experienced it at the teachers' training college in Wellington. I explored beyond the narrow confines of clinical psychology into the terrain of cultural anthropology and sociology. I took a special seminar with Percy Bridgman, the physicist whose theory of operational logic in *The Logic of Modern Physics* had left a deep imprint on me from Dunedin days.

I worked for the joy of learning and not to pass exams. I did not keep a systematic record of grades. The first time I needed a transcript of my academic record was years later when Maryland passed a law to license psychologists. It was only then that I discovered my course record had been one of straight A's.

In departmental examinations there was a different story. In one written examination, I wrote an essay that to my amazement was not acceptable. I had strayed too far from the party line as taught in the compulsory introductory proseminar. I had written about the universal inevitabilities of being human. To retaliate, I enlarged my essay and it became my second published paper, "Unanimity in the Social Sciences with Reference to Epistemology, Ontology, and Scientific Method" (1949).

Being in a hurry to graduate, I took the general qualifying examination a year sooner than was usual. I was not prepared for the persnickety detail and the potential ambiguities of true-false and multiple-choice questions, especially in sociology, and so I flunked. The amount of encyclopedic memorizing required was like having to pass or fail on a game of Trivial Pursuit. The task of preparing for a retake so overwhelmed me that for a time I was incensed enough to rehearse the possibility of quitting. Then salvation came in a pillbox. Amphetamines were newly on the market, and I was given a few by a fellow student. To this day I joke and say that I have a pharmaceutical Ph.D., thanks to the many extra hours of study, far into the night, the drug enabled me to accomplish.

Henry Murray's influential volume of *Explorations in Personality* and his *Thematic Apperception Test* (TAT), had helped to generate at Harvard, in the psychological clinic, the tidal change, namely the psychodynamics of personality, that swept over American clinical psychology in the postwar era. There was financial underpinning of the change from the newly created Veterans Administration hospitals where clinical psychologists were enlisted in the service of psychiatry. By 1950, a fair number of graduate students in the psychological clinic were innovators who would use their training in psychodynamics as Ph.D.'s in the practice of psychotherapy.

I was hot on the trail of psychodynamics, but not of their use to isolate psychogenic from organic causality in diagnosis and treatment. While in Pittsburgh, I had been impressed by a case in which the symptoms of a temporal lobe brain tumor had mimicked schizophrenia so well that for more than two years the case had been misdiagnosed as psychogenic. In New Zealand also, as a student working between semesters in the state mental hospital at Porirua, I had been keenly aware of the difficulties of differential diagnosis. Cautiously, my interest in psychodynamics was to investigate and find proof of their applicability, not to accept doctrine as truth.

One of my investigations of psychodynamics while at Harvard was for a seminar on research problems of social structure (under Stouffer, Parsons, and Florence Kluckhohn). The seminar was strongly oriented toward statistics. I was one of a pair of students (Arne van de Goot from Holland was my partner) who took on the task of evaluating the projective test (Rorschach and TAT) protocols obtained from two groups of men, one Navaho and one Zuni, in the Southwest. Our task was to perform various permutations and combinations of the test scores and to evaluate them statistically, so as to identify underlying psychodynamic similarities in the individuals of each group that might explain the widely divergent social structures of Navaho and Zuni communities.

We scored and rescored these protocols and analyzed and synthesized the scores, singly and combined, in so many ways as to have positively tortured them. Yet no semblance of a basic personality structure emerged. A maxim that I frequently quote is: Don't fight if you can't win, so I quit the psychodynamic arena of projective tests and basic personality structure. I would not expend any more of my research energy and time so unproductively. I was through with reading auguries from the entrails of inkblots, and with making divinations from the mountain peaks and ocean trenches of multivariate pencil-and-paper personality tests. The alternative, hidden in my brave new world of science fiction since undergraduate days, was a thought-reading machine that would give direct access to cognition as it was taking place in the brain.

Then along came the bonanza on which a research life could be spent very productively. I was one of half a dozen graduate students in a tutorial, "Fieldwork and Seminar in Clinical Psychology," under the psychoanalyst George Gardner, director of the Judge Baker Guidance Center on Beacon Street in Boston. The title accepted for the term paper I would write was "Psychosexual Development in Relation to Homosexuality." The outline was far enough advanced for me to know that it would be not a term paper in length, but a weighty monograph. Then George Gardner saved the day by presenting a case on which he had been a consultant. It was a case of hermaphroditism (nosologically, male pseudohermaphroditism) of the type subsequently known as testicular feminizing syndrome. By changing the focus of my paper to hermaphroditism, I made it far more manageable within the time available. The new title became "A Survey of Psychosexual Theory, Part I: The Evidence of Human Hermaphrodites."

In my paper, I included four case examples. This is what I wrote about case 2, the Gardner case:

Joseph, a high school student of 15, the second case, is reported in unpublished form from the Peter Brent Brigham Hospital. The patient is the youngest of three children: he has an unmarried sister of 25 and a brother 23, with whom he shares a bedroom The parents are of Italian birth and the family lives in a small New England town where the father is a small business man of moderate means. At birth the patient was declared first a girl, then a male by the obstetrician, and the father insists that up till the age of eight he possessed a scrotum and one descended testicle on the left, which the father was able to feel himself. Joseph is now 5'9" tall and weighs 193 lbs. He has well developed breasts and female genitalia. Physical examination revealed that he possesses well defined labia majora which are separated by a shallow recess, a large clitoris (or hypospadic penis) 1–2 cm long and a urethral orifice opening beneath the clitoris which requires his sitting down to urinate. No evidence of a prostate, vagina or uterus was found. Pubic hair was of feminine distribution, there was no facial hair, and there was some deepening of the voice which the father believed had been increasing during the preceding six months. Subsequently, laparotomy revealed an absence of internal female genitalia and atrophic testicles. Skull films indicated a normal sella turcica and there were no gross signs of adrenal or pituitary disturbance. The child had always been considered a boy and felt himself to be one. He denied that he had feelings about being different from other boys until about the age of 12, when his breasts began to develop. "Even now I don't think about it, or try not to." The examining physician found that the boy was superficially at ease, answered direct questions readily, smiled pleasantly, but was extremely reticent and anxious, particularly when the subject of his abnormality was approached. He blushed readily moved in his chair, tapped restlessly with his fingers on the table, and was uneasy with silences. Although reluctant to come to the hospital, he had wished to do so for a long time. He denied embarrassment about the examinations: "Whatever the doctors do is for my own good." He had difficulty in discussing the nature and emotional significance of his abnormality: "I think the most important thing, the thing that bothers me most, is my chest; if I could be fixed so that I wouldn't be self-conscious about being seen, that would be the most important thing. Then perhaps they could do something about the rest. I don't know whether they can or not. I wouldn't mind an operation, or anything they want to do, perhaps to open up and discover what's inside. In fact, if they're really going to do it, I would be glad to get it over with as soon as they can." Except to say that something wasn't right, he could not discuss his genitals. Since the development of his breasts, he has refused to permit his parents to see his genitalia. He tied a towel tightly around his chest, and became increasingly shy and seclusive, his few friends being boys. Formerly he had been active in customary boys' games and sports. He devoted increasing amounts of time to reading and study. He reported particular interest in mathematics and science, and had taken a college preparatory course in his first year of high school, where his grade average was 92%, with the intention of going to Yale and eventually studying medicine. The reporting physician commented that it did not appear that the patient had made a feminine identification. The father was described as a tiny, quick-moving, bird-like man; soft-spoken and extremely ingratiating in manner, expressing warm, obviously sincere concern about the condition of his son, from whom he had apparently succeeded in concealing his tremendous anxiety concerning the boy's sexual development. He had always considered the child a boy and although he was willing to agree to suggestions from the hospital, preferred that the child remain a boy: "But if you can't really change him, don't spoil him; let him stay like he is, as much a boy as he can." It was said that the mother did not visit the hospital because of her poor control of the English language. Psychiatric treatment after discharge from the hospital was recommended.

Then follows a paragraph in which, comparing case 2 with case 1 (a case of female pseudohermaphroditism secondary to congenital virilizing adrenal hyperplasia), I specified the significance of hermaphroditism for sexual theory.

> Both of these patients are pseudohermaphrodites. The first possessed ovarian tissue, bodily features and secondary sexual characteristics of a strongly masculine type, and had been reared as a girl from which psychosexual orientation she did not wish to change. The second possessed testicular tissue, bodily features of a strongly feminine type, and had been reared as a boy from which psychosexual orientation he did not wish to change. In both cases the problem confronting the patients was not that they felt themselves to have been reared in the wrong sex and that they had an inappropriate psychosexual orientation; but that their bodily features belied their psychosexual awareness and orientation. Here is strong evidence to support the thesis that the psychological phenomena of psychosexual orientation are a universe of discourse which should not be confused with that to which belong bodily features and processes. Of course it may be argued on the basis of these two cases alone that psychosexual orientation was congruent with the kind of gonad tissue possessed, paradoxical as is the relationship between the gonads and other secondary sexual features of body build in each patient. However, Albert Ellis (*Psychosomatic Medicine* 7: 107–125, 1945) records in tabular form many instances of pseudohermaphrodites whose psychosexual orientation and rearing was inconsistent with the type of gonad tissue present. In some of these cases bodily features and gonad tissue were congruent, in others not. The conclusion is obvious: in hermaphrodites there may be many inconsistencies and paradoxes among those features of body build and functioning which are commonly considered characteristic of either sex: but whatever the somatic features, they have very little to do with psychosexual orientation and awareness.

Becoming a Medical Psychologist

By summer 1950, I had completed the course work requirements and began writing my dissertation. The topic was "Hermaphroditism: An Inquiry into the Nature of a Human Paradox." Part 1 would be a review of hermaphroditism in the medical literature of the English language, 1895–1950. Part 2 would be ten case studies representing different varieties of hermaphroditism. I would see each of the ten hermaphrodites in person, administer a standard battery of psychological tests, and record on a disc rcorder (tape recorders had not yet been invented) several hours of biographical interview. The same schedule of inquiry would be used for each person and would cover a wide range of topics from which masculinity or femininity of lifestyle and sex life could be systematically construed, and then compared with the sexual morphology of the body and the sex of the gonads and hormones (the technique for ascertaining genetic sex had not yet been discovered).

George Gardner became my dissertation advisor. He introduced me to Stanley Cobb, chief of the Psychiatry Department at Massachusetts General Hospital and a Harvard professor. The approach to his office in the historic Bullfinch Building was through the "Ether Dome" amphitheater, the place where a dentist administered an anesthetic, ether, for the first time in history in 1846. I could not shake hands with Dr. Cobb, as his joints were afflicted with the gruesome pain of rheumatoid arthritis. A stoical and friendly man, he welcomed me cordially and gave me a student appointment in his department, thus legitimizing my research presence in the hospital and giving me access to its library.

Thus legitimized, I was able to establish contacts with physicians responsible for the care of hermaphrodites in pediatrics, gynecology, endocrinology, and, at Children's Hospital, plastic surgery (Dr. Donald W. MacCollum). There were some misgivings about exposing patients to psychology, though not in the endocrine clinic.

The director of the endocrine clinic, Fuller Albright, was one of the founders of clinical endocrinology. He was a clinical research genius, noteworthy for recognizing and naming new syndromes. He defied the handicap of early-onset Parkinson's disease until eventually it restricted his movements so greatly that he took the do-or-die promise of experimental brain surgery as a cure. Alas, it neither cured nor killed, but left him brain-damaged and aphasic, unable to respond though probably able to comprehend, for eight interminable years.

Albright recommended me to Fred Bartter, who would later become chief of the National Heart Institute, his senior assistant in clinical research and treatment for hermaphrodite females with congenital virilizing adrenal hyperplasia (CVAH). One of Bartter's patients, whose case became one of the ten in my dissertation research, manifested psychologically problematic behavior, notably kleptomania. It was a great embarrassment to herself and her parents when she pilfered from the houses of friends.

This girl had made medical history when on a clinical treatment trial after a test with ACTH (adrenocorticotropic hormone) at the end of December 1949 that produced a negative result, she was tested at the beginning of January 1950 with the new hormone, compound S (dihydrocorticosterone), which by contrast produced a positive result. Thus, with this new hormone, the masculinizing effect of the CVAH syndrome could be suppressed and replaced by a release of feminization.

In the search for this new treatment, Albright and Bartter at Massachusetts General in Boston had been running in a friendly and neck-to-neck race with Lawson Wilkins at Johns Hopkins in Baltimore. By the coincidence of fate, his first test with compound S had been during the same period of time. Though the race had ended in a draw, Wilkins was the one who made the CVAH syndrome his major speciality, for which he became very well known.

Wilkins had established the world's first pediatric endocrine clinic on a part-time basis in the 1940s in the Harriet Lane Home for Invalid Children at Johns Hopkins. He gave up private practice to run the clinic full time in 1946, after his only son was killed at age 16 in an auto crash. His clinic became heir to the CVAH patients that the late Hugh Young, first professor of urology, had tried unsuccessfully to cure surgically with adrenalectomy. The Wilkins clinic became known nationally as a prime referral center for newborn and infantile hermaphrodites.

At the 1950 meeting in Boston of the American Academy of Pediatrics, Lawson Wilkins gave an all-day workshop on pediatric endocrinology. Fred Bartter arranged an appointment for me to meet him. One item on my agenda was a request to visit Johns Hopkins and to be permitted to search for additional social and behavioral information in the files of several hermaphroditic patients whose cases could be traced from various medical publications, and possibly to test and interview one or two patients for my dissertation.

In January 1951, I went to Baltimore by car on two-lane roads that by comparison with today's multilane superhighways were mule tracks. I spent a week on the fifth floor of the now-demolished Harriet Lane Home and in the record rooms of pediatrics and urology, taking notes from patient's charts. One chart was that of a black youth diagnosed at puberty as a true lateral hermaphrodite, with a unilateral ovary (left) and testis (right) and with breast development on the left side only. There are infinitesimally few such cases on record, even today. Thus, the significance of my research series was greatly enhanced when the young man came to Boston for two days of tests and interviews.

I had an experience with vocabulary while writing my dissertation that strongly impressed me. I wrote to a gynecologist in England, Professor W.I.C. Morris of Manchester, for a follow-up on a hermaphroditic baby girl. Her case was of great importance to me because she was one of only six known cases in which a daughter fetus had been masculinized because of an ovarian or other masculinizing tumor in the mother during the pregnancy. The gynecologist replied by first apologizing that he could not provide me with a psychologic report of the sort he presumed I would need. Then in short and simple sentences, he proceeded to describe the girl's appearance, pose, manner, and conversation on the occasion of her most recent checkup at age 9. She had a ragdoll. It wore winter clothing, which she had sewn onto it herself. His letter left me in no doubt about what I wanted to know. The child appeared socially as a girl and not as a tomboy or as a child wanting to e changed to a boy. A report of psychologic testing alone almost certainly would not have given me that information.

The jargon-free information of this letter strengthened my already established professional resolve to use pediatric and vernacular English and to avoid psychological and psychoanalytic English. I further resolved that my reports, written or spoken, should be comprehensible to the clinicians and others to whom they were addressed and thus pragmatically of value in case management and patient care.

Before Lawson Wilkins took his first measure of me in Boston, at Johns Hopkins he had already singled out Joan Hampson as his top-priority psychiatrist whenever he needed a psychiatric consultation for one of his hermaphroditic patients. British by origin and early training, she was the most brilliant of the psychiatric house staff and also one unencumbered by the rising tide of American psychoanalytic vocabulary and principles. She presented her findings in a language that Wilkins could understand. But the exigencies of her schedule made her frequently unavailable. Wilkins contrived a plan to alleviate this situation. He answered a letter from me as if he had misread it.

My letter was actually a request, in advance of January 1951, to be a research visitor in his clinic. His reply was to tell me that he had accepted my research request and that he anticipated being able to obtain a research grant from the Commonwealth Fund. It would be sufficient to support me full-time and Joan Hampson half-time.

During the course of my visit in January, I was interviewed in the Department of Psychiatry, in which I would be academically appointed. The impression I was left with was, on the whole, of a rather lackluster department, its research stranded in the doldrums. Apart from pediatric endocrinology, I would be without spiritual kin in clinical psychoendocrinology, not only at Johns Hopkins but in general.

I had the competing enticement of a full-time faculty appointment teaching psychology at Bryn Mawr College in Pennsylvania. A third alternative would have been to prolong my existence as a graduate student. I had been offered a research assistantship by Henry Murray at Harvard. But I was impatient to graduate. It was time to finish—up and out. Henry Murray exercised so much charisma that my saying no to him was a bit like disregarding the royal command.

I weighed the pros and cons of Hopkins and Bryn Mawr with fellow Harvard students and faculty advisers, until I was persuaded not to underestimate the prestige in American psychiatry of John Whitehorn, successor to Adolf Meyer, the founder of the Phipps Clinic at Johns Hopkins. I did not yet have a clear image of psychohormonal research, but rather of being a standard clinical psychologist assigned to a children's endocrine clinic as a postdoctoral fellow, with no teaching appointment. It was rare in that era for a Ph.D. in psychology to do a postdoctoral fellowship before taking up an academic appointment. It was a possibility, however, and all the more so as I was able to negotiate with Bryn Mawr for a prart-time appointment. For the academic year 1951–52, I taught undergraduate physiological psychology there, one day a week, and spent the other five working in Baltimore.

Confirmation of a Commonwealth Fund grant dragged on and on, far beyond the expected date. John Whitehorn, I later discovered, was an administrative procrastinator, a man chronically depressed ever since his only son had been killed in World War II. The Commonwealth Fund application forms on which his signature was required lay in his urgent file for three months. By then the due date had passed.

Lawson Wilkins saved the day by contacting Frank Fremont-Smith, president of the Josiah Macy, Jr., Foundation. I recall very clearly the early spring day when he and I talked as we walked around the yard in front of the Bullfinch Building at Massachusetts General Hospital. My dissertation research was by now far enough along to reveal its significance and future potential. I was enthusiastic to tell about it, and Frank Fremont-Smith was an enthusiastic listener. That was my oral examination as a candidate for a postdoctoral research grant. Nothing was required in writing, no forms to be filled out, not even a signature to guarantee my appointment at Johns Hopkins.

I took my almost completed dissertation with me to Baltimore in the fall of 1951. In February 1952, I returned to Cambridge for the final oral examination and graduated.

Limerence and Power

As a new graduate student at Harvard, I had an agenda, the priority item of which was study and a Ph.D. To survive, I became a part-time interviewer in the Boston area for the Center for Survey Research of the University of Michigan. The center surveyed a national probability sample for the Federal Reserve Board with respect to family income, expenditures, prospective purchases, and attitude toward the economy. Although I knew nothing of Kinsey's sex surveys at that time, I was serving an apprenticeship in sex interviewing, insofar as personal income is as taboo a subject as personal sex. The ideal refusal rate was zero. There were fewer refusals at nights and weekends when the head of the household was available.

Surveying and studying, together with a tight budget, restricted my recreational life. I did not go to bars, movies, or other places of entertainment. With antipodean yearning to hear the great Boston Symphony Orchestra under Koussevitsky, I stood in line one afternoon, but to no avail. There were many empty seats reserved for season ticket holders who failed to appear. Those in line were turned away. I never did get to hear the Boston Symphony.

I lived not in Cambridge but in an apartment across the Charles River in Boston's West End, behind Massachusetts General Hospital, at 104 Brighton Street. This was the neighborhood of Whyte's *Street Corner Society* (1943). The apartment had been found for me by a New Zealand student at Harvard, Sigmund Gruber. It occupied the first floor of a nineteenth-century tenement house. A converted coal-burning stove had to be filled with heating oil from a five-gallon can every day in winter. Only the large kitchen was kept heated. Every morning in summer, I heard the iceman's street cry, "Eye-yiss," as he brought a new block of ice for the icebox. These outmoded conveniences were offset by the exceptional affordability of the place, for it was located in a rent-controlled zone.

Living there was like being on an urban camping trip, and I was well used to camping trips and climbing in the alpine mountains of Otago's lake and fiord region in New Zealand. I liked urban camping. For the first time I had the privacy of living in my own place.

Although living alone, I was not isolated. I kept in touch with people in person and by mail. One correspondent, an authoress whom I had first met in Pittsburgh, wrote from England. In connection with a story proposal, she asked for my ideas about the American woman. My reply was dated March 1, 1950.

I think the thing which strikes me most about the American woman is the ambiguity of her role. Educationally and vocationally, on the one hand, she is emancipated; executive of her own ego and controller of her own destiny if she wants to be. In sex and love, on the other hand, she doesn't know where she stands. Traditionally she should be submissive to the male, and although this tradition is changing, it is by no means moribund. Men do think of women as chattels, to some degree, often treating them as little more than instruments of their sexual pleasure, subject to their often capricious domination. Commonly their attitude toward a woman sexually is that of making her "come across." Emancipated to the degree that she is, the woman resents such treatment. She would like to feel emancipated enough to be able to make the man "come across." But the weight of custom is against her, so that she must adopt a weeping violet reaction which, contradictory as it is of the emancipated role, also holds some intrinsic charm for her. Perhaps it is that the weighty responsibility of emancipation becomes too great for her. Anyway, she is always left to carry the baby!

There is another factor, however, and that is that the weeping violet uses her technique to tyrannize over the male: once she has got him, she can become capricious and domineering. It seems as if the proposition is always that of who is going to dominate whom, and by what technique. There is almost a complete lack of any conception of genuine sharing and functional equality. By equality I do not mean identity of role; it is something like the equality in status but not in stature within the British Commonwealth. It is commonly observed that the woman is first fiddle; and in this respect I think there is a difference between the American and European families. In the latter the man is the leader. It is uncommon to find a genuine duo.

The struggle as to who dominates whom is a basis of much of the hostility and distrust in relationships between the sexes. The little boy grows up with a nucleus of fear and distrust toward the powerful woman, who in fantasy is a kind of ogre, vagina dentata, alluring him to its capture. Then in youth he finds that custom supplies him with all the weapons, and he can allure the woman. But he still has a quite deeply engrained disrespect and hostility, aptly expressed in the alliteration "find her, feel her, fuck her and forget her." His almost compulsive preoccupation is to prove his own none-too-sure virility with little concern for the woman as a personality.

The little girl, with the example of her mother before her, builds a conception of her feminine role which has to be demolished when she reaches adolescence. Her competence and achievement will count for nothing, unless her upbringing has permitted her to become a competent and achieved sex partner without too much guilty conscience, and she will have to adopt the subservient violet role if she wants dates and marriage. It is a disillusionment, and she loses respect for the man in having to be so two-faced. But she goes through with it because the social pressures demand that she have dates and get married. Difficult as it is not to be popular and frequently dated, it is much more difficult to reach the middle twenties with no prospect of marriage. Under these circumstances a woman is liable to become desperate, social pressure being so strong, and she will play weeping violet with exaggeration in order to get a man, despising him all the more for having to do so.

The rivalry and hostility which exists in relationships between the sexes helps to explain the peculiarly American phenomenon of dating. It is a product of a half-achieved emancipation, a pushing need to appear sexually normal, and a social sanction against overt sexuality. Unable to accept the reality for what it is, youth is obliged to make a game out of it. And it is a competitive game in which the one exploits the other for self-enhancement. The man is motivated to prove his virility and his power over women who have previously been a threatening power over him. The woman is motivated to prove her ability to meet social demand and get married, meanwhile being apprehensive of accepting her femininity and sexuality, and scared lest she lose the battle for domination.

The man uses his car and his money, together with his more favorable social and occupational status as a male, as coin of the realm in his game of exploitation. The woman uses her charm and her body. The fact that she gains a man's body and its charms is only incidental to her at this time. The fact that a man gains a potential home- and family-maker is only peripheral to him, for at this time he is only interested in thrills, and stories of glorious conquest to be told in bull sessions to gain the envy and admiration of his buddies. Thus neither gives much thought to the primary things of sexuality, home, and family-making. Little wonder that so many wake from a kind of daze to find themsleves married, and wonder what they will do next.

Those who have transcended the folkways, and have no guilty conscience about sexuality, are few and do not often cross paths. For such a woman is it especially disastrous if she does not meet a man who appreciates her point of view, for then she will be considered a slut. She will be the type to have a good time with, but not to marry. A clear dichotomy between these two categories is made especially by youth of the lower classes, in contrast to college youth. There are still many who regard it a kind of moral law to marry a virgin, regardless of the wild oats they have sown.

When I wrote this letter, I omitted from the equation of the masculine-feminine relationship the factor of having fallen in love, being love-smitten, being lovesick, or just being in love. There was no noun with which to name this state of being until Tennov (1974) coined the term *limerence*.

Eventually, my studies of hermaphroditism would guide me to the realization that the ultimate criterion of a hermaphrodite's gender-identity/role as masculine or feminine is the body sex of the partner who, whether male or female, evokes limerence and erotic attraction. In this respect, limerence supersedes the other criteria of masculinity/femininity that would eventually enter the medical dictionary and that I partialed out from my hermaphrodite data—namely, chromosomal sex, gonadal sex, hormonal sex (prenatal and pubertal), genital sex (internal and external), and sex of assignment and rearing. Each one of these criteria of masculinity/femininity may be discordant with one or more of the others, and no single one of them can be counted on to predict the sex of limerence.

One hermaphroditic patient in particular brought home to me the significance of limerence. Though reared as a boy and masculine in appearance, he had at age 12, before being referred to Johns Hopkins, been declared eligible to change to a girl, since there was effective feminizing hormonal and surgical treatment for his syndrome (CVAH). To resolve his vacillation, he submitted to his own test: he would have as a sexual partner both a boyfriend and a girlfriend. He discovered that he was more attracted to the boyfriend as a lover and so elected to change to live as a girl and woman. The relationship with the boyfriend eventually became a marriage that was societally defined, by all, as heterosexual. Then the marriage broke up and the patient made a new relationship with a girlfriend. In this relationship, the patient was defined by society as a lesbian. However, the same relationship would have been defined as heterosexual had the patient not changed sex but grown up to be a man with a masculine body build. It was the appearance and body build that people judged by, not the invisible sex differences.

With and without the inclusion of limerence, the issues in my letter on the American woman are issues for men as well as for women. They are issues for individuals as well as for society at large. They are also issues that to some extent are autobiographically derived.

I grew up in a family that identified politically with the Labor Party. The women of my mother's generation had an indomitable spirit of pioneer independence and a memory of the suffragette movement that, in New Zealand, achieved women's voting right much earlier than in Europe and America. I grew up to accept without questioning the political and civil rights of women. Many years later I thought of myself as a natural ally of the feminist movement. I was wrong. I was typecast as a proponent of the medical model and of biological and hormonal determinants of sexual differentiation.

Two of my mother's sisters were victims of the decimation of New Zealand's young male population, especially at Gallipoli, in World War I. After the war there was a surplus of marriageable young women who remained forever spinsters. For my two unmarried aunts, *spinster* was an unspeakable word. After my father's death, they came to live in my mother's house. They resented being single, envied their sisters-in-law by denigrating them, and never-endingly riled against the injustices of living in a man's world.

I suffered from the guilt of being male. I wore the mark of the best of man's vile sexuality. I wondered if the world might really be a better place for women if not only farm animals but human males also were gelded at birth. The antisexualism and the antimasturbation hysteria of Victorianism spread a sinister influence over me and my generation of youth. It was sinister enough to keep me, off and on, professionally and personally engaged in rectifying it over the full course of my career.

In 1939, when I was 18, I succeeded in obtaining a copy of Havelock Ellis's small volume *Psychology of Sex* (1933). It was extremely difficult to obtain such a book in the New Zealand of that era. All sex books in the university library were shelved in the librarian's office and were often stolen even from there.

The process of self-discovery took on an accelerated momentum when at Otago University I encountered the books of Karen Horney for the first time. Her analyses of the psychodynamics of self and others in interaction lent themselves to self-application and self-analysis—a process that continued with variations in degree of intensity and perspective indefinitely. I had already attended to religious issues and began to pay more attention to the psychological pathodynamics of people in my childhood and later life; and also to the dynamics of attraction and responsiveness in love and limerence, male and female. The psychodynamics of marriage and living together came into focus much later, when I was living in Boston.

By trial and error, I discovered the unstressfulness of self-sufficiency in both living and working, as compared with accommodating to supervision or being subordinate. Of course, I have never worked in total isolation but always with assistants and colleagues. Nor have I lived sexually abstinent, but in a give-and-take of sexual visitations and friendly companionships with compatible partners, some women, some men, some briefly, and some with continuity ending only in death.

The greatest forfeiture of this lifestyle is to have had no parenthood. I gave up on that after going through the invincible horror of separating and breaking up a long-term relationship with a woman brilliantly accomplished professionally, sexually, and as a homemaker. Years later, with the advance of psychiatric knowledge, I recognized that a wrong diagnosis of the source of the horror had been made. The correct diagnosis was toxic amphetamine psychosis from pills that she had been prescribed for weight loss to control orthostatic albuminuria.

I find it very congenial to live alone. The stress level is low, and the level of health and well-being is high. I like the freedom of being able to furnish my house as a museum of primitive art. I like being able to make my own schedule for social activities or for work marathons, and I like being able to set my own timetable for travel. I travel to many professional meetings domestically and abroad. I have set foot on every continent except Antarctica, visiting many cities and seeing many of the splendors of civilizations past and present.

From Psychohormonal Research to Dyslexia

When I took freshman psychology as an undergraduate in Wellington in 1939, endocrinology was a very young science. Thyroid hormone, with the longest history, had been in clinical use only since the turn of the century. The sex hormones had been isolated in the 1920s and synthesized and marketed in the 1930s. Most of the hormones in clinical use today had not been heard of. It was fashionable for psychology texts to suggest somewhat mysteriously that hormones might eventually be shown to be determinants of personality.

The mystery of hormones and personality still existed twelve years later when at the age of 30 I became a member of Lawson Wilkins's Pediatric Endocrine Clinic. I would cover in my research not only the syndromes of hermaphroditism, CVAH included, but all of the endocrine syndromes of childhood and adolescence, before and after hormonal treatment, and in long-term follow-up, for as long as I had research funding to keep going. Insofar as I had time available, I would evaluate patients irrespective of diagnosis, but each year I would concentrate on at least one diagnosis with a view to preparing a report for publication.

Initially, although my concentration was on hermaphroditism, I tested the intelligence of many patients with a history of treatment for hypothyroidism, which had been Wilkins's speciality before congenital virilizing hyperplasia. The earlier the onset of thyroid replacement therapy, the greater the potential for intellectual catch-up growth and IQ increase.

I evaluated also several patients with extremely early onset of puberty, before age 6. In their developmental histories, psychosexual age was closer to chronological age than to physique age.

The first publications on hermaphroditism were in 1955. Eventually they led to the Hofheimer Prize of the American Psychiatric Association for me and my two co-authors, Joan Hampson and her husband John. He had joined us upon his return from service in the Korean War. Later they would both move to Seattle and discontinue psychohormonal research. The major finding in the prize-winning publications was that gender role as masculine or feminine is not innate but is greatly influenced by postnatal socialization.

Every week was a race against time, for there were so many syndromes with which I needed to become acquainted and so many patients in each group. On Saturdays, Wilkins convened his outpatient follow-up clinic in a shabby annex of the Harriet Lane Home, which had long outlived its status as temporary. Attendance was compulsory. In addition to the Hopkins pediatric endocrine staff, there were many visiting pediatricians, international and national. Some, from local military installations, were seeking academic stimulation. The ratio of patients to physicians was no more than 2:1, whereas for all the patients there was only one psychologist. Despite the hectic pace, the Saturday clinics were my learner's diamond mine. Wilkins was a virtuoso of clinical teaching. He covered each patient's case history so thoroughly that after some years of follow-up one could practically recite all of them. In addition, he expounded all the theories of etiology and the latest in research developments. Often he could not stop before the doctors' dining room closed at 2 PM. Saturday clinics were a major source of my education in the endocrinology component of psychoendocrinology.

In the Saturday clinics, there were many patients with impaired statural growth and/or with pubertal delay or failure. In the 1950s, the very existence of a pituitary growth hormone was questionable. Thus, for children of dwarfed stature, the only effective hormonal treatment for those who were not only short but also failed to go into puberty at the appropriate age, was with sex hormone, male or female, to induce secondary sexual maturity.

Among girls, a large majority of those who would not mature without hormonal (estrogen) treatment were diagnosed with a syndrome named after its discoverer in Oklahoma, Turner's syndrome. Initially the defining features of this syndrome of variable multiple birth defects were dwarfism (adult height four and half to five feet) and ovarian agenesis.

Rapid advances in genetics research showed by the late 1950s that girls with Turner's syndrome have only one sex chromosome, an X, and no second X and no Y. With this new discovery, it became possible to link the developmental anomalies of Turner's syndrome not only with hormonal deficiency, but also directly with a major genetic deficiency—namely the absence of an entire chromosome. The technique of chromosome counting ushered in the new era of genetic exploration in 1956, and the launching of Sputnik on October 4, 1957, ushered in the new era of space exploration. Though both have become merged in my mind as being of equally momentous significance for the history of science, it was chromosome counting that affected me most. It ushered in a new era of psychocytogenetic research, a speciality branch of behavioral genetics.

The era of cutthroat competition for research funding from the National Institute of Mental Health had not yet arrived, and my research was by now supported by NIMH. It provided a salary for a young psychologist, John Shaffer, whose special interest was in statistics. His project was an analysis of the IQ subtest scores of girls with Turner's syndrome. His findings on Verbal/Performance IQ disparity led to the discovery that among the syndrome-related symptoms are specific space-form disability (dyspraxia), direction-sense blindness, and dyscalculia. Verbal IQ is not affected. On the contrary, it may be at the superior level, despite a grossly deficient Performance IQ.

My publications on intelligence and specific cognitional disability in pediatric hypothyroidism, sexual precocity, and Turner's syndrome had an unanticipated outcome. I was requested by the professors of pediatrics and opthalmology to help the dean's office save face with the NIH by revising a rejected application for the funding of a clinic for reading disability in the Department of Opthalmology. I agreed to work by moonlight so as to obtain funds and people to run the clinic. Nine years later, the entire project collapsed through the capricious withdrawal of governmental funding for the running of the clinic. Two books had been published: *Reading Disability* (1962) and *The Disabled Reader* (1966), as well as several journal articles. The data that forever remain incomplete and unpublished supported the hypothesis that in many instances a child with severe and bizarre manifestations of dyslexia has parents who have a catastrophic sexual life. The child's allegiance to one and not the other of the parents may entail dyslexia—being unable to read about the other's version of the catastrophe in the relationship.

Even though the reading clinic folded, the nine-year venture had demonstrated, academically and professionally, that I was not narrowly restricted to either psychoendocrinology or sexology. All of my research was positively endorsed by Seymour Kety, the head of the department who succeeded Whitehorn. After a test trial of one year, alas, he resigned and returned to his brain research laboratory at NIH. Under him, for the first and only time in my academic career, I had received for one year a strong sense of belonging.

His successor was Joel Elkes, who at departmental meetings identified my research only as dyslexia, never as psychoendocrinology or sexology. He was the victim of the man whom he appointed, despite widespread contrary advice, as his deputy chairman. I identified the deputy chairman as a Cardinal Richelieu, the power behind the throne, the first time we met. I classify him as the most contentiously destructive person I have ever known. His clandestine efforts to get rid of me failed. Thus, I have a lifetime of gratitude to Elkes, for he is also the one responsible for my promotion to a full professorship.

Joel Elkes is a great intellectual synthesist and a humanist in advance of his time. These virtues have also been his undoing. They cost him his professorship at Hopkins. He was sufficiently naive to trust his enemies.

Transexualism and Sex Reassignment

For many children, and their parents as well, referral to a psychologist or psychiatrist is the equivalent of having already been suspected of being insane. For children with a birth defect of the sex organs, my explanation to their parents, as to them, was that they needed a needle doctor, a cutting doctor, and a talking doctor, all three working together.

One of the cutting doctors who was a member of our team was the gynecological surgeon Howard W. Jones, Jr., now well known as the physician who did the first U.S. in vitro fertilization procedures after he reached retirement age at Johns Hopkins and began a second career at the newly established University of Eastern Virginia in Norfolk, Virginia.

World renowned as an expert in the surgical correction of hermaphroditism in the newborn, Howard Jones had had experience also in the surgical feminization of older hermaphrodites whose defect had been left uncorrected. In some instances the patient had been assigned and reared as a boy but had not differentiated a masculine gender identity and had required sex reassignment. In these cases, successful post-surgical rehabilitation as a woman gave support to the then very controversial idea that sex reassignment from male to female might be rehabilitatively successful for patients whose natal sex was male but who were transexuals. This term became widely adopted after Harry Benjamin published *The Transsexual Phenomenon* in 1966. I arranged for three patients who were under the care of Harry Benjamin and Leo Wollman in New York and who had been operated on overseas (one unsuccessfully in Naples and two successfully in Casablanca) to come to Baltimore and be examined by Howard Jones.

It was in January 1965 that the first sex-reassignment patient was admitted to Johns Hopkins for male-to-female reassignment surgery. However, the devoutly psycholanalytic deputy chairman of the department intervened and had the patient transferred from gynecology to psychiatry. The operation was thus, in effect, canceled. Another patient, a former Baltimorean, was referred from Harry Benjamin's clinic in New York. The first transexual surgery at Johns Hopkins was done on June 1, 1965. Phillip Wilson became officially and publicly known as Phyllis Avon Wilson.

By coincidence, it so happened that at this same time the professor of plastic surgery Milton Edgerton (long since at the University of Virginia) was devising female-to-male plastic surgery of the genitalia for a patient who had given an admission history of congenital hermaphroditism but who was congenitally a natal female. It was on Edgerton's suggestion that a committee was formed and a sex change clinic officially established within the hospital. I named it the Gender Identity Clinic, a name that I hoped would allow it eventually to encompass all problems of gender identity, including those of hermaphroditism, not only those of transexualism. That did not happen.

I have always considered transexualism in its literal sense, crossing sex, not as a diagnosis but as a method of rehabilitation for a small and special group of patients in distress. The lack of an absolutely clear-cut etiology for the condition may have had something to do with the Johns Hopkins policy of announcing in a press conference on August 10, 1979, but not in the professional literature, that the surgical operating rooms would no longer be available for transexual surgery. The irony of this announcement is that Howard Jones, no longer at Hopkins to make a rebuttal, had invariably used the operating rooms of his own Department of Gynecology for transexual surgery.

The press conference was scheduled without reference to any of the members of the gender identity committee. It was conducted by a man who had resigned from his former position as committee chairman. He did not act alone, but his superiors have not revealed themselves. His statement was based on his out-of-date and statistically flawed follow-up report, which in today's new climate of biomedical ethics would be subject to charges of fraud.

The contrivance of a press conference to announce the cessation of sex-reassignment surgery at Johns Hopkins was, in my judgment, a matter neither of science nor of medicine but of medical morals. It belongs in the same category of medical morals as does abortion. It may even have been designed to undermine the authority of the chairman of gynecology with a view to forcing closure of his abortion clinic. He lacked the power to counterattack. The Gender Identity Clinic did not disband. It has continued to evaluate candidates for surgical sex reassignment. The surgeon who performs the operations does so at a hospital in another part of town. The major hindrance is, as it always has been, financial. Hospital charges and professional fees are not covered by medical insurance.

In the annals of transexualism, the clinic at Johns Hopkins became famous not because it was the first in the field of sex-reassignment surgery in the United States, but because it made it respectable. There had been a few cases of transexual surgery, done by the urologist Elmer Belt in Los Angeles in the 1950s, but they had not hit the headlines. In 1930–31, the Danish painter Einar Weneger had been reassigned by Werner Kreutz in Dresden as Lili Elbe Hoyer, (*Man into Woman,* 1933). It was, however, the case of Christine Jorgensen in 1952 that hit the headlines when she returned to the United States after having been sex-reassigned from George to Christine in Denmark (*Christine Jorgensen: A Personal Autobiography,* 1967).

Antiandrogen, Paraphilia, and Sexual Identity

In July 1966, I was a guest lecturer at the University Hospital in Hamburg, West Germany. While there, I was introduced to Hans Giese and his staff at the Institute for Sexual Research. From them I learned about the use of an antiandrogenic hormone, cyproterone acetate (Androcur), newly synthesized by Schering in West Berlin. It had been given to a severely mentally retarded adolescent and had been successful in regulating perpetual masturbation that prevented him from appearing anywhere in public, including at school. There were preliminary indications also that intervention with the same hormone might be effective for a farmer affected with pedophilia involving prepubertal girls.

Toward the end of November of that same year, I was working very late when the phone brought in a call from the wife of a cross-dressing transvestophile who was known to me as the regional organizer of a support group for transvestites. The wife had overheard their 6-year-old son talking to his father asking him why his mother should not know their second secret. She already knew the first one: father and son cross-dressed as mother and daughter and played the game of being on television. The second secret was a penis game, in which the father fondled the boy.

In that era, compulsory reporting had not yet been legally mandated, so it was possible for me to work out a plan of prevention and rehabilitation involving all three members of the family. After a brief period of defiant denial, the father underwent a dissociative change of personality and begged for treatment. He had read extensively about his condition and knew that behavior modification treatment was a new vogue. He requested the aversive, punishment form of behavior modification. No one would accept him for treatment.

I discussed the case with Claude Migeon, a specialist in steroid hormones and one of the two codirectors of the Pediatric Endocrine Clinic since Wilkins's death in 1963. I told him about the use of antiandrogen in Hamburg. Then, as now, it was prohibited to use cyproterone acetate in the United States, as it had not been cleared by the Federal Drug Adminstration for the treatment of behavioral sex disorders. There was an available alternative, however: medroxyprogesterone acetate (Depo-Provera), manufactured by Upjohn. It had been used in the clinic to retard the velocity of pubertal maturation that began excessively at the age of 6 or sooner. Thus, it was known to be safe for clinical usage.

The patient had a favorable response to treatment with Depo-Provera (Money, 1970) that was maintained even after he was weaned off the hormone. In consequence, other cases of paraphiliac sex offending were referred for treatment.

As in the case of dyslexia and of sex reassignment, it was necessary to begin the new program without special funding, piggybacking on the research grant I had already received. Even though the sixties were the era of the so-called sexual revolution, the word *sex* in the title of a grant application would have been a kiss of death. There was wisdom of foresight, therefore, when I titled my first application, and all renewals, "Longitudinal and Related Psychohormonal Studies."

Taking care of patients with paraphilias is very demanding and time-consuming. It may require many hours of legal preparation and of appearing in court. By the late 1970s, the sex-offender program in which antiandrogenic injections and sexological counseling were combined had grown too big and too expensive to be carried on the same budget as all the rest of my clinical psychoendocrine research. It was therefore a blessing in disguise when the program was absorbed into the Department of Psychiatry as a new clinic under new management—even though the decision was unilateral and handed down without prior consultation. As in business and politics, one must adapt to academic power maneuvers.

The idea of a paraphilia as a sexological syndrome was and still is uncongenial to people who follow the ancient tradition of classifying sexual nonconformity as sin or crime, and the nonconformist as deviant or disobedient. Herein may lie an explanation of why medicine in general, and psychiatry in particular, especially as practiced within the judicial and penal system, has been slow to include antiandrogenic treatment in the case management of paraphiliac sex offending. There are cracks in the wall of resistance, however. Slowly, offensive sex is becoming decriminalized by becoming medicalized. In 1980, perversions were renamed paraphilias in the nomenclature of the American Psychiatric Association, but without including antiandrogen in the forms of treatment.

In my philosophy, the discordance between medicine and law in the treatment of sex offenders is irreconcilable, insofar as the adversarial principles of the law and the consensual principles of science constitute two irreconcilable systems of logic. The legal system is directed toward establishing guilt, blame, and punishment, which it cannot do without espousing the doctrine of free will and personal responsibility for all of one's actions. The scientific system, which includes biomedical science, is directed toward establishing origins, determinants, and causes, without espousing free will as a causal explanation and without making the individual personally responsible as the agent of all his or her actions.

The law is judgmental. Medicine is nonjudgmental. The law blames a person for getting sick, say with syphilis or AIDS, and enforces constraints and discipline. Medicine, by contrast, does not blame but intervenes with treatment: penicillin for syphilis and, as yet, nothing but palliative treatment for AIDS. Having no effective treatment for either the prevention or cure of AIDS, medicine follows the path of scientific research to discover one.

With an effective treatment, it is easy to be professionally nonjudgmental. Without one, it is easy to become professionally judgmental. Then one begins to admonish and blame the patient—for engaging in high-risk sexual behavior, for example, and so becoming HIV-infected and developing AIDS.

Medical students whom I have taught have difficulty, particularly with reference to sexual practices, in distinguishing professional nonjudgmentalism from self-applied nonjudgmentalism, which they interpret as an anarchistic lack of any personal moral principles by which to govern their own sexual behavior. They obey the dictates of their moral heritage—namely that their own sexual morality is absolutely correct, and it applies not only to themselves but to other people as well.

My own position with regard to sexual morality and the paraphilias is that there are more than enough people in the paraphile's life who pass judgment in the form of ridicule, stigmatization, vilification, assault, or arrest, singly or severally. By contrast, there may not be even one person who withholds judgment and is impartial, unless it is his doctor, or perhaps his lawyer, both of whom have the privileged, socially sanctioned role of impartiality. If I myself should fail to be professionally nonjudgmental, then the patient will be unable to disclose the data of his paraphilia in detail. Deprived of data, I will be deprived of the possibility of discovering the origin and determinants of paraphilia. Thus there will be no possibility of effective intervention. Above all, there will be no possibility of preventing the juvenile development of paraphilias in the next generation, and the next.

Becoming professionally nonjudgmental necessitates a self-imposed vigilance and discipline in the use of language. Idiomatic English is laced with words and phrases that attribute the cause of behavior to personal motivation and volition—words like *want, wish, desire, choose, prefer,* and *decide,* for example. Among the most sneaky offenders are clauses that begin with *because.*

Professional nonjudgmentalism may create the impression of condoning. This also has been a problem for medical students. Not all variations of human sexual behavior are playful or harmless to society. Serial lust murder is the example par excellence. The principle I have used is that the dividing line between harmless and noxious is based on the criterion of not invading the inviolacy of the other person, together with the criterion of informed consent. It is possible to give informed consent only if the beginning predicates the end. Walking to one's car at night does not predicate a sudden assault and violent rape. Therefore, mutual consent is impossible. Thus, in the absence of a guaranteed cure, the violent rapist today is comparable to the carrier of smallpox, who in the past had to be quarantined. Quarantine can be humanistic, however, not brutalistic like the typical American prison and the death sentence.

Scientific impartiality and moral nonjudgmentalism conflict not only with the law but also with the principle of academic freedom when the issue is one of sexual ideology. In my career, academic freedom became subject to controversy when the actualities of human sexual behavior were in conflict with the ideological morality of sex. Thus, controversy surfaced in connection with the programs I established for sex offenders and for transexuals.

Controversy raged also over the use of sexually explicit films in the teaching of medical students. Some of the films had been produced for academic distribution and some for commercial pornographic distribution. All of them had specific relevance to the lectures in sexual medicine, which in the academic year 1969–70 were an innovation in the completely revised curriculum of the introduction to psychiatry. The new curriculum was designed by Richard Allen Chase, under the then-new leadership of Joel Elkes.

For students of prior years there had been no such lectures and movies. To accommodate their requests, a slot was found in the section of the course reserved for special events. Invitations to my special event, a lecture with movies, was extended to all members of the academic community. Under the title of "Pornography in the Home," it addressed the concerns of parents regarding the effect of explicitly erotic materials on children and teenagers. It was immensely popular, as well as fiercely controversial. In its second year it drew an audience of fifteen hundred students and members of the Hopkins academic community and their partners.

Subsequently I learned on a quite direct grapevine that a potential benefactor had confronted the trustees of the university with a threat to withhold a proposed million-dollar bequest if I continued to remain on the faculty. This threat was confirmed by the benefactor's grandson after he subsequently became a medical student. I did not, however, suffer the fate of my illustrious predecessor, John B. Watson, author of the theory of behaviorism. In 1920, he had been forced to resign from his professorship over an issue of medical morals, but the true source of his disgrace remained concealed until H. W. Magoun (1981) uncovered the evidence. Watson, who trained only two graduate students, Curt Richter and Rosalie Rayner, had been investigating, in the style of Masters and Johnson, the physiology of the vaginal orgasm, with his female graduate student, later his second wife, as the subject.

The time allocated to the teaching of sexual medicine in the psychiatry course was progressively eroded after Joel Elkes resigned his professorship in 1973. In 1983, I was advised by a secretary that my course outline would not be needed. No longer would I be teaching. Mysteriously, in that same year, the announcement of my human sexology course was dropped from the printed catalog of the School of Continuing Studies, with no further explanation forthcoming. It was an evening course open to undergraduate and graduate students and was always fully enrolled. By the 1980s, explicitly erotic sex education had become a danger to the morals of Johns Hopkins students, medical and nonmedical. This is the way it remains in the era of AIDS, as the epidemic insidiously expands itself into the heterosexual population of university students.

What the students at Johns Hopkins have lost has become the gain of students around the world. For them I now have more time to write. There are future journal articles on my agenda, as well as books that have not yet been written.

Causality Is Not One-Way

For several decades prior to 1967, from different disciplines and places, a number of investigators working independently of one another on the problems of failure to thrive in infancy and childhood, came very close to putting two and two together and making the discovery that failure to grow both physically and mentally may be not only correlated but may also share a common origin in parental deprivation, neglect, and abuse. It was in a two-part report in the *New England Journal of Medicine* from the Pediatric Endocrine Clinic at Johns Hopkins in 1967 that the connection was finally made.

These two papers demonstrated that there is a syndrome in which the body fails to grow, so that the child becomes a dwarf; that the failure to grow originates in a failure of the pituitary gland to secrete growth hormone; and that the failure of growth hormone can be reversed by the simple expedient of transferring the child to another place to live—even a hospital ward. Then, within a period as short as two or three weeks, growth hormone reappears in the bloodstream and catch-up growth begins.

Analogously, if the child is old enough to be pubertal, after transfer to the new living place, the gonad stimulating hormones (the gonadotropins FSH and LH) from the pituitary gland begin to be secreted into the bloodstream, and the signs of pubertal growth and development appear for the first time.

The factor responsible for growth failure was attributed to maternal deprivation, and the syndrome was referred to as *deprivation dwarfism.* Then the name was generalized to *psychosocial dwarfism,* a term too diffuse according to my standards, but still in use. Soon I came across cases in which the psychosocial factor was not only deprivation and neglect but also indisputable abuse. I began using the term *abuse dwarfism* and gave it a priority position on the list of syndromes under active investigation.

For clinical psychology, abuse dwarfism has special significance in etiological theory, for it reverses the direction of cause and effect—from behavior to hormonal change, instead of from hormones to behavioral change. There is, as yet, no systematic, step-by-step neuroendocrine explanation of how neglect, deprivation, and abuse turn off the hormonal regulatory centers of the brain, notably in the hypothalamus, which then turn off the secretion of growth hormone (and gonadotropin) from the pituitary gland.

My own early search for an explanation pointed to sleep deprivation as a possible etiological consideration. Sleep impairment was shown to be prevalent in abuse dwarfism, the significance of which is that the maximum secretion of growth hormone is during deep sleep.

In addition to implicating sleep deprivation, the same early search implicated impairment of the sense of pain (pain agnosia). The significance of this finding is that pain agnosia is attributable to an increased secretion of the brain's own painkillers, its own morphine-like opiates, which in turn may interfere with growth. Increased opiate secretion may also account for the paradoxical finding that children with the syndrome of abuse dwarfism may become addicted to abuse and thus may invite more of it, even after rescue.

One of the more recent findings from animal studies is the relationship between skin stimulation and growth hormone secretion. The mothers of newborn rats lick their babies. Deprived of licking, the babies do not secrete growth hormone, fail to thrive, and die. Premature babies react similarly if they are deprived of skin stimulation by not being smoothed, patted, and cuddled.

Physical growth failure in the abuse dwarfism syndrome is not the only growth failure. Three important findings from my psychohormonal research unit are that failure of statural growth correlates with failure of intellectual growth (and lowering of the IQ), sociobehavioral growth, and erotosexual growth (including the actual onset of puberty). All of these growth failures are subject to partial catch-up growth following rescue from abuse.

Neither a purely organic theory of causation nor a purely psychological one was adequate to accommodate the phenomena of the ause dwarfism syndrome, nor the directionality of its cause and effect from behavioral environment to neurohormonal secretion. By contrast, exigency theory was adequate. It has served me well.

Cornerstones

Looking back, I think I always entertained the idea that to have a career in research is to be in society's debt, for the cost of research is in the long run, one way or another, a capital investment of funds from the commonwealth, earmarked for research instead of for something else. Society's research dividend is distributed as knowledge made available not only to professionals but also to the public at large— not only in professional periodicals and meetings but also in the lay press and electronic media. I came to envisage public relations as one of the cornerstones of a research career and made an effort to accept requests for media interviews and appearances. It had been time-consuming, but overall, my experience in the dissemination of knowledge to the general public has been positive.

Overall, my experience in disseminating the results of research among professionals and scientists has also been positive, apart from the usual scorecard of having manuscripts rejected by one editor but accepted by another. If I considered an editor's rejection grievously biased, I submitted subsequent manuscripts elsewhere. I wrote on the assumption that a particular piece of research is unfinished until it has been kiln-fired in writing. Then I see no point in withholding it from publication in order to present it first at a professional meeting. Thus, my presentations at professional meetings, of which there have been a great many, nationally and internationally, have been by invitation and not in response to a program committee's call for papers. The many chapters I have contributed to edited books have also been by invitation, whereas in the case of my own books I write them first and then find a publisher for them.

As in the case of meetings addressed, I have joined societies more often upon invitation than by application. Politicking for position on the ladder of profesional or academic sovereignty has never lured me, though I have served when appointed or elected. I did four years of grueling service evaluating behavioral science grant applications for a study section of the National Institute of Child Health and Human Development; and a two-year stint as president of the Society for the Scientific Study of Sex. At Johns Hopkins, I have been singularly free from committee obligations.

Generation of knowledge, dissemination of findings, and service in research organizations are three of what I have come to regard as the cornerstones of my research career. A fourth cornerstone is teaching and training. Having been trained as a teacher, I have always known that teaching in a classroom is also performing for an audience. The audience may approve or boo. There is always an adversarial tension, epitomized in the tyranny of the examination that does less to admit youth into the sanctuary of knowledge than to exclude it, for the young dispossess the elders of their waning authority.

I dislike giving examinations, and I have a deep mistrust of true-false or multiple-choice tests designed to be electronically scored. I favor tutorial teaching and learning. I regret that tutorial matching of teacher and student is rarely achieved. Mismatching creates the stresses and strains of disconformity, misunderstanding, and error that may, at worst, become stubbornness, defiance, and deceit. Then my intolerance inflates until it may explode. All to no avail! The blast creates an ogre and a legend of implacable demands that no one will ever be able to satisfy.

To this legend, my response has been that in a hospital, any miscalculation or defect, no matter how trivial, may mean the difference between life and death. Likewise, a seemingly trivial error in the numerals or syntax of a psychological report may mean educational, occupational, or social ruination for the patient. An inference wrongly stated as fact may lead to a costly lawsuit. In the practice of my psychohormonal research, I do not suffer fools gladly.

The fifth among the cornerstones of my clinical career has been the provision of clinical service. There are a few people (transexuals and people with other body-image conditions are among them) who proudly offer themselves to be, in the language of their own research vernacular, guinea pigs, but only for the special treatment that they demand, and so as to receive it, usually, free of charge. By contrast, the majority of people come to a clinic, or bring their children to one, to receive treatment but not to be guinea pigs. Provided with the benefits of treatment, however, it is then to the further benefit of each patient to have his or her record included in a research study of the efficacy and outcome of that treatment. Outcome research is so beneficial, in fact, that all patients would be well advised to consent to a hospital admission only on the condition of a guarantee that the hospital routinely practices outcome research.

Even at the outset of my dissertation studies of individuals with a syndrome of hermaphroditism, it was self-evident to me that since they had given me the right to ask them questions in order to discover things about themselves, then I should give each one of them the right to ask me what it was I discovered. The two of us were embarked on a cooperative enterprise. Even today, I do not deny patients the right to see their own records. There are two provisos. One is that the transcripts of interviews with living kin are withheld until those kin give signed consent. The other is that the record be read in my office so that its contents can be explicated and its personal impact dealt with as needed at each reading session.

The ten patients who contributed to my Harvard dissertation research were volunteers. By definition, a volunteer sample is a biased, not a random, sample. To avoid sampling bias, my plan when I began working with Lawson Wilkins was to have a complete census, with no refusals, of all the patients in each diagnostic group that I would follow. Patients who were considered psychologically healthy, as well as those who were not, would be referred to me for evaluation.

Many patients, parents and children alike, were antagonistic toward a psychological (or a psychiatric) evaluation, for the referral alone was tantamount to already having been stigmatized as mentally not normal. By contrast my position was that it would be as beneficial to have a pediatric talking doctor as to have a pediatric hormone doctor. I was already committed to the Wilkins policy of long-term outcome follow-up, so that my services would include not only present counseling and guidance but also preventive intervention and crisis intervention. They would receive these benefits of psychological health care, and I would receive the benefit of having on file the psychological test records and the verbatim transcripts of interviews and summary interviews.

I respected the principle of confidentiality of interviews, irrespective of age. Mother, father, and, as soon as old enough, child, all were given a chance to talk alone, concurrently, or sequentially, dependent on available staff. Then, in a joint interview, the findings of all the interviews, unless already declared confidential, were pooled. Thus, they became shared informational property for use within the clinic and the family.

I knew from experience that there are no well-kept secrets in patients' clinical histories. Hospital doors have ears. Patients read their charts in the examining room when the doctor leaves them for an urgent call. Then they are likely to learn only enough to be traumatized. Since medicine makes its living from pathology, medical charts celebrate the identification and description of disease, as well as its treatment. Treatment is directed to an attack on the agent of the patient's disease, not on the patient himself, unless the patient is considered to be, at least in part, the responsible agent—which may happen if, for example, the disease is related to smoking, eating, or drinking too much.

In clinics of psychology and psychiatry, the agents of disease that have long been in vogue are emotions, attitudes, drives, needs, wants, and conflicts, conscious and unconscious. As determinants of disease, these agents inevitably place a burden of motivational responsibility on the patient as the agent of mental disease. They do so by reason of the idiomatic construction of the language, which dictates a vernacular philosophical doctrine of personal responsibility for one's own states of mind and behavior.

Herein lies an insoluble problem in reciprocal communication: I can taste orange juice better than you can, and I defy you to prove otherwise! How can I know the taste of your taste? How can I know the world of your vision, if you are colorblind and I am not? Years ago, I increased my understanding of this problem of solipsism when I interviewed a man known in the clinic since early childhood to have a congenital absence of the sense of pain (pain agnosia). Neither of us comprehended what the other was talking about when the words *pain* and *hurting* were used. Since infancy, he had had a lifetime of ridicule for being indifferent to injuries that were noxiously painful for others. He agreed to be tested for sterility and a chromosomal aberration, since both are known to be associated in some cases of congenital pain agnosia. He made the conditions of his agreement contingent on having the required testicular biopsy operation without anesthesia. He had no pain response to the surgery. Thus did he triumph over the mistrust of medical skeptics.

Before I broke away from the dictates of vernacular philosophy, the transcripts of my interviews and my written reports came across, like those of everyone else, as diagnostic indictments rather than as diagnostic documents, as divinations rather than prognostications, and as being judgmental rather than impartial. They insidiously estranged doctor and patient as adversaries, instead of uniting them as allies against the common adversary, namely the disease. For the patient they were offensive and traumatizing instead of informative and therapeutic. If subpoenaed, under legal cross-questioning they would be easily dismissed as doctrinal, not accepted as factually conclusive.

The first exercise in escape from vernacular philosophical doctrine was to put all interviews and reports to the test of being defended, if challenged by either an attorney in court or the patient in one's own office. I made it a rule that all documents pertaining to a patient would be worded in the expectation that a carbon copy (later xerox) would be made for and read by the patient concerned, and that for him or her it would be beneficial, not harmful. This rule has proved that there are two ways of conveying the same information, one offensive and alienative and the other respectful and allegiance-inducing. The one decreases and the other increases well-being, irrespective of the portents of the disease.

A clinical document that increases a patient's well-being is one in which its originator does not fall into the trap of using linguistic idioms that attribute causality to a motivational state. For example: Q. Why did you do it? A. Because I was angry. In this example, instead of the cause-and-effect contingency implied by the conjunction *because,* the implied contingency should be either spatial or temporal. For example: Q. When did you do it? A. When I was angry. The responsibility for establishing a causal relationship between the temporal contingency established by the two *whens* belongs to the professional, not the patient. The anger may have been secondary to an enlarging hypothalamic tumor, for example, or to a posttraumatic flashback, or to a low rage threshold secondary to the genetic defect of a supernumerary Y chromosome (47,XYY syndrome), and so on. There is always a different list of hypotheses to be set in place. One alone is not enough. At a minimum, it should be paired with itself in reverse. Never be satisfied with platitudes. Question everything!

Questioning everything has a long history in my life. My oldest Morrinsville cousin recently confirmed that from the time when I first learned to talk, I had a reputation for asking questions—too many of them.

The last of the cornerstones of my research career, the sixth, pertains to a research strategy that has been longitudinal and developmental rather than cross-sectional, as well as ethological and observational rather than interventional and manipulative, and oriented toward investigation of syndromes rather than toward applied testing and measurement.

With no guarantee of a lifetime's research endowment, in 1951 I had no way of predicting how long I would be able to follow the development of the patients I would be following. There was no doubt that I should follow them, for Lawson Wilkins had an established tradition of pediatric endocrine follow-up that he applied not only to clinical care but also to his own clinical research.

As time went on, instead of going on the job market, I took the risk of being able to get a research grant renewed every three to five years (only once was it seven years) and so to extend the duration of developmental follow-up and outcome. I've had gambler's luck that has now persisted for forty years, of which twenty-nine coincide with the existence of the National Institute of Child Health and Human Development. In 1987, when NICHD celebrated its twenty-fifth anniversary, it was discovered that mine was the only grant continuously funded for all twenty-five years.

Retrospectively retrieved developmental data are deficient and distorted as compared with the data prospectively entered into the same patient's longitudinal record. Too much is lost, scientifically and financially as well, if outcome studies are terminated prematurely. The avenue of longitudinal developmental outcome is a route for clinical psychology to follow in the twenty-first century.

Whereas ethological and observational studies of animals are optional, in human beings they are imperative, insofar as the principles that regulate interventional research in animals are totally unacceptable for the developmental understanding of children. Thus, one may inbreed pure strains of mice but not of human subjects for double-blind crossover studies; and one may subject mice to invasive, even lethal, interventions and manipulations that are prohibited in children.

My response to the lack of uniformity in observational and interview data was not to devise questionnaires and rating scales as substitutes. Instead, I constructed a systematic Schedule of Inquiry, with adaptations for age, sex, and type of syndrome. It ensured that the same range of information would be documented in each patient's file, in the form of observational notes or transcripts of audiotaped interviews, each well punctuated with subheadings.

When a file is due to be used for a research report, its contents are indexed according to the conceptual classifications of the report. Thus, information required for the report can be readily located, classified, and transferred to the appropriate flow sheet. On each sheet there is a data-reduction column on each row of which is entered a symbol (for example, for country or state, sex, religion, socioeconomic class), number (for example, age, income), or rating (for example, frequent, rare, never; strong, medium, weak). Ratings are made by two or more staff members trained and practiced in applying the same criterion standard from one file to the next. By contrast, when patients themselves fill out a rating scale, each patient uses a criterion standard that is personally idiosyncratic to an unknown degree. When a patient's file is one of several to be used in a research report, then the ratings, numbers, and symbols from each are transferred onto a master or summary chart.

In some instances, a file is processed for publication as a report of the clinical biography of a single case of a rare syndrome or unusually significant outcome of treatment. Alternatively, two files are published as a matched pair, each case being a reciprocal or contrast case for the other, but each having a clinical biography sufficiently rare that no other exactly similar pairs are known. When there is no shortage of similarly matched pairs, then the published report is one in which two clinical groups (or a clinical and a nonclinical group) are used, each a comparison or control group for the other.

Over the years, the principle of syndrome selectivity has always been integral to my research strategy. Otherwise I would have been distracted by a haphazard diversity of diagnoses. I would have been distracted also had I taken on too many patients by taking on too many syndromes. Thus, I excluded juvenile diabetes and juvenile obesity. There were plenty of psychological problems in the case management of children with these two diagnoses, but neither syndrome yielded up a significant and specifically psychoendocrine hypothesis. Investigation of these syndromes would have been too narrowly confined to testing of personality profiles only.

There were many pediatric endocrine syndromes that did yield up a psychoendocrine hypothesis—too many, in fact, from the point of view of work overload—and that were included on my research agenda. "Know your syndrome" became my catch cry, as it became evident that there is a psychology of syndromes that is generic to the syndrome. When I know my syndrome, I know a good deal about the psychology of a child who has that syndrome, even before the first appointment is made. Moreover, I may even be the first person to suspect the diagnosis. Knowing the psychology of syndromes is another route for clinical psychology to follow in the twenty-first century.

Epilogue: The Dissident

From as far back as the day when I first went to school, there has been ample evidence that I do not have a talent for establishing dominance in the power hierarchy. Thus, I have on several occasions been a sitting duck for the potshots of other professionals. Some colleagues and students, female as well as male, intramural and extramural, have been, I would say, rather shamelessly exploitative. Nor have the media been exempt from taking potshots from time to time.

I have been, however, a survivor, not a martyr. I have survived by putting into practice my own maxim and have not been lured into declaring a war that I had no possible chance of winning. Instead of mounting a direct counterattack, I would adopt a policy of disengagement and redirect my energies into an alternative channel of achievement. There have always been more alternatives in my work than could be attended to at any one time.

I look to the lessons of history and ask myself whether the practitioners of dominance may be those whose special talent is for ascendancy in the power hierarchy. My personal impression is that they are lacking in the special talent for original thinking, for formulating new concepts and hypotheses, and for making new discoveries. Maybe the two talents are incompatible. Whether they are or not, those who dominate me in the power hierarchy frequently characterize me as one who is controversial and dissident.

I interrupted the writing of this chapter to participate in the Third International Berlin Conference for Sexology, July 10–15, 1990. As the successor to the 1926 conference, it was a historic occasion for those in attendance, made all the more so by the recency of the currency conversion on July 1 and the fall of The Wall on November 9. The mood of unification was everywhere. By contrast, when I returned to Baltimore, I encountered a reminder of being separated. It was in the form of a letter (reproduced with permission) from a patient now in his thirties, whom I had first seen at 1 year of age. It informed me that as a sequel to his 1990 psychohormonal follow-up appointment, he had taken it upon himself to address a letter to the chief of psychiatry, which he quoted as follows.

> I have been meaning to write to you for some time to express my unhappiness about the fact that Johns Hopkins seems to be trying to will Dr. Money's unit out of existence by moving his unit four blocks from the hospital proper. I am an intersex patient who has been followed for some 31 years by Dr. Money's unit and the Endocrine Clinic. I have received much help over the years from Dr. Money and his staff, in terms of supportive counseling and information provided at appropriate times. I feel that it is important to insure that Dr. Money's unit remains in existence at Johns Hopkins, at the very least as an adjunct to the Endocrine Clinic. I hope that you will do your best to see that this unit continues to exist at Johns Hopkins.

In his letter to me, he then quoted the reply he had received.

> Thank you for your letter. I do not understand your concerns. Dr. Money's unit is in active practice and I am delighted that you found him helpful. I consider him a genius.

Working as an off-campus exile, in a green subterranean jungle that flourishes under artifical light, I have a sense of kinship with dissidents like Galileo, who by order of the Vatican lived as an exile under house arrest.

References

Benjamin, H. (1966). *The transsexual phenomenon.* New York: Julian Press.

Bridgman, P. W. (1946). *The logic of modern physics.* New York: Macmillan.

Ellis, H. (1933). *Psychology of sex: The biology of sex—The sexual impulse in youth— Sexual deviation—The erotic symbolisms—Homosexuality—Marriage—The art of love.* London: Heinemann.

Hoyer, N. (Ed.). (1933). *Man into woman.* London: Jarrolds.

Jorgensen, C. (1967). *Christine Jorgensen: A personal autobiography.* New York: Paul S. Eriksson.

Magoun, H. W. (1981). John B. Watson and the study of human sexual behavior. *Journal of Sex Research, 17,* 368–378.

Money, J. (1947, May). *Basic concepts in the study of personality.* Paper presented at the meeting of the British Association for the Advancement of Science, Wellington, New Zealand.

Money, J. (1948). Delusion, belief, and fact. *Psychiatry, 11,* 33–38.

Money, J. (1949). Unanimity in the social sciences with reference to epistemology, ontology, and scientific method. *Psychiatry, 12,* 211–221.

Money, J. (1957). *The psychologic study of man.* Springfield: Charles C Thomas.

Money, J. (1962). (Ed.) *Reading disability: Progress and research needs in dyslexia.* Baltimore: Johns Hopkins Press.

Money, J. (1966) (Ed.) *The disabled reader: Education of the dyslexic child.* Baltimore: Johns Hopkins Press.

Money, J. (1970). Use of androgen-depleting hormone in the treatment of male sex offenders. *Journal of Sex Research, 6,* 165–172.

Money, J. (1986). *Venuses penuses: Sexology, sexosophy, and exigency theory.* Buffalo: Prometheus Books.

Money, J., Hampson, J. G., & Hampson, J. L. (1955a). An examination of some basic sexual concepts: The evidence of human hermaphroditism. *Bulletin of The Johns Hopkins Hospital, 97,* 301–319.

Money, J., Hampson, J. G., & Hampson, J. L. (1955b). Hermaphroditism: Recommendations concerning assignment of sex, change of sex, and psychologic assignment. *Bulletin of The Johns Hopkins Hospital, 97,* 284–300.

Murray, H. A. (1938). *Explorations in personality.* New York: Oxford University Press.

Murray, H. A. (1943). *Thematic Apperception Test.* Cambridge: Harvard University Press.

Powell, G. F., Brasel, J. A., & Blizzard, R. M. (1967a). Emotional deprivation and growth retardation simulating idiopathic hypopituitarism. I. Clinical evaluation of the syndrome. *New England Journal of Medicine, 276,* 1271–1278.

Powell, G. F., Brasel, J. A., Raiti, S., & Blizzard, R. M. (1967b). Emotional deprivation and growth retardation simulating idiopathic hypopituitarism. II. Endocrinologic evaluation of the syndrome. *New England Journal of Medicine, 276,* 1279–1283.

Tennov, D. (1974). *Love and limerence: The experience of being in love.* New York: Stein & Day.

Whyte, W. F. (1943). *Street corner society: The social structure of an Italian slum.* Chicago: University of Chicago Press.

Julian B. Rotter

Professor of Psychology
University of Connecticut

◆

Expectancies

Since social learning theory emphasizes the importance of previous experience and cultural milieu for understanding an individual, I will begin this biography with a broad survey of some of the important variables in my early background.

I was born in October 1916, the third and last child of Abraham and Bessie Rotter, in Brooklyn, New York. My brother Saul, five years older, went on to become a physician; Norman, the middle child, two years older than I, became a businessman. Because of the closeness in age, Norman was both the closer sibling and the one with whom I was more rivalrous.

Born into the same culture that Alfred Adler knew best, we not surprisingly fit quite well into Adler's descriptions of the oldest, the middle, and the "fighting youngest child." My mother came to the United States from Lithuania at the age of 1; my father, from Austria at age 13. They were Jewish, observed the Jewish religion and customs, but were not deeply religious. My father, in particular, believed that religion was a necessary part of civilized life but not to be taken literally. Both parents completed high school with outstanding academic records. Our circumstances were comfortably middle class until the Great Depression, when my father lost his wholesale stationery business and we became part of the masses of unemployed for two years.

The Depression came at a critical time in my own development. It began in me a lifelong concern with social injustice and provided me with a powerful lesson on how personality and behavior were affected by situational conditions.

My first acquaintance with psychology came in my junior year of high school, when, while browsing in the local branch of the public library, I noticed a shelf labeled "Philosophy and Psychology." Some of the titles seemed interesting to me. I do not remember the order in which I read them, but the first three books I took out were Adler's *Understanding Human Nature* (1927), Freud's *Psychopathology of Everyday Life* (1917), and Menninger's *The Human Mind* (1920). The first two impressed me, and I went on to read Adler's *Practice and Theory of Individual Psychology* (1924) and Freud's *Interpretation of Dreams* (1933). In my senior year of high school I was interpreting other people's dreams (I was very good on balconies and horses) and wrote a senior thesis entitled "Why We Make Mistakes." By the time I entered Brooklyn College, I was seriously interested in psychology. I found that Adler's insights into human nature made a great deal of sense in my efforts to understand myself and the people around me. But there was no profession of psychology that I knew of; and in 1933, during the depths of the Great Depression, one majored in a subject that would enable one to make a living. In general, I was a good student in science and math, and I had earned some honors in biology and chemistry. Chemistry seemed my best bet for future employment, so I chose that as my major. My primary interest, however, remained in psychology and philosophy; I took all my electives in these two subjects, completing my B.A. with more credits in psychology than in chemistry. In retrospect, however, the hard science background, along with courses in vertebrate biology, logic, epistemology, and math, were an excellent preparation for graduate training in psychology.

At Brooklyn College the faculty members in psychology were young and enthusiastic. In 1933 there was no Psychology Department as such at Brooklyn College. Psychology courses were taught in the Philosophy Department by young, recent Ph.D.'s. Two teachers in particular influenced my development as a psychologist. Austin B. Wood's lectures on the scientific method were inspiring, and Solomon Asch introduced me to the fascinating controversy between Gestalt and Thorndikian approaches to learning theory. It was Asch, also, who got me interested in the work of Kurt Lewin. The honesty and involvement of both these teachers made me consider a possible career in teaching.

When I began my junior year in college, I discovered that Alfred Adler had come to the United States and had accepted a chair in medical psychology at Long Island School of Medicine, whose campus was in downtown Brooklyn. Adler, a socialist, had left Vienna on short notice after the socialist government fell and when Vienna was no longer a healthy place for socialists to work and thrive. Adler taught his course to medical students at the third-year level; but at the request of fourth-year students, he gave a similar course to seniors and faculty at night. I began to attend these lectures. Once, when I stayed after the lecture to ask a question, he invited me to attend the clinic demonstration he gave each week at the medical school. I explained that I was not a medical student, which did not seem to bother Adler. Eventually this led to invitations to attend his child and family clinic in uptown Manhattan and monthly meetings of the Society of Individual Psychology in his home.

The controversy between Freudians and Adlerians was still going strong in 1937. At the end of one of these meetings in his home, Adler suggested that the group attend a public lecture by a prominent Freudian at Columbia University the following week. There was a collective gasp from the group, and Adler said, "But we must listen to what they have to say."

Adler looked like a teddy bear and his rapport with young children was amazing to me. His wife accompanied him wherever he went. In his conception of both position in the family and "masculine protest" he recognized the psychological costs of the inferior role of women in our society.

Adler died in the summer of 1937, the year that I graduated from college. With no money and no steady work or career qualifications, I planned to stay in New York, try to find a job, and continue my studies at night wherever I could. Adler's death, talks with Asch and Wood, and the presence of Kurt Lewin at the University of Iowa convinced me at least to attempt to go there and see if could survive financially. With a round-trip railroad coach fare of about $25.00 and tuition of about $35.00, I could survive two or three weeks on the money left over from a summer job as a camp counselor.

Lee Travis, chairman of the Psychology Department, was sympathetic, but told me with certainty that all Psychology Department funds were gone, and I soon learned that no other job was available in Iowa City. Nevertheless, I decided to stay there until my money ran out. I did get to know Travis better—mainly on the tennis court—and after two weeks he managed to find $200 for a part-time research assistantship. So began my graduate career as a psychologist.

The year at Iowa was profitable in many ways. Kurt Lewin's course, which focused on his theory, and his weekly seminar dealing with current research generated excitement and controversy. His basic interactionism and purely psychological approach influenced me greatly, although I was somewhat surprised at the scant attention Lewin and his students paid to individual differences. I also came to disagree with his belief that psychology was or could be an ahistorical science.

Wendell Johnson, whose main interest was in the study of stuttering, was a general semanticist, a follower of Korzybski. Johnson viewed stuttering as a semantic problem; from his work and that of Korzybski (1941), I learned about abstractions, referents, and the problems that arise when two or more people use the same words but have different meanings in mind. Herbert Feigl's excellent and exciting seminar on the philosophy of science consolidated my interest in theory building in psychology. My own first research study (Rotter, 1938) was an investigation of stuttering and position in the family, undertaken from an Adlerian point of view. My master's thesis, with Lee Travis as my advisor and Wendell Johnson as a committee member, was undertaken as a test of Travis's theory of lack of cerebral dominance as the main cause of stuttering. It was not surprising that with

Travis committed to an organic theory and Johnson to a psychological theory of etiology, the results of this study of the motor integration of young adult stutterers were ultimately interpreted as equivocal.

Toward the end of the year at Iowa I learned that applications were being accepted for an internship in clinical psychology at Worcester State Hospital in Massachusetts. The notion of an internship in clinical psychology was a new one at the time. Lee Travis was leaving Iowa, and although I could have had a full assistantship with Wendell Johnson, the internship opportunity seemed too intriguing to pass up.

I knew nothing about Worcester State Hospital when I arrived there in the fall of 1938. As far as I knew, no other institution in the country offered a formal internship, and very few universities offered the Ph.D. degree with a major in clinical psychology. Worcester State Hospital was an important center of research and training in both psychology and psychiatry. David Shakow was chief psychologist, and the staff included Eliot Rodnick and Saul Rosensweig. In addition, there were two assistant psychologists and four other interns.

One of these interns was Clara Barnes. I had the good fortune to marry Clara two years later, in 1941, when we were both graduate students at Indiana University. Spring vacation began on April 1, but we were married on April 2, since for obvious reasons we both wished to avoid the implications of an April 1 marriage. In 1947, our first child, a daughter named Jean, was born; she is now a special education teacher. Our second child, Richard, was born in 1949; he is an exercise physiologist.

Much of the modern emphasis on graduate training in clinical psychology derived from two articles by Shakow (1938, 1945), dealing with the internship year and with trends in clinical training. These articles had a strong influence on the ideas and focus of the Boulder Conference, which was held in 1949 and set the pattern of clinical training for many years to come.

David Shakow was a gentle but very orderly man, and he arrived at the psychology office precisely at 8 AM every morning. He would walk through the office, apparently looking neither right nor left, and disappear into his office. About two minutes later he would buzz his secretary and say, "Ask Rotter to step in to see me." His secretary would say, "He has just stepped out." Then my roommate, W. V. Snyder, would rush down the hall where our sleeping quarters were, shake me awake, and tell me, "Shakow wants to see you!" I would crawl out of bed, throw on some clothes, and go to his office, where he would ask me inconsequential questions and I would give some brief answer and depart. I would then retreat to my room, remove my clothes, go through my morning ablutions, remove a pint of milk from a water cooler in the hall, drink it, and be ready for work about 8:30. Although we played out this script many times, Shakow never directly complained to me that I was supposed to be at work at 8 AM.

It was at Worcester that I began to have doubts about the whole approach to psychopathology, abnormal psychology, and psychiatric diagnoses. Every week I attended a diagnostic staff conference. The clinical director would question the patient, as would the rest of the psychiatric staff, all of whom had read the case history. The patient was then dismissed. A psychologist would be called upon to provide information from the diagnostic testing based on a battery of tests usually including the Stanford Binet, the Rorschach, and the Wells' Memory Test. Sometimes other projective measures and the Kent-Rosanoff Word Association Test were also used. Then the psychiatrists would decide upon and defend their diagnosis, with the clinical director making the final "official" diagnosis. It was not unusual for five or six psychiatrists to provide five different diagnoses, and the clinical director might add yet another. After attending several of these conferences, I found that most of the diagnoses were more predictable from the psychiatrists' biases than they were from the patients' behavior.

In 1939 no psychologist at Worcester practiced psychotherapy on patients. For almost all psychiatrists, psychotherapy meant psychoanalysis, and psychologists, in any case, were not considered eligible to do any treatment because of their not having a medical degree. Because I was interested in knowing more about patients than their psychiatric diagnosis, I was allowed to "talk" to a few patients on a regular once-a-week basis, but no one considered this treatment and no notes were entered into the case record to reflect these meetings.

At Worcester I began my work on developing an individual difference measure of level of aspiration, which later evolved into my dissertation. I also began research with the TAT, using an early experimental set of pictures of H. A. Murray's that Saul Rosensweig had shown me. Within psychiatry, psychoanalytic, disease entity, and organic approaches to psychopathology battled for dominance as explanations of etiology. Although none of these approaches satisfied me, the controversy was exciting.

In 1936 C. M. Louttit, a professor at Indiana University, had written a textbook entitled *Clinical Psychology* that identified a field of application involving the diagnosis and treatment of psychological disorders of all kinds in children and adults. The book summarized existing data and attempted a kind of integrated approach to topics ranging from speech problems in children to adult psychoses. Because of this book, I applied to Indiana for my Ph.D. work and in 1939 was given an assistantship with Louttit, working in the university's psychological clinic.

In 1939 very few universities granted a degree in clinical psychology or in psychology with a formal specialty in clinical psychology. However, in the big midwestern universities with their emphasis on application, many more courses that we would now refer to as clinical were taught. Almost all clinical psychologists in practice worked for public institutions and either dealt primarily with children's problems (speech, auditory, learning disabilities, conduct disorders), juvenile delinquency, and mental retardation, or with incarcerated criminals or hospitalized mental patients. University programs with some training in clinical work mostly or entirely focused on intelligence testing and children's problems. The University of Indiana was no exception.

C. M. Louttit was my dissertation advisor. His method of teaching was essentially a willingness to discuss anything at any time in an open and egalitarian manner. Although he contributed much to my intellectual growth, as a friend and advisor he contributed even more to my personal growth. At that time J. R. Kantor was very influential at Indiana with both staff and students. Courses with Kantor furthered my education in philosophy of science and the nature of theory in psychology. My dissertation was on level of aspiration; it included a series of studies begun at Worcester State Hospital and continued throughout my two years at Indiana, where I completed my work in 1941.

At Brooklyn College and again in graduate school, I had been warned that Jews simply could not get academic jobs, regardless of their credentials. The warnings seemed justified. There were few academic positions open in 1941; I received a single offer of an academic job, teaching at a branch of a midwestern university. However, I was interested in clinical work as well as in research and teaching, so I turned the offer down. Instead, I was hired as a clinical psychologist at Norwich State Hospital in Connecticut, where I remained for thirteen months before going into the army. At that time the University of Connecticut and Wesleyan University both had M.A. programs that included a year's internship at Norwich State Hospital, and my job included training the interns and assistants. Although I had taught a course on personality at Indiana University, this was my first experience in one-to-one, long-term teaching. I found it to be very satisfying. For me, it is still the most rewarding part of my professional experience.

Wiliam Bryan, who had been superintendent at Worcester State Hospital, was hired to revitalize Norwich Hospital, following an exposé of the sad condition of Connecticut mental hospitals. The clinical director, Louis Cohen, an expert on psychopathic personality, had come to Norwich from Yale College of Medicine, where he was professor of psychiatry. However, nothing had changed in the role of psychology. Our clinical function was to give tests to aid the psychiatrist in making a diagnosis. Research typically dealt with analysis of test results for groups with different psychiatric diagnoses. No challenge to the disease-entity approach to psychopathological behavior had appeared on the mental hospital scene. However, the limited value of this elaborate process of diagnosis became more and more clear to me, partly because of my training with Adler, Lewin, and Kantor and partly as a result of experiencing the poor reliability of diagnoses and the poverty of treatment methods related to the diagnosis. The diagnosis, however, did have a relationship to management within the hospital and to the issue of whether or not hospitalization was mandatory.

I entered the army as a private in 1942 (having failed a year earlier to obtain a commission in the navy because of partial red-green color blindness). However, after a month I was transferred to the Armored School at Fort Knox to work in the Office of the Military Psychologist. Except for the seventeen weeks of training in Officer Candiate School as an armored officer, I spent the rest of my three and a quarter years in the army and air force working as a psychologist. The military psychologist at Fort Knox was Milton B. Jensen, a Stanford Ph.D. who had worked with Terman and who had the complete confidence of the commanding general of the Armored School. Our job was to see every individual who had charges preferred against him or who was being considered for discharge for psychological reasons, and to make recommendations regarding overall problems of the school and officer candidate selection.

Since our recommendations were almost always carried out, it was a remarkable, informal field study of the value of the environmental treatment of young adults. I found the results astonishing. A set of recommendations for reducing the numbers of those who were absent without official leave (AWOL)—a serious problem among base personnel—were followed to the letter and succeeded in reducing AWOL to less than 25 percent of its former rate in a two-month period. Students failing in their courses could show remarkable changes as a result of simply being allowed a three-day pass to go home to settle a personal problem not officially recognized by the army as meriting special consideration. Drunkenness and AWOL by soldiers on permanent kitchen duty was reduced remarkably when the status of their jobs was increased and their working conditions improved. The permanent kitchen personnel were given one day off after two days' work. Previously they had been lucky to get a weekend pass every two weeks. This remarkable bonus was to be lost if they did not return on time. I suppose this "treatment" would now be considered a successful behavior modification approach. The range of problems that could be dealt with by environmental manipulation was extensive, and I learned the lesson well.

As the war wore on, psychological casualties mounted and the armed forces were not prepared to deal with them. The surgeon general's department began a two-month training program in psychiatry for servicemen who were recent graduates of medical schools. The graduates of the program were referred to as "60-day wonders," and it fell to many of these physicians to make the diagnoses for the services. Here the diagnosis was important because the choices were discharge from the army, return to duty, or convalescence followed by return to duty.

These young and inexperienced M.D.'s needed help, and a parallel program of training clinical psychologists was started at the air base in San Antonio, Texas. The army also began a new program of direct commissioning of older, experienced clinical psychologists. In true army fashion, after long and expensive training as a tank officer, I was transferred to the air force to work as a psychologist in the Air Force Convalescent Hospital Program and following some directive or other was sent to the San Antonio school, although my training and experience exceeded that of most of the instructors. The students were mostly psychology graduate students who were pulled away from other assignments and a few recent Ph.D.'s, such as Sol Garfield, Abraham Luchin, and myself. The course consisted primarily of an analysis of Wechsler patterns, TAT, and Rorschach as aids to diagnosis. Nevertheless, the graduates of this program made a sufficiently good impression to have an effect on the support for clinical psychology training by the Veterans Administration and the United States Public Health (USPH) immediately following the war. Psychological casualties were particularly high in air force crews, and a program of convalescent hospitals sprung up to deal with this problem and try to return as many men to duty as possible.

It was at one of these hospitals that I began working with Ben Willerman on an objective scoring system for an incomplete sentence test as a measure to determine suitability for return to duty (Rotter & Willerman, 1947). Later at Ohio State this work served as the basis for construction of the Incomplete Sentences Test, a measure of college student adjustment (Rotter & Rafferty, 1950).

In several of these hospitals group therapy was instituted. The therapy was usually based on an oversimplified Freudian notion that the patients' problems were due to repressed hostility. The sessions, therefore, were structured to encourage the expression of hostility. Usually the groups were too large and difficult to handle. Psychiatrists and psychologists were the therapists, although in one hospital where John Spiegel was the chief psychiatrist, psychologists were again forbidden to do psychotherapy.

It was my impression that these sessions did little or no good and in fact reinforced, rather than dissipated, the hostility toward the army. The "patients" came in angry and left raging mad. One problem of course, was that hostility toward the army was quite overt before therapy, and the real problems of depression following the death of buddies and fear of their own death were based on very real events.

Following the war, both the Veterans Administration and the USPH began to heavily support graduate programs in clinical psychology in the universities granting Ph.D.'s in psychology. They supported students, provided salaries for new staff members, and provided consultant funds to supervise the students' placement in Veterans Administration clinics and hospitals. The universities happily accepted these funds and tried to meet the demands of the granting agencies. The result was a rapid expansion of academic positions in clinical psychology, accompanied by much internal stress within university psychology departments as the dominant experimental psychologists clashed with the upstart clinicians.

As one of the relatively few Ph.D. psychologists trained as a clinical psychologist in 1946, I found myself sought after for academic positions. After a brief return to Norwich State Hospital in Connecticut, I went to Ohio State University as an assistant professor. Ohio State was a happy, productive, and rewarding situation for me. I was soon deeply involved in teaching, research, participation in regional and national psychological organizations, and consultation with government agencies.

During my army days I had been attempting to integrate current learning theory and personality theory in my spare time, and at Ohio State I began to work more systematically to construct a social learning theory of personality (Rotter, 1954). Weekly meetings with a group of bright, dedicated, and otherwise marvelous graduate students were an important part of the process. Also of great help was my friend and colleague Delos D. Wickens, from whom I continued to learn about the data and current thinking of learning theorists. On the "softer" side, a close association with Melvin Seeman, a sociologist, kept me involved in broader social constructs and social issues.

C. M. Louttit had gone into the navy and from there to Ohio State University as director of their psychological clinic and training program. He left one year after I arrived, and George A. Kelly was hired to replace him. Along with Victor Raimy, we developed a broad training program. If success of an educational program can be measured by the productivity and prominence of its graduates, it was a highly successful program. Our philosophy was to provide the student with as many theoretical approaches as possible in an atmosphere of friendly controversy. We paid more than lip service to the notion that a clinical psychologist was first a psychologist and then a clinician; we placed a heavy emphasis on understanding theory and research methods as well as clinical practice.

The great acceleration of graduate training in clinical psychology led to a conference on graduate training in Boulder, Colorado, in 1949. Although the conference was run by the American Psychological Association, the strong influence of the government granting agencies was always present. In fact, the high bill for the conference was picked up by the USPH. The results of that conference, known as the Boulder Model, are well known (Raimy, 1950). What is perhaps not so well known is that there was a movement afoot to move the training of clinical psychologists into medical schools and consequently under the control of the medical profession. In one of the sessions a resolution was introduced to this general effect. Laurence Shaffer, Seymour Sarason, and I spoke strongly against such a move, and with support of the department chairmen present at the conference this resolution was defeated.

One major effect of this government support was to change the emphasis at the universities from children's problems to adult problems. The Veterans Administration wanted graduates who would staff their clinics and hospitals, and the early emphasis was again on diagnostic testing, with many universities providing a year-long course focusing on the study of the Rorschach test. At Ohio State I resisted this emphasis on techniques for diagnosing adult psychopathology and put much more emphasis on methodology for construction and validation of psychological measuring instruments.

The influx of refugee psychologists from Europe shortly before the outbreak of World War II resulted in a great increase in interest in projective techniques, and a great variety of these techniques flourished in the postwar era. However, the new batch of clinical psychology students had to do something for their theses and dissertations, and under pressure form the experimentalists they undertook to establish the validity of these projective tests, which usually were based on clinical insight and special case reports rather than hard data. The results were not encouraging, and the projective test movement eventually lost favor in the university setting, although its influence continued for a much longer time in clinical settings.

The work on internal versus external control of reinforcement, which has proved to have a great deal of heuristic value, was the product of an integration of science and practice. The concept arose in applying some ideas that occurred to me in explaining some of our findings regarding how expectancies change following success and failure, and in supervising E. Jerry Phares, who was treating a challenging patient at the Columbus VA Clinic (Rotter, 1989). More specifically, an expectancy approach to learning theory and previous research on level of aspiration, particularly a dissertation by Alvin Lasko, had raised questions regarding the automatic or mechanistic effects of reinforcement on acquisition, extinction, and performance. Phares's client was a young man we had prodded into some new experiences that should have, but did not, raise his expectancies of acceptance by the opposite sex. In trying to explain this failure it occurred to me that the idea of internal versus external control served to explain both the client's behavior and several earlier laboratory studies. It is still for me a good example of the value of the scientist-practitioner model.

When George Kelly gave up the clinical directorship in 1951, I became clinical director. This made little difference in the program, however, since we continued to work in reasonable harmony as a congenial committee of all the clinical faculty, including at different times my valued colleagues and friends Boyd McCandless, Paul Mussen, Alvin Scodel, and Shepherd Liverant. The usual conflict between clinical psychology and experimental or general psychology did not develop at Ohio State, partly because we insisted that clinical students be broadly trained; and no time or effort was wasted in fighting with one's colleagues. Most of my own time was spent in directing dissertations and master's theses, and it was primarily through this research that social learning theory was tested and modified.

It was in these early years after World War II that the war with psychiatry over psychologists' right to do therapy unsupervised by an M.D. took place. The war was finally won by psychologists in a state-by-state fight. Usually it was the support of other groups who did counseling, such as lawyers, social workers, and the clergy, that made the difference. This victory had a strong effect on clinical psychology. The emphasis on diagnostic testing began to give way to an ever-increasing interest in psychotherapy and from broad theories to therapeutic techniques. Many of the techniques had and have little in the way of theory or empirical findings to support them. Several clinical psychology programs became single-technique programs in which other approaches were disparaged or simply not taught.

Ohio State did not give sabbaticals, but several times I took leave to teach elsewhere as a visiting professor, sometimes for a summer and sometimes for the full academic year. In this way I continued to interact with and learn from colleagues in many institutions, including the University of Minnesota, the University of Colorado, the University of California at Berkeley, UCLA, and the University of Pennsylvania.

McCarthyism found fertile soil in central Ohio. Although it did not affect the day-to-day work of the Psychology Department, both in the city of Columbus and in the university administration the attempts to suppress radical ideas were a constant irritation. Partly because of this and partly because of a desire to return to New England, I left Ohio State in 1963 to come to the University of Connecticut and direct the clinical training program they were in the process of rebuilding.

Toward the end of my time at Ohio State I took part in an interdepartmental faculty seminar on disarmament. We had guests who had negotiated with the Russians, three-star generals, and members of the U.S. disarmament commission. All of these guests expressed such strong distrust of Russia that I was prompted to ask, "What if the Russians came up with a proposal that was the same as one of our own? Would you accept it?" The answer was always no, because the proposal would certainly contain some advantage to the Russians that we had overlooked. This experience got me interested in interpersonal trust and I began to think about the costs and problems of distrusting too much. After moving to the University of

Connecticut, I began a research program dealing with interpersonal trust in earnest (Rotter, 1971, 1982).

With the move to Connecticut, the emphasis of my writing and research changed in some subtle ways. It has been a period devoted mostly to consolidation of previous ideas and application. I put together a thorough analysis of published and unpublished work on internal versus external control in a monograph (1966), and I began work on interpersonal trust more with a view toward application than toward new theoretical development. Nevertheless, I have continued to elaborate and revise previous theoretical conceptions (Rotter, 1982). I have also become more involved in national and regional organizations.

I continued my work in selection with the Peace Corps. During these years I served a second term on the APA Education and Training Board and APA Council, as well as a term on the psychology training committees of the United States Public Health Service. I also served terms as president of the APA Division of Social and Personality Psychology, the APA Division of Clinical Psychology, and the Eastern Psychological Association.

My years at the University of Connecticut have coincided with greater and greater emphasis on practitioner skills at the national level. APA accreditation and the power of internship facilities to turn down applicants with limited field experience has forced the lengthening of the training programs from four to five years, including internships. During this period Psy.D. programs have proliferated, and private practice has changed from a rarity to a major source of income for clinical psychologists.

The clinical program developed at the University of Connecticut continued the Boulder Model and still does, although many schools have opted for programs and degrees emphasizing the practitioner role at the expense of the scholar and scientist role, a development I consider premature and mistaken.

It is not surprising given my background and history that I have some misgivings about the shift in emphasis in clinical psychology from research to practice. The proliferation of therapy techniques, therapeutic fads, and the practice of single technique therapy almost independent of the characteristics of the client, seem to be more a groping process than genuine growth in the field. Research supporting the techniques is sparse, inadequate, and often absent. Theories supporting the techniques are based mostly on assertions rather than tested principles.

Sooner or later, good therapy practice will surely be understood to require an analysis of the triple interaction of therapist, method, and client. When this is recognized, it will be necessary to return to an analysis of the relevant variables and their measurement, a process that will be facilitated with sound, tested theoretical principles of complex implicit and explicit human behavior.

The conflict of scientist versus practitioner within the field has now developed to the point that two new national organizations have sprung up to counter the perceived domination of APA by practitioners. It will be the problem of the next generation to resolve the issue of whether or not clinical psychology will split into two groups, scientists and practitioners, or return to the Boulder scientist-practitioner model.

References

Adler, A. (1924). *The practice and theory of individual psychology.* New York: Harcourt Brace.

Adler, A. (1927). *Understanding human nature.* New York: Garden City Publishing Co.

Freud, S. (1917). *Psychopathology of everyday life.* New York: Macmillan.

Freud, S. (1933). *Interpretation of dreams.* New York: Macmillan.

Korzybski, A. (1941). *Science and sanity* (2nd ed.). Lancaster: Science Press.

Louttit, C. M. (1936). *Clinical psychology.* New York: Harper.

Menninger, K. A. (1920). *The human mind.* New York: Knopf.

Raimy, V. C. (Ed.). (1950). *Training in clinical psychology.* Englewood Cliffs, NJ: Prentice-Hall.

Rotter, J. B. (1938). Studies in the psychology of stuttering: IX. Stuttering in relation to position in family. *Journal of Speech Disorders, 3,* 143–148.

Rotter, J. B. (1954). *Social learning and clinical psychology.* Englewood Cliffs, NJ: Prentice-Hall. (Reprinted NY: Johnson Reprint Col, 1973, 1980.)

Rotter, J. B. (1966). Generalized expectancies for internal versus external control of reinforcement. *Psychological Monographs, 80*(Whole No. 609).

Rotter, J. B. (1971). Generalized expectancies for interpersonal trust. *American Psychologist, 26,* 443–452.

Rotter, J. B. (1980). Trust, trustworthiness, and gullibility. *American Psychologist, 35,* 1–7.

Rotter, J. B. (1982). *The development and application of social learning theory.* New York: Praeger.

Rotter, J. B. (1989). Internal versus external control of reinforcement: A case history of a variable. *American Psychologist, 45,* 489–493.

Rotter, J. B., & Rafferty, J. E. (1950). *The Rotter incomplete sentences blank manual: College form.* NY: Psychological Corporation.

Rotter, J. B., & Willerman, B. (1947). The Incomplete Sentences Test as a method of studying personality. *Journal of Consulting Psychology, 11,* 43–48.

Shakow, D. (1938). An internship year for psychologists. *Journal of Consulting Psychology, 2,* 73–76.

Shakow, D. (1945). Training in clinical psychology. *Journal of Consulting Psychology, 9,* 240—266.